"This team of authors integrates their international leadership on adapting evidence-based couple therapy to couples in which one partner has a major psychiatric disorder, along with a wealth of clinical wisdom as therapists, supervisors, and trainers, to create this exceptional volume. When I teach my graduate course in couple therapy at UCLA, I believe it is essential to include this work; otherwise, I would be negligent. The current book should be on the bookshelf of couple researchers and therapists, particularly those interested in psychopathology."

—**Andrew Christensen, Ph.D.**, Distinguished Research Professor of Psychology, University of California at Los Angeles

"This outstanding text, which is written by international experts, provides detailed guidance in how to flexibly deliver cognitive-behavioural couples therapy with distressed couples and with individuals in a relationship who are also suffering with a mental health problem. Thoroughly recommended for both trainees and experienced practitioners."

—**David M. Clark**, **DPhil**, Professor of Experimental Psychology, University of Oxford

"An oft-repeated truism in psychology is that there remains an elusive bridge between the practice of psychotherapy and the empirical evidence for this work. Nowhere have I seen this bridge navigated as deftly as in this volume. Through the authors' wealth of clinical experience, as well as the extensive body of literature that they have jointly and individually developed, this volume presents a groundbreaking model for treating relationship distress and psychopathology within a couple context. It is a must-have for clinicians, researchers, educators, and teachers in both the couple and psychopathology domains."

—**Tamara Sher, Ph.D.**, Clinical Professor, The Family Institute, Northwestern University

Treating Relationship Distress and Psychopathology in Couples

Close relationships and mental health are two key ingredients to living a meaningful, fulfilled life. These two domains are the central focus of *Treating Relationship Distress and Psychopathology in Couples: A Cognitive-Behavioural Approach.* As expert clinicians, trainers, and researchers in the field of cognitive-behavioural couple therapy and couple-based interventions for psychopathology, the authors offer a highly accessible volume for experienced clinicians and trainees alike.

This book details the most recent innovations in CBCT, a principle-based, flexible treatment approach for couples with a wide range of relationship concerns, circumstances, and stages of life. Based on a clear conceptual framework, readers learn how to address individual and couple functioning in an integrated, comprehensive manner and how to apply principle-based interventions that directly flow from this framework.

Treating Relationship Distress and Psychopathology in Couples was written by a team of five authors, born in four different countries and working together as a team for a number of years, providing a cohesive framework based on work in a variety of contexts. While staying close to research findings that inform treatment, they provide a text for clinicians at all levels of training and experience in working with couples.

Donald H. Baucom is Distinguished Professor of Psychology and Neuroscience at UNC-Chapel Hill. He is one of the developers of cognitive-behavioural couple therapy and its application to treating relationship distress and psychological and medical concerns in one partner. He is an active researcher, clinician, teacher, trainer, and supervisor in the area of couple functioning.

Melanie S. Fischer is a clinical psychologist at the Institute of Medical Psychology at the University Hospital Heidelberg. Her research specializes in psychopathology in a relationship context and the development, evaluation, and dissemination of couple-based treatments. She also is a clinician and provides training and supervision in couple therapy in Germany, the U.S., and England.

Sarah Corrie is a Consultant Clinical Psychologist and Programme Director at Central and North West London NHS Foundation Trust and Royal Holloway University of London. She is a trainer and supervisor in cognitive-behavioural couple therapy, a Visiting Professor at Middlesex University, and a Fellow of the British Association for Behavioural & Cognitive Psychotherapies.

Michael Worrell is a Consultant Clinical Psychologist and Head of Department, CBT training programmes, Central and North West London NHS Foundation Trust and Royal Holloway University. He is Visiting Professor at Regent's University London. Michael works clinically with couples and is a trainer and clinical supervisor in cognitive-behavioural couple therapy.

Sara E. Boeding is a clinical psychologist in the Durham VA Health Care System. She is an active clinician and supervisor with a specialty in couple-based interventions for relationship distress and psychopathology. She has trained others in couple-based interventions both locally and internationally.

Treating Relationship Distress and Psychopathology in Couples

A Cognitive-Behavioural Approach

Donald H. Baucom, Melanie S. Fischer, Sarah Corrie, Michael Worrell, and Sara E. Boeding

Routledge
Taylor & Francis Group
LONDON AND NEW YORK

First published 2020
by Routledge
2 Park Square, Milton Park, Abingdon, Oxon OX14 4RN

and by Routledge
52 Vanderbilt Avenue, New York, NY 10017

Routledge is an imprint of the Taylor & Francis Group, an informa business

British Library Cataloguing-in-Publication Data
A catalogue record for this book is available from the British Library

Library of Congress Cataloging-in-Publication Data
A catalog record has been requested for this book

ISBN: 978-1-138-12398-4 (hbk)
ISBN: 978-1-138-12402-8 (pbk)
ISBN: 978-1-315-62641-3 (ebk)

Typeset in Times New Roman
by Swales & Willis Ltd, Exeter, Devon, UK

Visit the eResources: www.routledge.com/9781138124028

Contents

Figures and tables

Figures

Tables

Foreword

Douglas K. Snyder, Ph.D.

PROFESSOR, DEPARTMENT OF PSYCHOLOGICAL AND BRAIN SCIENCES

TEXAS A&M UNIVERSITY, USA

The mental health field has been needing, and waiting expectantly for, a clinical textbook exactly like this—a theoretically grounded and evidence-based approach targeting *both* couple relationship distress and individual psychopathology from an integrative framework.

Couple distress is prevalent in both community epidemiological studies and in research involving individual treatment samples. In both the United Kingdom and the United States, the most salient indicator of couple distress remains a divorce rate of approximately 40–50% among married couples. Independent of divorce, many, if not most, intimate relationships experience periods of significant turmoil that contribute to personal suffering and risk for a variety of mental health disorders. Indeed, the most frequently cited causes of acute emotional distress are couple relationship problems. Couple distress covaries with overall life dissatisfaction even more strongly than does distress in other domains, such as health, work, or children.

Compared to individuals in satisfying relationships, distressed partners are significantly more likely to experience major depression, generalized anxiety disorder, social and specific phobia, panic disorder, and alcohol or other substance dependence or abuse. Moreover, adverse effects of couple distress are not confined to the adult partners. Couple distress has been related to a wide range of deleterious effects on children, including depression, anxiety, withdrawal, poor social competence, health problems, poor academic performance, and a variety of other concerns.

What are the implications of these findings for mental health practitioners and needs of the profession for this clinical textbook?

First—neither couple therapists nor therapists working with individuals can afford to ignore incontrovertible evidence regarding the recursive and mutually reinforcing interactions between individual disorders and couple relationship dysfunction. Rarely would one anticipate encountering someone with significant psychopathology for whom there are not also significant implications for that person's intimate relationships. Hence, couple-based therapies represent not only a viable intervention for a broad spectrum of individual emotional and behavioural disorders but, in many cases, also comprise the preferred treatment. Similarly, couple therapists should anticipate a strong likelihood that many of the partners they treat will also exhibit significant individual dysfunction. Individual psychopathology in either partner may cause or exacerbate existing relationship problems, may interfere with or detract from couple therapies targeting interpersonal functioning, or may require specific interventions aimed at individual mental health problems before interventions emphasizing relationship issues can be effective (Snyder & Whisman, 2003).

Second—effective treatments targeting either individual or couple distress, but especially their co-occurrence and interaction, will be more effective when they integrate interventions addressing contributing factors across a variety of domains (e.g., emotional, cognitive, and behavioural), across multiple system levels (e.g., individual, dyadic, extended interpersonal, and cultural), and broad temporal perspectives (e.g., developmental histories as well as current exigencies). Most individuals and couples in treatment exhibit complex and diverse amalgamations of contributing factors in their presenting complaints including individual dynamics, interpersonal relationships, and situational stressors—any of which may function as predisposing, precipitating, or perpetuating causal influences. Although many alternative theoretical approaches to couple therapy have been advanced (Gurman, Lebow, & Snyder, 2015), few of those can credibly proclaim to be integrative in this manner. Moreover, among the genuinely integrative approaches to couple-based treatments with evidence supporting their efficacy, none has the breadth of empirical support for extension to individuals with psychopathology as does the comprehensive cognitive-behavioural approach detailed in this clinical textbook.

What will the reader find here?

First, the book offers a thoughtful structure and sequencing of material intended to promote (a) a conceptual grasp of fundamental principles for understanding individual and relationship dysfunction from a broad cognitive-behavioural framework, (b) specific clinical skills for targeting behaviours, cognitions, and emotions in couple functioning—with consideration of both individual and broader systemic dynamics influencing their development and potentially informing their treatment, and (c) extension of couple-based interventions to the treatment of individual psychopathology—either by targeting specific aspects of the couple relationship interacting with individual dysfunction, or by drawing on one partner to offer support or engage in specific behaviours aimed at alleviating the distress of the other. Specific disorders featured in the text include depression, various anxiety-related disorders (including obsessive-compulsive disorder and posttraumatic stress), eating disorders, and a spectrum of other mood and emotion-regulation disorders. However, perhaps more important, the book promotes a way of conceptualizing, assessing, and addressing the interplay of couple and individual distress from a generalizable framework that transcends any specific disorder.

Second, the reader will find a treasure trove of clinical wisdom interwoven throughout the exposition of theory, empirical evidence, and description of specific interventions. All five authors are therapists, trainers, and supervisors who bring personal insights to both their research and teaching. Donald Baucom, from the United States, has published prolifically on cognitive-behavioural couple therapy and is recognized internationally as the premier clinical scientist developing and documenting the efficacy of couple-based treatments for a broad spectrum of mental and physical health problems. In England, Michael Worrell and Sarah Corrie have published valuable clinical guides related to cognitive-behavioural treatments and supervision for individual or couple dysfunction, and run intensive training programs in cognitive-behavioural therapy through the National Health Service in Great Britain. Melanie Fischer (from Germany) and Sara Boeding (from the United States) bring extensive research and clinical expertise both in treating relationship distress and in couple-based interventions for numerous disorders such as depression, OCD, emotion dysregulation, eating disorders, and posttraumatic stress. The result is a *tour de force* that integrates scholarship and clinical experience in exquisite fashion. And because the co-authors hail from different parts of the world but have worked together for years on a project to train therapists to work with couples experiencing depression, the book reflects both coherence and sensitivity to the myriad social and cultural factors influencing the development, expression, and treatment of both couple distress and individual psychopathology.

This book advances both the understanding and treatment of couple distress and individual psychopathology and their complex interaction. The text is clear and sequential, each chapter building incrementally on material that precedes it. Readers should approach the text as they might an elaborate meal with numerous courses—each distinct, each marvelous on its own, yet each reflecting what has already been encountered as well as that which is to come. This is a feast to be embraced!

References

Roz Gurman, A. S., Lebow, J. L., & Snyder, D. K. (2015). *Clinical handbook of couple therapy* (5th ed.). New York, NY: Guilford.

Snyder, D. K., & Whisman, M. A. (Eds.). (2003). *Treating difficult couples: Helping clients with coexisting mental and relationship disorders*. New York, NY: Guilford.

Foreword

Roz Shafran, Ph.D.

PROFESSOR OF TRANSLATIONAL PSYCHOLOGY

UCL GREAT ORMOND STREET INSTITUTE OF CHILD HEALTH, UK

I opened the newspapers this morning to the blazing headline that a new study has found that married women are physically stronger than single women. The newspapers speculate on the reasons for this and whether being in a relationship is good for you or not. They need not speculate, they could just refer to this comprehensive, accessible book written by world expert clinician-scientists that provides the answer on the first page about the central importance of healthy relationships to all aspects of life. The authors then turn the question around to discuss the potential damage, including accelerated death and impact on children, caused by the absence of meaningful relationships. It's a fantastic hook and strong foundation on which to introduce the central concept that relationships and individual psychopathology are bedfellows. Strong relationships can protect against mental health difficulties and poor ones can exacerbate them. The same is true in reverse—having mental health problems such as anxiety or depression can impact negatively on relationships. Using the relationship as the basis to improve individual psychological functioning and integrating the fields of couple therapy with the evidence-based treatment of individual psychopathology is such an obviously sensible way to proceed that it is no wonder that the approach is so compelling from theoretical, scientific, clinical, and human standpoints.

The book divides roughly into two halves. The first comprises Parts I and II (Chapters 1–9), and concerns the couple relationship and techniques for understanding and improving relationship distress in the cognitive, emotional, and behavioural domains. Within this section, there is a testable, integrated model that provides a visual aid to clinicians to help understand the different contexts that contribute to relationships. There is a chapter on how to conduct cognitive-behavioural couple therapy which is essential because it's not as easy as it might seem! For experienced therapists used to addressing individual psychopathology, it might seem as though the "common factors" of therapy and key principles of cognitive-behavioural therapy (collaboration, empiricism and Socratic dialogue) might make the transition easy, but the book makes it clear that such factors are necessary but not sufficient. Specific skills such as helping clients take a "dyadic perspective" are helpfully described and made explicit. The three subsequent chapters are devoted to explaining the basics of cognitive-behavioural couple therapy, including a focus on behaviour and communication as well as cognition and emotion. It is refreshing that behaviour and communication are given such prominence as it reflects the concerns that couples come with, as opposed to the rather more abstract but equally vital notion of cognition. Couples do not live in a vacuum, however, and understanding their individual, couple, and environmental context is fundamental and fully addressed in three separate chapters. Of the many wise words in the book, my personal favourite is in Chapter 8: "Frequent late nights out and partying with other couples likely will not serve them well as a young family." The examples given to illustrate points throughout the book are illuminating, including the description of the challenges to the relationship brought by transition to parenthood, illustrated by the example of Aliyah and Ernesto in Chapter 9. The book truly addresses the full spectrum of human experience including same-sex couples, work stress and empty nest syndrome, and the uniqueness of each couple.

The second half of the book (Parts III–V, comprising Chapters 10–15) focuses on psychopathology, and it is made explicit that the goal of couple-based treatments for psychopathology is to treat the mental health disorder. The chapters explain how to do this, using evidence-based principles from both cognitive-behavioural couple therapy and individual CBT to address a specific disorder. The close, reciprocal association between relationship functioning and psychopathology is presented before drawing on extensive experience and data on couple therapy for depression, anxiety, OCD and PTSD, and other disorders. The authors are gentle in the way they guide therapists through the various options of how to address such psychopathology. They are not proposing that couple-based treatments are the solution for all people with depression, nor are they suggesting that even in couples with relationship distress that "one-size fits all." Instead, they provide essential aids for clinical decision-making. It is this flexible, pragmatic approach that will ensure this book is used optimally rather than it being just another treatment manual gathering dust on the bookshelf. Being married to someone with social anxiety will require a different approach to being in a relationship with someone who is repeatedly begging you for reassurance that the house is locked. Both these scenarios and many others are tackled head-on in the chapters. The chapter on the various disorders includes a transdiagnostic perspective, including emotion regulation difficulties, and ends with key points about the importance of having a general treatment plan that is personalized to the presenting problem and couple seeking help.

Many would consider it strange to have the penultimate chapter on assessment, conceptualization and treatment planning, but the authors make it clear up-front that it is essential for clinicians to know what they are assessing prior to assessing it. This makes good sense, and I can only imagine the prolonged discussions prior to coming to the decision to have it close to the end of the book. It works brilliantly, links back to the model, and is an example to others to "buck the trend" to maximize the impact. The authors' confidence in their expertise that is apparent in such a decision is well-founded. They are an international "dream team." Don Baucom from the United States combines his unparalleled, wide-ranging clinical scholarship in couple therapy with decades of experience in research and education. His kindness and humour are a key part of his exceptional ability to share this work with students, clinicians, and academics. Melanie Fischer and Sara Boeding are central to the U.S. contributions to this book, bringing their individual research, clinical, and training expertise to share with the reader. Working from both the United States and Germany, Melanie Fischer provides leadership regarding the role of emotions in close relationships and individual psychopathology, integrating research with her treatment experience. In addition to her broad-based clinical and research experience with couples in multiple contexts, Sara Boeding contributes a real world dimension of extensive work with military couples and veterans in the United States. Michael Worrell and Sarah Corrie, likewise, fly the flag for real-world implementation of couple therapy in the context of psychopathology and are widely recognized as the leading evidence-based trainers and supervisors across England with a strong commitment to effectiveness research, demonstrating that these interventions work in real world settings outside of universities. They have provided notable contributions to health care in England by implementing these couple-based interventions in the National Health Service.

This book really has it all as far as I am concerned. Excellent writing enables difficult points to be understood; clear principles allow the techniques to be flexibly applied according to individual presentations; wonderful examples bring the book to life; the main points at the end of every chapter help remind and clarify the essentials; there is strong evidence in support of the approach; the book is a synthesis written by expert clinician-scientists with decades of experience in different contexts reflected in every chapter, and it is truly original. Most importantly, this book has the power to help clinicians transform the lives of millions of people affected by relationship distress and mental health problems. Happy reading!

Acknowledgments

Writing a book is a challenging and rewarding process. First and foremost, it is crucial to have something valuable to say to an appropriate readership. Second, as we describe throughout this book, human behaviour, including "book writing behaviour," has to be understood in context, taking into account the individuals, their relationships, and the context within which they operate. Third, writing a book is not a static phenomenon; it is a dynamic process that evolves over time. So, how did five co-authors born in four different countries come together to converge on what they believe to be the essence of healthy and maladaptive relationships, which often includes one or both partners with psychopathology?

By 2010 the five of us had been working as two teams: Baucom, Fischer, and Boeding in the United States, and Worrell and Corrie in England. For a number of years, the U.S.-based team had been intrigued by the intersection of individual and relationship functioning, how they went awry, and how to use the couple as the base of intervention to address distress in both of these domains, conducting both basic and treatment research to approach these issues. In England, Worrell and Corrie were centrally involved with efforts to bring empirically supported interventions to the public through the innovative and massive program entitled Improving Access to Psychological Therapies (IAPT) within the National Health Service (NHS). Given their own background in couple therapy and leadership in training and supervision of cognitive-behavioural therapy, the seeds of collaboration were planted and needed a stimulus to take shape. As we often ask couples, "So, how did you meet?" At that time, Phillip Tata in the NHS was a mastermind in facilitating effective partnerships. He invited the U.S. team to come to London to offer workshops on working with couples in which one person has depression, a treatment approved for dissemination within IAPT. Given that Roz Shafran had earlier introduced Don Baucom to the joys of training couple therapists in England, this seemed like a worthy venture. The two teams met in London, began offering the training workshops along with year-long clinical supervision, and the rest is history, realizing that history is truly dynamic. Operating within a large national system such as the NHS is complex, and it would not have been possible without the ongoing support of David Clark and Richard Layard, who helped to spearhead IAPT and helped us navigate this ongoing process. Our deepest gratitude to Roz Shafran, Phillip Tata, David Clark, and Richard Layard in England for creating the context and supporting our efforts to make this international collaboration a reality.

While offering our trainings on couples and depression, workshop participants continued to ask for appropriate readings to supplement the training. Among us, we had written numerous articles, book chapters, and books on couple therapy, psychopathology in a couple context, and training and supervision of cognitive-behavioural therapists. Yet, we had not created a single comprehensive, integrated source that brought these various clinical and research observations together. One day during one of these workshops, Michael Worrell casually proposed, “Why don’t we write a book on this?” “Sure, sounds great” the rest of us casually replied, kicking off a several-year international effort. Routledge agreed and has provided ongoing support, encouragement, flexibility, and expertise throughout this process, so our sincere thanks to our publisher for their assistance over these years of work on the book.

Co-authoring a book with five authors living in England and the United States (and later in Germany as well when Fischer returned to her home country) with different writing styles, different cultural experiences personally and professionally, and varying time zones to navigate requires good will, flexibility, and perspective to work effectively as a team. Through countless videoconferencing calls, emails, and in-person discussions, we have attempted to work in an integrated manner throughout this journey. Going beyond our collective perspectives, we highly valued integrating the perspectives of trusted colleagues and friends: Their input and expertise regarding various aspects of the book has been essential throughout. Therefore, our true appreciation to colleagues who know a lot about couples and psychopathology and were willing to give us valuable input and ideas about various chapters in the book: Brian Baucom, Emily Carrino, Carlton Coulter, Jessica Cuellar, and Doug Snyder. Anyone who has ever taken on the task of writing a book will know that a final detailed edit throughout from start to finish from someone with knowledge of the area who also is a professional editor is invaluable and often hard to come by. For us, Linda Baucom was the sole person who could do that, and we gratefully express our appreciation for the enormous effort that she put into that editing process.

As the authors, we hope this book is a valuable contribution to the field and is a “good read.” To whatever extent we have been successful in these efforts, to the above people we say, “Thanks for your help and for being part of the journey.”

Abbreviations

AN	anorexia nervosa
BA	behavioural activation
BED	binge eating disorder
BN	bulimia nervosa
CBCT	cognitive-behavioural couple therapy
CBI	couple-based intervention
CBT	cognitive-behavioural therapy
CBTI	cognitive-behavioural therapy for insomnia
DBT	dialectical behaviour therapy
ED	eating disorder
EE	expressed emotion
EFT	emotion-focused therapy
EOI	emotional overinvolvement
EST	empirically supported treatment(s)
OCD	obsessive-compulsive disorder
PTSD	posttraumatic stress disorder
SCT	stimulus control therapy
SRT	sleep restriction therapy
TTP	transition to parenthood

Part I

An introduction and overview of cognitive-behavioural couple therapy

Throughout this book, we discuss committed relationships, what contributes to optimal relationship functioning, and how some relationships become distressed. Second, we emphasize how to understand individual adult psychopathology within the context of intimate relationships and how relationships and individual functioning influence each other in a reciprocal, circular manner. With this understanding in mind, we then provide a wide range of interventions for clinicians to assist couples in addressing relationship distress and individual psychopathology. In doing so, we place a primary emphasis on empirically supported intervention principles from both the cognitive-behavioural couple therapy (CBCT) and individual therapy realms. Thus, the treatments described in this book are principle driven and are not presented as a treatment manual with a given number of sessions unfolding in a set fashion. Instead, with a clear understanding of intimate relationships and adult psychopathology, the clinician develops a conceptualization and treatment plan tailored to each couple. In order to accomplish these goals, the first section of this book lays the groundwork and provides a foundation for everything that follows. First, Chapter 1 provides the rationale for why to focus professional efforts on addressing relationship distress and psychopathology in an integrated manner. In proposing that psychopathology be treated at times with a couple-based approach, we are advocating for a broadened paradigm for the field of psychotherapy, and a strong justification needs to be made for such a fundamental shift. We believe that evidence from multiple disciplines exists to justify this continued broadening and strengthening of our approaches to treating human suffering.

Chapter 2 follows and presents our overall model for how to understand healthy committed relationships from a cognitive-behavioural perspective. This model integrates two frameworks. First, our contextual framework emphases that it is crucial to understand each partner as an *individual*, how the two partners come together to form a *couple* as a unit that is more than the sum of the two individuals, and how each partner and the couple live in a broader *environment*. The second framework described in Chapter 2 integrates and enhances the individual cognitive-behaviour therapy (CBT) perspective by addressing how one person's behaviours, cognitions, and emotions are impacted by the other partner's behaviours, cognitions, and emotions, creating a reciprocal feedback loop between the two partners. Likewise, these two frameworks are integrated into the complete model, discussing how these interrelated behaviours, cognitions, and emotions between and within the two partners relate to individual, couple, and environmental factors. This model serves as the foundation for CBCT for couples presenting with relationship distress and cognitive-behavioural, couple-based interventions (CBIs) for psychopathology.

Chapter 3 discusses what implementing CBCT and CBIs actually looks like and the role of the therapist as an integral factor in optimal treatment. We believe that, along with specific intervention techniques, the therapeutic relationship and the manner in which various interventions are presented are essential elements of optimal treatment. We provide a discussion of common factors in psychotherapy that are important in treatment outcome, including treatment enhancing factors that transcend specific theoretical orientations, factors common to different CBT approaches, and factors common to couple therapy. We present this chapter before delving into specific therapeutic interventions beginning in Part II because the specific interventions must be considered within the context of these common factors. As a therapist, it is not just what you do, but how you do it. This book is about relationships and their potential to optimize quality of life; consistent with this perspective, the therapeutic relationship has great potential to assist couples, particularly when paired with empirically supported intervention principles.

Chapter 1

Introduction

When people reflect on their own and their family's hopes and dreams, what do they see? Often they wish for a fulfilling life, happiness, good health, rewarding relationships, and opportunities to contribute to the world around them. At the end of life, people often cite these same areas of individual and interpersonal well-being as what made their lives the happiest and most fulfilling. So, the question remains, how do we get there? What leads to a full, enriching life? What makes people happy? Conversely, what factors contribute to broad dissatisfaction and even poor health?

These questions have been asked innumerable times across centuries and cultures, by people in all walks of life. Philosophers, writers, religious leaders, mental health professionals, and scientists have attempted to address this question in a multitude of ways. Although there are undoubtedly many influences, findings from several disciplines seem to converge on at least one set of factors that is vital to our well-being—the centrality of strong, caring, close relationships. Human beings are social creatures, and meaningful connections with others are essential for most people to live their lives to the fullest. This conclusion seems to surface again and again.

For example, the Harvard Study of Adult Development began in 1938 when male undergraduate students were assessed across multiple domains, including physical, psychological, and relationship well-being. That assessment has broadened and continued to the present, with some of the participants now in their 90s. Because this sample was not representative of society at large, men with lower socioeconomic status were later added to the investigation. Strikingly, a major conclusion after decades of gathering voluminous amounts of data seems surprisingly straightforward, as stated by the director of the investigation, Robert Waldinger (2015):

> When we gathered together everything we knew about them at age 50, it wasn't their middle-age cholesterol levels that predicted how they were going to grow old . . . It was how satisfied they were in their relationships. The people who were the most satisfied in their relationships at age 50 were the healthiest at age 80.

Or, as the previous director of the Harvard Study George Valliant noted, "When the study began, nobody cared about empathy or attachment. But the key to healthy aging is relationships, relationships, relationships" (Mineo, 2017).

From a very different perspective, Richard Layard, an economist at the London School of Economics, spent many years pioneering research on happiness, the economy, and other aspects of life across different countries. Although happiness is not the only goal in life, it is of paramount importance for many people and is closely related to overall life satisfaction. The associations between economic standards of living and reported quality of life are complex;

clearly, poverty and living financially below what individuals experience to be a reasonable level adversely impact an individual's well-being (Payne, Brown-Iannuzzi, & Hannay, 2017). When Layard looked beyond economic factors, he found that across cultures, genders, and walks of life, the *quality of family relationships* is one of the most important predictors of happiness (Layard, 2005). These findings are consistent with the Harvard study described above: Individuals who have rewarding, satisfying close relationships tend to be the happiest.

Whereas healthy relationships contribute to well-being, is the reverse true as well? Does the absence of meaningful relationships place individuals at risk for negative outcomes? Consistent with this notion, Holt-Lunstad, Smith, and Layton (2010) investigated the role of social relationships in mortality. Evaluating the findings of 148 studies, which included more than 300,000 participants in total and followed participants for an average of 7.5 years, they found a 50% increased likelihood of survival for individuals who had stronger social relationships. This finding was robust across age, sex, initial health status, and cause of death. In essence, successful relationships are about more than feeling good; they have implications for one's very survival.

The above findings demonstrate the importance of close relationships in promoting well-being and the lack of such relationships in predicting death. Yet, relationships are not the sole factor influencing how individuals fare over their lives. It seems likely that issues which focus more explicitly on the individual would impact distress or suffering. Layard and Clark (2014) explored which factors contribute most to human suffering (note that the absence of suffering does not imply the presence of happiness and well-being). Integrating findings across countries and studies, they concluded that the greatest source of human misery is mental illness, even more so than physical illness. Consistent with this conclusion, the World Health Organization recently ranked depression as the single largest contributor to global disability (World Health Organization, 2017).

The findings across these various lines of research are striking and point to two responses to the question: "How do we live and help others live in a way that leads to the most rewarding lives possible?" First, close relationships are central in psychological and physical well-being and overall happiness, and a lack of meaningful relationships predicts a shorter life expectancy. Second, mental health is essential in order to avoid suffering. Hence, the two major foci of this book—intimate relationships and psychological well-being—are key to experiencing a full and rewarding life for most people. Furthermore, not only are these two domains important, but they also are inextricably intertwined.

The impact of relationship adjustment on individual functioning

In most cultures, a large proportion of adults form committed relationships at some point in their lives, with implications for themselves, their nuclear and extended family, and their wider community. Although marriage rates have been declining in many Western countries, marriage remains common and also has become legal for same-sex couples in an increasing number of countries. In 2018, 71.2% of adults 18 years and above in the United States were married at some point in their lives (U.S. Census Bureau, 2018a); in addition, other adults never married but were in a committed relationship. In England and Wales, 81.7% of men and 87.5% of women born in 1960 had married by the time they were 50 years old (Office for National Statistics, 2015). Thus, intimate relationships are an important aspect of the lives of most individuals, and the quality of these relationships can have wide-ranging impact on all family members.

Impact on individual partners

Strong relationships can contribute to individual well-being in a multitude of ways, largely by (a) increasing positive experiences for both partners and (b) improving individuals' ability to cope with negative experiences, stressors, and risk factors. For example, people in satisfied relationships are more likely to have positive emotions and enjoyable experiences such as love, companionship, affection, physical and emotional intimacy, social support, and rewarding joint couple and family activities. In addition, being in a committed relationship tends to afford certain social and practical benefits, including greater financial resources and stability, shared family responsibilities, and social status.

Satisfying romantic relationships also buffer the individual against negative experiences and stressors in profound ways. While it is easy to think of practical examples of how partners might care for one another, such as taking on extra household chores when one's partner is sick, it is also important to understand that social bonding is ingrained in human biology. That is, a person's subjective emotional experiences, physiological responses, and behavioural reactions become interdependent with one's partner in close relationships, which has the potential to assist the individual during difficult times (Coan, Schaefer, & Davidson, 2006; Diamond & Aspinwall, 2003; Sbarra & Hazan, 2008). The message is truly, "You don't have to do this alone."

The positive effects of healthy relationships are also demonstrated when one person has a psychological disorder. Many research studies and clinical observation confirm that close relationships influence the course of psychological disorders, either by helping to alleviate distress and facilitate recovery, or by contributing to the maintenance and exacerbation of symptoms (Fischer & Baucom, 2018). Across many disorders, appropriate support from a partner can be restorative and assist an individual in overcoming distressing symptoms. On the other hand, distressed relationships can serve as a broad chronic stressor on the individual. If one partner has a vulnerability to a condition such as depression, living in a chronically stressful social environment can contribute to the precipitation of a disorder or impede recovery.

However, even in satisfied relationships, well-meaning partners can inadvertently contribute to the maintenance of an individual's disorder. Loving partners often seek to decrease the affected person's psychological distress but do so in counterproductive ways. Termed *symptom accommodation,* this set of behaviours includes actions that partners may knowingly or unknowingly take to alleviate or prevent distress for the affected person in the moment, which ultimately help to maintain the disorder in the long term. For example, partners might take over roles and responsibilities or help the person avoid anxiety-provoking situations. As will be discussed at length in the current volume, accommodation takes various forms, in large part as a function of the disorder itself. Although the specific form of accommodation might vary, research on couples and families has consistently shown that accommodation to psychological symptoms is associated with more severe symptoms and poorer treatment outcomes (e.g., Boeding et al., 2013; Calvocoressi et al., 1995; Fredman, Pukay-Martin, et al., 2015; Sepulveda, Kyriacou, & Treasure, 2009). Thus, couples' relationships have great potential to impact the course of an individual's psychological disorder in both positive and negative ways.

Impact on children

At the family level, the impact of relationship problems appears to continue throughout the life span of children with relationally distressed or divorced parents, even for several generations. For example, children of high-conflict or divorced parents are more likely to experience internalizing and externalizing problems, academic difficulties, and low self-esteem. In addition, they are more prone to drop out of school, commit acts of juvenile delinquency, and engage in substance abuse. When these children reach adulthood, they tend to have lower socioeconomic status, relationship problems of their own, and increased divorce rates, compared to children of nondivorced parents (Amato, 2001; Hetherington & Elmore, 2004; Zimet & Jacob, 2001). Perhaps most poignantly, a follow-up study of Terman's classic study of gifted children found that children from divorced families died on average four years earlier compared to their peers with nondivorced parents (Friedman et al., 1995). In summary, a couple's distressed relationship or relationship termination can extend beyond themselves and impact their children in the present and for years to come, with the majority of evidence suggesting that it is relationship discord rather than divorce per se that might be the more important factor (Sbarra, Bourassa, & Manvelian, 2019).

The impact of individual functioning on relationship adjustment

As noted above, the level of relationship adjustment impacts both partners as individuals and their children. The reverse is true as well. Within a couple's relationship, each of the two individuals influences the quality of the relationship. Being with a partner who is happy, well adjusted, skilled, flexible, and generous can be a huge asset to the other individual and to the relationship. Consistent with this perspective, Baucom and Aiken (1984) found that when both partners had strong leadership skills, were task-oriented, and were interpersonally attuned, those couples had particularly high levels of relationship satisfaction. On the other hand, individual psychological problems experienced by one person can be a major stressor for the other partner and the couple's relationship. For example, findings confirm that when one partner is depressed, such couples have a highly elevated risk of developing subsequent relationship distress (Davila, Bradbury, Cohan, & Tochluk, 1997). This finding is not surprising because low energy and depressed mood can interfere with positive interactions between partners, decrease intimacy, and result in the redistribution of household chores. Other disorders often impact the couple's relationship functioning in unique ways as well. Therefore, in considering how to help a couple alleviate relationship distress or optimize relationship functioning, it is important to understand how each individual's well-being impacts the other partner and the relationship as a whole.

Treating relationship and individual distress—a dyadic perspective

Given the complex interplay between individual and relationship functioning, what is the most appropriate way to think about psychological interventions for various presenting concerns? If a couple presents with relationship distress, the couple itself often is considered to be the client, and some form of couple therapy or counselling is likely to be recommended. However, if a client presents with what traditionally has been considered to be an "individual psychological problem" such as an anxiety disorder or depression, then individual psychotherapy is often seen as the gold standard for treatment. Finally, if both individual and relationship concerns are present, the client might receive two separate forms of therapy simultaneously, employing an additive approach to addressing each concern. Thus, relationship difficulties are traditionally addressed in couple therapy and individual problems in individual therapy.

In essence, viewing adaptive and maladaptive functioning as existing solely on either a relationship level or an individual level can lead to overly simplistic conceptualizations of a client's concerns and less than optimal treatment. A major premise of this book is that, in order to optimize treatment for a wide range of concerns, a clinician will benefit from understanding the complex interplay between relationship and individual functioning. Thus, many clients with psychological difficulties that have previously been viewed as individual problems might benefit notably from including a partner in treatment. Similarly, when assisting a couple with relationship distress, a clinician will likely have the greatest impact if they know how to integrate individual functioning into a thorough conceptualization and treatment of relationship concerns. To further contextualize individual and relationship distress, and to address other relevant factors that often maintain the distress, both demands and resources in the couple's physical and social environment need to be attended to as well.

Hence, this book focuses on how to conduct couple-based interventions, meaning that both partners attend sessions together and both are integral to treatment. When the primary target of treatment is relationship distress, this intervention is best conceived of as *couple therapy* with the goal of improving the relationship. When the primary focus of treatment is one partner's psychological concern, these interventions are termed *couple-based interventions for psychopathology*. This term is employed to indicate that the couple is considered the basis of the intervention, with the goal of improving one (or both) partner's psychological condition. When couples seek intervention because both individual and relationship difficulties pervade their lives, these two approaches are integrated.

In order to be effective in offering couple-based interventions that incorporate an emphasis on both relationship and individual distress, clinicians will benefit from the integration of skills across several areas. First, an in-depth understanding of romantic relationship functioning and the major intervention techniques employed in couple therapy to promote behavioural, cognitive, and emotional change in one or both partners provides a solid foundation for this work. Thus, in this volume, we provide a sound background in understanding and treating relationship distress from a cognitive-behavioural perspective. Cognitive-behavioural couple therapy (CBCT) has an extremely strong research and clinical base and includes a focus on normative individual factors such as personality traits and individual needs and motives (Epstein & Baucom, 2002).

Second, the clinician needs to understand specific forms of individual psychopathology and be knowledgeable about the changes needed for an individual to recover, improve, or cope effectively with the disorder. Within this context, the current volume draws upon empirically supported treatments (EST) from an individual treatment perspective, with an emphasis on cognitive-behavioural therapy (CBT), due to its strong empirical track record (de Jong & DeRubeis, 2018). These well-founded individual intervention principles are drawn upon in couple-based interventions for psychopathology.

Third, the clinician must know how to integrate these two factors. The approach encompasses an integration of (a) working effectively with couples in general, and (b) promoting individual change when one partner is struggling. This integration involves understanding how individual difficulties exist within the relationship. It also includes understanding how to employ the relationship to promote individual well-being.

At first, developing all the skills needed to be an effective therapist could seem daunting, but that has not been our experience in training hundreds of therapists internationally (D. H. Baucom & Boeding, 2013). Across a multitude of training sessions, we have encountered four types of therapists. First, some therapists have previous training and experience in working with couples. They tend to be comfortable with managing two clients in the room at one time and providing a relational lens for viewing problems. In many instances, such therapists need to focus on understanding individual psychopathology and the interventions that have been used successfully to treat these disorders, and then learning how to integrate these individual cognitive-behavioural treatment principles into their couple work. Second, many therapists have experience in individual CBT for various disorders but little or no experience in working with couples. These therapists need to focus on how to work with couples, manage the high levels of negative affect that often occur in therapy sessions, and give a "relational lens" to what they already know about CBT. Third, some therapists have experience in both couple therapy for relationship distress and individual therapy for psychopathology. For them, the challenge is learning to integrate these two somewhat separate modalities into a couple-based treatment. Finally, some therapists are beginning this journey with little experience in either couple or individual therapy. If you are one of these latter therapists, you are in luck—there is very little that you will need to unlearn!

To complicate and enrich matters further beyond the individuals and the couple level, most people live in relationships within complex environments (e.g., neighbourhoods, work environments, social networks); individuals encounter a variety of relational, social, and environmental influences. Thus, our goal in this book is to propose something of a paradigm shift within a cognitive-behavioural framework—employing couple-based interventions to address relationship discord, along with psychological disorders, while explicitly taking into account individual, relationship, and environmental factors.

In order to accomplish these goals, this book addresses two major topics. First, we focus on understanding couples' relationships and how to treat relationship distress. Although they often overlap, for heuristic purposes these intervention strategies are differentiated into treatment strategies focused on the behavioural, cognitive, and emotional domains. These interventions are also placed within a contextual framework, stressing the importance of attending in treatment to the two partners as individuals, the couple as a unit, and the environment within which they live. The second portion of the book places an emphasis on individual psychopathology within an interpersonal context. An overall interpersonal model for understanding and treating psychopathology is provided with a particular emphasis on depression and anxiety disorders, given their high prevalence. Additional disorders such as eating disorders, bipolar disorder, insomnia, substance use disorders, and broader emotion regulation difficulties also are addressed, demonstrating how to develop effective treatment plans across a wide range of individual concerns. Next, strategies for assessing the couple are discussed. Although it might seem unusual to cover assessment near the end of the book, it is necessary to have a clear understanding of relationship distress, individual psychopathology, and various interventions strategies prior to explaining how to conduct an assessment; in essence, the clinician needs to know what to assess before doing so. The initial assessment then leads to a case conceptualization and initial treatment plan, and the principles for developing these reports are provided. Throughout the book, the empirical status of the work is noted; we have a strong commitment to providing empirically supported interventions to couples. Thus, it is important to know the extent and limits of our empirical knowledge and where we need to go next, both as clinicians and as relationship scientists.

Our belief is that the best hope for providing thoughtful, clinically sensitive interventions to couples results from addressing the complexity of life that people experience. Thus, our approach involves integrating empirical knowledge of interventions for relationship functioning and individual psychopathology while attending to behavioural, cognitive, and emotional factors within a contextual framework, along with what we know about the nonspecific factors that are important in conducting therapy. The next chapter provides an overall model of relationship functioning and serves as an important building block in this process.

Chapter 2

A cognitive-behavioural model for understanding relationship functioning and individual well-being

Chapter 1 points to the centrality of healthy intimate relationships for the well-being of the relationship itself and for an individual's well-being and happiness. The resulting challenge is to understand what factors contribute to fulfilling relationships, how the relationships are maintained successfully over time, and how they go astray. When couples seek treatment for relationship problems, some partners are precise and clear about what is going wrong, how their difficulties developed, and what they think might help (suggestions usually involve having the other person "shape up" in some way). More frequently, couples are not clear about what is going wrong, as reflected by Samantha when asked about why she and Paul had decided to seek therapy: "I don't know; everything just seems to have fallen apart. We can't talk about anything without it turning into a major fight. And our physical relationship—nonexistent. I don't understand it; I just know it isn't working anymore."

In many instances, the therapist plays a major role in helping the couple get past this confusion—or the mutual blame—and delineate an understanding of how they might work to make their relationship better. In order to conceptualize the couple's difficulties and develop an appropriate treatment plan, the therapist needs a theoretical model of relationship functioning. Our approach draws heavily from existing models of individual functioning while incorporating appropriate adaptations and extensions to understand relationships. More specifically, we have adopted a broad, cognitive-behavioural approach both to understand relationship functioning and to implement couple-based interventions. Thus, an understanding of central behaviours, cognitions, and emotions, as delineated in cognitive-behavioural therapy (CBT), is retained in conceptualizing couples' relationships. Whereas mastering CBT concepts and interventions can be challenging when considering only one individual, this process is further complicated because with couples there are, by definition, two individuals to consider. Moreover, when exploring a couple's relationship, each individual's behaviours, cognitions, and emotions of central interest often are *about* the other partner, the couple's relationship, or oneself within the context of the relationship. Therefore, these couple-oriented reactions from each individual are important to take into account when conceptualizing a couple. Most importantly, couple-oriented cognitions and emotions typically do not remain internal to the individual. Instead, an individual's thoughts and feelings routinely influence that person's behaviour toward a partner, who then reacts with corresponding cognitions, emotions, and behaviours. This reciprocal, bidirectional, ongoing set of actions and reactions between the two partners then creates a unique relationship between the two partners that we call "a couple."

As a result, there are important patterns unique to the couple as a unit that go beyond a CBT understanding of individuals. For example, one person's behaviour typically influences the partner's subsequent behaviour, such that the second person is more likely to respond similarly to how the first person behaved. This couple-level pattern is referred to as *reciprocity* (Gottman, 1979), and it can be either negative or positive. That is, when one person is critical toward a partner, the partner is more likely to respond with a critical or other negative response, and the couple becomes trapped in a negative cycle, a hallmark of relationship distress.

In addition, each partner and the couple must be viewed in a larger context; each person is part of multiple systems that include the couple itself, each individual's immediate and extended family, and their interactions with their broader physical and social environment. Therefore, the current model also incorporates aspects of systems theories, such as Bronfenbrenner's ecological systems theory (1989) and Nichols and Schwartz's systems perspective (2001).

Likewise, while acknowledging each person's prior experiences or learning history as an important factor, CBT generally emphasizes the present and the future. Other models, such as psychodynamic theories, place relatively more emphasis on how one's past influences the present. Within CBT, past experiences and learning histories are represented in the notions of *schemas* and *core beliefs* that individuals might develop over the course of their lives (A. T. Beck, Rush, Shaw, & Emery, 1979; J. S. Beck, 2011; Young, 1999). In cognitive-behavioural couple therapy (CBCT), we emphasize the impact of learning histories, core beliefs, and schemas that might significantly impact current relationship functioning, such as a core belief that "people can't be trusted." Schemas or core beliefs that existed prior to the relationship might influence the couple in ways that they do not recognize; for example, such a core belief could underlie discomfort with intimacy even if the person generally has a high need for intimacy. Many behavioural patterns within a relationship develop over time and are, in part, the result of the person's earlier relationships and experiences. Therefore, the current model takes into account not only recent factors in understanding relationships but also more historical influences when appropriate.

The above discussion highlights that for any couple, there are broad themes that are important for understanding the couple and for treatment planning. In addition, a hallmark of cognitive-behavioural approaches has been an emphasis on specificity. Both levels of understanding are incorporated in the current model; they are referred to as *macro* and *micro* levels of functioning, respectively. On a micro level, the couple might argue about how to use their free time, how to balance couple versus individual time, and whether to use their couple time talking over a leisurely dinner or going to a movie. On a macro level, disagreements about what to do during their free time might be part of a larger pattern regarding different desires for intimacy. This broader theme of intimacy might also be a source of conflict concerning the extent to which the partners disclose vulnerable information to each other, how they relate physically to each other, and in other micro-level disagreements. Optimal understanding and intervention attend both to specific domains of concern and to how these specific concerns might fit into broader patterns, which can help to guide treatment planning and ongoing intervention.

In summary, our approach to understanding relationships and individual functioning within those relationships flows from a comprehensive, cognitive-behavioural conceptualization. The model includes not only individual behaviours, cognitions, and emotions that are typically explored within CBT. It also emphasizes those same elements as they are focused on the couple. Thus, the focus is not only on the two persons as unique individuals but also on the couple as a unit. Therefore, new constructs and patterns at the couple level must be introduced, building on and expanding beyond the constructs central to understanding individual functioning. Finally, the couple does not exist in isolation, so the role of their social and physical environment must be considered as well.

The CBCT model of relationship functioning and couple therapy

As described above, the current model draws heavily from individual cognitive-behavioural models, while asking the question, "What is new or unique about relationship functioning from a CBT perspective that cannot be gleaned from an individual model?" Essential to the CBCT model is the recognition that relationships have to be understood in context; they do not exist in isolation but rather in an ecological milieu. Within this contextual perspective of the CBCT model, three domains or units of functioning notably impact the relationship and provide the focus for applying a CBT framework. Moving from smaller to larger units, these domains are: (a) the well-being of each partner as an individual in the relationship, (b) the couple's ability to function as a unit, and (c) the couple's interactions with their social and physical environment, along with a consideration of how these three domains influence each other. Therefore, it is helpful first to consider these three contextual domains and then explore the behavioural, cognitive, and emotional factors relevant to each of these domains.

Several characteristics are important to all three domains. First, each domain must function well in its own right. It is certainly preferable that both individuals are well adjusted without significant psychopathology, both for that individual's well-being per se and because psychological distress in either or both partners often places stress on the couple's relationship. Moreover, for the couple to thrive, they need to be able to function well as a unit; they need to be able to make decisions effectively, accomplish tasks, and create a caring, loving atmosphere unique to that couple. Likewise, although couples might have limited control over certain aspects of their environment, the nature of that environment might strongly impact the couple. For example, couples living through a national financial crisis (or natural disaster, or death of a parent, or living in a low-income area) are affected by these forces that exist beyond themselves.

Second, the three domains must exist relative to each other in some sense of balance. Many couples lead complex lives and deciding how to devote energy to themselves as individuals, as a couple, and in interaction with others around them is a significant challenge. Often, life is a balancing act for which there is no easy solution. For some couples, life consists of a string of activities to attend to in one domain before moving on to the next. For other couples, the balance might have been tipped toward one area for a long time, making it difficult to imagine how things could be different despite the problems this imbalance creates. For example, it is not uncommon for one partner—in different-sex relationships often the female partner—to become the "family manager," keeping up with everyone's schedules and day-to-day needs, and putting those needs before her own. As Sena responded when asked what she wanted for herself, "I have no idea. That doesn't seem like a relevant question; I don't even consider what I want." For other couples, their lives seem to be devoid of meaning and gratification in any of the three domains; they experience themselves as merely existing. Furthermore, many couples do not know what a balanced life means for them. Is it devoting equal time, energy, and resources to each domain? Such a strategy is likely to prove simplistic and unsuccessful. Instead, balance implies allocating time and energy in a manner that is consistent with their goals and values at a given point in life, while also taking into account the demands of each domain and the long-term impacts on the couple. Translating this broad perspective on balance into concrete decisions and daily life is a complex process.

Third, a healthy relationship must be able to adapt to changes over time. Although a couple might be successful in attending to each of the three domains with a good sense of balance at a given point, life changes and individuals grow or struggle in different ways throughout adulthood. What each person wants from the relationship changes, and the environment provides different challenges and opportunities over time. It is not unusual to find that a couple has been doing well until they enter a new phase of life, but then they struggle when they are unable to meet new, unfamiliar demands. For example, when a couple reaches the *empty nest* stage of life after children have left home, they might experience difficulties because they previously spent much of their time as a couple attending to their children. Now they are uncertain about how to relate to each other or what to talk about when the children's activities are no longer central in their daily lives. In some instances, couples seem to be aware that they are in a new phase of life that requires change, yet they are uncertain about how to accomplish such changes. Other couples, in the face of new difficulties, continue to behave as they have in the past and might not fully recognize the need for change. For example, continuing to spend money without much thought after a financial setback does not work, although it might have been appropriate in the past.

The above discussion acknowledges the complexity of factors to consider in understanding a couple's relationship: attending to each of three domains of life simultaneously, maintaining some sense of balance among them, and adapting over time as life changes. This set of tasks is complex enough if there is a unified perspective that both partners share. Yet in many instances, two somewhat or two very different perspectives or preferences regarding these domains must be taken into account. Thus, what is balanced for one partner might be very skewed for the other partner; for example, one partner might prefer a great deal of solo time while the other wants to spend most of their time together as a couple. Differences in perspective might be a function of personality, individual upbringing and learning histories, or the cultural identity of each partner, among other factors. Consequently, the relationship must take into account two different perspectives on all the factors noted above, and a couple's effectiveness in integrating the two perspectives greatly impacts their satisfaction and functioning. Many couples are successful in doing so, but others struggle as each person attempts to have their own needs and preferences met, at times at the expense of the other partner.

In order to understand how couples might navigate the above challenges, an overview follows of each of the three contextual domains of individual well-being, couple functioning, and environmental integration (see also Figure 2.1). Consistent with our cognitive-behavioural theoretical orientation, the cognitive, emotional, and behavioural responses of each partner must be understood across these domains. Each will be discussed separately in subsequent chapters. The current chapter provides an overview of our integrated model which considers (a) three contextual domains focusing on the individual, couple, and environment as relevant to the couple's relationship, and (b) the cognitive, emotional, and behavioural responses of each partner across these various domains.

The couple in context—individual, couple, and environmental factors

Meeting the needs of the individual and addressing individual differences

As noted above, relationships involve two people, and for a relationship to be successful, it needs to contribute to the growth and continuing development of both partners as unique individuals. Therefore, optimal relationships help both partners grow and feel good about themselves, bringing out the best in each person, and contributing to both individuals'

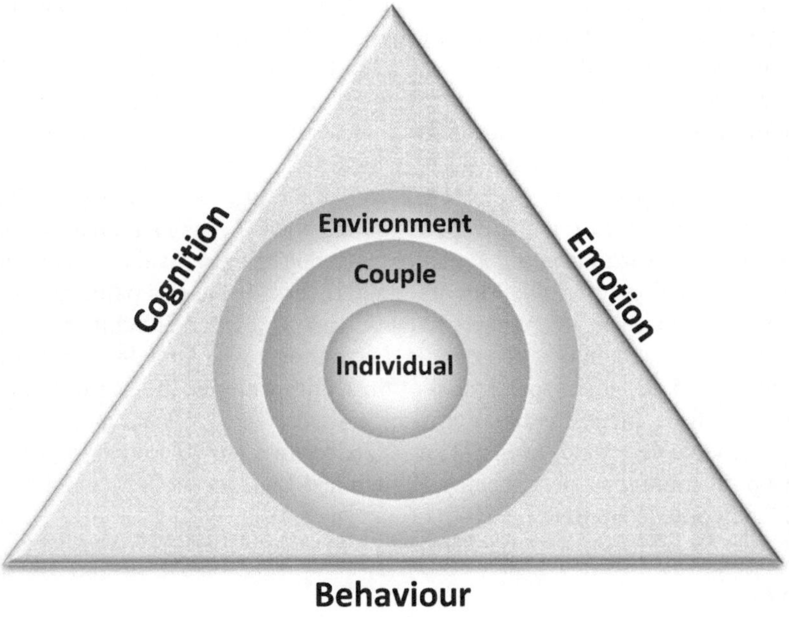

Figure 2.1 The CBCT model of relationship functioning

well-being. In order to provide such benefits to each partner, it is important to understand what individuals seek from relationships. A common source of relationship distress involves one or both partners' experience that their relationship is not meeting or, worse yet, is stifling some of that person's important motives/needs[1] and goals in life, or the partner or relationship does not seem to respect who that person is as an individual and how that partner wants to live.

Individual and communal motives or needs

Although no relationship can be expected to meet all of an individual's needs, partners often develop interdependent lives in which their individual well-being and overall life satisfaction are greatly influenced by their relationship. Based on a variety of influences such as cultural norms and individual differences, individuals seek to have many needs met within their relationship context, either directly or by developing a relationship that allows each person to get some of their needs met elsewhere in an adaptive fashion. Although there can be debate regarding what is a need/motive, a desire, or a preference, we use the term *motive* consistent with McClelland's (1987, p. 132) definition of a motive as a "learned, affectively charged anticipatory state aroused by various cues." That is, individuals have emotional responses to various situations or cues that motivate them to seek certain goals, and these behavioural responses tend to occur in patterns that become well ingrained over time. For example, upon seeing one's partner, one might frequently have a strong, warm emotional response that triggers a desire for closeness. Because different people have different learning histories, they might seek that closeness in different ways, for example, through meaningful conversations, physical proximity, or joint activities. The strength of these motives, the ways in which each individual seeks to satisfy those motives, and the receptivity of the partner are all important in how adaptively these motives are met within the couple's relationship.

Individuals vary widely in terms of the strength and importance of their motives, and there is no explicit healthy or adaptive level for each motive. Thus, if one person has a particularly strong need for achievement, that motive by itself is not maladaptive. Instead, *how* individuals attempt to fulfil their needs is what matters, i.e., whether they do so in an adaptive or maladaptive manner. For relationships to work well, each partner must be responsive to the other person's needs as well as their own, attempting to meet those needs in a manner that is respectful and sustainable over time and that conforms to both persons' values. While it might seem obvious that relationship difficulties are likely to arise if the two partners vary widely in their most salient motives, the partners likewise can experience difficulties when the two people are similar to each other. For example, two partners who both desire a great deal of intimacy with each other might spend most of their time with just the two of them, resulting in hurt feelings from friends and family members who feel devalued, along with social isolation of the couple over time. In CBCT, we consider two sets of motives that are central to relationship functioning as described by Epstein and Baucom (2002): communal motives and individually oriented motives.

COMMUNAL MOTIVES

Communal motives refer to an individual's desires that are relationship oriented and involve interactions with other people, including their partner. These motives often involve a wish for strong stable relationships with others, a sense of belonging, and being part of a social network. Epstein and Baucom (2002) have delineated four core communal motives: (a) *affiliation*, a need to be with people rather than engaging in solitary activities; (b) *intimacy*, a need for close contact, mutual disclosure, and other forms of sharing in another person's world; (c) *altruism*, a need to take care of other people's needs, even when it involves personal sacrifice; and (d) *succorance*, a need to be nurtured by others.

Often partners vary regarding their communal motives, and these differences can be challenging for couples. For example, when two partners vary notably in their desire for intimacy, they often experience a push-pull pattern. This dynamic will be described below in its more extreme form, a demand-withdraw interaction pattern, in which the person wanting more closeness attempts to "pull" the other person closer while the person wanting less closeness attempts to "push" the other person away. Such patterns can lead to feelings of rejection or suffocation, respectively.

INDIVIDUALLY ORIENTED MOTIVES

In addition to having various motives that are focused on relationships, people want to feel good about themselves and experience meaningful lives as individuals. Epstein and Baucom (2002) note three central individually oriented motives that are important in relationship functioning: (a) *autonomy*, a need to operate freely within one's environment, pursuing one's personal interests and goals independently of other people; (b) *power or influence*, a need to exercise influence and experience impact on one's environment; and (c) *achievement*, a need to perform well on tasks, gaining mastery and improved status in one's own or others' eyes.

Just as with communal needs, differences between two partners on individual needs can be challenging for the couple to navigate. For example, if one person has a strong motive for achievement and the other person does not, the latter partner might feel unloved or second priority and perhaps express, "Your job is more important to you than I am." Likewise, a very achievement-oriented person can start to lose respect for a partner who does not have a similar drive to excel. As with communal motives, even when the two partners have similar individual needs, such similarity can result in an imbalance in the couple's life. Thus, if both partners are extremely achievement oriented, they might each spend a great deal of time engaged in individual pursuits but then experience a lack of intimacy between them. This lack of closeness can result, not from a desire to avoid closeness, but rather because the partners' focus on achievement in other realms diminishes their time to foster intimacy. That is, they are struggling to find a way to balance each partner's motives, which has a subsequent impact on their relationship.

Other individual differences

In addition to the above needs/motives that can drive individual behaviour, other individual differences, personal styles, and personality attributes also can impact relationship functioning. Although there is likely an endless list of such characteristics, some tend to be particularly salient and require negotiation between two partners. For example, partners often differ in the degree to which they prefer spontaneity versus careful planning. At times, partners report that they found these differences appealing in their initial attraction to each other but later found their partner's characteristics to be a source of frustration. For example, a very planful individual might initially seek out a carefree partner to add spontaneity to their life yet later view that same individual as scatterbrained and disorganized. Likewise, the more spontaneous individual might think of a planful, detail-oriented partner initially as providing stability and a sense of groundedness, only later to experience the same person as rigid and tedious.

In summary, for a relationship to succeed, it must be responsive to the motives and needs of each partner, accommodate personality and other differences between the two partners, and be attuned to risks that come from being too alike on some dimensions. Hopefully, each partner has an experience that makes them feel, "Being with you allows me to be me and respects who I am." These and other individual factors are discussed in Chapter 7. In addition to normative individual differences, individual functioning might also be strongly impacted by a psychological disorder, with consequences for the relationship; this situation is discussed further in Chapter 10.

Couple processes

Most couples would agree that they are more than the sum of the two partners as individuals; they form a unit that has its own distinct style and attributes—a couple. That is, there is not only a *you* and *me* as two separate entities who come together to define the couple; there is a *we* that transcends the sum of the two. A number of factors help to define and maintain the couple as a unit; when these basic functions and aspects of the *we* are not operating well, relationship distress often ensues. Satisfied couples have a clear sense of "we-ness" (Sullivan & Baucom, 2004) and have translated what their couple identity means into concrete behaviours, routines, and ways of living that maintain that identity. As discussed below, in defining themselves as a unit, couples need some sense of boundaries around their relationship, that is, who and what aspects of their lives and sets of behaviours are solely theirs and what aspects incorporate others. Within those boundaries, they need an investment of effort and energy from both partners so that the relationship functions well, remains vital, and is a high priority for both of them. Yet, these factors do not clarify how the partners actually operate as a unit, how they relate and accomplish tasks. More specifically, how do they make decisions? How is authority and power allocated around various domains? How do they communicate with each other to make these decisions and to stay connected? The above factors help to define how a couple functions at a given point in time. In addition, the couple needs to be able to balance stability and change to be responsive to the complex, evolving context within which they operate.

Relationship boundaries

First, for the couple to exist, a set of *boundaries* must be established around the couple that separates and differentiates them from their social environment, including family members and friends. Couples either explicitly discuss or implicitly attempt to define what belongs to us only, and where others are not allowed, thus facilitating a sense of commitment, closeness, and attachment. For example, couples might decide that certain topics such as their finances are not discussed with anyone else. Or they might decide that when taking a holiday or vacation, no one beyond their immediate family is invited to participate. Likewise, couples often have strong feelings about where to set boundaries regarding physical contact and extent of interaction with other individuals. That is, a brief hello hug with a friend whom a partner has not seen for some time might be acceptable, but a long embrace with a co-worker each morning could be taboo. Sometimes, couples have not discussed these issues but rather have assumed that they agree on where to set such boundaries. One person then becomes upset when the partner behaves outside of the presumed boundaries: "You do not do that with other people!" On other occasions, one or both partners knowingly violate a boundary and become involved in a sexual or an emotional affair, with a potentially devastating impact on the couple. Thus, helping couples clarify and navigate relationship boundaries is important in therapy since boundaries help to define the limits for the couple.

Investment in the relationship

Whereas boundaries help to define who and what are part of the couple, the relationship must be kept alive within those boundaries. Both partners need to be invested, and both need to give to the relationship. In the absence of investment by either partner, the relationship starts to feel devitalized, leading the couple or the therapist to comment that there is "not much there." Difficulties for couples also can arise when, overall, one person seems to be more invested in the relationship than the other. In such circumstances, the person investing more can start to feel devalued, along with having a sense of unfairness that he or she is responsible for keeping the relationship afloat. Additionally, there are multiple ways that partners give to a relationship, and one major distinction is the degree to which each person invests instrumentally and emotionally (Epstein & Baucom, 2002). That is, a person can invest by engaging in a variety of instrumental or practical tasks that are important for the couple, such as earning money or taking on household responsibilities. Or, a partner might demonstrate investment through acts of caring and love, thus attending to the emotional aspects of the relationship. Many couples find successful ways to incorporate these various types of investment into their relationship, but others struggle because one person does not value the type of investment the other person provides or because competing demands and stressors drain an individual's capacity to invest energy in the relationship. Thus, comments abound, sometimes humorous, sometimes not, such as, "Thanks for the kiss; now would you take out the garbage?"

Control and power

Investment in the relationship is crucial to keep it alive, but in some fashion the couple has to decide where to focus that energy and how decisions are made, including who has authority, control, or power in various domains in the relationship. Some couples share decision-making in most areas of their lives, yet operating in this way can require extensive discussion to make certain that both partners agree on how to move forward in a given domain. Either for efficiency, because of expertise or interest in certain domains, or because of cultural beliefs and preferences, the couple might delegate decision-making authority to a given partner in certain areas. Sometimes this delegation is based on explicit, mutual consent; yet at other times, it seems to evolve gradually without discussion, either satisfactorily or not. Thus, the couple might decide that one person is better at monitoring the details of finances, and that person agrees to maintain the budget for the couple. However, problems can arise if one person assumes authority in a given area without mutual consent, or if one partner generally seems to dominate decisions regarding how the couple operates in multiple domains. The couple might have heated arguments about power and control, even if the arguments are not labelled as such. In this context, depression can result when one partner experiences little or no control over important aspects of their life, often referred to as *learned helplessness* (Seligman, 1975). Therefore, issues related to control and power can have notable effects on both relationship and individual functioning.

Communication: An important process and outcome

Couples need to be able to negotiate all the issues discussed above. One of the main ways that adults accomplish this negotiation is by communicating with each other. Effective communication is a fundamental component of healthy relationship functioning, and communication difficulty is one of the most frequent complaints of couples seeking therapy (Geiss & O'Leary, 1981). In addition, observations of couples' communication consistently demonstrate that distressed couples have less effective communication than nondistressed couples (Heyman, 2001). Relationships serve different important functions and, as a result, couples need to have different types of conversations to serve them well. More specifically, there are at least two major reasons that couples communicate with each other: (a) to share thoughts and feelings with each other and feel understood, and (b) to make decisions. The first type of conversation often is important for strengthening the emotional aspects of relationships, whereas effective decision-making or problem-solving conversations are vital for the instrumental aspects of relationships. Some couples are effective with both types of communication; some have strengths in only one; and other couples struggle to communicate in either manner. The focus of both types of conversations can vary, at times focusing on some aspect of the couple's relationship or their environment, including other family members. Other conversations might address concerns or successes of one partner, somewhat unrelated to the relationship per se, such as difficulties at work. These latter conversations are typically viewed as social support conversations in which one partner is responding to the other, either attempting to be of assistance to the distressed partner or joining in celebrating the partner's triumphs. The role of appropriate social support becomes paramount when one partner is experiencing some form of a major stressor. Among couples with communication difficulties, it appears that some couples or partners have actual skill deficits in communicating, while other couples appear to have communicated effectively in the past but struggle to maintain effective communication in the context of relationship distress (i.e., a performance deficit).

As will be discussed in Chapter 4, a number of problematic communication patterns can be observed among distressed couples. These problems can include both an excess of negative communication behaviours such as criticism and a lack of specific positive communications behaviours. In addition, some patterns of interaction can create communication difficulties, such as when one partner is less engaged or withdraws or avoids during the conversation. Moreover, it is crucial to understand the skill with which partners communicate during such interactions. For example, both partners might be very engaged during the conversation, demonstrating *mutual engagement*. If they do so with effective communication, such conversations might be rewarding to the couple or be productive in resolving difficult issues, even if the conversation itself is distressing. However, mutual engagement with poor communication skills might involve long, protracted arguments as the conversation spins out of control. A frequent communication pattern among distressed couples is a *demand-withdraw* pattern, in which one person attempts to engage the other person, who withdraws from the interaction (e.g., B. R. Baucom et al., 2011; Christensen & Shenk, 1991). Often such a pattern becomes more extreme during a given interaction or over time across interactions. As one person tries even harder for engagement, the other withdraws more, which leads to stronger attempts from the first person to engage, and so on. The attempts at engagement can become extreme as one person exhibits increasing volume, a negative tone, and hurtful comments while the other person shuts down. Finally, some couples demonstrate a *mutual withdrawal* interaction pattern in which both partners avoid engagement or stay distant from each other. This pattern is often seen in devitalized relationships in which the partners no longer turn to each other for rewarding interactions or as a source of support.

Thus, communication between partners is a process that is vital to address a wide variety of issues that couples confront on a regular basis. In addition, communication is an important behaviour that carries a great deal of meaning in itself. Major sources of rewards and punishments for adults are socially based. That is, people central in our lives have the ability to impact our mood, how we think about ourselves, and our behaviour. What each person communicates to their partner can serve as a prominent reinforcement or punishment. Does one partner praise the other, bolster their sense of efficacy, make them feel loved and cared about? Or does the partner deride the other person, tearing down their self-esteem? The expressed emotion literature demonstrates that high levels of hostile and critical comments from family members can alter the prognosis for adults who struggle with a variety of psychological disorders, such as mood disorders and schizophrenia (Hooley & Miklowitz, 2018). Furthermore, difficulties with communication interfere with the couple's ability to resolve other substantive issues in the relationship, such as negotiating different levels of needs for intimacy. Therefore, both the process and the content of communication between partners is a major emphasis in assisting couples who either are experiencing relationship distress or are struggling with one partner's psychopathology.

Balancing stability and change

The above areas help to define who the couple is and how they operate at a given point in time. In addition, couples need to be able to adapt as life changes for them as individuals or as a unit, or as the environment places new demands or provides new opportunities for them. Thus, couples as a unit must be flexible to allow for change as they progress through different stages of life, yet maintain some consistency so that there is an acceptable level of predictability.

Couples attempt to maintain consistency and predictability for various reasons and in different ways. First, consistency is efficient in that both partners know what to expect, and the couple does not have to negotiate each aspect of life on an ongoing basis. One way that couples create consistency is through defined roles. In this way, each partner understands how they are to contribute, perhaps with some agreement about how and when the role is to be fulfilled, along with clarifying who will have input regarding decisions in a given domain. Frequently, couples learn to define roles through observations of others, either in their personal lives or in society more broadly; thus, difficulties can result when appropriate role models have been absent for one or both partners. For example, defining roles can be particularly problematic for same-sex couples who often grew up with heterosexual parents and where most examples in society still define a relationship as between a woman and a man. Consistent with this lack of role clarity for same-sex couples, couple therapists report that it often takes same-sex couples up to 10 years to define their roles within the relationship (Green & Mitchell, 2015), which requires additional energy and effort from them, compared to different-sex couples with clearer role models, who are able to focus their efforts elsewhere. Similarly, any couple involving individuals who have grown up without good role models or for whom those role models do not apply to their circumstances or personal preferences might well struggle to define the roles that the two partners will assume in the relationship.

In addition to consistency for the sake of efficiency, some couples create consistency through rituals in order to give special meaning to their lives. Thus, there might be a particular restaurant that the couple visits on certain occasions, or a weekly ritual such as an extended Saturday morning breakfast. For many couples, such places, actions, or phrases that only they share can create a sense of closeness or specialness between them.

On the other hand, some couples complain that their relationship has lost its vitality, has become boring or stale, or is filled with a routine set of activities. In such instances, couples might need to infuse their lives with a sense of novelty, whether that involves each person individually exploring new activities that they can bring back to the relationship or the couple together engaging in new activities (C. L. Gordon & Baucom, 2005, 2009). Each couple must find their own balance between consistency and novelty, which can be a challenge if the two partners differ notably in their preferences along these lines.

The above domains help to describe how a couple defines themselves and how the two partners relate to each other as a unit. In addition, the couple also exists within a broader environmental context.

Relationships in an environmental context

As discussed above, couples need to establish boundaries to define themselves as a unit, distinct from others around them. These boundaries are essential, not to permit them to withdraw from the environment, but rather to facilitate their functioning within it while maintaining a sense of "coupleness." Therefore, in order to understand a couple's functioning, it is important to consider how they relate to their physical and social environment. The couple's interaction with their environment is reciprocal; that is, the environment impacts the couple, and the couple influences their environment, potentially in both positive and negative ways.

The environment as a stressor or resource for the couple

The couple interacts with the environment in multiple ways and at various levels, including their physical environment such as the home in which they live, their neighbourhood, their workplace, their community, and their society and political system more broadly. Likewise, they are embedded in a social environment, typically including other family members, friends, work associates, strangers with whom they interact, and the broader culture. All these aspects of their environment have the potential to influence the relationship. For example, if a couple lives in a resource-deprived or unsafe neighbourhood, then going for a walk after dinner might not be a positive, relationship-enhancing activity; instead, the couple might need to direct considerable attention toward monitoring their children's whereabouts and safety. Likewise, family members who drop by to visit unexpectedly might be well intended but inadvertently disrupt the couple's attempt to have time alone. On the other hand, those same family members might serve as a resource to babysit and give the couple an opportunity for a date night, and being part of a tight-knit extended family might be an important aspect of life for the couple. In essence, the couple's environment likely includes a complex mix of stressors and resources.

THE ENVIRONMENT AS A STRESSOR ON THE COUPLE

While it can be easy to understand how a major stressor such as an ailing parent might impact the couple, it is equally important to understand how ongoing minor stressors or daily hassles can have a negative influence. Living in cramped, noisy quarters which provide little opportunity for time alone can have a negative cumulative effect, particularly for individuals who have a strong need for individual time to rejuvenate. Similarly, stressors that might seem invisible to some individuals can be detrimental to other couples. For example, same-sex or racial-minority couples might experience subtle or institutionalized forms of discrimination that other people might fail to recognize or even deny, perhaps making it increasingly difficult for the couple to cope with such stressors and find supportive communities.

In addition to environmental stressors experienced by the couple as a unit, often one or both partners experience stressors as individuals during the day, which they then bring into the relationship. Bodenmann and colleagues have documented how daily hassles, such as difficulties in the workplace, influence that individual's mood, which can then spill over into negative interactions with the partner (Bodenmann, 2006; Falconier, Nussbeck, Bodenmann, Schneider, & Bradbury, 2015). Even within the family unit, conflictual couple interactions appear to disrupt subsequent parent-child interactions (e.g., Jouriles & Farris, 1992). In essence, there often is a transfer or contagion from one person's experience and resulting mood that is carried forward into the couple's relationship.

Cultural factors as salient stressors for subsets of couples Many environmental stressors might impact any couple, yet certain couples are at particularly high risk for experiencing additional stressors as a function of living in specific cultures or subcultures where they are likely to experience discrimination. In addition to minority stress and oppression related to an individual's cultural background or identity (e.g., race/ethnicity, sexual orientation, gender identity, religion, class, disability status, immigration history, etc.), the couple constellation involving the two partners can further increase experiences of discrimination. That is, in most cultures some of the majority population have implicit norms or explicit values regarding who should comprise a couple. If a couple differs from such norms based on visible characteristics, adverse responses from their environment might be particularly likely. For instance, in many cultures, couples are expected or preferred to include one woman and one man of the same approximate age with the man perhaps being slightly, but not too much, older, and frequently of the same race/ethnicity or class. When a couple does not conform to these or other norms, they might be subjected to discrimination in overt or subtle ways. For example, a same-sex couple might conceal their relationship to protect one partner's career prospects in an organization with a homonegative culture. However, this decision could also create tension in the relationship if the partner makes a different attribution for the concealment (e.g., "If you loved me, you'd be open about us. The reason you haven't told people at work is because you're ashamed of me!"). In more extreme cases, they might be the targets of overt hostility or threats. In the above examples, the couple as a unit is experiencing the negative effects of being a minority couple. In addition, these culturally salient experiences might be directly experienced by only one partner, which then affects the couple.

THE ENVIRONMENT AS A RESOURCE FOR THE COUPLE

The couple's environment also can serve as a rich resource that can provide support and add meaning to their lives. Within our model, we refer to the couple as the two partners together, and everyone and everything beyond as the environment. Thus, the couple might be able to call upon their environment in the form of family support to help with child care when both parents have returned to work. Also, a couple can help to create an environment that emphasizes or sustains their values and lifestyle. For example, some couples might affiliate with a religious institution that provides them with an opportunity to live consistent with their faith and to interact with others who share their values. Thus, within the constraints of reality, couples have the capacity to shape their environment and do not simply inherit their circumstances. Couples vary in the degree to which they proactively select and invest with other individuals, groups, and institutions that can facilitate their well-being. Even though resources might exist in a couple's environment, the couple will not necessarily access those resources for a variety of reasons. First, couples might not know that such potential resources exist. For example, couples might not know what organizations within their community can assist on an immediate basis if they are experiencing financial hardship. Second, even if a couple is aware of potential resources, they might not avail themselves of those resources because they might believe that asking for help is a sign of weakness and they must manage on their own. Thus, informing other people that a partner is depressed and needs contact with and affirmation from other people might violate both the couple's boundaries regarding private information and their standard that couples must be self-reliant in confronting life's adversities.

In summary, it is important to understand not only what happens within the couple as a unit, but also how their environment influences the couple in both positive and negative ways, and the extent to which the couple and both partners proactively help to create and alter that environment.

The couple as an agent in influencing their environment

Not only does a couple's environment continuously impact a couple, but the couple knowingly or inadvertently influences their environment as well, both positively and negatively, and for various reasons. At times, the couple might make decisions with the explicit goal of creating a new environment or altering their existing environment. Thus, they might move to a new location to assume a new job or to be closer to extended family. Or they might decide to have a conversation with family members, requesting a phone call before family members drop by for a visit. At the same time, some of their decisions might have inadvertent negative consequences. In this example, the conversation with family members might not be well received, and the couple might find themselves the subject of family gossip. Likewise, deciding to be assertive and resist committing to extra work hours could result in the lack of a much-needed promotion or additional professional opportunities. Thus, the couple's attempts to influence their environment often have a subsequent influence on how the environment responds to the couple, for better or worse.

A couple's decision about how to interact with the environment might not always be intended to promote the well-being of the couple explicitly but rather be aimed at having a positive influence on the world around them. Many couples have a prosocial perspective in which they want to improve certain aspects of the world for others. Thus, the couple might decide to devote their time and resources to environmental causes, or focus on activities that contribute to the well-being of their extended family. Engaging in activities that improve the world for others often can have an unexpected positive influence on the couple. Engaging in activities that are consistent with their core values can help partners feel closer to each other and reaffirm their sense of identity. In essence, such activities can contribute to the couple's experience of living a value-based life and having a shared sense of purpose. Such activities can also be valuable to the individual partners. For example, depressed individuals often experience a lack of meaning and direction in their lives. Helping that individual and the couple clarify what is important to them and how their actions can embody those values can benefit a depressed individual, a form of what we would call *value-based behavioural activation.*

While contributing to the environment can be beneficial for the couple, it is also important for them to balance their allocation of time and energy. Partners who are heavily involved in supporting others around them consistent with their values can inadvertently skew their lives such that there is little time or energy left for the couple. Moreover, the optimal balance likely shifts over the course of the couple's relationship. Young couples who are trying to establish their careers and start a family might have less time available to contribute to their environment compared to couples whose children have left home and who are financially secure. Thus, a couple's contribution to the environment must be understood within the context of other needs and priorities.

As can be seen, a couple's relationship is a complex entity. It includes two unique individuals, each with their own desires, preferences, and needs, who come together to form a relationship in which the couple is more than the sum of the two partners. These individuals and the couple as a unit interact with the environment with reciprocal influences in an ongoing fashion, and these interactions change over time as the couple attempts to promote consistency while also recognizing the need for adaptation and change. While this discussion highlights spheres of influence that must be considered to understand a couple, it also is important to address how the two individuals and the couple experience and respond to these various demands, challenges, and opportunities. Our approach to understanding these phenomena is based on a broad cognitive-behavioural theoretical perspective, integrated with systemic and emotion-focused perspectives. In discussing a CBT perspective on intimate relationships, particular emphasis is given to those aspects that are relationally focused. At the same time, it is important to recognize that each person's individual behaviours, cognitions, and emotions unrelated to the couple impact their relationship; this sphere of influence will become increasingly clear as the interaction between relationship functioning and individual distress is addressed in the second section of this text.

Cognitions, emotions, and behaviours: Application to relationships

Individuals have cognitions, emotions, and behaviours that exert reciprocal influences on the person on an ongoing basis. Therefore, it is somewhat arbitrary to select one of these factors as the beginning point to understand this interactive process. For example, an individual might notice some event or action in the environment, have thoughts about that event which lead to an emotional response, and these thoughts and emotions combined then encourage the person to behave in a certain way (cognitions lead to emotions, and the two result in a behavioural response). Or one could begin with an individual who is in a bad mood (negative emotion) and is therefore anticipating that any interactions will be negative (cognition), then deciding to stay at home rather than venturing out to interact with others (behaviour). In addition, often individuals experience cognitions and emotions together in an integrated internal subjective manner without distinguishing between the two. Each of these factors will be discussed in more detail in subsequent chapters. In this overview, we begin by exploring an individual's cognitions relevant to their relationship, with the recognition that any of these three factors, or two factors in combination, could serve as the starting point for discussing or understanding an individual.

Not only do cognition, emotions, and behaviours exert a reciprocal influence *within* an individual, but similar interactive processes also occur *between* the two partners in the relationship. For example, one partner's behaviour, such as coming home late at night without an explanation, will likely give rise to cognitions in the other partner, perhaps thinking about that individual as rude or thoughtless. Those negative cognitions might trigger anger in that person, who then responds behaviourally in a verbally attacking manner. Next, the partner who came home late will likely respond to that anger, initiating a new phase of the interaction within and between partners. Finally, both partners and the couple interact with other individuals and groups in their environment, who will likewise respond to the individual or the couple, setting off a whole new chain of reciprocal interactions. Thus, the reciprocal interactions among cognitions, emotions, and behaviours that are the central focus of a cognitive-behavioural model of individual functioning become geometrically more complex when the two partners and their interaction with the environment are taken into account. This rich interplay can prove confusing to distressed couples, who often experience more broadly that "things are not going well between us," so it can be valuable for the therapist to help the couple understand which of these factors is most salient in understanding their current distress.

Below is a brief introduction to the primary elements emphasized within the CBCT model of relationship functioning with a major focus on the cognitions, emotions, and behavioural responses of individuals in distressed relationships. It is important to recognize that although an almost purely behavioural model of relationship functioning provided the groundwork for this perspective beginning in the 1960s and 1970s (e.g., Stuart, 1969; Weiss, Hops, & Patterson, 1973), the model has evolved over the decades, first to incorporate cognitive elements, and then in recognition of the centrality of emotions in intimate relationships. These internal experiences and behavioural responses of relationally distressed individuals are not arbitrary; instead, in many ways, relationally distressed individuals experience their relationship in negative, distorted ways, similar to what is seen in a variety of psychological disorders. These negative filters act to maintain and even exacerbate relationship distress over time. Thus, while there are a vast number of relevant types of cognitions, emotions, and behaviours in relationships, we focus on those aspects that appear to be most central to relationship functioning and that serve as potential points of intervention.

Cognitions in relationships

One of the most central factors in an individual's experience of a relationship is how they think about it, process what happens on a daily basis, and anticipate the future. For many people, thinking about their partner and their relationship in these ways is highly rewarding. However, for individuals in distressed relationships, their thoughts about their partner and relationship can be upsetting and discouraging, and contribute to individual difficulties such as depression. In an attempt to provide greater clarity regarding the types of cognitions that contribute to the development, maintenance, or exacerbation of relational distress, Baucom and colleagues (D. H. Baucom, Epstein, Sayers, & Sher, 1989) differentiated among several categories of cognitions. Four of these categories involve an individual's thoughts that are focused on specific events: (a) selective attention, (b) relationship schematic processing; (c) attributions, and (d) expectancies. The final two categories involve broader relationship beliefs that transcend specific situations: (e) assumptions and (f) standards. Although they are distinct categories, these various cognitions frequently become intertwined in distressed individuals, who experience one or both partners, the couple as a unit, and their interaction with the environment in negative ways.

Selective attention

Selective attention refers to what an individual notices in their daily experiences, based on the recognition that an individual cannot attend to everything that goes on around them. As a result, an individual selectively attends to some aspects of reality while ignoring or de-emphasizing others. In many instances, individuals selectively focus on aspects that seem particularly relevant and tend to confirm their views of the world. Therefore, selective attention can lead to a somewhat distorted experience of the world and contribute to a self-fulfilling prophecy, particularly in distressed individuals. Similar to depressed persons (A.T. Beck et al., 1979), individuals in distressed relationships frequently attend to negative aspects of their partner or the couple as a unit. For example, a relationally distressed person might be quite aware each time the partner does not fulfil their household responsibilities but rarely notice when that same person accomplishes agreed-upon chores. On the other hand, an individual in a happy relationship might selectively attend to positive events, perhaps even ignoring negative behaviours (e.g., not recognizing a partner's subtle insults because the person wants to maintain the image of the partner as caring and supportive). Thus, selective attention can exist in either a positive or negative direction and can lead to a distorted experience of the couple's relationship or of a partner.

Relationship schematic processing

An important aspect of cognitive processing that is related to selective attention involves how the different elements that are noticed are integrated with each other. This process issue is referred to as *relationship schematic processing* (RSP), which is the tendency and ability to think in relational terms—that is, the degree to which partners view and interpret events from a relational perspective rather than an individual perspective. For any individual, this issue raises the following question: once some event or behaviour is noticed, is it believed to reflect something about only an individual or about an interpersonal process? Some individuals view the world through "relationship lenses" whereas others are more individually focused. For example, while on a date to attend a ballet performance, if one person focuses on the performance and says little to their partner, the person might interpret their own behaviour as indicating, "I am watching the performance; my lack of conversation with you means nothing about us" (individual schematic processing). For a more relationally oriented partner, the same experience might result in hurt feelings: "This was an opportunity for us to enjoy a special evening out together, but you just don't see things that way, do you? You might as well have gone by yourself!" (relationship schematic processing). Not surprisingly, this individual versus relational approach to organizing information and one's experiences has a notable influence on the meaning or attributions given to an event.

Attributions and expectancies

Whereas selective attention influences *what* events an individual attends to, attributions involve how that person explains *why* the event occurred. Consistent with the overall negative filter that is part of relationship distress, a relationally distressed individual often explains an event in a way that maintains the distress. Thus, one individual might view the other partner as responsible and explain it in a way that emphasizes negative aspects of the partner or the relationship. For example, if a conversation becomes contentious, an individual might explain it as being due to the partner's inattentiveness, which results from the partner's self-centredness, lack of caring, and lack of effort to improve the relationship. An explanation that emphasizes self-centredness focuses on the partner as the basis of the problem. Such an explanation is unlikely to change, and it is likely to influence many aspects of the couple's relationship. Additionally, this explanation might lower motivation to make efforts to improve the relationship, since such efforts seem unlikely to lead to change.

In a similar vein, individuals not only attempt to explain events that have occurred, they also tend to predict what *will* happen in the future, with distressed individuals again often having a negative bias in their predictions. Consequently, many distressed individuals predict that things will never get better: "You will never change, and we are doomed to misery if we stay together." Not surprisingly, when an individual ascribes to this belief, it can be difficult to motivate that person to make an effort to improve the relationship, which then, in a self-fulfilling manner, confirms their prediction that the relationship will not improve.

Assumptions and standards as broad beliefs

The degree to which an individual focuses on a specific event in the relationship, explains why that event occurred, and predicts what will happen in the relationship in the future will result, in part, from what has transpired within the couple's relationship so far. However, these situational cognitions also are rooted in broader beliefs that the person holds. These broader beliefs often have evolved over time, perhaps across other personal relationships, or they might have their origins in early life and derive from observations of how primary caregivers and other key adults treated each other. Based on this learning history, individuals often develop assumptions about the nature of individuals, relationships, and the broader environment, as well as form standards for what relationships *should* be like. These broad beliefs which have formed over time might be adaptive or maladaptive for conducting a relationship in the present.

Assumptions are strongly held beliefs regarding what people, relationships, and various aspects of the environment are actually like, and on occasion these assumptions can seem extreme or distorted. An assumption might be about one's partner, such as that they were raised in a dysfunctional family and therefore will never understand how to treat other people well. On the other hand, assumptions can be optimistic and pro-relationship, such as the belief that if a couple is struggling, other people in their environment can be counted on to support them. A person's assumptions about relationships and partners are broad in nature, yet they can provide a lens that sets the stage for selective attention and for making attributions regarding specific events that have occurred as well as predictions about what will happen in the future.

Individuals not only have assumptions about how things actually are; they also have broad standards about how relationships and partners *should* be. For example, an individual might hold the standard that within committed relationships, partners should share everything they are thinking, or the standard that partners should spend all free time with each other. Such standards might be viewed as extreme because of their possible consequences or the difficulty the couple would have in attempting to carry out such standards. In other instances, the two partners might each have reasonable standards, but the standards are different from each other in ways that are difficult for the couple to accommodate. For example, if one person believes that having fun and enjoying oneself is the most important thing in life (while still meeting major responsibilities), and the other partner believes that meeting daily responsibilities should come before play or relaxation, the couple might struggle in deciding how to allocate their time, although each person might live successfully according to their standards if they were not in the relationship. Regardless of whether a person's standards are extreme or are merely different from their partner's standards, individuals often become distressed if their standards are not met.

In summary, it can be valuable to differentiate among categories of cognitions in order to understand more fully how each person experiences their relationship, both with specific events and on a broader level. At the same time, an individual's various cognitions typically are related to each other in some thematic fashion, and in many relationally distressed individuals, this overall pattern reflects a negative perspective on the partner, the relationship, their environment, and at times, on themselves. These various cognitions understandably influence that partner's emotional reactions.

Emotions in relationships

The way that an individual processes and thinks about various aspects of their life has a major influence on their emotions, a basic tenet of a cognitive-behavioural model. These emotional responses to their partners and their relationship as well as how they feel about themselves within the relationship often are a central part of what gives value to life. People have emotional responses to other aspects of their lives such as their work, family, and friends, which are discussed within their committed relationship as well. Therefore, intimate relationships often are the source and the context within which important emotions occur and are addressed.

In considering emotions in a relational context, a number of factors need to be taken into account. First, it is important to recognize that positive and negative emotions are not on opposite ends of the same continuum, but instead can be viewed as independent dimensions. For example, some couples who might be described as passionate experience a high level of both positive and negative emotions about their relationship, whereas other couples who are more devitalized experience few positive or negative emotions about their relationship. Other couples who describe themselves as happy might experience many positive emotions and few negative emotions about their relationship, but many unhappy couples have a surplus of negative emotions and a paucity of positive ones.

Second, partners vary in the extent to which they are aware of their emotions, can label them, and know how they arise. Some people are attuned to their own emotions, can label and differentiate subtle differences in their emotional states, and can describe the environmental or internal stimuli that have given rise to their emotions. Often these same individuals are skilled at reading and understanding the emotions of others, including their partners. In fact, they might be more perceptive of their partner's emotions than their partners are themselves. Other individuals do not live in this same emotionally attuned world. They do not focus on emotions as a central part of life, might not value emotional expression, or perhaps even view emotions as detrimental, preferring rationality instead as the basis for making good decisions and more generally guiding their lives. Whereas partners might initially be attracted to each other because of these differences ("She was so stable and rational and kept me grounded." And, "He was so much fun; he freed me up to play and feel things."), over time these tendencies can become problematic ("She is so dull; I can't get her to talk about important things, how she is feeling about our kids, and the fact that we're making more money than either of us ever thought we would have. Can't you get excited about that rather than just tracking the stock market trends?").

Third, not only does an individual experience moment-to-moment emotional responses; individuals also appear to have a dispositional tendency to experience positive and negative emotions which is relatively consistent even over decades, sometimes referred to as *positive affectivity* and *negative affectivity*, respectively (Watson & Tellegen, 1985). This tendency is consistent with the notion that some individuals seem to be basically happy and upbeat, but other people struggle and are prone to experience levels of depression and anxiety beyond what might be explained by the current circumstances of their lives. This notion can be conceptualized as an individual difference that persists across time and setting. Furthermore, some people have overall very strong emotional experiences while others have more muted emotional reactions, and both of these emotional levels often fall within a normative range. This recognition of individuals' broad tendencies to experience emotions in certain ways is important for the person and the partner to understand.

Fourth, people vary considerably in the degree to which they are able to regulate their emotions adaptively. Even if they have strong emotional responses, some people are comfortable with their emotions and can integrate them with their cognitions and behavioural responses without considerable effort. Other individuals struggle to regulate their emotions, particularly negative ones. As a result, their negative emotions become easily activated, reach a higher level of intensity, and remain intense for considerable time (Linehan, 1993). During these times of intense negative emotions, they might behave in ways that are detrimental to themselves or others, contributing to both individual and relationship difficulties, for example, responding to their angry feelings with strong insults toward the partner which they later regret. In fact, for most individuals, relationship distress is emotionally dysregulating, and they might be at their worst when around their partner. Consequently, the ways that individuals behave in a couple therapy session might be quite different from their emotional reactions and behavioural responses with other people and in other aspects of their environment.

On the other hand, when relationships function well, they can fulfil important functions in regulating emotions. At times, individuals rely on themselves to regulate their emotions. In addition, a potentially valuable role of intimate relationships is that individuals can draw upon their partner and their relationship to regulate emotions, which is referred to as *interpersonal emotion regulation* (Butler, 2011; Butler & Randall, 2013). Thus, one person might have a clear awareness that, "When I'm upset, I know I can turn to you to help me deal with my feelings. Sometimes we need to talk, but sometimes I just need to be with you." In healthy relationships involving two well-adjusted partners, each individual likely learns both individual and interpersonal emotion-regulation strategies. However, within the context of relationship distress or individual psychopathology, these emotion-regulation strategies might be compromised such that one person withdraws from the other person and tries to address emotions solely on their own, or, alternatively, relies too heavily upon the partner to regulate their emotions (Fischer et al., 2017). Such maladaptive attempts at regulating emotions might further strain an already distressed relationship.

Fifth, emotions are not merely an internal, subjective experience, but they serve an important communicative function with the partner and others as well. What an individual experiences subjectively is not automatically communicated to others. Instead, an expression of emotion in part results from a person's beliefs about emotional expression and how their emotional expression has been received by others previously, including both their partner and other important people in their lives. For example, an individual might believe that it is inappropriate to express anger or that expressing fear is a sign of weakness, even though that person frequently experiences both anger and fear. These beliefs are likely to be shaped by a variety of factors, including the person's gender, culture, and family of origin. Moreover, the beliefs might have arisen from direct personal experience; that is, that same individual might have been made to feel guilty when they expressed anger or fear, or they were ignored, invalidated, or punished in other ways for that expression. As with other domains of relationship functioning, couples might struggle when they hold very different beliefs about the expression of certain emotions. For example, based on family of origin, one partner might believe that strong expressions of anger are "no big deal," but for the other person, that expression of anger is very hurtful: "You just don't say things like that to someone you love."

In summary, emotions give colour and vitality to life. Yet, some individuals struggle with their own emotions in a variety of ways. Even when both people are within the normal, adaptive range, similarities and differences in their experiences and expressions of emotions can create challenges. Additionally, emotions do not exist in isolation; they are related both to the individual's and couple's cognitions and their behaviour—the final domain to which we now turn.

Behaviours in relationships

Cognitions and emotions represent the internal, subjective experience of each person. In many instances, these internal experiences serve as the basis for each partner's subsequent behaviour. Behaviours are the explicit, outward expression of an individual's attempts to fulfil needs, express personality, respond to the other partner's actions, and engage in relationship-focused actions, whether positive or negative. Furthermore, consistent with the former discussion of the individual, the couple, and the environment, an individual's positive or negative behaviour can be directed at any or all of these facets. Many of the issues raised in the above discussion of emotions apply to behaviour within a relationship as well.

First, as is the case with emotions, positive and negative behaviours are not opposites but can exist simultaneously, or a relationship might be somewhat devoid of both, resulting in a potentially boring, lifeless experience. Although both couples and therapists might wish otherwise, it appears that overall, negative behaviours have a greater impact on relationship satisfaction than positive behaviours (for a review, see Epstein & Baucom, 2002). A high level of positive behaviours appears to be important for couples to reach an optimal level of functioning. However, what seems to spell doom for many relationships is a high frequency of negative behaviours, or even a lower frequency of negative behaviours when those behaviours are highly aversive. When a partner declares, "I can't keep living this way; something has to change, or I have to get out," typically that person is indicating that life contains so many negative behaviours that they are considering terminating the relationship. Yet, decreasing these highly aversive behaviours does not mean that more positive behaviours automatically occur. Helping couples begin to engage in more positive behaviours often needs to be addressed separately in treatment. In thinking about the presence or absence of positive behaviours, it is important to differentiate between smaller, more frequent positive acts, such as giving a hug or initiating a brief contact during the day, versus "big-ticket" positive acts, such as going away together on a holiday. The latter is nice, but frequent, sustainable, smaller positive behaviours are essential. Going away together only to return to daily life devoid of caring, thoughtful daily behaviours typically is unfulfilling.

Second, couples often develop routinized ways of behaving in which one or both partners appear to respond automatically, what can be called *mindless behaviour*. This type of response can be adaptive if the automatic behaviour toward one's partner is positive. The person does not even need to think about it; they seem to treat their partner well and attend to the relationship on a routine basis. However, for distressed couples, these automatic, mindless behaviours often are negative. For example, a couple might be nasty to each other in social situations, oblivious to how they are coming across or unaware that their actions are making others uncomfortable.

Furthermore, the behaviours of one partner are not independent of the behaviours of the other. In fact, reciprocity between partners, or the tendency to respond to one person's behaviour with a similar behaviour, is an extremely important aspect of relationship functioning. Often this reciprocity seems to operate at a mindless level as well. It is important to recognize the type of behaviour that is being reciprocated. Negative reciprocity (an increased likelihood of responding to a negative behaviour from one partner with a negative from the other partner) is a particularly strong characteristic of distressed relationships (Heyman, 2001). Often the magnitude of the negative responses increase as the interaction continues. Thus, an explosive argument between the partners might be characterized as rapidly escalating, negative reciprocity. Even if the partners are aware of the exchange of negatives and the importance of breaking that chain, often they struggle to do so while feeling defensive or angry. Positive reciprocity also exists, although it might not be as strong or immediately impactful as negative reciprocity in that it tends to evolve over a longer period of time. In fact, this delay in reciprocating positives might be a characteristic of a healthy, trusting relationship in which partners believe that each person will be caring and responsive over time, but there is no need to have one's act of kindness immediately reciprocated (Gottman, 1999; Murstein, Cerreto, & MacDonald, 1977). However, among distressed couples, a lack of immediate positive reciprocity can be interpreted as being taken for granted: "Why try? I'm the only one making an effort here."

Third, couples engage in discrete moment-to-moment behaviours, yet these behaviours also fall into broader patterns that frequently are related to their needs, preferences, and personal style. For example, one partner who wants more intimacy in the relationship might make a number of specific requests of their partner, including spending more time talking to each other, having more frequent date nights, being more affectionate with each other, and so forth. Although understanding each of these specific issues separately might be beneficial, understanding the broader themes in their relationship can help bring order to what sounds like a long list of specific concerns. These broader relationship themes might be directed toward one individual, the couple's relationship, or interactions with the outside environment. For example, specific concerns about the extended family might reflect boundary issues for the couple: how to spend holidays, how to respond to frequent telephone calls from family members, and whom to designate as godparents for a newly arrived baby. It is important to help the couple recognize whether requests for change in some broad area will contribute to a greater sense of balance among important areas of functioning or perpetuate an imbalance in their lives.

The empirical status of cognitive-behavioural couple therapy for relationship distress

The cognitive-behavioural model of relationship functioning described above and the CBCT interventions resulting from this model are the authors' most recent version of an evolving and broadened perspective on how to assist distressed couples, employing a framework based in a behavioural tradition. The current, expanded model, informed by advances in relationship science, is an evolution and expansion from what was originally called behavioural couple therapy (BCT or BMT for behavioural marital therapy). CBCT is a theoretical perspective that is practised in multiple variations by different clinicians (for example, Worrell, 2015, describes CBCT largely consistent with the current presentation yet with unique perspectives and integrations still within a CBT framework). Given the diversity of needs among couples and diversity in how various CBT-oriented research groups and clinicians apply these principles, there is no single treatment manual that provides a session-by-session approach to CBCT. The current authors believe that such diversity in implementation is essential in order to provide optimal couple therapy that is individualized for each couple, based upon empirically supported treatment principles. An important implication of this approach is that when efforts are made to summarize the overall effectiveness of CBCT or behaviourally oriented approaches to treating relationship distress, conclusions are based on multiple investigations that vary somewhat in how CBCT or BCT was implemented.

Taking this variability into account, several meta-analyses and major reviews have been conducted to examine the efficacy of couple therapy across the United States, Europe, and Australia (e.g., Snyder, Castellani, & Whisman, 2006). All these reviews reach the same conclusion: behaviourally based couple therapies, including CBCT, are efficacious for the treatment of relationship distress, and the findings are similar across countries (see Fischer, Baucom, & Cohen, 2016 for a review). Moreover, the evidence also largely points to equal efficacy among various forms of couple therapy including insight-oriented couple therapy

(Snyder & Wills, 1989) and emotion focused couple therapy (Johnson & Greenberg, 1985), with all behavioural approaches creating large effects (Shadish & Baldwin, 2003). Also promising, Christensen and colleagues conducted a large-scale study comparing two behaviourally based couple therapies for relationship distress and found large effects for both approaches similar in magnitude to meta-analytic findings; most importantly, the improvement gains were maintained five years after treatment was completed (Christensen, Atkins, Baucom, & Yi, 2010). Thus, well-controlled treatment outcome research conducted across several continents by numerous investigators over several decades consistently points to the efficacy of behaviourally based interventions such as CBCT in assisting distressed couples. Although beyond the scope of the current book, these same behavioural principles have been adapted with promising results to address specific, complex relationship concerns, such as infidelity (K. C. Gordon, Khaddouma, Baucom, & Snyder, 2015), intimate partner violence (Epstein, Werlinich, & LaTaillade, 2015), and medical concerns (D. H. Baucom, Porter, Kirby, & Hudepohl, 2012; Schmaling & Sher, 2000; Sher et al., 2014). Likewise, these principles have been employed successfully with satisfied couples as well within the context of relationship education (Halford et al., 2015; Markman, Halford, & Hawkins, 2019), impacting not only relationship satisfaction but perhaps adaptive physiological changes as well (Ditzen, Hahlweg, Fehm-Wolfsdorf, & Baucom, 2011). This strong, broad established empirical base serves as our inspiration for sharing this current, most recent rendition with the reader.

Concluding comments

Long-term, committed relationships are complex, yet many couples navigate this complexity such that their relationship is one of the most important and rewarding aspects of their lives. This is no simple feat, given that a multitude of factors can influence relationship well-being. In this chapter, we presented our CBCT model of relationship functioning, which integrates two different perspectives: (a) an ecological, contextual model and (b) a cognitive-behavioural model. The contextual approach delineates the various units of analysis that need to be taken into account in understanding the couple, moving from smaller to larger units incorporating (a) the individual, (b) the couple, and (c) their environment. Thus, a couple must attend to both partners' individual needs and stylistic differences, learn to function well as a couple, and interact effectively with various aspects of their social and physical environment. The cognitive-behavioural perspective clarifies how each person's cognitions, emotions, and behaviours affect the couple in each of the three contextual domains. Not only do these factors interact with each other within an individual, but they also impact the partner, setting off a reciprocal chain of cognitions, emotions, and behaviours. In addition to forming the basis for conceptualizing a couple's relationship, the interventions described in subsequent chapters are directly based on the model described here. That is, CBCT techniques are categorized by their major focus of intervention—behaviours, cognitions, and emotions—and are applied to address targets across the three domains of the individual, the couple, and the environment.

Although many couples navigate this complexity effectively, it is not surprising that other couples struggle in these endeavours. The above model might seem daunting for a therapist or a couple to keep in mind. Yet, for any given couple, it is likely that only a few factors are particularly pertinent, and significant facilitative effects can be achieved if the couple can make appropriate changes in those domains. Furthermore, these specific salient factors typically are not unrelated or independent of each other; instead, they form a meaningful pattern that can help to create a conceptualization of the couple's relationship strengths and weaknesses, along with treatment planning in a clinical context. The remainder of this text is devoted largely to explicating these factors, describing how they can be assessed effectively, and discussing how an individualized treatment plan can be developed and carried out to help a couple optimize their relationship. Before we turn to these specific factors and related interventions, a broader perspective on implementing CBCT will be presented in the next chapter.

Note

1 As noted in Epstein and Baucom (2002), the terms *needs* and *motives* are at times used interchangeably and at other times differently. On occasion, *needs* is used more narrowly to refer to tension reduction whereas *motives* often is used more broadly to describe a goal-oriented behaviour extending beyond tension reduction. In the current book, the terms are used interchangeably.

Chapter 3

Conducting cognitive-behavioural couple therapy

During debriefing at the end of a successful course of couple therapy, the therapist asked a couple what was helpful about their work together, and they replied:

Sandra: I think it was a lot of different things, and it's hard to put my finger on it. On a very concrete level, you helped us communicate with each other, and that was huge. We were stuck in some horrible patterns, and you helped us see those and made us face what each of us was doing that kept those going and how to change them. That wasn't easy, but you made it safe enough for us to take a hard look at ourselves. But it was much more than that. Without being unrealistic, you gave us our hope back and helped me to remember the good things about William that are still there. I couldn't see them before because of how nasty we were to each other all the time. It was all so confusing when we first came, and I think you helped us step back and see it more clearly and figure out what we want and how to do it.

William: I agree. I'll never be the greatest communicator, but I think I'm better, and she knows I'm trying. Really important for me, you helped us get the fun back. I really dreaded coming here at the beginning, and although we dealt with hard stuff, at times our sessions were actually fun. I sure didn't expect that we'd laugh this much during therapy. At one point, she even called me a "hot potato," and I was thinking, "Yes, the potato is back!" To be honest, lots of this therapy talk sounds like psychobabble to me, but you actually seemed to understand us and had lots of ideas to share, without dictating what we had to do. I expected that I was going to look like the idiot male mucking things up, but you seemed to respect both of us and kept things balanced. Sandra and I had to do a lot of work and we did, but it was you too.

A therapist in training watched a videotape of an experienced CBCT therapist during a training workshop and remarked:

> That was really helpful, and I think I understand the technique. But what strikes me the most is not so much *what* you did, but *how* you did it. At one level, I can see links to the theory of CBCT, but at another level, there is so much in the way that you put it into practice with the couple that made it a successful intervention. What you said seemed really smooth and sounded very caring, while you were actually saying some really difficult things that I wasn't sure the couple would be able to hear! At the moment, I don't know how I would figure out precisely what words to use in the room, or how to put it across in order to have that effect. I guess my question is, "*How* do you do that?"

Much psychotherapy research has been dedicated to the question of what makes treatments effective. Is it (a) specific techniques, or (b) common factors (also referred to as therapist–client relational elements) that cut across theoretical orientations, or is it (c) both techniques and common factors and the integration of the two? If there are common factors, which ones are most central, and are there some aspects of therapeutic style that are essential for a theoretical approach such as CBCT? Most treatment manuals focus on techniques, and this book does as well. Yet, there is a good reason for our waiting to present the techniques until after we have presented our model of relationship functioning (in Chapter 2) and the process of conducting CBCT in the current chapter. Specifically, we present this chapter before multiple chapters on interventions because we do not want the following message to get lost in the midst of theoretical frameworks and multiple intervention strategies: *The most effective CBCT is provided by therapists who attend to important therapist–couple relationship factors that are common across psychotherapy approaches, along with therapist behaviours unique to CBCT.* Thus, techniques, the therapeutic relationship, *and* the integration of the two are crucial in CBCT. Notably, the therapeutic relationship involves more than the therapist and couple liking each other; rather, it becomes a tool itself that relies on the judicious use of therapist verbal and nonverbal behaviours. During every session, the therapist makes many decisions about when to intervene, how to intervene, and how to balance the therapeutic relationships between the therapist and each partner. Just as the couple's relationship is characterized by an overall tone in addition to how the partners interact around specific domains, the therapeutic relationship also has an overall tone and interactions around discrete moments in therapy.

Moreover, attempting to capture effective CBCT with techniques alone does not match the research regarding common factors in psychotherapy. Although almost all research on common factors is based on individual therapy, the findings likely hold for couple therapy as well. The research findings consistently demonstrate the importance of common therapist–client relationship factors in understanding therapeutic change (Ackerman et al., 2001; Norcross & Wampold, 2011). These common factors are likely one reason that meta-analyses indicate no significant differences in efficacy among empirically supported approaches to couple therapy (e.g., Shadish & Baldwin, 2003). Yet, given the well-entrenched maladaptive patterns in relationship distress and psychopathology, relying on the therapist to be warm and accepting is not enough to effect change. Thus, couples themselves, therapists in training, and empirical findings in the broader psychotherapy field, all seem to converge on this belief: along with the techniques of evidence-based treatments, *how* the therapist relates to the couple, delivers particular interventions, and interacts with the couple during a given session and across the course of treatment is crucial for effective treatment (for a thoughtful text devoted to common factors in couple and family therapy regarding the importance of the therapist–couple relationship, see Sprenkle, Davis, and Lebow, 2009). Therefore, how does a therapist deliver CBCT interventions in an optimal manner?

Adapting general and CBT-specific therapist–couple relationship elements to CBCT

Kazantzis, Dattilio, and Dobson (2017) reached similar conclusions regarding the centrality of both techniques and the therapeutic relationship in CBT overall, not unique to couple therapy. In doing so, they discuss two types of client-therapist relationship factors: (a) general relationship elements across various theoretical models of therapy, including CBT, and (b) CBT-specific relationship elements. The general relationship elements (often referred to as "common factors") have been investigated empirically by the American Psychological Association's second Interdivisional Task Force (APA Divisions 12 and 29), which identified empirically supported relationship factors that are important in therapy across orientations. Among those factors with the strongest support for their importance in predicting treatment outcome are: the therapeutic alliance, therapist empathy, collecting client feedback, and creating cohesion in group therapy. General relationship elements with some, yet not as strong, empirical support include: goal consensus, collaboration, and positive regard (Norcross & Wampold, 2011). Consistent with these findings, we believe it is crucial that a CBCT therapist be empathic with a couple, demonstrate genuine positive regard, and create cohesion between two partners who often are not working collaboratively toward common goals. While focusing on goals relevant to a given couple, the therapist's own style needs to come across as genuine. Some CBCT therapists have a great sense of humour and are somewhat playful; at times they can use their personal style effectively to help the couple relax in the sessions and think more flexibly, while still addressing serious concerns. Some CBCT therapists are energetic and optimistic and use their personal style to help demoralized couples become more active, while acknowledging the challenges and constraints that many couples face. Other CBCT therapists have a steady, calm demeanour which can be facilitative in slowing the pace for partners who are highly reactive to each other. Thus, while attending to the important common factors described above, CBCT therapists adapt and use their own personal styles and strengths in a genuine manner to attend to the needs of particular couples.

Kazantzis et al. (2017) point out that in addition to the common factors above that transcend theoretical orientations, there are CBT-specific relationship elements, including:

- Collaboration: The therapist and client work together as a team in a positive, collaborative manner to explore the client's cognitions, emotions, and behaviours, rather than the therapist coming across as an authority to challenge and evaluate the legitimacy of the client's experience.
- Empiricism: The therapist and client adopt an empirical approach, meaning that they gather information from the client's everyday life and the sessions to guide their work together. The therapist does not act as a distant scientist who is interested only in "hard data"; instead, the therapist helps the client step back and re-evaluate based on what is actually happening rather than remaining fixed in their views based on the distress the client has been experiencing.
- Socratic dialogue: Much of the therapist and client discussion evolves through Socratic dialogue as a way to help the client explore new ways of approaching concerns.

To a large degree, these same CBT-specific relationship factors are adapted in CBCT. For example, often the therapist asks the couple to try new ways of interacting during the coming week and "see how it goes" with plans to discuss their experience during the next session, a form of gathering "data" to evaluate what is and is not rewarding for the couple. These general and CBT-specific elements often are more complex when working with a couple as a result of having two individuals in the room who might be experiencing their relationship in quite different ways. In building empathy, the couple therapist might demonstrate understanding of one person's perspective regarding their relationship difficulties. Yet, if not carefully managed, this expression toward one person can be interpreted by the other partner as the therapist "taking sides." Thus, the couple therapist often makes comments that seek to validate both partners' perspectives without having to consolidate them, such as the following:

> Given how you interpreted what happened, it is very understandable why you felt sad and devalued; that must have felt so discouraging. And at the same time, we've heard from Mehmet that he interpreted the situation very differently and therefore had a different emotional reaction. So, each of your reactions is very understandable, given that you experienced the situation so differently.

That is, empathy and understanding for each person often is demonstrated by acknowledging and accepting each person's reactions, given that person's subjective experience. Likewise, in empathizing with the couple as a unit, the therapist conveys how difficult it is for the couple to have such different experiences as individual partners.

In a similar vein, using an empirical mindset to gather new information with a client can be more complex with distressed couples. Empiricism often involves going into the world, having experiences, "collecting data" about what happened, and bringing it back to the session. However, the often highly discrepant experiences of the same situation by two distressed partners mean that the data that one person "collects" can be immediately disputed by the other partner as being untrue, distorted, or only a portion of the full picture, making it difficult to use that information as grist for the cognitive mill. As a result, cognitive restructuring based on gathering information about events outside of the session often can be compromised when the partners argue about what did and did not occur. In such instances, the therapist might focus on the partners' discrepancy per se, or at times rely more on what happens during the session with everyone present, helping the couple process what just occurred. Thus, the elements that seem to be important in therapy in general, and in CBT, need to be adapted when applied to couple therapy or couple-based interventions for psychopathology.

Employing CBCT-specific, therapist–couple relationship elements

The third domain of therapist–couple relational elements is specific to working with a couple rather than an individual from a CBT perspective, referred to as CBCT-specific, therapist–couple relational elements. Addressing these elements in CBCT involves recognition of two important characteristics of the treatment. First, therapy involves working with a couple with both partners present, and there are common factors for couple therapy that apply across theoretical orientations. Second, in our approach, these common couple therapy factors must be incorporated into a cognitive-behavioural framework (i.e., CBCT-specific common factors). Below we first discuss therapeutic relationship factors that are common to couple therapy across theoretical orientations.

Important functions of healthy relationships

As Halford and Snyder (2012) note, there are multiple ways to interpret the finding that several theoretical approaches to couple therapy demonstrate comparable outcomes. One likely possibility is that there are important common factors across theoretical orientations. Sprenkle et al. (2009) and Christensen (2010) concluded that in all forms of couple therapy, the therapist relates to the couple in a manner that facilitates achieving broad goals, such as (a) providing a dyadic perspective on the couple's relationship and (b) curtailing dysfunctional interaction patterns. In addition, Christensen noted the importance of fostering effective communication, emphasizing strengths, and promoting positive behaviour. These common factors of couple therapy are aimed at restoring/developing important functions of a close, committed relationship that often have been disrupted in the presence of relationship distress and psychopathology.

One key function of healthy, committed relationships is to provide each partner with a safe place in the world, a place where each person feels understood, accepted, and valued. Whether it is viewed as unconditional positive regard or a secure attachment, having an experience that one's relationship is a constant in the midst of a complex, changing world is one of the true assets of a committed relationship. Unfortunately, this safe base from which to operate often is disrupted in distressed couples (Greenberg & Johnson, 1988); instead, partners come to view the other person as a source of hurt, disappointment, and pain. Therefore, couple therapy employs the therapist–couple relationship to create a safe environment in the therapy room so the couple can do the difficult and vulnerable work needed to improve their relationship. Likewise, the therapist helps the couple begin to (re)create a similar relationship environment in their everyday lives.

Feeling safe and secure is not a vague, internal experience that exists independently of how the two partners behave. Therefore, another important function of committed relationships is to provide both partners and the couple as a unit with a high degree of positive experiences while minimizing unnecessary negative interactions. These positive behaviours have value in themselves, along with contributing to a safe environment. On the other hand, as the expressed emotions literature points out, individuals do not function well when there are frequent hostile and critical exchanges (Hooley & Miklowitz, 2018). Thus, the CBCT therapist places a premium on fostering interactions during the session, both between the partners and with the therapist, that set a respectful tone, minimizing ingrained destructive interactional patterns and optimizing the opportunity for positive interactions. Because communication is a central part of how couples interact, creating adaptive communication between partners and between the therapist and couple during the session is central in treatment. These communications are essential not only to help partners feel understood and safe but also to help couples decide how to meet the demands that are part of their ongoing lives, as described in detail in Chapter 4. Furthermore, because CBCT operates on the premise that relationship quality is highly dependent on how the couple interacts in their daily lives, the therapist likewise interacts with the couple in a manner that fosters a sense of couple efficacy and exploration. This approach involves a mind-set of the partners being willing to interact in new ways, recognizing that their new efforts might not be successful at first, and embracing opportunities for fine-tuning in the future (also consistent with the notion of empiricism). Overall, the CBCT therapist interacts with a couple to help them (re)create these qualities of safety, respect, and exploration in their relationship, and, if needed, teaches the couple the skills and provides the knowledge required to accomplish these goals. That is, in CBCT there is an assumption that even with an ideal, safe, facilitative context established in therapy, couples do not necessarily have all the knowledge and skills to make needed changes in their relationship (e.g., due to poor relationship models in their families of origin). Thus, the therapist can serve as a valuable resource in providing guidance to the couple when appropriate. In doing so, the CBCT therapist does not dictate what a healthy relationship must look like for a given couple; rather, the therapist provides expertise on important *principles* of relationships (such as ways that relationships can be a "safe place"), with the couple discussing their own interpretation of the *what* they would like to build into their own lives.

Fostering a dyadic perspective

In well-functioning relationships, there tends to be a strong couple identity that involves the two members of the couple being a unit (with many variations of what this concept means practically), or, in other words, the couple experiences strong "we-ness" (Acitelli, Rogers, & Knee, 1999). Thus, difficulties are appraised as "our" problem, with a prominent dyadic component. For many distressed couples, "our" problem becomes "you are the problem." For example, in a couple with some difficulties related to personality differences, a dyadic perspective might be, "We are two very different people, and we haven't found a way yet to make that work for us in this area of life." In a distressed couple, however, partners are more likely to adopt an individual, blaming perspective when referring to personality differences: "You are just too stingy!"

A dyadic perspective on a couple's difficulties tends to reduce mutual blame and attacks. With less critical judgment about each person, individuals tend to be more willing to admit their own contribution to what has occurred (e.g., "I'm sorry I snapped at you. Your comment rubbed me the wrong way, but I had already had a rough day so I overreacted"). On the contrary, losing a dyadic perspective and blaming the other person is in and of itself distress-maintaining, as avenues for joint problem-solving are blocked and partners become gridlocked in defending and attacking. Thus, as noted in the literature on common factors in couple therapy (Davis, Lebow, & Sprenkle, 2012), helping couples jointly view their problems in dyadic terms seems to be a mechanism of change across theoretical orientations, with various ways of accomplishing this goal.

As described in Chapter 2, a major emphasis of CBCT is identifying the couple's interaction patterns and exploring how they maintain or exacerbate relationship difficulties, along with individual and environmental factors. In doing so, the roles and contributions of each individual in those patterns are discussed in therapy, recognizing the influences of each person's personality, motives, and individual well-being, along with the environmental context. Helping the couple shift (back) toward a dyadic conceptualization of their problems accomplishes multiple goals, including: (a) helping each person take responsibility for their own contributions and focus on changing their own behaviour, (b) decreasing distorted negative attributions about the other partner's behaviour, and (c) externalizing the interaction pattern such that a joint focus on addressing the maladaptive pattern is possible.

Even if each partner is able to describe their own role during a problematic interaction, often they do not see how this interaction reflects repetitive patterns. In such instances, the therapist might offer a broader conceptualization of that pattern: "So it sounds like when you strongly disagree about some topic, either one of you might raise the concern, but if it seems that either of you could get upset during the conversation, you quickly shut it down and both withdraw, regardless of the topic being addressed. And then your problems rarely get resolved. Is that what happens?" Similarly, during the feedback session with the couple (see Chapter 14), the therapist often provides brief psychoeducation about whatever domains are central in the couple's functioning or in an individual's psychopathology. Some discussion is included of how individual, relationship, and environmental factors influence each other, and how those factors influence the couple's current maladaptive interaction patterns, using examples from the couple to bring the message to life.

While providing a dyadic perspective on relationship difficulties, it is also important for the therapist to convey the notion that it is very difficult for either person to change the other partner's behaviour directly. What each partner can control is their own individual behaviour, and given the pervasive impact of reciprocity in couple's relationships, changing one's own behaviour often is the most effective way to promote change in a partner. Consequently, at multiple times throughout treatment, the therapist might ask:

> What do each of you think you might do individually to change things and impact the pattern you are describing? I know you really want the other person to change, but that is hard to control. What you can control is your own behaviour. You both are quite reactive to each other, so behaving in a more positive way probably creates the optimal context for your partner to change as well.

That is, individual responsibility to change dyadic interaction patterns is a frequent theme in comments from the therapist.

In discussing these dyadic interaction patterns, the therapist often integrates each person's cognitions, emotions, and behaviours as well, emphasizing the subjective nature of each partner's experience. "If I understand correctly, your thought was, 'He's ignoring me.' That seemed so unfair, and you became angry. And then in response to feeling angry you snapped at him, and then he immediately withdrew even further. Is that right?" Thus, the cognitive-behavioural model of individual functioning is integrated into the dyadic conceptualization. Not only is a dyadic perspective valuable in helping to identify ways that each partner might alter dysfunctional interactions, but it also can contribute to creating a safe, secure environment for both partners. When relationship difficulties are viewed as the result of malice or a lack of caring from the other person, the relationship is experienced as an unsafe place. However, if a couple can see that at least to some extent their relationship difficulties are the result of maladaptive interaction patterns, then the relationship can seem more predictable and amenable to change. Negative exchanges do not mysteriously erupt, and the relationship difficulties are not viewed as the result of an inherently hurtful or self-centred partner. Thus, helping the couple develop a dyadic perspective on their difficulties externalizes the problem, such that the partners can have a shared view of it, even if they disagree on the specifics and have different preferences regarding the pertinent issues. This approach can facilitate joint, respectful steps to finding a way forward. Additional therapist interventions can further facilitate the externalizing process. For example, in multiple ways throughout treatment, the therapist provides psychoeducation regarding broad patterns that often typify distressed couples. The therapist then explores collaboratively with the couple how these patterns operate in their relationship, identifies what each person might do behaviourally to alter the patterns, and pauses the process to identify and celebrate when maladaptive patterns are broken or positive exchanges occur. As therapy proceeds across sessions, the therapist gives the couple increasing autonomy to identify and alter these interaction patterns with decreasing input from the therapist. Yet, without a great deal of effort both within and outside of the sessions, such maladaptive patterns continue or couples quickly revert to them when interactions go awry, even when both partners want their relationship to be different.

Disrupting negative interaction patterns and promoting positive interactions

If CBCT therapists merely helped couples identify their maladaptive interaction patterns and pointed out what they might do to change while optimizing constructive interactions, couple therapy would be extremely brief. However, both therapists and couples know that changes rarely occur rapidly, and if they do, they are rarely maintained over time. Instead, distressed couples and couples experiencing psychopathology seem to be stuck in entrenched patterns and rigid behavioural repertoires, and much effort is needed to help them alter the patterns and maintain changes. All the strategies discussed above regarding a dyadic focus are relevant here, given that a dyadic focus is central in helping the couple alter dysfunctional interaction patterns and promoting rewarding interactions. There are several additional ways the therapist can interact with the couple to promote changes in these entrenched patterns, with particular attention to the amount of *structure* and *guidance* introduced into the session.

Optimizing structure

For many distressed couples, when entering into a therapy session, each partner is ready to report on the other person's inappropriate behaviours. Similarly, during the session, often one person says or does something that the other person reacts to negatively, and the interaction quickly deteriorates. One major overall strategy for helping couples alter their emphasis on negatives and related interaction patterns is for the therapist to provide more structure for the couple so that they do not "get off track" without even realizing it. In doing so, it is crucial for the therapist to optimize important common factors in the therapist–couple relationship, such as positive regard and a collaborative approach.

Thus, the therapist does not become a taskmaster for the couple, telling them what to do, or providing them with lists of rules regarding how to behave or communicate. Instead, the therapist discusses with the couple what they already experience—their tendency to move quickly to maladaptive interaction patterns, both during the session and in daily life. Often the therapist explains that when an individual or couple is attempting to change well-ingrained behaviour patterns, good intent is not enough. The therapist might provide examples, such as the reality that fitness centres have long membership rosters of people who made a New Year's resolution to get in shape, only to abandon it soon afterward. As with many other aspects of life, providing more structure and articulating clear plans are strategies that appear to be of assistance, along with careful monitoring of times when things veer off course. In a collaborative fashion, the therapist and couple decide what level of structure will be helpful to the couple in making desired changes. In addition, it is important to recognize that providing structure does not mean acting in a cold, authoritarian manner as a therapist; instead, structure and warmth are highly compatible and often facilitative, similar to findings in the parenting literature (McKee, Jones, Forehand, & Cuellar, 2013).

> Great, so you are planning to play tennis together sometime this week since you enjoyed that so much in the past. You know yourselves better than I do; is that enough detail so that it is likely to happen, or will you be more successful if you get more specific about when you might play tennis and consider what might happen to disrupt your plans?

In the above example, the therapist and couple decide together what level of structure might facilitate their desired changes. In addition, the CBCT therapist builds structure into the sessions in other ways, adapting to the needs of a particular couple. For example, just as in individual CBT, the session typically includes several elements that unfold in a regular order: (a) checking in with the couple about the week in general and how homework from the previous session unfolded; (b) setting an agenda for the session; (c) engaging in the agenda;

(d) wrapping up the session, including a review of how the session went; and (e) discussing agreed-upon homework or activities for the couple before the next session. This structure can be helpful in keeping the couple and therapist on track to address the important issues in the couple's relationship. Otherwise, the session can easily dissolve into a discussion about the "argument of the week" as the couple reports what has happened since the last consultation. Certainly reporting on such mishaps is appropriate during the initial check-in. Yet after a brief discussion, the therapist and the couple decide together whether a further conversation about what occurred outside of the session would be important to put on the agenda, and if so, how to approach it so that it is not a rehash of who said and did what and who was at fault. Thus, the structure of the session often can keep the couple and therapist on track so that they do not mindlessly slide into an unproductive use of session time. Similarly, the therapist often uses the initial check-in to help the couple step back and look at the "big picture" of where they are in their joint work in therapy and how the relationship or psychological concerns of one person are proceeding. This focus on the big picture also can help to focus the couple and therapist on how to use the session time to address central issues and themes rather than attending to one-off negative interactions.

Structure often is built into CBCT interventions as well. For example, significant time is spent with the two partners having conversations with each other, sharing thoughts and feelings or problem-solving (see Chapter 4). To facilitate this process, the therapist often provides a list of guidelines that couples find helpful in having these conversations but never insists on rules that the couple must follow. These guidelines are adapted to the couple's needs and style, often serving as reminders to keep them on track and away from maladaptive interaction patterns, along with promoting a positive experience. For instance, one guideline for being an effective listener is that while the other person is speaking, the listener's role is merely to listen, to attempt to understand the other person's experience, and to accept the other person's right to have their own point of view. In essence, this guideline does not ask the listener to agree but rather to accept. For some couples, this guideline is particularly valuable in helping the listener refrain from responding immediately with counterarguments and thrusting the couple into an antagonistic debate. Moreover, feeling heard and understood on both an emotional and a cognitive level can be quite rewarding for the speaker and contribute to a more caring and validating interaction between the partners. In this instance and in other contexts, structure is not employed for its own sake or because "that is the way we do it in CBCT"; structure is employed when needed to help the couple make changes when they are struggling to do so.

Whereas structure is explicit in the above examples, at times the therapist behaves during the session in a way to provide or increase structure without labelling it as such. For example, if the couple starts to interact in an unproductive manner, the therapist might stop the couple's interaction to intervene and prevent further escalation. In deciding how to stop the couple's conversation, the general guideline is to use the least amount of therapist "force" needed to do so. In many instances, the therapist might gently ask the couple to stop for a moment or hold up a finger in the couple's view to signal a request for the therapist to speak. If the couple is more emotionally aroused, the therapist might need to speak more forcefully or lean forward toward the couple and hold up a hand in a stop signal gesture. Rarely is a therapist harsh, but it is important to halt unproductive interaction sequences, and most couples value that the session is a safe place to explore difficult issues without the risk of discussions becoming destructive. Again, over the course of therapy, the therapist generally intervenes in a less demonstrative manner as the couple increasingly monitors their own behaviour, cognitions, and emotions. In addition to stopping destructive interaction patterns, therapists provide structure by guiding where the interaction goes next. In this way, the therapist takes gentle leadership to help the couple interact in more helpful ways or gain new insights, rather than just providing a structured context in which the couple is left to their own devices to determine next steps.

Providing guidance

Within the structure provided by the therapist as discussed above, another consideration becomes how to adapt the amount of guidance to the needs of a given couple. When the partners are talking directly with each other and the therapist wants to intervene, the therapist's response typically involves three components. In addition to (a) stopping the couple's interaction, the therapist (b) provides whatever intervention is appropriate, and finally (c) puts the couple "back on track" to continue with their conversation. The interventions employed might vary considerably as discussed throughout this book, and if the couple's conversation is to continue, the therapist often suggests to the couple where they resume their conversation and what might be productive. Putting the couple back on track is one instance of providing guidance combined with structure to alter the interaction in a more productive manner. For example, the therapist might suggest to the couple:

> Grace, I think you were trying to tell Frederica how you felt when she came home late without informing you. Why don't you pick up at that point, but try to express what we were just discussing, letting her know how worried you were rather than focusing on the fact that she didn't call you, okay?

Alternatively, the therapist might provide guidance in a subtler way if the interaction is productive otherwise (e.g., brief prompts such as "say more about the worry" without stopping the conversation), or in helping them set the stage for a conversation (e.g., by heightening vulnerable emotions before the couple begins their interaction; see Chapter 6 for more detail).

The above examples are part of a broader way of interacting with the couple during the session, in which the therapist serves as a guide to steer the couple in a direction that is likely to be productive. Thus, rather than implementing some form of rote communication training, the therapist guides the couple's conversation to emphasize the important aspects of the issue that need to be addressed and will allow the partners to join with each other. More broadly stated, the therapist needs to use the case conceptualization, along with their knowledge of the couple and their therapeutic relationship, in order to "work the material," decide where to pause, and consider what to accentuate, while addressing the current issues and how they relate to broader treatment goals. This approach might involve helping the couple focus on more vulnerable emotions, such as sadness, around which they can join rather than focusing solely on difficult emotions, such as anger or a partner's withdrawal during the session.

At times, the therapist might not actually stop the couple's interaction to have a three-way discussion but instead offer a brief suggestion to one partner or the couple without breaking the flow of their conversation. This comment could take the form of "affirm and redirect," as in this example: "Jared, this was really frustrating for you, but a moment ago you had started to tell Amanda how excited you had been to surprise her. Tell her what you wanted to do for her." Other brief prompts might take the form of brief questions, such as, "Okay. Lots of frustration. Any other feelings you also experienced?" Thus, in small and subtle ways, the therapist might gently steer the couple to more productive interactions during the session, a less direct form of providing guidance and structure.

Whereas structure and guidance are frequently used to help the couple decrease or eliminate negative interactions, excessive structure can be counterproductive when applied to positive behaviours that rely on a partner's internal motivation for their meaning. Thus, attempting to structure laughter or playful interactions can seem artificial to the couple. Even in these instances, the therapist and couple can discuss what the couple might do in their daily lives that would provide the context for fun and laughter. That is, the couple can control what they do and the procedures they put in place to maximize the likelihood of positive interactions, even when they often cannot control the outcomes themselves.

Using the therapist as a therapeutic tool

The discussion thus far has focused to a large extent on how the therapist relates to the couple and conducts sessions in order to present various interventions optimally. In addition, the therapist is an important therapeutic tool beyond delivering CBCT-specific interventions in an effective manner. In many instances, couples who are distressed or have one partner with psychopathology arrive for treatment confused, discouraged, and unclear if or how they can improve life. In such instances, the therapist might serve as the initial source of encouragement, hope, and reinforcement for change because partners cannot provide these important motivational efforts for each other. The therapist hopefully is perceived by the couple as a knowledgeable professional who has a valued perspective, as well as being a social reinforcer as a caring individual who knows the couple well, often in ways unknown to anyone else. Therefore, through a careful conceptualization and treatment plan, the therapist can provide a realistic basis for the couple to consider how their lives might change, without promising certainty or unrealistic outcomes. The therapist is not a cheerleader who encourages the couple in the abstract without a basis for realistic optimism and does not give a generic message that "you're great; you can do this!" Instead, the therapist seeks to inspire realistic hope through a well-articulated road map for understanding relationship and individual distress, along with strategies for making good decisions with regard to how to proceed with life, whether together or apart. As a result, while being appropriately tentative about outcomes, it can be facilitative for the therapist to express true confidence in understanding the couple and how these interventions have been successful with other couples and might be of assistance to this couple. At the same time, the therapist readily acknowledges concerns about various factors that might be barriers to improvement while discussing how those barriers might be addressed.

While always being realistic, the therapist at times needs to help motivate or even inspire the couple to be their best. At the extreme, this concept is exemplified in an apocryphal story about Michelangelo, who reportedly once stated, "In every block of marble, I see a statue as plain as though it stood before me, shaped and perfect in attitude and action. I have only to hew away the rough walls that imprison the lovely apparition to reveal it to the other eyes as mine see it." This phenomenon, known as the Michelangelo effect, embodies the importance of being able to see the potential in others that they might not even see in themselves and helping them to become the best versions of themselves that they can be, even going well beyond what they thought was possible. Without going over the top, the therapist can challenge the couple and both partners to become their best selves and see where it takes them. An important element in this process is the clear road map incorporating various relationship and individual psychological principles that the couple can put in place to assist them.

This approach also means that the therapist might directly reinforce and join the couple in celebrating their successes and acknowledging the efforts they are making, both during the sessions and in their daily lives. For example, when they are successful in implementing new guidelines, the therapist might focus on the specifics and respond, "Excellent! You two really did it! I know that was hard, and you stuck with it." Likewise, when the couple made strong efforts but did not achieve the desired outcome, the therapist might similarly reinforce the efforts, "That did not go well, did it? But I'm so impressed that you tried, and hopefully we can pinpoint what went wrong so it can go better the next time." Or when an unexpected devastating event happens during the course of therapy, such as a diagnosis of cancer for one partner, the therapist might be explicit in expressing sorrow and join with the couple in exploring worry about the unknown future. Certainly, the therapist needs to maintain perspective and not put the focus on their own emotions. Yet, validating concerns that the couple and therapist share can give the couple courage to explore what is frightening, knowing that a skilled professional is there with them, cares, and understands what they are facing.

In response to hearing that CBCT therapists at times expresses their own emotions, therapists in training ask, "Would you really laugh like that with a couple? I thought we were supposed to be serious." Or, "Would you actually allow your sadness to be evident when they told you the hopeless news about their child? We're supposed to be professional and maintain our boundaries, aren't we?" Indeed, therapists need to respect professional boundaries and avoid dual-role relationships, yet there is great latitude regarding how to respond to a couple. The CBCT conceptual framework emphasizes that couples are impacted by their social and physical environment; during treatment, the therapist is a crucial part of their interpersonal environment. CBCT therapists should gauge their own emotional reactions according to what they are attempting to accomplish with the couple, using selected CBCT interventions and creating an atmosphere that encourages couples to be their best. Most importantly, CBCT therapists are not merely conductors or technicians who apply various interventions with the couple. Therapists are rich sources of reinforcement, support, and encouragement to couples, and they should be aware of their impact and use it effectively as a potentially important therapeutic tool to address relationship discord or individual psychopathology.

Concluding comments

CBCT makes use of a variety of interventions to assist distressed couples and couples in which one or both partners are experiencing psychological difficulties. However, these interventions are provided in an interpersonal context, and understanding that interpersonal therapeutic context is important for at least two reasons. First, the therapist is relating to two unique human beings who have created a unique relationship, and CBCT interventions can be implemented most successfully when the therapist is attentive to these characteristics of the couple and relates to the couple in a way that encourages them to engage in these interventions. Common factors in the therapist–couple relationship include: (a) common factors that are important across most or all forms of therapy; (b) CBT-specific relational factors; (c) common factors relevant to various theoretical approaches to couple therapy; and (d) CBCT-specific therapist–couple relational elements. Thus, the therapist relates to the couple in ways that generally are facilitative in various forms of therapy, while adapting and extending these relational elements to interventions that are employed within CBCT. Furthermore, the therapist–couple interactional style must integrate effectively with the CBCT model of healthy couple relationships and the interventions specific to CBCT. These various factors combine to dictate what CBCT "really looks like."

Second, the therapist–couple relationship is important beyond providing a context for optimal implementation of particular interventions. The therapist is a person, a knowledgeable professional who can serve as a source of motivation, encouragement, and social reinforcement to the couple. CBCT therapists are fully cognizant of the couple dyad as the focus of treatment; there also is a triad that includes the therapist, who works to assist the couple. Recognizing and employing the CBCT therapist as an important therapeutic tool when appropriate allows the couples to make full use of the couple therapy context. To a large extent, the remainder of this book focuses on the interventions available to the CBCT therapist. It is important to keep in mind that these interventions are always implemented with these relational factors in mind.

Part II

Working with the "fundamentals" of CBCT—behaviours, cognitions, and emotions

Everyday life consists of an ongoing, intertwined series of emotions, cognitions, and behaviours. Emotions can drive cognitions and behaviour. When someone is happy, the world and everyone in it might seem a bit more benevolent, and they treat them as such. Alternatively, cognitions can drive emotions and behaviour; if a partner seems to have behaved unfairly, the other person might well get angry and let them know it. Finally, behaviour can result in cognitive and emotional change. When a person pushes themselves to go to dinner with their partner despite not feeling like it after a fight, they might enjoy the dinner and become more hopeful about the future. A central premise in CBCT and as demonstrated in these examples, one person's emotions, cognitions, and behaviours often are about the other partner, the relationship, or oneself within the relationship and are directed toward the partner. That partner is likely to respond with their own emotions, cognitions, and behaviours, again, often directed toward the other person. It is this complex set of interactions within each person and between partners that give relationships their richness, complexity, and vast capacity to serve as sources of fulfilment or suffering.

Part II emphasizes this interplay within and between partners, yet in order to provide a thorough foundation upon which to understand this complexity, Chapters 4–6 address the importance of behaviours, cognitions, and emotions focal to intimate relationships separately. Given the interconnections among these three factors, each provides a "portal of entry" to intervene with a couple, recognizing that intervening in one domain will likely have notable impact on the other domains as well. That is, altering the partners' behaviour toward each other is likely to change their emotional reactions and thoughts as well. Each chapter includes extensive discussion of how to intervene directly in that domain; for example, behavioural interventions primarily target behaviour change. In addition, how to employ interventions to take advantage of the "cross-fertilization" among the domains is discussed, for example, how to employ cognitive and emotional interventions to promote behaviour change. Thus, when a therapist is developing a treatment plan or intervening at the moment, a variety of behavioural, cognitive, and emotional interventions are available, and guidelines are provided to assist in making these clinical decisions.

Chapter 4

Behavioural factors and communication

Good relationships bring out the best in each partner, allow the couple to function well as a unit, and are meaningfully embedded in the couple's environment. Both partners invest time and energy in the relationship, often with a notable focus on "making life good" for each other. Even when both partners are making their best efforts, optimal relationships also require that the two partners are able to communicate well to integrate their efforts, problem-solve, and express love and care. Many couples readily endorse these aspirational goals for a relationship, but how do such notions translate into daily life? Likewise, at the opposite end of the spectrum, how do severely distressed couples create misery on an ongoing basis? Critical comments, ridicule, or thoughtless acts, such as keeping the only umbrella to oneself during a rainstorm, all send a strong message. All these situations involve behaviours, and they stand out to others very quickly, giving the impression that the relationship is not functioning well. Similarly, an overall sense of "they are such a great couple" often is based on behaviours. At times, the behaviours might be encoded in small gestures—a hand briefly placed on a partner's back, statements of pride and encouragement in the face of a partner's recent success, or the ability to tell a story together that keeps others laughing. At other times, behaviours might involve more extensive efforts, such as one partner taking on additional responsibilities so that the other is able to accomplish important goals, such as completing an academic degree.

Thus, behaviours in relationships define how couples function as a unit and how their values and goals are lived out day by day. Admiring one's partner or professing deep feelings becomes almost meaningless if the two members of the couple continually treat each other poorly, or if they cannot coordinate efforts so that the tasks of life proceed smoothly ("We have a lot of fun together, but the house is a mess, and now we have been evicted because of the mice!"). How one person treats the other and how the couple functions as a unit determine whether life is uplifting and successful or becomes an exhausting experience to endure. In addition, an individual's behaviours in a relationship impact that same person's sense of self; that is, "Do I like who *I* am in the relationship? Does it bring out the best in me?" Thus, attempting to maximize constructive behaviours from each partner and decrease maladaptive couple interactive patterns is a major focus in CBCT.

Conceptualizing behaviours in relationships

The *content* of behaviour, or what couples actually do, and the *process* of how the two partners interact with each other are both essential components of relationship well-being. Couples presenting for therapy might have particular content-related complaints, such as one person wanting the other partner to take a more active role in parenting or disagreements about finances. However, the most frequently cited concern of distressed couples is communication difficulties (Doss, Simpson, & Christensen, 2004), often unrelated to specific content ("We just don't seem to be able to talk about anything. Even the slightest comment leads to eruptions"). Extensive research over the past decades has elucidated adaptive and maladaptive communication and broader interaction patterns, which are common treatment targets in CBCT.

The current chapter discusses behavioural and communication factors in relationships from a CBCT perspective and interventions focused on these factors. First, a conceptualization is presented of *discrete* communication and noncommunication behaviours central to relationships. Second, because these discrete behaviours of the two partners do not occur independently of each other, a discussion follows of the interactional behavioural patterns that evolve in relationships and that are central to relationship well-being.

Discrete relationship behaviours: Positive and negative behaviours

Most individuals begin their committed relationships with an abundance of good feelings, yet many of these same couples develop significant distress over time. Often it is hard for them to articulate the basis for their distress beyond knowing that they dislike their partner's behaviour, are not getting along, and experience a void of rewarding experiences. In essence, often many negative behaviours are occurring, and important positive behaviours are missing from the couple's life.

While the distinction of positive versus negative behaviours is a broad one, it is highly relevant for therapists and couples alike. Intuitively, many people think of positives and negatives as polar opposites of one dimension. However, positive and negative behaviours function as two separate dimensions in relationships (Epstein & Baucom, 2002; Gable & Reis, 2001). Well-adjusted relationships typically involve high levels of positive, rewarding behaviours. Conversely, few couples thrive in the context of high levels of negative behaviours. Research findings confirm that partners who are happy with their relationship report a greater number of gratifying behaviours and fewer dissatisfying behaviours than their distressed counterparts (e.g., Gottman & Notarius, 2000; Heyman, 2001). The nature and content of the positive and negative behaviours vary widely among couples, depending on factors such as personality, relationship history, cultural background and identity, and the stage of the relationship. Yet, these very basic findings demonstrate that most healthy relationships include a great number of positive (adaptive) and few negative (maladaptive) behaviours between partners (Gottman & Notarius, 2000; Heyman, 2001).

A couple might display any combination of positive and negative behaviours—both occurring at a high frequency, both low, a high frequency of positives and low negatives, or low positives and high negatives. As a result, not all relationships with a high rate of either negative or positive behaviours are alike. If there is a lack of positives in the presence of high rates of negative behaviours, the relationship is likely to be experienced as pervasively antagonistic. If the negative behaviours are accompanied by high rates of positive behaviours, a couple might describe their relationship as turbulent, stormy, or passionate. Likewise, when a couple engages in high rates of positive behaviours with few negatives, they are likely to find the relationship to be rewarding and easy to manage. Table 4.1 outlines some of the common characteristics of various combinations of positive and negative behaviours, recognizing that

Table 4.1 Combinations of positive and negative behaviours and their implications for a couple's relationship

Low positives, high negatives The relationship is likely to be experienced as difficult, unrewarding and undermining of each partner's well-being and the well-being of the couple as a unit. The relationship creates a pervasive sense of negativity such that it serves as a chronic, diffuse stressor.	**High positives, high negatives** The relationship is likely to be experienced as "stormy." While there are moments of closeness, tenderness, and passion, these can be overshadowed by periods of negativity, rejection, and hostility. Depending on the nature of the negative behaviours and how contained they are, some couples might be happy and view the relationship as "passionate," while other couples might view the relationship as unpredictable.
Low positives, low negatives The relationship is characterised by few, if any, negative behaviours such that outward conflict might be rare. However, the lack of positive behaviours means that the relationship is somewhat lifeless and might be experienced by the couple as stale, boring, or perfunctory.	**High positives, low negatives** The relationship provides an interpersonal environment where both the couple and the individuals within it have the potential to thrive. The relationship brings out the best in each partner, helps each partner feel valued, affirmed and cared for, and is likely to be experienced by both partners as rewarding and fulfilling.

many relationships do not involve symmetrical behaviours between the two partners. Thus, one partner might express many positive and few negative behaviours while the other individual is more volatile. Furthermore, not all behaviours have the same impact; the context and severity of the behaviours determine their impact on the relationship. For example, an isolated, major negative incident such as infidelity can dramatically change an otherwise positive relationship. Thus, there is no ratio of positive to negative behaviours that defines an adaptive versus maladaptive relationship.

Positive behaviours

Adaptive relationship behaviours can be differentiated in many ways. Often distinctions have been made in terms of instrumental versus expressive behaviours (Epstein & Baucom, 2002); the discussion below adapts these domains slightly to emphasize the important relationship functions that those behaviours serve. Thus, positive communication and noncommunication behaviours might serve the vital function of helping life run smoothly for each partner and for the couple as a unit. Indeed, many couples remark, "We are a good team; we work well together and get things done." Yet, few individuals select a lifetime partner because they are efficient together. A central aspect of close, committed relationships involves positive behaviours that lead to each partner feeling cared about, valued, and loved by the other person; in other words, these actions contribute to a sense of well-being, security, and contentment. These behaviours might include the "feel good" moments in a couple's life, but they are not only about feeling good. Positive, adaptive behaviours also are essential to address difficulties that arise in the relationship and to address challenges external to the couple.

Positive behaviours to help life run smoothly

Successful, happy couples develop ways to make life run smoothly within the constraints of their circumstances, with an appropriate level of defined roles and routines that minimize the need to improvise constantly. Frequently, these roles involve a host of task-oriented behaviours. Positive instrumental behaviours include concrete, tangible actions that are concerned with the pragmatics of life, such as completing household chores, paying bills on time, and bringing the children home from school.

Although some instrumental actions are focused on the couple as a unit, others are directed at supporting the other partner as an individual, typically referred to as *social support*. Commonly, different types of social support are categorized as *instrumental (tangible) support* and *emotional support* (see below). Instrumental support refers to task-oriented behaviours, including concrete assistance and giving advice. For instance, instrumental support could take the form of temporarily taking over the running of the household to enable the partner to focus on preparing for a job interview or getting the car repaired. Extensive research has demonstrated the positive impact of social support on individuals' psychological and physical well-being (Cutrona, 1996; Taylor, 2011). In addition to these behaviours that make life easier for the couple or one partner, other behaviours are explicitly focused on making the other person feel special, cherished, or loved.

Positive behaviours to affirm the partner and the couple

Positive *expressive behaviours* are closely connected to the emotional "tone" of the relationship. Expressive behaviours cover a wide range of verbal and nonverbal behaviours. Within adult romantic relationships, positive communication behaviours (such as verbally expressing love or commitment, intently listening to find out what is on the other person's mind, etc.) tend to be particularly central to relationship well-being. Research shows that, compared to distressed couples, happy couples communicate in a way that includes more assent, approval, empathy, humour, laughter, and positive physical touch (for a review see Osgarby, 1998).

Positive, caring behaviours typically are welcomed by partners at any time, yet they can be particularly important when one partner is struggling. *Emotional support* often is aimed at joining with the other person so that they do not feel alone in a difficult situation ("I'm here for you") and they know that the other person understands and validates their experience ("That sounds incredibly difficult, and I can tell how much it weighs on you") [see Cutrona, Suhr, and MacFarlane (1990) for a review of the different forms of support-intended communication in couples]. On the other hand, emotional support need not be restricted to difficult situations; in fact, cheering a partner on and celebrating a partner's successes can be affirming: "You did it! I'm so proud of you!"

While positive, affirming behaviours might be adaptive in many types of relationships, *intimacy-enhancing behaviours* that help partners feel close and connected have unique importance in romantic relationships (Reis & Shaver, 1988). Many unhappy couples report a sense of feeling disconnected as one of their most distressing concerns (Doss et al., 2004). Individuals vary in terms of what types of behaviours will create a sense of intimacy for them, but all of them provide some way to connect with a partner. Common positive behaviours that enhance intimacy include, but are not limited to: (a) open, in-depth conversation about personal feelings or vulnerable topics; (b) physical affection and sexual behaviour; (c) joint activities or couple "rituals" in which the partners focus on each other (e.g., date nights for fun, exercising together, accomplishing a task together); or (d) joint activities focused on the couple's environment consistent with the couple's value system (e.g., an experience of working together as a team to help others). What creates intimacy for one couple might be less rewarding for another; caring, loving acts need to be tailored to the preferences and needs of each person. Thus, it is important for each couple to find specific behaviours that promote their desired level of closeness.

Not only do couples vary in terms of what makes each person feel special and close, but couples and individual partners also differ in their abilities and desires to carry out these caring behaviours, as well as more task-oriented behaviours. Whereas some couples excel in both instrumental, pragmatic behaviours and behaviours that contribute to a positive tone in the relationship, other couples have distinct strengths in one area yet struggle in the other domain. Some distressed couples struggle in both areas, such that they experience feeling disconnected emotionally, and the pragmatic aspects of life lag. It also is important to recognize that various couples and partners differentially value these domains, such that for some, frequent acts of caring are essential whereas for others, "getting the job done" is the first and foremost aspect of being a good partner. Relationship distress can arise when each person behaves in a manner to achieve what they value but minimizes the types of positive behaviours valued by the partner.

Negative behaviours

While a high frequency of positive behaviours appears to be important for couples to reach optimal functioning, a high frequency of negative behaviours, or low frequency but highly destructive negatives, can spell doom for relationships. In fact, if there is one general characteristic of distressed relationships, it is the presence of many negatives—negative behaviours, negative cognitions, and negative emotions. When one or both partners report, "I can't take it anymore! Something has to change, or I'm leaving," typically they are indicating that the relationship contains so many negative behaviours that everyday life has become unbearable. Indeed, research shows that negative behaviours tend to be more predictive of how a relationship fares than positive behaviours (Weiss & Heyman, 1997).

Communication is one major category of behaviour, and the majority of research comparing behaviours between distressed and nondistressed couples has focused on communication. The findings with regard to negative communication are consistent: distressed couples use negative communication behaviours much more frequently and reciprocate their partners' negative behaviour at higher rates, such as criticizing, blaming, denying responsibility, or expressing hostility (Gottman & Notarius, 2000; Heyman, 2001). Thus, both negative communication and noncommunication behaviours are a hallmark of relationship distress. Understanding the basis for these seemingly self-defeating behaviours is important because the different bases of the behaviours call for different intervention strategies.

First, many negative behaviours are *maladaptive behaviour-change strategies* that one person uses in an attempt to alter the other person's behaviour. In every relationship, partners knowingly and unknowingly influence each other and need a way to request changes from the other person. Such strategies might be adaptive (e.g., asking for a conversation to discuss concerns about the increasing amount of time spent at work) or maladaptive (e.g., giving one's partner "the silent treatment" when they come home late). Partners might use maladaptive behaviour change strategies because prior attempts with more adaptive methods have not worked, because they had early relationship models that suggested hostile methods are normal or necessary, or because they lack the skill for more adaptive strategies. Unfortunately, negative behaviours to effect change often are inadvertently reinforced by short-term positive consequences (D. H. Baucom & Epstein, 1990). For example, the other person might eventually give in and temporarily provide the desired response: "The only way I can get her to listen to me is to shout."

Second, once negative behaviours emerge, the cycle can become self-maintaining and difficult to break. Once a behaviour has occurred multiple times and has been reinforced, it often is repeated almost automatically when similar circumstances occur. Such behaviours might be thought of as *mindless behaviours* (i.e., behaviours that occur without the individual being fully aware or able to self-monitor). "Being on autopilot" can be adaptive if a relationship is functioning well; however, for distressed couples, these mindless behaviours often are negative (Epstein & Baucom, 2002). Other mindless behaviours might not have started as behaviour-change strategies, but rather have "crept in" to the relationship over time, perhaps because stress has increased in other areas of life and the capacity for self-monitoring has decreased. For example, general irritability and strain due to financial hardships may wear partners down, increasing the likelihood of partners "snapping" at each other over minor issues that they would otherwise be able to respond to more effectively.

Third, the above patterns might be exacerbated by particular types of psychopathology or subclinical symptoms. For example, as discussed in Chapter 12, a person with obsessive-compulsive disorder (OCD) might become angry if the partner "contaminates" their home with germs—an attempt to alter the partner's behaviour which becomes particularly rigid and pronounced within the context of the disorder. Thus, the context for negative behaviours must be understood so that effective treatment can be planned.

Magnitude of negative behaviours

Not all negative behaviours are the same in magnitude or type: an isolated, thoughtless remark ("That looks like the dress your grandmother wore in that photo from 30 years ago!") has a different impact than gambling away the family savings. Thus, we distinguish three broad "magnitudes" of negatives: (a) minor annoyances, often stemming from individual differences, which serve as "irritants" (e.g., a partner's mannerisms, forgetting to close the door of the refrigerator) and take on greater significance in the presence of the other categories of negative behaviours; (b) moderate, frequent negative behaviours (e.g., consistently coming home much later than agreed upon); and (c) major relationship violations or traumas that strike at the very core of one's beliefs about one's partner or the relationship (e.g., infidelity, physical aggression). Moreover, regardless of their magnitude, negative behaviours can interfere with the same aspects of life that positive behaviours promote. That is, they (a) interfere with the smooth running of life—partners make life more complicated and difficult for each other and for the couple as a unit, and (b) undermine each partner's self-worth, foster negative feelings about each other and the relationship, and create an environment in which one or both partners feel emotionally and/or physically unsafe.

Negative behaviours that make life more difficult

Just as there is a multitude of ways that partners can invest positive effort to ensure that the relationship functions well, there also are many ways in which negative behaviours can negatively impact a couple's functioning. These behaviours often fall into at least one of three domains, and understanding their basis is important to effect meaningful change:

(a) not following through with agreed-upon behaviours that are necessary for smooth couple functioning, (b) making unilateral decisions, or (c) engaging in behaviours directed toward others or the environment that make life more complicated for the couple.

One major complaint among distressed couples is that one partner does not follow through with commitments, chores, or responsibilities, such as completing household tasks or paying bills, which complicates life or creates an unpleasant environment. This lack of follow-through can occur for multiple reasons, including an overall style of avoiding unpleasant tasks, subclinical or clinical levels of attention deficit disorder, agreeing to do something to keep the peace but with no intention of engaging in the behaviour, or "payback" for being upset with the partner for other reasons. For other couples, the cause may be a dyadic one, such as difficulties reaching decisions together. For example, the partners might not have reached clear agreements regarding who does what in the home.

Second, although the couple needs to function effectively as a team, some partners act independently at inappropriate times or make unilateral decisions that impact the couple negatively. Not surprisingly, Liu Yang was furious when Zhang Wei told her that he had signed a contract for a new house without discussing it with her; in fact, they had not even talked about buying a house. She was shocked that he would independently take such a major step that would greatly affect the whole family. While some individuals seem to understand intuitively when to consult with a partner and make joint decisions, other partners are not adept at making this judgment, or they are aware but proceed with a solo decision as "payback" or because they fear what the partner might say if consulted. In some couples, partners disagree about which domains are appropriate for unilateral decisions and who should make them, and they have not been able to reconcile these different perspectives.

At other times, overt negative individual behaviours from either partner can complicate the context within which the couple lives. Thus, being rude to the neighbours when it is important to gain their agreement regarding putting up a shed can be self-defeating in helping the couple improve their living situation.

Sometimes, the difficulty in moving forward in life stems not so much from one person's behaviour but from having the experience that almost nothing in the relationship seems to be easy—everything has to be debated rather than moving forward with ease. In many instances, such difficulties result from being in a relationship with someone who has reasonable yet very different perspectives on the world, different values regarding how to behave, and overall stylistic differences as described in Chapter 7. In such instances, couples experience that the relationship is "so much work. Everything is an effort; why does it have to be like this when other couples seem to be able to get things done without huge debates?"

In essence, there is a range of negative behaviours focused on the couple or the environment that make life seem effortful. Some are self-focused and others result from a lack of perspective or normal individual differences between the two partners. On the other hand, many negative behaviours have their impact not by making life complicated but rather because they are hurtful and erode the individuals' and couple's joy and pleasure, replacing these experiences with ones of hurt, anger, sadness, and a lack of safety.

Negative behaviours that make one or both partners feel bad about themselves, their partner, and the relationship

The healthiest relationships are affirming; partners demonstrate belief in each other and help both people grow and be their best as individuals. Caring partners often overlook the other person's shortcomings and vulnerabilities, instead focusing on their partner's strengths, efforts, and good intentions. In addition to affirming the other person as an individual, partners in healthy relationships convey messages about the value of the individual within the context of the relationship: "You are special to me as a partner," or "I carry you in my heart." Unhealthy relationships often do just the opposite. They tear down the other person as an individual, undermine their sense of worth, and focus on their failures and shortcomings. In unhealthy relationships, partners engage in behaviours that make each other feel unloved or unimportant within the relationship: "You and our relationship are not that important to me," or "You and our relationship are very important to me, just not measuring up to what I had hoped."

There is a myriad of ways in which partners can undermine each other's sense of worth and value as an individual or as part of the couple. Many of these negative behaviours fall into the frequent, "moderately negative" category, meaning that they are harmful, yet as a single occurrence, they are likely not devastating to the individual or the couple. Instead it is the persistent, cumulative effect of many such behaviours that wreaks havoc on relationships. Often such behaviours occur during conversations in the form of both verbal and nonverbal putdowns. Some nonverbal behaviours such as eye rolls are not clear as to their precise meaning, yet they are hurtful because of their broad devaluing message. Yet, other negative behaviours are not so subtle; a verbal comment might be an explicit putdown: "Do you really believe that? I can't see how any reasonable person could possibly support such a stupid idea." Thus, across domains of functioning, one person makes statements that question the skill and value of the other person as an individual, as part of the couple, or the relationship more broadly.

Other "negatives" can involve omissions of behaviours that convey the same message. For example, François and Janine sat down at an outdoor cafe overlooking the French Riviera on a picturesque summer evening. The moment was set; they were served their drinks, and then both pulled out their phones and proceeded to text without saying a word to each other for the next 40 minutes. When they finished their drinks, François and Janine nodded to each other, got up, and left. There was no overt verbal hostility, nor even a disapproving glance from either of them; yet their behaviours seemed to carry a strong message of how they regarded each other and their relationship in the context of what seemed like a "made for movies moment." Thus, both commissions and omissions of behaviours can carry the hurtful message that "you and our relationship are not important to me."

Major, relationally traumatic behaviours

The above examples demonstrate how hurtful comments and actions can have a detrimental cumulative effect on an individual or the relationship. In addition, major negative events that fall into the category of *relational traumas* can be devastating, such as sexual or emotional infidelity or physical aggression. Relational traumas disrupt important assumptions (basic beliefs regarding what one's relationship and one's partner actually *are* like) and standards (beliefs regarding what the relationship and both partners *should* be like), as discussed in Chapter 5. Such violations can shake a person to the core. For example, in responding to a recently revealed affair, a partner might say, "I realized my entire adult life has been a lie. You are not who I thought you were all this time; I've been such a fool!" In such instances, typically it is not enough to end the affair or other traumatic behaviour. Instead, the shattered assumptions and standards must be addressed before the injured partner can move forward in a healthy manner. Couple therapy for these relational traumas is complex, and describing the treatment approaches for infidelity, for example, is beyond the purview of the current volume. Baucom and colleagues (D. H. Baucom, Snyder, & Gordon, 2009; Snyder, Baucom, & Gordon, 2007) have written books both for therapists and for couples that build on the model currently being presented. When such interpersonal traumas have occurred, they typically must be addressed before the couple can move forward and confront other less traumatic aspects of their relationship that also merit attention.

When considering the various positive and negative behaviours that occur in relationships, it also is essential to attend to the fact that individuals' behaviours do not occur in isolation; instead, the two partners respond to each other's behaviour in an interdependent manner. Below, important process factors and interaction patterns are discussed that emerge when examining longer sequences of these behaviours in everyday life.

Behaviour and communication in relationships: Dyadic interaction patterns

One of the unique rewards and, simultaneously, challenges in relationships is that the two individuals *relate to* each other. In other words, the two members of a couple enter an intricate web of actions, reactions, and recurring interaction patterns. Relationships could not exist without this interdependence, which reaches from macro patterns ("We do a good job of keeping a good work-life balance. When one of us has to put in extra effort at work, the other person gives more time to the children.") to the smallest micro behaviours—e.g., synchronization of facial expressions during a conversation that fosters a sense of closeness. While relationships would not exist without this interdependence, there also is an inherent risk for the development and continuation of persistent, maladaptive interaction cycles. Many distressed couples experience rapidly escalating arguments about seemingly trivial topics and often cannot explain how they ended up shouting at each other. Often, such interaction cycles become a source of distress in and of themselves, almost independent of the topic at hand. Below is a description of the most important interaction patterns in intimate relationships that are essential for addressing behaviours in CBCT.

As outlined in Chapter 2 and discussed in more detail in Chapter 8, couples need to navigate a variety of macro-level processes in order to be successful, such as transitioning through different stages of relationship development and balancing stability with change. Many of these macro-level processes are concerned with how couples operate as a system. In addition to these larger themes and tasks that couples navigate, understanding the micro-level processes through which partners impact each other on a moment-by-moment basis clarifies how the macro-themes operate. That is, patterns that are exemplified during a given interaction often are consistent across time and content issues for a couple; thus, understanding these discrete interaction patterns often provides insight into the broader themes that characterize and maintain relationship distress.

The remainder of this chapter focuses on communication and behavioural interaction patterns at this more detailed, micro level. Before discussing couple interaction patterns, we first focus on couples' communication. This emphasis on communication is important because conversations between partners is one of the most important contexts within which specific interaction patterns occur and which serve as a basis of intervention, as discussed later in this chapter.

Communication as a central process and a context for interaction patterns

Communication is crucial to relationship success for at least two reasons. First, communication represents an important relationship behaviour in and of itself; second, effective communication serves as the vehicle to address a variety of substantive issues that arise in relationships (Epstein & Baucom, 2002). Within this broad domain of communication, two major types of couple conversations can be differentiated. Each brings its unique challenges and context for adaptive and maladaptive interaction patterns.

Types of conversations and communication difficulties

CBCT conceptualizes two fundamental types of conversations that couples have, with each contributing to the two central behavioural functions of experiencing oneself and the relationship as valued and of making life run smoothly, as discussed above. These conversations include the couple's ability to (a) share how they think and feel, and (b) make joint decisions or solve problems (Epstein & Baucom, 2002). The first domain is concerned with letting the other person know one's views on an issue, perhaps sharing what has happened during the day, or engaging in more in-depth conversations about each partner's emotions and thoughts about important domains of life (e.g., how they feel about their child's behaviour problem). There is no instrumental outcome from this type of communication. Rather, these conversations fulfil a variety of purposes, ranging from allowing each partner to gain a more in-depth understanding of the other person's experiences and perspectives (which might inform subsequent decision-making), to fostering connection and closeness, to providing a safe context to address disagreements. Couples with good communication skills are able to use this context to promote positive experiences as well as understand and accept each other's perspectives without becoming defensive or critical, even if they disagree. Distressed couples frequently "skip over" this type of conversation and instead engage in premature problem-solving (e.g., demanding changes) or engage in this type of conversation but do so in a way that comes across as trying to "win" an argument. Criticism and verbal attacks make it extremely difficult for partners to listen to each other, such that each individual tends to be preparing a rebuttal rather than trying to understand the other's perspective. Other distressed couples report that they rarely share their thoughts and feelings at all.

The second domain is concerned with making decisions and solving problems. This domain encompasses the small and mundane ("Who will do the supermarket shopping?"), the more significant ("What type of mortgage will best suit our circumstances?"), and the major, life-changing decisions ("Shall we try to start a family together?"). As such, although the content varies, the process involved in reaching joint decisions in an adaptive fashion typically is quite consistent. Couples who struggle in this domain often do not take both partners' perspectives into account in deciding what to do. Instead, partners frequently fall into the trap of entering the interaction with a preferred solution in mind and then trying to convince the other person to agree with this solution. Alternatively, couples might struggle with other aspects of joint problem-solving, such as attempting to resolve too many issues at once or failing to implement agreed-upon plans.

Couples might be effective in one, both, or neither of these two types of conversations. Often, a major stumbling block occurs when the two partners are attempting to have these two different kinds of conversation simultaneously (i.e., when one partner wants to share thoughts and feelings while the other partner offers solutions or tries to problem-solve). Typically, the interaction becomes dissatisfying for both partners, with a vague experience that "we're not on the same wave length." For example, when Lauryn came home after a particularly difficult day and wanted to share how exhausted she was dealing with biased comments toward her and other co-workers who were people of colour as well, Roy offered suggestions for how she might approach her department of human resources. As a result, Lauryn felt that Roy did not listen or understand her situation. At the same time, Roy became exasperated because Lauryn was "complaining" about her job but was unwilling to consider his suggestions. Neither understood why the other person was becoming upset.

Even when partners are attempting to have the same type of conversation, a variety of adaptive and maladaptive interaction patterns can develop within conversations. These interaction patterns, described below, can become well-ingrained and either facilitate or compromise the individuals' and the relationship's well-being.

Categories of couple interaction patterns

Broadly speaking, dyadic interaction patterns can be characterized in terms of whether each partner is "moving away" (withdrawing, avoiding) or "moving toward" (engaging) the other person during the interaction, with various combinations resulting from the two partners' actions (see Figure 4.1). Engaging and withdrawing are not inherently adaptive or maladaptive responses; instead, their effect depends on the context of the interaction and how the behaviour is enacted. For example, reaching out for constructive discussion and attacking the partner are both approach behaviours. These patterns can be seen both in communication and non-communication behaviours (e.g., withdrawal might include saying "I'm done with this conversation!" or going to the pub every night to avoid confrontation).

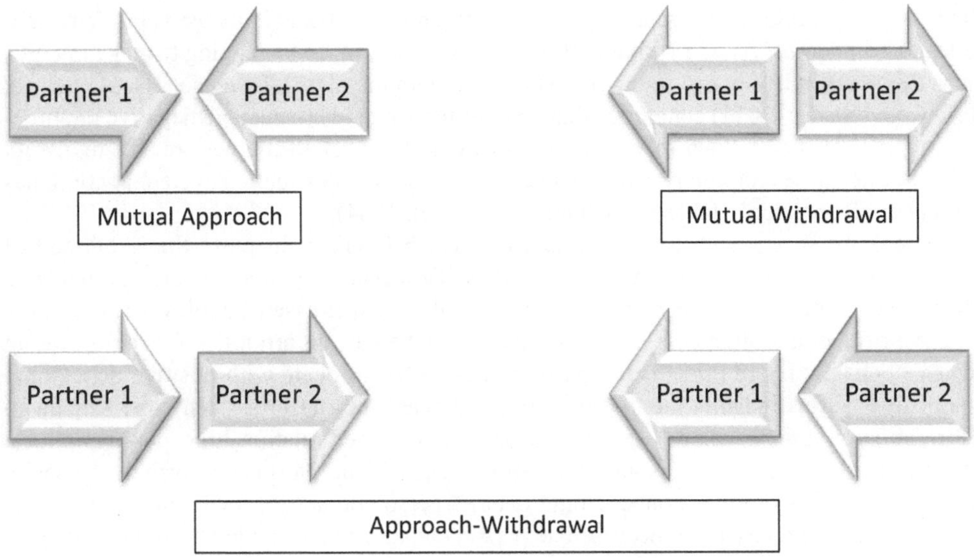

Figure 4.1 Combinations of partners moving away and toward each other during interactions

Mutual approach

For happy couples, mutual approach is a common pattern, adaptive when dealing both with positives and with negatives. With positive emotions and behaviours, mutual approach allows both people to enjoy their relationship fully through interaction such as joint leisure activities, engaging conversations over dinner, and physical intimacy. With negative emotions and behaviours, mutual approach helps couples deal with difficult topics and problems constructively by being able to express displeasure with the other person's behaviour, make difficult decisions in areas where partners hold different values, or respond to health crises. Under such circumstances, partners might disagree about what to do, or experience and express distress related to the issue. However, being able to grapple respectfully with such issues is essential for effective long-term relationship functioning. Indeed, some studies have found that, particularly for women in relationships with men, being "too positive" and not expressing important concerns or preferences for the sake of "keeping the peace" predicts poorer relationship functioning long term (D. H. Baucom, Hahlweg, Atkins, Engl, & Thurmaier, 2006; Schilling, Baucom, Burnett, Allen, & Ragland, 2003).

When dealing with negative emotions and behaviours, however, mutual approach can backfire if the couple does not do so skilfully. Many heated arguments are characterized by mutual attacks, criticism, blame, and negative nonverbal behaviours. In distressed couples, each partner tends to respond quickly to the other's negative behaviour with another negative behaviour. In a long tradition of observational research on couple conflict discussions in laboratory settings, this pattern is called *negative reciprocity* (Gottman, 1979), which often distinguishes distressed from happy couples. Negative reciprocity in couple interactions means that if one person says or does something negative, the other person is increasingly likely to respond with a negative behaviour, and so forth, rather than responding in a way that might diffuse conflict and disrupt the chain. Negative reciprocity can occur outside of a particular argument and stretch over time; if one person criticizes the other partner, the latter might be more likely to respond harshly to situations days later that they would have otherwise let slide. Negative reciprocity occurs with non-communication behaviours as well ("You cancelled our dinner reservation without asking me last weekend, so I am going to make my own plans this weekend. You can figure out what to do with the kids"). Levenson, Haase, Bloch, Holley, and Seider (2014) concluded that couples who are able to manage negative reciprocity are more satisfied in their relationships. For example, satisfied couples are able to disrupt a chain of negative reciprocity rather than getting stuck in a destructive cycle that continues to escalate (Revenstorf, Hahlweg, Schindler, & Vogel, 1984).

Reciprocity occurs with positives also: positive behaviours increase the likelihood of the other partner responding in positive ways. However, negative reciprocity tends to "drive itself" more easily than positive reciprocity. In distressed couples, reciprocating negative behaviours often occurs almost instantly, whereas opportunities for reciprocating positive behaviours are missed. If a partner does not reciprocate with positive behaviours in a distressed relationship, the first person might cease their efforts: "Why try? I made an effort, and you didn't even notice!" In essence, in distressed relationships, partners have a tendency to "keep score." This pattern means that even when effort is put forth, it can easily be abandoned if positive responses from the other person do not follow immediately.

Cycles of reciprocity often occur if one person engages in a behaviour and the other person responds in kind; however, that is not always the case. Instead, the other person might "move away" from the other person, leading to an approach–withdraw pattern.

Approach–withdraw

The approach–withdraw pattern (also referred to as demand–withdraw when it is more extreme) is the most extensively researched pattern and a hallmark feature of many distressed relationships. It occurs when one member of the couple attempts to engage the other person, to have conversations, or to get important needs met, while the other person does not engage or withdraws (Eldridge & Christensen, 2002). Both strategies can be enacted with varying degrees of negativity (e.g., seeking out discussion in a calm way versus shouting), but in combination, they are detrimental to relationship satisfaction (Eldridge & Christensen, 2002). Consistently shutting down any attempts at engagement is referred to as *stonewalling*, which tends to be destructive, similar to the more "active" counterparts of hostile or contemptuous attacks (Gottman, 1994). In the back-and-forth of approaching and withdrawing, the couple ends up in a "tango across the room": the more one person seeks engagement, the more the other person withdraws; the more one person withdraws, the more the other person seeks engagement. In different-sex couples, women are more likely to be in the approach/"demand" role, although the pattern might shift depending on who is more invested in the issue at hand (Eldridge & Christensen, 2002).

It is important to note that under some circumstances, when carried out adaptively, "withdrawal" might be useful; for example, if one partner recognizes that a discussion is beyond repair or that a requested change is not possible, decreasing the intensity of the interaction to de-escalate or prevent an argument might be beneficial. In fact, findings indicate that among socioeconomically disadvantaged couples with fewer resources for making requested changes, husband withdrawal was beneficial to wife satisfaction (Ross, Karney, Nguyen, & Bradbury, 2019). Furthermore, the approach–withdraw pattern is not limited to negative behaviours. Positive approach behaviours have been described as *bids for engagement* (Driver & Gottman, 2004), to which the other person might or might not respond. If the other partner either does not respond or rejects the bid, this action can be hurtful for the partner who made the bid (e.g., initiating physical affection). Partners might fail to recognize positive bids or decline them for many reasons, such as needing solo time at that moment, wanting to punish the other person, or simply not recognizing that a bid was made.

The variations in approach–withdraw patterns described thus far assume that at least one partner is approaching. Another pattern in distressed couples is mutual withdrawal.

Mutual withdrawal and avoidance

A final interaction pattern involves both people withdrawing, or avoiding interaction with each other. This pattern can reflect different couple dynamics, such as: (a) happy yet conflict-avoidant couples, (b) unhappy couples who are still invested in the relationship but want to avoid further negative interactions, and (c) disengaged couples who have largely given up on their relationship. First, some couples with mutual avoidance appear to be "nice couples" composed of partners who do not want to hurt each other or come across as demanding. They might be quite invested in the relationship and have many positive feelings toward each other. Often such couples consist of two generally conflict-avoidant individuals who function well until negative events occur, when they find that they lack the skills to address problems together. Second, some distressed couples are still engaged in the relationship, but in the face of multiple aversive interactions and failed attempts to address concerns, they avoid further potentially destructive interactions. Third, some couples have fundamentally given up. They might still be together "because of the children" or due to their cultural or religious beliefs, lack of perceived options, or resistance to confronting the difficulties of ending a relationship.

In summary, major couple interaction patterns can be characterized by the approach or withdrawal behaviours of each partner, leading to two symmetrical patterns (mutual approach, mutual withdrawal) and one asymmetrical pattern (approach–withdraw). While many couples engage in a variety of interaction patterns across situations and time, the approach–withdraw interaction pattern is a common feature of many distressed relationships and predicts future declines in relationship functioning.

The discussion of maladaptive or hurtful interactions poses another question: what is needed when an interaction has gone awry or the couple has been going through a "rough patch?" Avoiding all conflict is neither possible nor recommended. If a couple attempts to address difficulties that inevitably arise rather than sweeping them under the rug, some interactions will be effective, and others will not. Thus, even the healthiest couples will face situations in which they have been hurtful to each other. Healthy couples develop adaptive ways to get back on track.

Getting back on track: Repair strategies

When couples have negative interactions that are not effective and are hurtful to one or both partners, they often withdraw or engage in retribution. At such times, positive behaviours could serve not only to "balance out" negatives but also to repair the hurt, anger, or other negative feelings. These positive behaviours, called *repair strategies* (Wilson & Gottman, 2002), are genuine messages of care for the other person, expressing a desire for the relationship to improve, a wish for greater closeness, or regret if one has behaved badly. If couples do not have healthy repair strategies, negative interactions can accelerate over time; the partners can hold grudges, or an icy distance can continue between them. Repair strategies that might adaptively help couples "get back on track" after negative interactions are discussed in the intervention section later in this chapter.

Summary

A major component of couples' relationships involves their positive and negative behaviours, including discrete positive and negative behaviours from each partner, communication and non-communication behaviours, and micro- and macro-interaction patterns that help to define what it means to say, "A couple is more than the sum of the two individuals." Therefore, each partner's behaviours and the couple's prominent interaction patterns become a major focus of intervention in CBCT.

Intervening on behavioural factors and communication

Intervention principles

Given the critical importance of communication and non-communication behaviours in determining the essence of a relationship, behavioural factors and patterns of communication often are central targets of intervention in CBCT. A wide range of interventions can be used to achieve improvements in this domain and the choice, implementation, and sequencing of interventions will depend on the therapist's conceptualization of a couple's primary areas of need. For example, a couple might benefit from addressing *specific behaviours* in an important relationship domain, such as developing positive behaviours so that their life functions more smoothly (instrumental behaviours), providing each other with greater affirmation and validation (expressive behaviours), or addressing negative behaviours that result in both partners feeling bad about themselves, their partner, or the relationship. Alternatively, a couple might need assistance with *behavioural interaction patterns*, such as an approach/demand–withdraw communication pattern or interactions characterized by negative reciprocity.

In practice, the therapist typically draws on interventions that target both communication and non-communication behaviours. As discussed above, rather than representing isolated events, each individual's behaviours reflect a complex mix of interdependent actions and reactions. In supporting behaviour change and promoting effective communication, the therapist therefore selects, implements, and sequences interventions in ways that take account of relevant individual, couple, and environmental factors. Thus, rather than viewing behavioural interventions in a simplistic or formulaic way (i.e., "nice behaviour = a happy relationship"), therapists need to exercise good judgment and creativity in helping partners devise new ways of behaving toward each other that will foster a more positive emotional climate in the relationship, feel meaningful and rewarding, help life function more smoothly, and facilitate more effective ways of communicating, both immediately and long term.

For the purpose of clarity, the primary strategies for targeting communication and non-communication behaviours are described separately below, even though therapists might combine them. A description of communication skills training is presented first, given that communication difficulties are the most frequently cited concern of distressed couples. Often, focusing on communication between the partners also means that their most central interaction patterns (such as approach–withdraw patterns) are likely to occur during a session and can be modified in real time. Additionally, encouraging an adaptive communication process in a session also provides a platform for a variety of other treatment targets to be addressed. That is, while communicating, the couple is addressing substantive issues that are important in their relationship.

Improving couple communication through communication skills training

Within the broad domain of communication, two main categories of couple conversations were identified earlier in this chapter: (a) couples seeking to share how they think and feel, and (b) couples seeking to make decisions or solve problems. Most couples presenting for treatment are not effective in having one or both these conversations on their own, either due to a skills deficit or a performance deficit in which relationship distress, strong emotions, and ingrained interaction patterns interfere with the application of existing good communication skills. Even when the partners have strong communication skills, very few couples can explicitly distinguish between these two types of conversations. As described above, a hazard of being unaware of this distinction is that frequently the two partners unknowingly attempt to have both types of conversations concurrently, leading to hurt and frustration on both sides. Thus, it can be important to help partners learn to "cue" each other regarding the type of conversation they would like to have (e.g., "I've had a rough day and just need to vent," or "I could really use your advice on something"). Many couples will benefit from at least some communication interventions. Indeed, in CBCT, understanding and practising these two conversation types frequently is an important mode of intervention in which the partners speak to each other, assisted by the therapist.

Typically, utilizing the two types of conversations has one or both of the following goals: (a) skills training, and (b) addressing substantive/content issues. Because effective joint decision-making partially relies on the ability to understand each other's perspective, the guidelines for sharing thoughts and feelings are often practised first. A common sequence of communication skills training involves a brief discussion about the guidelines tailored to the difficulties of the couple, followed by a first in-session practice with the two partners speaking directly to each other about an "easy" topic (depending on the couple, a positive topic or a topic that involves some negative feelings at a manageable level). Less problematic issues are addressed early so that the main focus can be on grasping the communication guidelines. Couples then are asked to practise having similar conversations at home. In these early sessions, the therapist acts as a teacher and coach, explaining the guidelines, providing guidance and feedback as the couple puts them into practice, and providing content prompts in order to direct the conversation.

As couples become more adept at communicating, there is less emphasis on skills training and more focus on the content of the conversation. The therapist continues in a "coach" role, but as the sessions progress, couples increasingly learn to self-monitor, and the therapist's and the couple's attention increasingly turns toward other therapeutic goals that can be achieved using this format (e.g., guiding the conversation to more vulnerable topics to foster emotional intimacy, using decision-making conversations to help a couple develop new routines to adapt to parenthood, etc.). Frequently, sharing thoughts and feelings and decision-making conversations will be used throughout treatment, at times for small portions of sessions, and at times as the major intervention for most of a session. Many couples begin to use these formats or some variation quite naturally during sessions and in their daily lives. Chapter 6 discusses additional considerations relative to the issue of focusing on "process-versus-content" and its impact on the emotional experience of an interaction.

In CBCT, communication skills training is usually introduced with a discussion of written guidelines, which are described below. See Appendices 1 and 2 for the complete guidelines for sharing thoughts and feelings and decision-making, respectively. It is crucial to emphasize that they are guidelines, not rules. If the couple experiences them as rules, the resulting conversations can feel contrived. Many couples react against such artificiality, or become preoccupied with following the rules at the expense of learning how to communicate effectively. Guidelines are generally useful recommendations and should be adapted to the couple's particular needs, style, and culture. As such, they need to be discussed with the couple in a collaborative manner, with all three persons commenting on how the guidelines apply to the couple and how they can help identify the couple's strengths and areas for further growth. The guidelines are not intended to be presented as a list which the therapist merely reads to the couple or hands to the couple to read in silence.

Improving skills for sharing thoughts and feelings

In many ways, sharing thoughts and feelings between partners can be seen as fundamental to any conversation. In essence, the couple uses these skills to address any topic in a way that is respectful, in both the delivery and the reception of the message. Such exchanges can be valuable in helping each partner experience that they know and understand each other. When partners are expressing positive feelings about each other or the relationship, such conversations serve the important function described earlier of affirming the individuals and relationship. Likewise, the couple might discuss their hopes and dreams and how they would like to interact to make life function more smoothly. On the other hand, couples often need to address negative feelings about each other or the relationship. Helping couples express negative feelings adaptively is a major focus of much couple therapy. Finally, these types of conversations can be modified to help couples alter maladaptive interaction patterns, such as a well-ingrained demand–withdraw pattern.

As described above, the aim of a thoughts-and-feelings conversation is to create an interpersonal context in which (a) each individual shares their thoughts and feelings in an appropriate way and (b) each individual listens attentively, with the intention of understanding the situation from their partner's perspective without judgment, and showing the partner that they understand. In the "speaker role," the task is for the individual to identify and label their internal experiences and communicate them in a way that increases the likelihood that the partner will be able to listen and understand without feeling attacked or becoming defensive, even if the listener disagrees with the speaker. In contrast, the role of the listener is to demonstrate genuine interest, acceptance, and understanding of the speaker's perspective.

The guidelines for sharing thoughts and feelings are separated into two sets—one for the speaker and one for the listener (see Appendix 1). A cycle of communication involves one person speaking and the other listening, then reflecting. After this cycle is complete, the speaker might continue with additional comments, or the partners might switch roles with the listener now becoming the speaker. The overall goal is to develop effective speaking and listening skills, integrate them into a comfortable interaction style, and use them when needed.

SPEAKER GUIDELINES

The speaker guidelines discussed with couples are as follows:

1 *Describe experience subjectively.* The task for the speaker is to express their perspective in a way that conveys the subjective nature of their experience, rather than expressing their view as a statement of fact. The former increases the likelihood that the listener will be able to understand and appreciate the speaker's experience. For example, the speaker might say, "After everything we've talked about in therapy, when you forgot to call to say you would be home late, I felt so low. In that moment, I had a terrible feeling that you just didn't care." In contrast, the following statement decreases the likelihood that the listener will be able to accept the thoughts and feelings that are being expressed: "After everything we've talked about in therapy, when you forgot to call to say you would be late home, it showed yet again what a self-absorbed person you really are!" The latter also increases the likelihood of a combative response that derails the interaction through escalating negative reciprocity.
2 *Include emotions in what is expressed.* When the speaker describes their emotional experience and feelings, the interaction is typically more impactful. The listener is better able to enter the internal world of their partner, which not only enhances understanding but also might foster empathy and emotional intimacy. Emotions carry a great deal of information and meaning, so including emotions helps to clarify the experience of the speaker.
3 *Specificity and pacing.* It is easier for individuals to be understood, and conversations are generally more productive, when partners express their experience in clear and specific terms. Consider, for example, these two alternative statements: "When I got home last night and saw all the dirty dishes in the kitchen, I felt really stressed thinking about my parents arriving in less than an hour" versus "You *always* leave stuff *everywhere*!"

Additionally, the speaker is encouraged to pace themselves and "speak in paragraphs," whereby a single idea is expressed and then elaborated only so far as it enables the listener to absorb what is being conveyed. Although the listener needs to refrain from interrupting, if the speaker talks for an extended period, the listener might start to feel overwhelmed and tune out due to emotional or cognitive overload.

4 *Sharing underlying positives.* Particularly when a couple is experiencing conflict, it is often easier for partners to express negative thoughts and feelings than positive ones. However, it is important that partners provide a balanced perspective and not focus solely on negatives; including positives or desired positives can be quite helpful, even when there is significant distress in discussing a given domain. For example, it would be more helpful to say, "I care a lot about you and really miss our time together" instead of "You never spend time with me anymore, and I'm frustrated." Similarly, expressing underlying vulnerable emotions rather than only "hard" emotions (e.g., sadness versus anger) can lead to enhanced understanding as well as lower the listener's defensiveness (Sanford, 2007). Through sharing thoughts and feelings, one partner might come to appreciate that what sounds like an angry statement ("I can't believe you came home late again! How hard can it be!") might be masking more vulnerable feelings, such as fear ("When you came late home, I thought something had happened to you"), sadness ("When you go out with your friends so often, I feel sad because I remember how you used to want to be with me"), or jealousy and worthlessness ("Seeing you flirt with my colleague at the Christmas party made me feel unattractive, worthless, and jealous"). In all these examples, the feelings of fear, sadness, and jealousy that underpinned an outwardly angry response communicate something tacitly positive: "I care about you and our relationship and love spending time with you." Hearing a partner express these underlying vulnerable emotions opens up a much greater opportunity for the couple to join together in approaching the issue. Even when the current situation is largely unsatisfying, expressing the desire for a more rewarding future can help facilitate a couple's sense of connectedness and, consequently, their willingness to discuss challenging aspects of their relationship in a more adaptive fashion.

5 *Where appropriate, include reference to the partner and/or the relationship.* Depending on the nature of the experience that the speaker wishes to share, the communication is typically more meaningful if the speaker includes references to the partner and/or the relationship, including "interpersonal emotions" (see Chapter 6). This guideline is particularly applicable when a conversation is positive, or when the couple has the potential of joining around difficult experiences. Thus, merely indicating that an experience was enjoyable in general terms ("It was a great day out; I really enjoyed the museum") might be less meaningful than stating that the experience was pleasurable because of the partner's presence ("It was a great day out. It was so good to spend time with you doing things that we love to do together").

6 *Tact and timing.* Effective communication also requires a degree of tact. The speaker needs to consider how best to express certain thoughts and feelings, and whether they should be shared at all. Especially when a couple is experiencing high levels of conflict, individuals can share their thoughts and feelings as a means of criticizing their partners, in order to vent pent-up frustrations. At times, these harsh criticisms are presented under the guise of, "I'm just being honest; don't you want me to be honest?" In some instances, harsh statements can be delivered with more consideration, yet some comments might not be helpful at all (e.g., "I wish you were a couple of inches taller; I've always been

attracted to tall people"). Couples also are encouraged to consider the best time of day or setting for difficult conversations. They are asked to anticipate obstacles that might hamper productive engagement and to avoid beginning a conversation when there is insufficient time or resources to complete it, or when such conversations might have a negative impact on either partner who has competing demands. As a general rule, for example, couples might avoid difficult conversations late at night when both are tired or in the morning when either person will soon be leaving for work.

LISTENER GUIDELINES

The listener also greatly impacts how a couple's interaction unfolds. It is important for the listener to contribute constructively both (a) while the partner is speaking and (b) through their response after the speaker has completed what they wish to say. In doing so, the listener's goals are to adopt the speaker's perspective rather than their own while listening and then to demonstrate understanding and acceptance of the speaker's message. The following guidelines can facilitate these goals.

1 *Consider the situation from the speaker's perspective.* This first guideline is a mindset for the listener to adopt while the partner is speaking. It is important for the listener to understand that the aim of listening is not to judge the accuracy of what is being said from the listener's perspective. Instead, the goal is to understand the speaker's message from the speaker's perspective without adding the listener's own judgment. It is important to reassure the listener that acceptance is not synonymous with agreement; both partners will have legitimate perspectives, and agreement is not a prerequisite for understanding and acceptance. Rather, what is being asked of the listener is an acceptance that the speaker is entitled to their own perspective and a willingness to try to understand how the speaker might have arrived at a particular point of view.
2 *Show understanding and acceptance of the speaker's experience while listening.* In addition to adopting a mindset of listening and acceptance, it is important for the listener to convey this attitude to the speaker. To accomplish this goal, the listener can use a variety of forms of nonverbal communication, including an open and nondefensive body posture, facial expressions that indicate interest and concern, appropriate eye contact, and other paralinguistic gestures that convey active listening.
3 *Summarize/reflect.* Having listened to the speaker, the listener is asked to respond in a way that confirms accurate understanding of the speaker's core message, including both the content and the emotions that have been expressed. This step can be achieved in various ways, but one of the most effective, particularly when couples are in the early stages of acquiring this skill, is to provide a reflection or summary of what has been heard that captures the speaker's most important feelings, preferences, hopes, and thoughts. The ability to provide a reflective summary confirms that active listening has taken place and if there is misunderstanding, the speaker can provide clarification. It is important for the couple to understand that the reflection is not a memory test; instead, the goal is for the speaker to feel heard, understood, and accepted. Thus, a verbatim listing of what the speaker said in a neutral or implied negative manner might "meet the letter of the law, but not the spirit." When the speaker believes that the core message has been understood and that the listener has accepted and respected the speaker's perspective, a greater sense of emotional connection is possible, even when the two people hold

different perspectives. It is important, therefore, that during this stage of summarizing and reflecting, the listener refrains from expressing their own viewpoint or from interpreting or otherwise judging what has been said. An added benefit for the listener is that the task of summarizing helps focus attention on the speaker's message (in order to be able to summarize later), instead of the common reaction in which the listener begins planning a rebuttal at the cost of actually listening.

Sharing thoughts and feelings is an essential component of helping partners understand each other, potentially achieving a greater sense of emotional connection and addressing areas of concern. However, to organize their lives effectively and have their individual needs and preferences met, couples also need to exercise decision-making skills, which are considered next.

Helping couples make good decisions and solve problems

In addition to understanding each other, couples also need to be able to collaborate to make good decisions and solve problems. In many instances, decision-making might be oriented toward managing the practical aspects of their lives effectively. However, decisions might also focus on the emotional aspects of the couple's relationship (e.g., deciding to reserve Thursday evenings as a date night to help them feel connected) or meeting one partner's individual needs.

Because there are multiple ways that couples might experience difficulty in making decisions, the therapist adapts the guidelines below to emphasize changes in the couple's particular interaction pattern, as well as addressing the manifest content of the conversation. As with communication interventions focused on sharing thoughts and feelings, the therapist's explicit focus on skills training versus facilitating the content of the conversation will vary strategically depending on the couple, the issue at hand, and the stage of treatment. In any case, therapists are explicitly encouraged to take an active role in assisting the couple to engage in an adaptive process: "Let's make sure both of you are ready to move on to generating solutions. Was there anything else either of you wanted to share first?" Moreover, therapists are encouraged to provide perspectives that might guide the content of the conversation and suggest solutions when appropriate. Doing so might include offering ideas for solutions the couple has not generated yet without implying that this would be the "best" solution: "Based on what the two of you have said so far, I am wondering if another option would be . . . " Similarly, the therapist might help the couple think about the pros and cons of a solution they are selecting and consider whether it is consistent with treatment goals, important relationship themes, and psychological principles (e.g., highlighting the need for caution if one partner offers to take on additional responsibilities when an existing theme is an unsatisfactory imbalance in how tasks are distributed). The guidelines for decision-making are presented in Appendix 2.

1 *Defining the issue.* Before a couple can begin to identify potential solutions, it is important to agree on the issue that needs to be addressed and to make sure that both partners are willing to discuss it. Of course, many issues do not come neatly packaged as single decision-making events but are multi-layered challenges that will entail many decisions at different stages. Larger or more complex decisions can be divided into a series of smaller decisions that are more manageable to address, which can help couples

appreciate that even situations that feel overwhelming might be amenable to effective joint problem-solving. This first step of defining the issue can be a stumbling block for many couples. Often, instead of clearly stating the issue or problem, the couple jumps to proposing a solution. Such a strategy can limit the options that are considered and skew them in a given direction. For example, rather than clearly stating, "We need to figure out how to build more exercise into our lives," a partner might instead say, "We need to figure out how to get up earlier in the morning, so we can go for a run before work." Thus, the goal in this first step is simply to identify the issue to be addressed as clearly as possible, without proposing a solution. Often an area of concern is raised when one partner blames the other for the problem: "We need to figure out how to get you better organized so you do your share of the household tasks and don't keep taking advantage of me." Such a statement does not contribute to a collaborative approach to problem-solving. Instead, the issue or problem to be addressed is to be stated in terms of behaviours that are occurring or not occurring or that need to be addressed, without focusing on blame: "We need to decide on a division of household tasks."

2 *Clarify why the issue is important and what each person needs or hopes for in relation to the situation.* Many decision-making scenarios contain a "higher order" level of meaning for each partner. After the couple has arrived at a shared definition of the problem, the next stage entails having each partner explain why this issue matters to them and what is important to them to consider. This step might include having each individual clarify their core needs, values, and motives (such as a need for solo time or the experience of fairness in how the couple operates) or hopes for the future. Frequently, the speaker and listener skills described above are useful during this part of the conversation. Couples often overlook this stage of the process and want to move immediately from stating the problem to attempting to identify solutions. However, when couples understand more about what is significant to each individual, mutually beneficial options can be generated. For example, if one partner unexpectedly resigns from an unsatisfactory job, arguments about financial pressures might appear to lead to solutions for curtailing spending and identifying options for interim work. However, if the other partner feels pressure to work longer hours to make up the shortfall in the couple's income and regards such a shift as emerging inequality in the relationship, the range of factors to be considered is somewhat different. Approaching the issue as a purely financial one would miss an important point for at least one of the partners—impending inequality in the relationship. Many decisions in committed relationships have a deeper or unanticipated meaning and require a more complex response than the enactment of a simple behavioural action plan. Moreover, including what is important to each individual can foster empathic understanding and connectedness, even when the decision to be made is emotionally laden. Importantly, at this stage, couples do not need to agree on the factors to consider. In fact, each partner might have very different preferences or experiences; such a situation does not preclude the partners' eventually reaching a mutually agreeable solution, if the process is handled well.

3 *Generating possible solutions.* The next step is for the couple to generate possible solutions. The aim is to create a range of options that accommodate both partners' needs, wishes, and preferences, as discussed in the step above. This approach transforms the task from one in which each partner identifies options that suit their own personal needs and then tries to persuade the other that theirs is the better approach, into a task that is explicitly organized around attempting to address the needs and wishes of *both* partners.

When each individual generates options that take the preferences of the other into account along with their own, the likelihood of identifying a solution that is mutually acceptable is increased. Additionally, by taking the other person's wishes into consideration, an individual is conveying that their partner's happiness and well-being are a priority. In practice, brainstorming many possible solutions might not always be necessary, especially when the options are clear or when a couple is able to generate solutions that take each other's preferences and needs into account. Nonetheless, brainstorming methods can help couples extend their thinking and prevent a narrow focus that might reflect the presence of cognitive biases. Brainstorming might also be useful when there is a tendency for partners to resort to "persuasion tactics," or when one person tends to dominate the decision-making process.

4 *Choosing a solution and creating a plan of action.* Once a variety of options have been identified, the couple selects a solution and devises a plan of action. This plan needs to be sufficiently specific such that both partners are clear about what the solution is and how it is to be implemented. It can be helpful to encourage couples to write down their preferred option and how they propose to implement it. Even though it is impractical for couples to keep a written record of all their decisions, this strategy can be useful when couples are developing their decision-making skills or when high levels of emotion or conflict are involved. Agreed-upon solutions might have multiple components, represent a combination of suggested solutions, or include a decision to postpone the final decision in order to gather more information first.
5 *Developing a trial period.* It is helpful for couples to think of the implementation phase as a process of trial and error, recognizing that a solution might sound very positive but have pitfalls that become obvious only when the plan is put into action. Also, a trial period can increase a couple's willingness to experiment with new ideas. If partners believe they are committing to a solution for life, they are likely to be much more hesitant and inflexible. Once a solution is adopted, the couple is encouraged to think about possible obstacles that might impede the solution and take them into account in their action plan.

Combining types of conversations

As noted earlier, partners often become confused if one partner is attempting to share thoughts and feelings while the other person is attempting to reach a decision on the issue. However, it is very feasible for both partners to share their thoughts and feelings first, and then proceed to making a decision. Couples often ask if it is acceptable to combine the two conversations, or whether it might be more adaptive to keep them separate and pursue each on a different occasion. There is no hard-and-fast rule that applies across topics or couples; rather, the couple and therapist should assess what is likely to be most advantageous in any particular context. Sharing thoughts and feelings about an area of disagreement sometimes leads to high levels of negative emotional arousal, especially when couples are refining their skills in this type of conversation. This situation poses potential challenges for decision-making, given that high negative arousal impedes many people's ability to think creatively about new, mutually advantageous outcomes and can interfere with an overall attitude of cooperation. Thus, couples might benefit from having two separate conversations in order to allow negative emotions to decrease and provide an opportunity for both partners to gain some perspective on the issue and absorb what they have heard from each other. On the other hand, some couples who manage emotions effectively or who are addressing less distressing issues can share their thoughts and feelings effectively and move directly to problem-solving. Thus, the guidelines are adapted flexibly to assist the couple in communicating successfully.

Summary

At the heart of both types of conversations—sharing thoughts and feelings and decision-making—lies a willingness to try to appreciate the situation from the other person's point of view and to recognize that the other person's perspective is equally valid to one's own, even when the two perspectives are different and seem irreconcilable. Once understood, the communication guidelines can be used by couples to discuss a wide variety of topics. Additionally, teaching couples good communication skills typically is not the sole behavioural intervention that is used with distressed couples. Rather, the therapist might decide that non-communication behaviours also need to be targeted. The use of behavioural interventions to achieve this goal is considered next.

Improving couple relationships through targeting non-communication behaviours

Providing guidelines to assist couples in communicating focuses on the importance of *process* aspects of interpersonal behaviour. In part this focus on process is emphasized because communication itself is a major way that partners reinforce or punish each other. In addition, there are many behaviour changes that couples might make to improve their relationship that are not a part of the communication process per se. These changes typically take the form of increasing various types of positive behaviours and decreasing maladaptive, negative behaviours that have been identified during the initial assessment (see Chapter 14). Such changes might include any of the domains discussed earlier in the current chapter, including positive and negative behaviour changes that help life proceed smoothly, as well as actions that affirm a partner or the relationship. Therefore, helping couples implement such behaviours when needed can be central in improving their relationship.

In doing so, we caution against a simplistic understanding of behavioural interventions to "be positive" and "not be negative," instead emphasizing a thoughtful use of methods that are informed by the case conceptualization. The intervention of choice will need to take account of the balance of positive and negative behaviours occurring (see Table 4.1) and the magnitude of each. For example, an intervention aimed at increasing the occurrence and impact of positive non-communication behaviours will likely be different for a couple whose relationship has become devitalized due to ongoing competing demands, compared to a couple in which one partner has withdrawn in response to major relationship violation (e.g., an affair) by the other partner.

Historical factors, including the developmental stage of the relationship, also are important to consider when selecting behavioural interventions. Even when a couple has historically engaged in a high frequency of positive behaviours, some adjustment might be needed if their stage of life or circumstances have changed. What is rewarding during the early stages of a relationship might be neither possible nor desirable later on. Thus, the nature of positive behaviours will likely change over time.

At times, couples seem to have an awareness of what changes are needed in some area of concern and how to go about making those changes. If so, they can use the communication skills they have learned to plan and implement these changes. On other occasions, the couple needs more assistance from the therapist in putting the concerns into a helpful perspective and considering various behaviour changes that might be beneficial. In such instances, the therapist focuses on the substantive aspects of the problematic area (e.g., dealing with in-laws) and provides information and some guidance to help the couple move forward, referred to as "guided behaviour change."

Guided behaviour change

As the label suggests, in guided behaviour change the therapist is guiding the couple in making behaviour changes; the therapist is not advising the couple on precisely what to do or not to do. Within this context, often the therapist provides some *principle* about relationships that seems pertinent to the couple's current situation which could take the form of brief psychoeducation (e.g., about support, trust, or intimacy, as described previously). Then the couple, often with the therapist's input, discusses how this principle applies to them and how they might make behaviour changes accordingly. This strategy emphasizes the expertise of both the therapist and the couple: the therapist has a broad perspective on important principles of well-functioning relationships, and the couple knows their current context and how the principle might apply and be enacted most effectively in their lives.

This strategy of the therapist providing information or principles about some domain of relationship functioning and the couple adapting it to their relationship is a major intervention strategy that is employed frequently throughout treatment. As will be discussed in Chapter 5, there are several strategies for providing relationship principles to couples, ranging from brief informal comments from the therapist ("Let's think for a moment about what it means to support another person emotionally") to more formal readings ("You are headed into a huge shift—retirement—and I think it is wonderful that you are approaching it so thoughtfully. As you've said, there are many parts to this transition. I have a brief article on dealing with changing roles at home when both people retire. What would you think about reading it before our next session, and then we can start to think about how it applies to you and what changes you might want to make, okay?"). In essence, the therapist provides the couple with a framework to use when considering their own relationship, and then the couple and therapist move forward with a variety of strategies to implement needed changes. For example, the therapist might initiate a brief discussion of the importance of maintaining small, caring acts toward each other, even in the midst of a busy life as follows:

> One of the things that strikes me is that you both are pretty unhappy with how things are going in your relationship, but it doesn't seem to be because you are doing lots of destructive, hurtful things to each other. Instead, it looks like the busyness in your lives has taken over, and you have "lost track" of each other in the process. It's clear that you still care for each other, but you rarely show that to each other through small kind, loving gestures, even though you mentioned that you used to excel at those. A relationship is like a plant; if you don't water it, feed it, and give it sunshine, it starts to wilt. At the moment, your leaves are not looking so healthy! I know life is full, but I am concerned that if your relationship always comes last after all the other demands, it will be very difficult to make it feel more rewarding in daily life. What would you think about finding some small ways to show each other that you care, things that wouldn't take much time or energy but still feel good to receive, things that you can do on a regular basis?

If the couple agrees that implementing this suggestion would be helpful, then they might have some ideas of how to initiate some small caring acts, or the therapist might introduce the concept of "caring days" (Stuart, 1980). This concept typically involves the partners taking turns engaging in one small, positive behaviour for their partner each day that could be easily incorporated into their routines long term. For instance, following discussion about what each might like from the other, Rodrigo agreed that on his "caring days" several times a week, he would send Javier a text from work to let him know that he was thinking of him. Likewise, on Javier's caring days, he agreed to bring Rodrigo a cup of tea in bed in the morning. Over time, the goal for the couple is to become more attuned to opportunities to perform caring acts for the other person, with the amount of structure in planning such activities decreasing. This example focuses on each partner focusing on the other person as an individual. If the couple has greatly decreased participating in pleasurable activities together, the strategy can be adapted to focus on regular "couple days" when partners engage in an activity that focuses on them as a couple, such as going for a walk together over the weekend, enjoying a cup of coffee at a favourite cafe, or having a "date night," with attention to the couple's preferences and circumstances (e.g., depending on where they live, Rodrigo and Javier as a same-sex couple might not show affection in public due to safety concerns). In essence, these behaviour changes might start to take the form of small rituals that couples value and can count on to happen regularly.

INCREASING POSITIVE BEHAVIOURS

As in Rodrigo and Javier's case, the emphasis might be on creating a broad, positive relationship atmosphere. Such a strategy might be employed when the therapist and the partners note the absence of an overall positive way of relating to each other, indicating that somehow the specialness of their relationship seems to be waning. This type of experience is common among couples who have been together for some time, for whom life has evolved into a set of routines to accomplish the tasks of living. Likewise, guided behaviour change can be employed for improving more specific areas of concern, for example, if the partners say they are pleasant toward each other but do not feel close. In such instances, the therapist might initiate a conversation about intimacy and how it evolves, as discussed earlier in the chapter:

Therapist: I know that one of your goals is to have an overall greater sense of closeness or intimacy between the two of you, right? So, let's think for a few minutes about how that sense of closeness happens in relationship. It involves more than being nice to each other. An overall sense of closeness usually develops as a result of having a number of interactions where people feel close to each other; over time, those experiences can lead to a general sense of intimacy. Different couples seem to find that different experiences create a sense of closeness for them. Can you think back to occasions when you felt close to each other? That could be a good starting point for thinking about what you might do.

[Couple gives some examples.]

Therapist: Excellent, so it sounds like having conversations where you both open up about really important things can help you feel close. But at other times, you don't need to say anything; just being together out in nature and feeling that you are with each other in this vast world helps you know that you've found your soul mate. Is that right?

[Couple responds affirmatively and elaborates.]

Therapist: So those are things we might want to help you get back to. Also we can think about whether there are new things that fit with your current stage of life. What is crucial is that each couple finds domains where they really connect, and I've had couples describe a wide range of what works for them. In addition to what you've already mentioned, couples have described just sitting and reading together in front of the fire; playing, dancing together in the kitchen, or going out for fun; physical intimacy; working together on projects at home; or taking part in volunteer work in their community to reaffirm their values. When you hear those, are there any that strike you that might fit for you or that you'd like to try out? Our goal will be to try some of these, to see if they help you feel closer to each other.

Often when couples are asked how they might build a more positive relationship environment or target some particular domain, they think in terms of "big-ticket items." While many people might find expensive gifts, weekends away, or holidays to romantic destinations intuitively appealing, for most couples these activities are occasional treats rather than behaviours that can be woven into the fabric of their everyday lives. Thus, any major actions that a couple believes will benefit their relationship need to be complemented by smaller, everyday acts that are realistic and attainable within their resources and which can be maintained over time.

Increasing positive behaviours also includes other adaptive behaviours that are not focused on demonstrating care or experiencing intimacy with each other. For example, a therapist might use a combination of structured decision-making conversations and guided behaviour change to help a couple develop a more adaptive approach to co-parenting or to develop a different weekend routine that accounts for a variety of needs and demands from all family members. In many cases, this intervention will involve both building positive/adaptive behaviours and reducing negative/maladaptive behaviours.

CONTAINING AND REDUCING NEGATIVE BEHAVIOURS

A high frequency of moderate negative behaviours or even a low frequency of highly aversive negative behaviours can undermine relationships. The choice of strategy to address such issues will depend on the therapist's conceptualization of the individual partners, the couple's patterns of interaction, and relevant environmental factors. For example, when frequent intense conflict is a function of skills deficits in one or both partners, the therapist might seek to introduce time-out strategies to enable partners to focus on reducing their own negative emotions and problematic cognitions before resuming their interaction, along with introducing whatever skills are needed. Alternatively, when negative behaviours result from *mindlessness* that comes from being on "autopilot," the therapist might introduce interventions that aim to improve partners' self-awareness and self-monitoring. This approach might involve asking them to write down what they as an individual were thinking and feeling, and how they responded when their partner did something they did not like. As discussed above, negative behaviour often can be understood as an attempt by one partner to alter the behaviour of the other, as a punishment-based behaviour-change strategy. In such instances, the therapist can help the couple think about more adaptive strategies to alter a partner's behaviour without resorting to punishment (e.g., sharing thoughts and feelings or having decision-making conversations).

Repair strategies: Responding to negative behaviours The above discussion is based on the notion that negative behaviours, when high in frequency or magnitude, have damaging effects on couples' relationships. As discussed earlier in this chapter, negative exchanges are inevitable, and couples need to address these experiences effectively and prevent a perpetuation of negative behaviours and emotions from one interaction to the next. Although couples vary in the behaviours that work best for them, effective repair strategies often demonstrate genuine care for the partner and the relationship, the desire to make things better, a wish for greater closeness, or regret if one has behaved badly. Accordingly, therapists might discuss the overall goals and principles of repair strategies with couples and then use guided behaviour-change strategies or structured decision-making to help couples develop their own repair strategies. At times, couples might need to hear a variety of examples from a therapist, especially if they have historically not had any repair strategies. Couples can choose their own repair strategies from a wide range of messages. Some couples might focus on the big picture and "trait" feelings about the partner, in spite of the current distress: "I love you. I hate it when we argue like that." Another partner might feel truly regretful for their behaviour and explicitly take responsibility for that behaviour, which can be healing: "I'm so sorry. I really am. I attacked you when you were already feeling down, and I should not have done that." Moreover, repair strategies can be nonverbal; one partner might bring the other person a food treat, which becomes a symbol of good feelings. Or the couple might share a hug that says, "I'm here," or they choose to engage in "make-up sex," which for some couples is a way of feeling close and being vulnerable after being distant. Gottman, Driver, and Tabares (2015) found that newlywed couples effectively used affection, humour, disclosure, agreement, empathy, taking at least partial responsibility for the problem, and reassurance as effective repair strategies during conflict.

Intervening in couple interaction patterns and broad relationship themes

The application of behavioural interventions thus far has emphasized how to promote specific, often individual behavioural changes that benefit the couple. In addition, it is important to attend to couple interaction patterns and broad themes central to relationship functioning. In fact, organizing interventions around broad relationship themes typifies much of the therapeutic work (see Chapter 14 on case conceptualization and treatment planning).

Applying behavioural changes to address broader themes typically is accomplished by first labelling a theme, including a discussion of the multitude of ways the theme is manifest in the relationship. Then, the therapist and couple define the couple's goals for making changes in this broad domain, and behaviour changes are enacted consistent with the overall goal. This broader theme and overall goals are kept in mind when the couple addresses particular aspects of their relationship. Thus, they implement a "top-down" approach, which encompasses remaining aware of broad therapeutic goals as they apply to specific domains of functioning. For example, Chapter 8 emphasizes that for a couple to define who they are, they need to create a set of boundaries between themselves and others, including what is discussed outside of the relationship and who is invited to participate in various activities, etc. One such couple, Shanequa and Nasim, experienced boundary concerns early in their committed relationship, without being able to identify them as such. Their distress resulted from differences in this important domain, which led to frequent arguments in other domains that seemed unrelated. Although they had never labelled it as such, the therapist helped them think about their concerns as involving where to place boundaries or "draw the line" around what was to be private to them as a couple and where others were allowed to join. Each of them had conducted their individual lives quite differently in this area before becoming a couple. Shanequa was outgoing, and prior to her relationship with Nasim, she told her female friends and mother many details about her dating experiences. Also, friends and family were always welcome on holidays—the more, the merrier. Nasim was more reserved, enjoyed his friends yet was more (in his view) "respectful" in what he shared verbally or when touching anyone. He cherished just being with Shanequa, and he wanted whatever happened between them to remain just between them. As a result, addressing relationship boundaries became a major theme of therapy, and specific aspects were addressed with this theme in mind. Thus, having a conversation about an upcoming holiday focused on boundary aspects of the holiday, including whether to invite parents, how the couple would have time alone, and how to have private time within a larger group. The full range of behavioural interventions was employed to address specific aspects of this broader theme of boundaries and was applied to other aspects of their lives which included boundary elements as well.

Similarly, a major focus for many couples in therapy might involve their broader interaction patterns. As noted earlier, a strong approach–withdraw pattern often occurs in distressed couples' conversations and other behavioural interactions. For example, Ben typically found himself in the approaching role, always asking for "more," while Sally often was withdrawing, feeling somewhat overwhelmed. For them, this demand–withdraw pattern was largely positively motivated. Ben adored Sally and just "couldn't get enough of her!" Before they finished any activity together, he was proposing their next adventure. Thus, he excitedly and proudly announced, "I am the luckiest man in the world. I found my soul mate, and I intend to live life with her to the fullest!" For Ben, *fullest* meant *more*, and it hurt his feelings that he was always the initiator. Likewise, Sally loved Ben very much, and she was fully committed to him, yet his exuberance and constant requests for togetherness left little alone time, which was important for her to rejuvenate. As a result, she felt guilty for hurting him but frequently said no to his requests for "couple time" and rarely initiated such interactions herself because she was already experiencing more than she needed.

In this case, the therapist and the couple discussed the partners' different needs for affiliation and intimacy (see Chapter 7) and how these contributed to their approach–withdraw pattern, both in their broader interactions across days and weeks, and within a given conversation. They discussed how this pattern might be altered in the couple's conversations, encouraging Ben to speak in paragraphs without long monologues and give Sally frequent opportunities to express her feelings as well. Typically, during problem-solving conversations, Ben would propose multiple solutions that involved being together, whether for enjoyment or to accomplish tasks, and Sally found it difficult to decline these caring proposals. The couple worked to ensure that in problem-solving conversations, Sally could express her own needs and that they were considered when the couple agreed on a solution. This approach allowed Ben to be more mindful of Sally's needs and not see them as a rejection of him. Similar behavioural approaches were employed to address specific non-communication behaviours that would alter their approach–withdraw pattern (e.g., Sally was encouraged to initiate affectionate behaviour, and Ben was urged to refrain from taking over when she did so; also, the couple began scheduling solo time for each person to get exercise).

In essence, many couples enter therapy with a wide range of concerns. A major goal of the therapist is to receive the large amount of detailed information provided by the couple; then, based on that information and in collaboration with the couples, the therapist delineates the important themes and patterns contributing to the couple's distress. These broader themes and interaction patterns are subsequently addressed by helping the couple make behavioural changes as described in this chapter, employing those changes to achieve the broader relationship goals central to that couple.

Main points

- Communication and non-communication behaviours comprise a significant part of the "essence" of a relationship and are commonly a target of intervention in distressed relationships.
- Positive and negative behaviours function as two separate dimensions in relationships, with satisfying, well-functioning relationships typically involving high levels of positive behaviours from both partners and low levels of negative behaviours.
- Both positive and negative behaviours can be differentiated in terms of instrumental and expressive functions, which serve the important goals of (a) making life as a couple run smoothly and (b) helping each partner feel cared about and valued. These categories are not discrete and can have significant meaning for partners on multiple levels. For example, instrumental support that makes life easier can also contribute to partners feeling valued.
- Major couple interaction patterns are characterized by the approach or withdrawal behaviours of each partner, leading to distinct patterns of mutual approach, mutual withdrawal, or approach–withdraw.
- Distressed couples need to acquire skills in two broad domains of communication: (a) expressive and listening conversations and (b) decision-making conversations.
- Behavioural interventions comprise a vast array of possibilities. Rather than teaching techniques in a mechanical or manualized fashion, the therapist exercises creativity in helping partners devise new ways of behaving toward each other that will foster a more positive emotional environment in the relationship, feel meaningful and rewarding, and facilitate more effective ways of meeting the demands of everyday life.

Chapter 5

Cognitive factors

A romantic relationship is one of the closest and most important relationships in adulthood for many individuals. Therefore, it is not surprising that many of us engage in ongoing intentional and automatic efforts to understand what is occurring in the relationship, how the partner is behaving, and what might be expected for the future. We do not just *behave* in our relationships; we *experience* them, and we strive to *understand* them as part of our internal experience of what is important in life. These internal experiences have the potential to add rich meaning to intimate relationships, but they also can create difficulties for couples, depending on how each member experiences and interprets both their own and their partner's behaviour.

As discussed in Chapter 2, an individual's internal subjective experience often consists of integrated cognitive-emotional responses, and many individuals do not distinguish clearly between their thoughts and emotions. However, for the purpose of clarity, in the current and next chapters, we differentiate cognitions and emotions in order to emphasize the salient aspects of each. The current chapter considers cognitions focal to interpersonal relationships. First, we focus on cognitive processes and content that are central to intimate relationships. Second, we present intervention strategies—cognitive, behavioural, and emotional—to facilitate cognitive change, along with guidance on when to use these interventions. The therapist's use of guided discovery as a vehicle for impacting the overlap between the cognitive and emotional aspects of a partner's subjective experience is also examined.

Strictly speaking, cognitions are individual phenomena; that is, an *individual* has thoughts, even when those thoughts are about their relationship or their partner. Consistent with a general CBT model, cognitions that impact relationship functioning are understood to be the product of a range of experiences, both in the current relationship as well as experiences outside of and prior to the current relationship. That is, beliefs about relationships are formed over time, likely with developmental contributions of individual experiences (e.g., a person's learning history such as early relationship models, including observing one's family of origin and experiencing prior romantic experiences), the couple's history (e.g., the couple's prior successes in addressing stressors or disappointments), and environmental influences (e.g., broader cultural messages about relationships).

An understanding of couples must also address the added complexity that emerges from the combination of two people's internal, subjective experiences, dyadic patterns of interaction, and the interplay between these and the couple's wider environment. Moreover, an individual's "relationally oriented" thoughts do not exist in isolation; they are closely integrated with that person's emotions and behaviours. Teasing apart the influence of this multitude of factors can be a challenge, for both the couple and the therapist. Therefore, in order to help the couple, the therapist needs a clear understanding of these different domains and the role that cognitive factors can play in perpetuating distress.

An important distinction in addressing cognitive factors is differentiating (a) how individuals *process* cognitions and (b) the *content* of their cognitions. Cognitive processing refers to the ways that information is attended to, absorbed, organized, and interpreted. Cognitions can also be differentiated in terms of their content and include *attributions* (explanations for relationship events that have occurred in the past or present, such as a partner's behaviour), *expectancies* (predictions about future relationship events), *assumptions* (beliefs about what people and relationships *are actually* like), and *standards* (beliefs about what people and relationships *should be* like) (see Figure 5.1).

Cognitive processing

Consistent with a general CBT model, each partner attends to stimuli relevant to their relationship, organizes the incoming information into categories that convey meaning about their relationship, and gives strong weight to certain aspects of what they perceive while

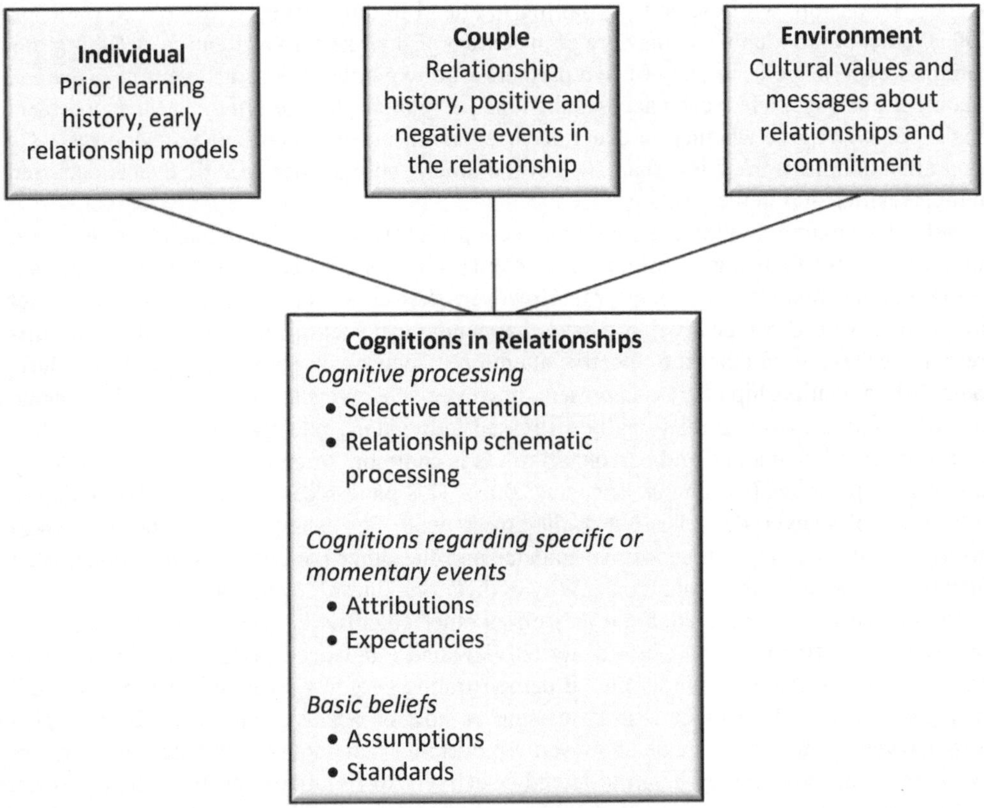

Figure 5.1 Cognitions of relevance in CBCT

minimizing other aspects of their experience of their relationship. Furthermore, just as an individual might have distorted cognitions that contribute to the development, maintenance, or exacerbation of psychopathology, distorted cognitions about the two partners and their relationship can contribute to relationship difficulties. In addition, some aspects of cognitive processing, such as relationship schematic processing, are more specific to relationships per se. Hence, what follows is a more delimited focus on cognitive processing that is central to understand and plan treatment for relationship distress or psychopathology in a couple context.

Selective attention

Human information processing entails filtering an enormous amount of sensory input that occurs at any given point in time. For example, most people are able to follow a conversation with the person next to them at a large social function; automatically "tuning out" other conversations and noises in the immediate surroundings facilitates this ability. Thus, selective attention is a natural and often adaptive process; however, if attention is consistently focused on certain types of events to the exclusion of others, difficulties can arise. In the context of relationships from a CBCT perspective, selective attention refers to the process of attending to certain aspects of one's partner, oneself, relationship events, and the environment relevant to the relationship, while selectively failing to attend to other aspects (Epstein & Baucom, 2002). Often, individuals are unaware of the extent of their selective attention, resulting in a common experience in therapy of two partners who remember the same event in disparate, incompatible ways, while each accuses the other of memory loss or lying. At times, partners might not even agree whether an event occurred at all: indeed, Jacobson and Moore (1981) found that couples agreed less than 50% of the time about whether specific events occurred in their relationship in the past day.

Selective attention within the context of a couple's relationship is not maladaptive per se; for example, not focusing on minor "bad" habits of one's partner might well be important in maintaining relationships long term. However, skewed selective attention that does not provide a balanced perspective on what is happening can fuel or maintain relationship distress, regardless of whether the selective attention is focused on negative or positive behaviours. When relationship distress is present, however, selective attention is typically directed toward negatives. Among relationally distressed individuals, selective attention to negative events, partner behaviours, and personality traits is common, often paired with the tendency to overlook positives (Epstein & Baucom, 2002). This pattern can become problematic not only in couples' everyday lives but in therapy as well. For example, if one person makes strong efforts to change in a positive manner and the other partner does not notice, such changes will be difficult to maintain ("Why bother? She doesn't even notice").

In considering selective attention as well as other cognitive processes and content, it is important to distinguish between a distorted view and a balanced perspective that leads to negative conclusions. If one individual is demonstrating very few positive behaviours toward their partner, then the partner is not "missing" a host of positives due to a distorted process. However, most individuals show some redeeming behaviours that distressed partners are likely to miss once they begin to attend selectively to negative aspects of their partner. Selective attention toward positive behaviours or partner characteristics can be problematic as well, particularly if negative behaviours that should be of concern are overlooked. For example, one person might be having an affair at work, and the couple's friends and colleagues all seem to be aware of what is happening. Yet the partner does not recognize obvious cues but instead selectively focuses on the caring behaviours from the person having the affair, ensuring that the image of a happy relationship remains intact.

Relationship schematic processing

A second impactful cognitive process is more unique to the interpersonal context. Relationship schematic processing (RSP) refers to the tendency and ability to think in relational terms; that is, the degree to which partners view the world and organize and interpret events from a relational perspective rather than in individual terms (Rankin-Esquer, Clayton, Baucom, & Mullens, 1997; Sullivan & Baucom, 2004, 2005). RSP can facilitate healthy relationship functioning because it includes an awareness of how one's own behaviour might impact the other person and the relationship. Therefore, it can be difficult for the couple if either partner is deficient in this capacity. Difficulties also can arise if partners are mismatched in their levels of RSP, which often leads the high-RSP partner to perceive the low-RSP partner as inattentive, uncaring, or selfish. For example, Jada was upset when Victor announced that he would be going to work the next day for an important meeting despite Jada having an oncology appointment where she would learn if her tentative breast cancer diagnosis was confirmed. Jada later told their therapist, "Would you believe he went to work as usual? It didn't occur to him that I might like my husband with me when I received my test results!" Victor, puzzled, replied, "How was I supposed to know that you wanted me to be there? If you had wanted me with you, you should have told me so that I could have made the necessary arrangements." Jada responded, "This appointment could have turned my life upside down and our family's as well. Of course I didn't want to go through that on my own! Do I have to tell you what would have been obvious to anyone who had a heart?"

Research based on behavioural observations of interactions among distressed different-sex couples (Sullivan & Baucom, 2004) suggests that as a group, women tend to exhibit more frequent and more complex RSP than men (Sullivan, 1999), which might be due in part to differences in gender-related socialization across the life span. Moreover, in different-sex couples, women's relationship satisfaction is positively associated with men's RSP (Sullivan, 1999), and if men's RSP improves with couple therapy, their female partners increase in relationship satisfaction (D. H. Baucom, 1999). Thus, it appears that RSP is an important cognitive processing construct to consider in couples presenting for therapy, and many interventions in CBCT include helping both partners adapt a more relational perspective on their behaviour.

However, it is not necessarily the case that more is better. The other extreme also can be problematic for couples if one or both partners default to interpreting most events excessively as having relational meaning when there is none. For example, as Theo explained, "I've told Nadine, I'm just not a morning person. This is not me being grumpy with her; it's just that I need a few more minutes and a shower to wake up. Nadine keeps thinking that I'm angry at her; she takes it so personally." In this example, Nadine is viewing an event as having interpersonal implications when it does not, and viewing the event as being more individually based would likely aid the relationship.

The factors discussed so far provide information regarding how relationship events might be processed, but this processing per se does not address the actual content of what is focused upon by both partners. Therefore, another important domain is the *content* of the cognitions, both in terms of momentary responses and broader beliefs, as discussed below.

Cognitions regarding specific or momentary events

Attributions

In CBCT, attributions refer to the explanations that individuals give for relationship events (D. H. Baucom et al., 1989; Epstein & Baucom, 2002). Similar to patterns of attributions that depressed individuals tend to make about themselves, among distressed couples, attributions about a partner's unfavourable behaviour are more likely to be viewed as internal to that person, stable, and global. That is, in a distressed relationship, even minor hassles, such as a partner leaving a cereal bowl in the sink after breakfast, can be interpreted as indicative of enduring characteristics (e.g., "You have always been such a slob!") (Fincham, Beach, & Baucom, 1987). On the other hand, individuals in satisfied relationships tend to interpret unfavourable behaviours in terms of circumstances that are external to the person, unstable, and situation specific (e.g., "I don't like you leaving dirty dishes, but I know this was a particularly hectic morning after the kids had been sick all night"). Ample research on such *distress-maintaining* versus *relationship-enhancing* attributions demonstrates that there are systematic associations with relationship distress in the expected directions, and higher levels of distress-maintaining and lower levels of relationship-enhancing attributions are associated with greater declines in relationship satisfaction long term (Bradbury, Beach, Fincham, & Nelson, 1996; Bradbury & Fincham, 1990; Holtzworth-Munroe & Jacobson, 1985). In addition to attributions about the partner or their behaviour, individuals also make attributions about themselves in the relationship and about the relationship itself. For example, if a couple struggles during a difficult time and one or both partners make the attribution that "it was only a matter of time; we weren't a good match from the start," more feelings of hopelessness and less proactive coping and joint problem-solving are likely to result. Similarly, a depressed person might take all responsibility for relationship difficulties: "You and the children would be better off without me; I've always messed things up, and I always will."

Expectancies

Whereas attributions are explanations about events that have already occurred, expectancies are predictions that partners make about the future of the relationship. Individuals might have positive or negative expectancies (which could be accurate or distorted) about how their partner is likely to behave in future situations or what the status of the relationship might be. As Naomi noted, "April got so busy with taking care of her mother, she'd barely pay attention to me. She rejected my attempts to be affectionate so many times that now I've given up. I've realized that things are never going to be the same again." As with this example, in most instances, negative, distorted expectancies are closely associated with emotions and behaviours that might inadvertently maintain relationship distress (e.g., hopelessness, criticism).

Basic beliefs

While selective attention, RSP, attributions, and expectancies refer primarily to responses an individual might have in the moment or in response to distinct relationship events, most of the time these processes and cognitions are not independent of each other. For example, repeated attributions that fall into similar themes (e.g., "My partner is uncaring") are likely to be associated with negative expectancies regarding the likelihood that the relationship will meet one's needs in the future. Selective attention then further emphasizes events that seem to support this conclusion. Emotions such as sadness or anger and behaviours such as withdrawal or criticism might follow. In addition, the individual is likely to form broader beliefs about their partner and relationships that are more global and stable, and those beliefs in turn impact cognitions that occur on a momentary basis as well as affect overall relationship satisfaction. The discussion below highlights two important categories of these broader and more basic beliefs: assumptions and standards.

Assumptions

Assumptions are a category of beliefs about what one's partner and relationship as well as people and relationships in general *are actually like*; that is, the person simply assumes, "This is how things are." Such broad beliefs are influenced by current circumstances, as well as a person's learning history and culture. For example, an individual with a stable, nurturing upbringing and a current relationship that is generally satisfying might hold assumptions that most people have their well-being at heart and that their current partner is trustworthy, loving, and supportive. Such assumptions likely contribute to an overall sense of safety, trust, and high relationship satisfaction (Epstein & Baucom, 2002). On the other hand, adverse life events prior to the current relationship or current relationship difficulties might shift these assumptions, and if the assumptions are inaccurate or extreme, they might contribute to the development or maintenance of relationship distress. For example, experiences of abuse or neglect prior to the current relationship could lead to the assumption that "anyone could end up hurting me, even if they say they love me." While such a belief might be well-founded in real and painful experiences, if the individual enters a relationship that is healthy and safe, such an assumption might lead the person to distance themselves maladaptively if they experience the relationship as becoming too close or intimate. As with other cognitive phenomena, overly optimistic assumptions can create difficulties as well. Thus, despite consistent, long-term, negative evidence to the contrary in their relationship, a partner might conclude, "People can change. I know that, and our therapist knows that, or she wouldn't be in this business. You can do this if you just set your mind to it."

Standards

In addition to assumptions about what people and life *actually are like*, most individuals also hold explicit or implicit beliefs about what their relationship and partner *should be* like. Often, standards are closely tied to a person's values and sense of morality, and, therefore, are deeply held beliefs which a person is reluctant to shift. Standards are influenced by a variety of contexts and experiences, such as family of origin, cultural beliefs, media, religion, and the immediate social environment. At times, standards might be taught explicitly, for example by one's parents (e.g., explicit conversations about what a "good" committed relationship should be like). At other times, individuals develop implicit standards by having various experiences themselves and by observing others around them. Many religions teach explicitly formulated standards for how individuals should behave and what the role of each partner should be. Findings that individuals who hold similar religious beliefs tend to report happier marriages might partially be due to a greater likelihood of sharing such standards with one's partner when both are members of the same faith community (Myers, 2006). In addition, many religions teach relationship standards that place a high value on family relationships, forgiveness, and ethical behaviour. In some contexts, standards within certain religious or cultural groups might run contrary to the couple's life circumstances or the well-being of one or both partners, thus contributing to individual or couple distress. The important message is that each partner's relationship standards can be deeply rooted, and the therapist must treat those standards with respect while noting ways in which they might also be contributing to the couple's relationship difficulties.

While standards can be deeply ingrained, explicit, and closely tied to daily behaviour, there is a fair amount of variability across individuals in terms of: (a) the degree to which individuals have a clear, well-defined set of standards about relationships and whether they are able to articulate what these standards are; (b) how closely their standards are associated with their behaviour; and (c) how distressing it is for the individuals if standards are violated or unmet. Not surprisingly, research suggests that overall relationship satisfaction tends to be higher if partners hold more "pro-relationship" standards (e.g., "Notable energy should be invested into a relationship"), have similar standards, and function consistently with each individual's standards (D. H. Baucom, Epstein, Daiuto, & Carels, 1996; D. H. Baucom, Epstein, Rankin, & Burnett, 1996; Ragland, Baucom, Burnett, & Schilling, 1996).

Couples' difficulties related to standards about relationships might arise for a variety of reasons and are not necessarily due to extreme or maladaptive standards. First, both partners might hold overall reasonable standards, but they differ in a way that creates difficulty for the couple; that is, the two partners simply have different blueprints for what life should look like. For example, one partner's standard might be that "family should come first; if one of our parents or siblings needs anything, we should respond immediately," while the other person might believe, "Family is important, but the highest priority should be us as a nuclear family that consists of you, me, and our child." Second, one or both partners might have standards that are too extreme or unrealistic to be met, such as, "Happy couples should never have any serious disagreements; if we do, that means there is something wrong with our relationship." Third, both partners might hold similar standards that inadvertently contribute to imbalance in their relationship. For example, if both partners believe that they should focus most of their attention on each other, they might become isolated from their extended family and friends in a way that later impacts them negatively.

Thus, rather than assuming that there are "good" and "bad" standards in relationships, within reason, couples' relationship functioning can be high even with a wide range of possible standards. Couples are likely to be more satisfied if their standards generally are compatible, if each partner overall behaves consistently with these standards, and if there are no adverse effects of the standards on the emotional well-being and behavioural habits of each individual or others.

Associations among cognitive factors

The various cognitive factors discussed above, including cognitive processes, responses to specific events, and more basic beliefs, are not isolated phenomena. Rather, they influence each other in a reciprocal manner. Furthermore, it is impractical to define a starting point for these cognitions from which all others evolve. For example, based on early life experiences, an individual might develop assumptions about how people treat each other in committed relationships. These assumptions might then influence the person's tendency to focus selectively on events that confirm those assumptions. Likewise, these assumptions might also serve as a filter for making attributions when certain events do occur and provide the basis for expectancies when the future is contemplated. In such an example, long-standing assumptions might be the driving force in understanding the complex cognitive functioning for that individual. However, in a different relationship, one person might behave frequently in such a negative, destructive fashion that the behaviour is in sharp contrast to previous, more benevolent assumptions that the other partner had. In response, the partner who has been the recipient of the negative behaviour might become hypervigilant to negative behaviours and no longer attend to sincere efforts the other individual is making to change. Thus in this instance, recent behaviours might be the driving force in influencing cognitive processing. By the time a couple comes for therapy, the clinician often confronts a comprehensive set of negative cognitions that encompass the various factors discussed thus far.

In summary, the variety of cognitive factors that help to create a rich internal life for each partner, and which reflect a fundamental human need to find meaning in our experiences, often are central in understanding a couple's relationship distress. Therapists need to be able to identify, conceptualize, and work with the variety of cognitive "lenses" that shape each individual's subjective experience of themselves, their partner, their relationship, and their wider environment. Helping partners understand the role of cognitive factors in their experience of the relationship and how they function as a couple often is a central aspect of couple therapy.

Intervening on partners' cognitions

As a principle-driven rather than protocol-driven therapy, interventions in CBCT are based on a conceptualization of the couple's needs and goals. In doing so, it is important to differentiate negative cognitions from distorted cognitions. Negative thoughts can be adaptive, serving the function of alerting individuals to an aspect of their world that is unsatisfactory or that needs attention. As noted earlier in the chapter, not all negative cognitions are distorted; an individual might have correctly concluded that a partner is very unlikely to change some destructive or undesirable behaviour. The couple must then decide whether the undesirable behaviour is acceptable or tolerable when the relationship is considered more broadly, or whether the behaviour is so upsetting or unacceptable that it is a "deal breaker," including separation as one possible way to move forward. As such, negative thoughts—and indeed positive thoughts—become a target of intervention when one person's experience becomes "hijacked" by cognitive distortions in ways that increase relationship distress or lead to avoidance of issues that warrant attention.

Intervention principles

Attempting to alter cognitions is complicated in part because cognitions can only be inferred, unlike patterns of behaviour which can be directly observed by the therapist. Although individuals are at times willing and able to verbalize what they are thinking, at other times they might withhold their thoughts. Furthermore, certain aspects of their cognitive worlds, such as selective attention and assumptions about relationships, might occur automatically, seem factual and "obvious" to the person, and are not easily recognized as an area that merits further consideration. As a result, the therapist needs to recognize that at least some of the cognitive themes that are relevant might be beyond the couple's immediate awareness and will need "unearthing" through a process of sensitive exploration.

While the challenge of exploring cognitions might be equally relevant to individual therapy and couple therapy, addressing cognitions in a couple context can pose several additional challenges. Although at times both partners' cognitions merit attention, often it is one partner's cognitions that need to be addressed (e.g., if a male partner strongly believes that if his female partner has any male friends, she *will* become romantically involved with them). Focusing on one person's cognitions can pose a challenge to therapists: "How do I intervene on one person's cognitions without doing individual therapy while the other partner just sits there? How do I intervene so that it doesn't seem that I'm taking sides with one partner against the other?" Avoiding individual therapy in a couple session can be particularly challenging for therapists trained in individual CBT due to the therapist's tendency to "click into" a therapeutic stance that is familiar to them. There are a number of steps that the therapist can take in order to facilitate addressing cognitions in a couple context.

First, the therapist should recognize that the triadic interactions during cognitive interventions can be quite different from other couple-level interventions, such as communication training where the therapist encourages the couple to talk directly to each other and facilitates the conversation, providing input along the way. In contrast, in many forms of cognitive restructuring, there are times when the therapist is addressing one person, and a brief conversation between the therapist and that person ensues while the other partner listens. Following this brief interchange, the therapist brings the other partner into the dialogue to obtain that person's perspective on the issue. Thus, while the therapist might begin by talking to one partner, they ensure that the other partner also is brought into the conversation and is not just sitting quietly for the duration of the session. Finally, the therapist helps the couple integrate these two perspectives and attempts to put this new information into a relationship framework.

In addition to ensuring that both partners are brought into the conversion, the therapist must take care when selecting what types of cognitive interventions will be used and in what manner. As will be further elaborated below, certain cognitive techniques commonly employed in individual CBT (e.g., identifying problematic thought patterns, learning formal ways to challenge thinking via worksheets) do not tend to work as well in couple therapy. Often, in a couple context, these strategies imply that the therapist has sided with one partner in identifying the other partner's thinking as "wrong" and can lead to partners' criticism of a given person for their way of thinking. Thus, the types of interventions used and the manner in which they are executed in CBCT are selected to minimize defensiveness from one person in the other partner's presence and are in line with the principles of guided discovery described in detail below.

As an example of the principles described above, while working with Kevin and Wendy to understand the factors that might have contributed to Kevin's recent affair (i.e., exploring attributions for his behaviour), the therapist proceeded as follows (note that there is no implication that Kevin was not responsible for his own behaviour):

Therapist: I know you both want to get a better understanding of how this happened, and I think it might be useful if we step back and try to see if there are any experiences in Kevin's history that might have made him more vulnerable to having an affair. So Wendy, for a few minutes, I'm going to talk with Kevin, and we definitely want to get your input to see if his perspective makes sense to you, along with important insights that you might have. Does this sound okay? (Couple nods.)

Therapist: So, Kevin, when we look back at your relationships with females in the past, growing up, and early dating, what is striking to you or stands out to you about those relationships in general? Did you have any atypical or even traumatic experiences?

Kevin: (after discussing various aspects of growing up and females in his life) Overall, I'd say my relationships with females have always been great. You know, I mentioned I have two older sisters, so I grew up hanging out with them and their friends. Actually, I think I understand women really well and have always been more comfortable with females than males, even as friends as well as romantically. I just get along with women; I enjoy being around them.

Therapist: And overall, how do you think women typically respond to you?

Kevin: I think they tend to like me as well. When I'm at social events, women often seek me out, but just as friends, nothing inappropriate.

(The therapist then brings Wendy into the dialogue, both to get her perspective and to maintain a couple framework in addressing Kevin's cognitions and behaviour.)

Therapist: Wendy, what is your perspective on what Kevin has said; do you see that?

Wendy: Absolutely, he's like a magnet for women. Kevin's very outgoing and sociable, and he simply seems to understand women. That is one of the main things that attracted me to him; he is so sensitive and understanding. And even my roommate in college said to me, "If you don't marry him, I will. You aren't going to find many men like Kevin."

Therapist: That sounds really striking. It seems you both agree that Kevin has a very easy and appealing way of interacting with women, not flirting, but just very engaging in a way that is delightful, right?

Wendy: I guess so, but are you saying that is part of the problem?

Therapist: I think we're just exploring a variety of possible factors, and I anticipate there are many things that have come together that led to Kevin's decision to get involved. But this is one that perhaps we'll want to keep in mind—does Kevin's comfort interacting with women contribute to some level of risk, given that many women will want to spend time with him? Kevin, what do you think?

In the above excerpt, the therapist exemplifies a dyadic perspective on addressing cognitions. The therapist focuses on Kevin's behaviour and what might have contributed to it, not from an accusatory perspective but from a standpoint of wanting to help the couple understand what has occurred, as detailed in the section on *guided discovery* which follows. Also, the ideas come from Kevin and Wendy to a large degree rather than the therapist. Although it is appropriate for the therapist to offer insights, the more the couple can do the work to develop a balanced perspective, the more they might "own" it. Additionally, the therapist brings the partner into the discussion to help develop a shared perspective, which might help influence her own initially catastrophic interpretation of the affair (e.g., "Our whole relationship has been a lie; you clearly are not the person I thought you were"). Thus, the goal is to create a collaborative discussion among both partners and the therapist, even when the focus is mainly on one partner. Furthermore, if the couple and therapist conclude that Kevin's style is a risk factor, at some point the couple would be asked to engage in problem-solving on how he can alter his interactions with women to lower the risk, while still valuing his positive qualities of being interpersonally attuned. In essence, the therapist takes brief interludes into one-on-one conversations with a given partner, brings the other partner into the dialogue, and then integrates this conversation into a broader couple-based set of cognitive, behavioural, and emotional interventions described throughout the book. Thus, rather than taking a full session or sessions to work on cognitions, cognitive work is integrated into sessions alongside other types of interventions.

Cognitive restructuring

In order for a person to change their cognitions about themselves, their partner, or their relationship, they need "new information" to take into account. Therefore, a major task for the therapist is to assist the couple in gaining new relevant information or ways of thinking about what they already know that can contribute to a more realistic and balanced perspective on their relationship. To assist in this process, the therapist can focus on strategies that provide new information and perspectives either (a) during a therapy session (e.g., conversations between partners in which new perspectives evolve) or (b) in the couple's everyday life outside of the therapy context (e.g., what the partners learn about each other on a thoughtfully planned date night).

The source(s) of the new information that can contribute to cognitive restructuring vary, providing the therapist with a multitude of strategies to facilitate cognitive change. First, the new information might initially come from a source outside of the couple, often from the therapist. For example, a therapist might explain that a decreased sense of emotional intimacy is common when a partner is traveling often and does not mean that their relationship is doomed. Second, the new perspective might evolve from a dialogue between the therapist and one or both partners. Third, the couple's new perspective might evolve from direct interactions between the two partners, such as a behavioural experiment during the week in which they go out together and agree not to talk about problems in their relationship.

In most instances, these sources of information are combined over time because typically changing a cognition does not result from a single intervention. Thus, after a behavioural experiment outside of the session, the couple and therapist might have a subsequent conversation in which they process this experience together and perhaps integrate it with other recent experiences. Below we describe a set of possible interventions that a therapist might employ to assist in cognitive restructuring, with examples for the various types of cognitions described earlier. At the same time, there is no set list of strategies to help modify cognitions in a couple context, and many practising clinicians devise creative strategies that are consistent with the principles of CBCT.

Guided discovery

Because of the diverse and potentially limitless number of cognitions that might arise, there are no formal, step-by-step guidelines. Instead, change in the cognitive domain is facilitated through a process of *guided discovery*. Guided discovery is a general therapeutic approach to engaging couples in a collaborative, discovery-oriented way of working. Here, we focus specifically on how guided discovery is used in the context of working with cognitive phenomena and, in particular, how the therapist uses this approach to assist with the process of cognitive restructuring.

In individual therapy, the use of guided discovery is predicated on the assumption that the individual's perspective, while initially seeming to that person to be both accurate and valid, might in fact contain distortions and biases. These biases help to maintain the individual's difficulties and, therefore, are an important target of intervention in CBT. Guided discovery proceeds in various ways to encourage the individual to think differently about their experiences. One common strategy in individual therapy involves a series of Socratic-style questions in which individuals are encouraged to examine the evidence for and against a particular cognition and to revise their initial interpretation in light of this evidence. When skilfully presented in a supportive therapeutic context, this process of "challenging" cognitions can be experienced by the client as liberating and empowering, opening up new perspectives on situations and events that the client has not previously considered. However, in CBCT, this form of guided discovery often is counterproductive. Distressed couples frequently are quite accomplished at challenging each other's cognitions in derogatory ways, being fully convinced that the other person's perspective is distorted or totally wrong. Any request by the therapist to consider how one person's attributions, assumptions, or standards might be distorted could lead to that person feeling "ganged up on," with the other partner quickly seizing the moment (e.g., "I was right all along! It's your messed-up thinking that's been causing our problems—even our therapist agrees!").

Thus, drawing attention to and directly challenging a distorted cognition might elicit the erroneous interpretation that the therapist has "sided" with one partner against the other, running the risk that one person will experience their perspective as being invalidated and will feel misunderstood, exposed, or even shamed in front of their partner because of their "flawed thinking." Far from empowering a couple, if delivered in this fashion, guided discovery risks triggering a defensive reaction in the targeted partner, will likely decrease that person's willingness to explore alternative perspectives, and might precipitate further mutual blame.

Thus, in CBCT, when undertaking guided discovery in the service of cognitive change, the therapist needs to remain acutely aware of the need for each person to "save face" in front of the partner. Therefore, the aim of guided discovery in CBCT is to help the couple create new experiences both in the session and in everyday life that enable them to learn about themselves, each other, and their relationship, and to revise their cognitions in ways that are more realistic and adaptive. Far from being a process centred around intellectual reconstruction, constructive guided discovery engages both "head and heart." This way, the techniques that are described below can provide couples with meaningful and impactful avenues to enhanced mutual understanding, caring, and growth. This new information or perspective can come from various sources in helping one or both partners experience their relationship differently.

ACQUIRING INFORMATION FROM SOURCES OUTSIDE OF THE COUPLE

When a couple would benefit from information or perspectives that they do not currently have, the therapist can provide that information for the couple, either coming directly from the therapist or from other sources such as readings or videos. Therapists also are in the unique position of being able to provide "outside input" that can include sharing observations about the couple that they might have previously overlooked. Rarely is this new information presented in a unidirectional manner. Instead, the couple likely processes this information as it applies to their lives, either between the two of them or with the therapist. This processing of newly provided information can be a starting point for cognitive change. Perhaps the most frequently employed intervention for providing new information is psychoeducation.

Psychoeducation Psychoeducation for the purpose of cognitive change typically involves providing new information or a different perspective on existing information with one of two foci: (a) information or a new way of thinking about cognitions themselves; that is, some aspect of cognitions per se is the focus of the conversation (e.g., selective attention and focusing on a partner's negative behaviour) or (b) information about some substantive domain of importance to the couple, such as describing the impact of having a child on a couple's sense of intimacy. When the therapist notes an ongoing pattern of thinking that is somewhat pervasive across topics, psychoeducation might focus on the cognitive processing itself. However, if the distorted thinking seems to result from a lack of information or perspective focal to a given topic such as transition to retirement, psychoeducation addresses the substantive domain of common challenges couples face as they move into this new phase of life.

First, therapists might provide psychoeducation about cognitions. At times, a focus of therapy is helping one partner or the couple change a more pervasive way of processing information relevant to the relationship. As a starting point, couples cannot change what they do not recognize. To help couples understand the impact of their cognitions on the relationship and to enhance their willingness to take responsibility for modifying unhelpful perspectives, it often is necessary to provide psychoeducation on the role that different cognitions and cognitive processes play in how individuals perceive and interpret their reality.

For example, the therapist might have the goal of increasing the extent to which a couple or partner thinks in relationship schematic terms, especially when at least one partner is low on RSP. Earlier in the chapter, the contribution of low RSP to couple distress was highlighted, including the increased likelihood of high-RSP individuals labelling their low-RSP partners as inattentive, uncaring, or selfish. When this dynamic occurs, the therapist can provide psychoeducation about how different people take in and organize information, pointing out the broad patterns of individual interaction and RSP. This information can help the high-RSP individual to consider alternative explanations for their partner's responses. Additionally, within this context the therapist can encourage both partners to consider how their own actions and responses play a role in shaping patterns of interaction, such as approach-withdraw and negative reciprocity. In essence, the capacity for RSP can be developed through encouraging partners to think about sequences of interaction in terms of circular, rather than linear, causality. This initial psychoeducation can be bolstered by encouraging the couple to reflect regularly on what they are learning about their patterns of interaction. Additionally, when partners appear to be interacting in a negative manner during the session and seem unaware of what they are doing, the therapist might stop the interaction and ask the couple what pattern of interaction is occurring in their current conversation, based on their knowledge of patterns that have previously been identified.

As another example, when one or both partners engage in selective attention that distorts their experience of the relationship, the therapist can explain how the ability to employ selective attention is adaptive in that it prevents our minds from becoming overwhelmed by information, helping normalize the ways in which the human mind also is prone to taking cognitive "short cuts" that in some situations prove problematic. The couple then can be given tasks to focus explicitly on positive behaviours from the partner during the week, perhaps writing down one positive thing the person does each day as a means of building on the psychoeducation.

Thus, whether it is delivered through "mini lectures" or relevant reading/video material, psychoeducation regarding cognitive concepts is an important form of intervention with distressed couples. Because distressed individuals excel in seeing how such distortions apply to their partners, typically the emphasis is placed on examining how the information applies to oneself, along with how it contributes to interaction patterns between the two partners. Such discussions might be followed up with behavioural assignments to help consolidate this new information.

Second, at times a couple or partner does not engage in ongoing distortions across domains of functioning but rather views a specific situation or domain in a rigid or distorted manner because they lack important information or perspective on that specific domain. For example, a couple might not know that significant vegetative changes such as lower sexual desire and sleep difficulties are a central part of depression. As a result, the partner might feel rejected and hurt that the depressed person wants to sleep in a bed alone and avoids sexual contact. The partner might inappropriately assume that these behaviours reflect serious relationship difficulties, thus engaging in distorted attributions and expectancies based on incomplete information.

ACQUIRING INFORMATION FROM COUPLE–THERAPIST INTERACTIONS (SOCRATIC DIALOGUE)

A further intervention is for therapists to engage the couple in a conversation that helps them think differently about the issue under consideration, such as through individual or couple-level Socratic dialogue. This strategy was employed in the example discussed earlier in this chapter when the therapist explored with Kevin how his long-term pattern of relationships with women might have contributed to his having an affair with a colleague. As noted earlier, the therapist must be cautious in using logical disputation per se due to the defensiveness it is likely to induce with a dissatisfied partner present. However, in line with Beck, Emery, and Greenberg's original recommendations (A. T. Beck, Emery, & Greenberg, 1985), Socratic dialogue (e.g., questions, summaries) can be used productively to clarify cognitions which might be vague or unknown, or to take new information and perspectives into account to create a more balanced perspective.

Whereas in individual therapy all questions in Socratic dialogue are geared toward the one client with the goal of potentially changing that one person's perspective, in couple therapy, the therapist might gear questions, reflections, and summaries toward one or both partners. Sometimes the dialogue is between one partner and the therapist only (as in individual therapy). However, in couple therapy, the therapist frequently takes advantage of having both partners present and includes them both in the exploratory process. For instance, when Amaad made the attribution that Haifa came home late because she no longer loved him or wanted to spend time with him, the therapist asked, "Haifa, it sounds like when you came home later than expected, Amaad experienced that as a signal that you no longer love him or care to spend time with him. Can you speak to that?" The therapist additionally asked follow-up questions to Haifa such as, "How *do* you feel about Amaad?" and "What is it like for you to spend time with Amaad?" In this line of questioning, Haifa clarified that she loves Amaad very much and also enjoys spending time with him but finds it difficult to balance her time between work, the children, Amaad, and herself. She noted that she came home late because she was trying to finish a big project at work so that she could spend time with the family the following day. The therapist then asked Amaad to comment on what he took away from what Haifa said (i.e., checked to see if and how Amaad's attribution shifted with this new information). Thus, the goal was to help Amaad think differently about Haifa's behaviour, and the therapist engaged in Socratic dialogue with both partners to accomplish this goal. Emphasizing Socratic dialogue involving both partners at once is one of the differentiating characteristics in addressing cognitions in CBCT versus individual CBT.

The inductive "downward arrow" method In cognitive therapy more generally, "downward arrowing" is one strategy within Socratic dialogue that is often used to elicit cognitions such as assumptions, standards, or core beliefs that the couple might not have been aware of and that lie underneath more readily apparent attributions or expectancies. Specifically, this intervention enables therapists to uncover deeply held beliefs which might explain the type or extent of an individual's distress that is not obvious from the situation itself. For example, Tyrone and his colleagues finalized a large business deal, so he called Sasha to tell her that he was going out with them after work to celebrate. Although Sasha expressed no explicit objection, Tyrone was puzzled by her cold manner on the phone, at a time when he thought Sasha should be happy for him. When they explored this situation during the subsequent therapy session, it became apparent that Sasha's reaction was a response to a perceived betrayal and the attribution that Tyrone had "chosen his colleagues over me." However, sensing that Sasha was experiencing a greater sense of emotional distress and vulnerability than her "coldness" implied, the therapist asked a series of questions including, "If it were true that Tyrone *had* chosen his colleagues over you, what would that mean?" and "What would that say about you and your relationship?" At this point, Sasha began to cry, revealing her fear that "he doesn't want to spend time with me anymore." When the therapist gently inquired as to what this would say about her and the relationship if it were true, Sasha replied, "It would mean that he is getting bored with me and is going to leave me in the end—and he's right because I am worthless and, in the end, everyone leaves." For Tyrone, what had been an uncomplicated, impromptu celebration with colleagues after work had been profoundly meaningful for Sasha, triggering her deepest fears about her relationship and herself. Through the use of the downward arrow technique, it was possible for Sasha to articulate the meaning of this event to her and for Tyrone to empathize with Sasha's distress in the context of his prior knowledge of her difficult upbringing and feelings of neglect from her parents. As Epstein and Baucom (2002) observe, the downward arrow method provides an opportunity for individuals to become more aware of the origins of particular beliefs, which in turn can increase their willingness to modify them. Recognizing that a partner's reaction is associated with an issue from the past rather than the relationship in the present can enable the couple to understand one person's strong emotional response in a new way, based on a revised and more accurate attribution.

Examining the advantages and disadvantages of a cognition At times, cognitive restructuring is needed not because available information has been integrated in an inconsistent or distorted fashion but because one's beliefs regarding how things *should be* are not working effectively for the couple (i.e., one or both person's standards). Helping a couple re-evaluate their standards can be accomplished by focusing Socratic dialogue on the benefits and costs of those standards. In essence, the message from the therapist is this:

> There are many ways to create and conduct your relationship, and any way you do that has the potential to create benefits for you, but it almost always has some costs as well. Our goal is to clarify your standards for your relationship and look at the pros and cons of living that way, and consider what, if any, adjustments you might want to make.

As noted earlier in the chapter, difficulties can arise when partners have conflicting assumptions or standards. For example, Ivan held a standard that "in a good relationship, partners should spend all of their free time together," which conflicted with Natasha's belief that "a healthy relationship accommodates time apart to socialize with friends." Problems also can arise if a couple shares a standard that skews their relationship in unproductive ways. For example, both career-oriented partners might believe that "work should always come before play." However, they might discover that over time, their relationship has become devitalized through a lack of shared leisure time, limited opportunities for fun, and increased separations due to the rigorous pursuit of individual career opportunities. Thus, even though the two partners agree on their standard, it might be the basis for their presenting complaint of not feeling close to each other and, therefore, is appropriate for reconsideration.

Epstein and Baucom (2002) have outlined suggested steps that the therapist can employ in helping a couple explore the advantages and disadvantages of a particular standard:

1 Clarify each partner's standard.
2 Discuss the advantages and disadvantages of each partner's standards, with input from both partners.
3 Search for overlap between the two person's standards and developing a modified, shared standard that both partners can endorse.
4 Translate the new standard into specific behaviours that the couple can enact to "try out" this new way of living, with additional alterations as needed.

In working through these steps, there are several considerations for the therapist to keep in mind. First, on many occasions, neither partner identifies that they are experiencing difficulties because of their standards; instead, they often report that they are experiencing difficulties in a number of specific, seemingly unrelated domains. Therefore, it often is up to the therapist to assess and ask whether there are broader issues or macro-level themes that serve as the basis for a number of their concerns:

Therapist: It seems like you are having a number of disagreements about how to spend your time, when to come home, and whether to include friends in your leisure time. Is that right? If so, it makes me wonder if you might have some different standards for how you should deal with time. That's a tough issue for lots of couples, and one possibility would be to step back and see what you both think about how you should be spending time as a couple and as individuals, rather than dealing with each of these concerns as separate, unrelated issues. Sometimes it's helpful to make sure you're on the same page on a big picture perspective regarding how you think you should conduct your relationship, and then we can move to dealing with specific aspects of that bigger issue. Does that seem reasonable to you?[1]

Once an individual's standards have been clarified, the therapist should recognize that these beliefs often are held with great conviction and can be based on a person's long-standing values. Therefore, both the therapist and partner must be respectful of an individual's standards rather than referring to them as extreme, inappropriate, or invalid. As a result, often the therapist can be more successful by having the couple consider small changes or shifts, rather than asking either person to give up their standard, which they are unlikely to do and which might lead to a polarization between partners. To counteract this tendency, it is helpful to have each person point out both the pros and the cons of their own standard before the partner provides input. Even when couples agree to revise their standards to a variation that sounds mutually acceptable, they often need to "try it out" by getting behaviourally specific and over time see what additional changes might be needed and if the new standard is acceptable to both people in the long term.

For example, Natasha and Ivan discussed the benefits and costs that came from spending all their free time together versus spending some of it apart with each person having time to spend with friends. They were able to agree that their time was limited, and they wanted to spend the great majority of it together, with just the two of them. In addition, they agreed there was value in other friendships, both because those friendships provided joy and because they offered another source, besides the partner, for meeting each person's interpersonal needs. Furthermore, they concluded that each partner's interactions with their own friends often provided interesting topics of conversation to bring back to the couple's relationship. As a result, they agreed that each of them would take an evening every couple of weeks to spend with friends without the partner being present. They tried their new approach and agreed that it actually enhanced their relationship rather than detracting from it. The therapist was able to help the couple accomplish this shift without a debate over who was right or wrong, but rather with a focus on thinking about how they wanted to live this phase of their lives together as a proactive perspective on relationship building.

ACQUIRING INFORMATION FROM COUPLE INTERACTIONS OUTSIDE THE THERAPY SESSION

Behavioural experiments have a long history within individual CBT and are equally important in CBCT in helping couples gather information that might enable them to revise existing, distorted cognitions. When a potentially problematic cognition is identified, such as a maladaptive assumption, standard or belief, the therapist might work with the couple to create a new experience to begin challenging that belief. While some therapists see behavioural experiments as merely providing information for cognitive processing, behavioural experiences also can serve an important broader, integrative function. That is, behavioural exchanges between partners often create emotional changes, along with new ways of considering the partner and the relationship.

For example, as described above, the process of revising an existing standard is likely to entail the therapist having the couple weigh its advantages and disadvantages, and then helping them consider the potential consequences of an adapted version of the standard. Subsequently, the couple is encouraged to behave in new ways that are consistent with the new standard (e.g., going out with individual friends without the partner present). The aim is to provide the couple with an experience of behaving differently and observing the effects, including the emotional and cognitive impact of this new behaviour. If these changes are experienced positively, the couple can reflect on what is working more effectively and choose to continue living according to the modified standard. If the outcome of these efforts is unsatisfactory, then the therapist can help the couple identify what was not effective and use this feedback to make further changes in their next steps.

In summary, cognitive restructuring has the broad goal of helping the couple experience their relationship in a realistic and balanced manner. Consequently, there are a number of cognitive interventions that might be employed in the service of this larger goal. Some interventions focus explicitly on cognitive processes per se, whereas other interventions address a substantive area in the relationship where inadequate information or how it is thought about contributes to relationship distress. The cognitive interventions might focus on what is happening during the therapy session, or the interventions might involve assignments to be carried out during the week. As demonstrated in the above examples, rarely is a single cognitive intervention used in isolation to address cognitive phenomena. A variety of cognitive interventions might be used together or sequentially to reinforce new ways to consider some aspect of the couple's relationship. However, cognitive shifts result not only from cognitive interventions. In addition, important cognitive changes can result from behavioural and emotional interventions where the primary focus of the intervention is in changing behaviours or emotions.

Facilitating cognitive change through behavioural and emotional interventions

As noted previously, cognitive change is often best achieved when partners are provided with experiences that provide new perspectives on the partner, the relationship, or some aspect of their lives together, rather than through a piecemeal, intellectual analysis of individual cognitions. Moreover, if the intervention targets cognitive change only or primarily, many couples respond with comments such as, "I understand what you are saying, and it makes sense logically, but it doesn't feel that way." In essence, what they are saying is that to promote broad meaningful change, they need to experience it across modalities, including their behaviours and emotions. In the next section, we consider some of the commonly used behavioural and emotional interventions used specifically in the service of promoting cognitive change along with behavioural and emotional change. Therapists should carefully consider how they might promote change across cognitive, emotional, and behavioural aspects related to an area of concern. At times, a single intervention might impact all three domains, but at other times, a series of interventions might be used that together impact these domains.

Behavioural interventions

Nearly any behavioural intervention employed is likely to have an impact not only on behaviours but also on cognitions. For instance, couples might develop the belief that it is not possible for them to enjoy themselves on a date night or that they are unable to have a constructive conversation. Thus, teaching communication skills and using guided behaviour change to facilitate date nights might be utilized primarily to facilitate behaviour change but can have a secondary positive impact on the partner's cognitions. Likewise, assisting the couple in negotiating roles and responsibilities can help facilitate their belief that they are able to discuss problems constructively, that they both do indeed have power and control in their relationship, and that both partners are motivated to improve their circumstances. Thus, behavioural interventions that have a primary focus on improving behaviours also tend to shift cognitions positively.

Emotional interventions

Just as there is a reciprocal association between cognitions and behaviours, there is a strong association between cognitions and emotions as well. That is, an individual's internal, subjective experience of their partner and relationship typically is some combination or integration of their thoughts and their feelings. However, the relative weight, clarity, and integration of cognitions and emotions in a person's internal experience vary widely among individuals and shift within an individual as a function of the context. Some people are able to articulate both their cognitions and emotions and clarify how these two domains relate to each other; other people struggle in various ways. Some individuals' internal experiences are dominated primarily by emotions (e.g., "I don't know what I'm thinking; I'm just upset") whereas other people live in what appears to be primarily a world of intellect (e.g., "I don't think it is very logical to drive to your parents' house for their 50th anniversary; we'll be seeing them in less than three months anyway").

Being aware of one's own emotions and cognitions (and one's partner's) and how they are related generally places an individual and a couple in an optimal position to take pleasure in that inner life or alter their internal experiences and related behaviours when appropriate. This emphasis on the integration of cognition and emotion is not unique to CBCT or CBT, but it is a central part of most theoretical models of psychotherapy, ranging from the concept of *insight* in psychodynamic models to *wise mind* in dialectical behaviour therapy. More specifically, because cognitions and emotions are closely related, if an individual is experiencing difficulty accessing cognitions, it can be helpful to encourage that person to access internal processing via the route of emotions instead. In such cases, the latter approach often can open up a more effective point of entry. Additionally, some partners' emotional experiences interfere with effective cognitive processing and thus intervening around emotions can simultaneously shift their cognitive experience.

ACCESSING COGNITIONS VIA EMOTIONS

Some individuals are fully aware of their emotions but have little awareness of their related thoughts. In such instances, the therapist can rely on the emotion-cognition linkage to facilitate clarifying cognitions by addressing emotions. This example illustrates that therapists have various "portals" for accessing cognitions, emotions, and behaviours. For example, the therapist might begin by encouraging the partners to share their experiences at the level of emotions, identifying specific emotions, and then helping make the connections between emotions and thoughts. This step might be achieved through psychoeducation (e.g., "Usually, when people are anxious, it is because something feels unsafe, dangerous, or perhaps unpredictable. You were saying you are anxious about sharing that with Alon. Is there something about sharing that with him that feels unsafe or unpredictable?") or by directly asking and accentuating what is being experienced (e.g., "I can see how anxious you feel. When you feel that anxiety, what goes through your mind; what are you concerned could happen? Can you tell me more about that?").

More broadly, recognizing cognitive–emotional–behavioural links helps equip a therapist to start "where the client is." If an individual or couple can more easily access emotions, the therapist can begin with emotions and then make the link to cognitions. For individuals more adept at identifying their cognitions, the therapist can focus on the cognitions first and then move to emotions that often accompany such thoughts. Likewise, for individuals who "experience by doing," it can be helpful to emphasize their behaviours and then relate those behaviours to their experience of the event.

CHANGING COGNITIONS VIA EMOTIONAL INTERVENTIONS

Sometimes, emotional interventions are used for the purpose of effecting emotional changes (see Chapter 6), but the same interventions also can assist in helping one or both partners think differently. For example, the therapist might seek to help a couple contain negative emotions because at a certain level of intensity, these emotions interfere with the couple's cognitive processing (e.g., increase selective attention and negative attributions in a distorted manner). Or, if one partner tends to think of the other as uncaring due to their lack of emotional expression, heightening and shaping that partners' emotional expressions might demonstrate that the partner does indeed care. As another example, helping partners express more primary, vulnerable emotions (e.g., hope) versus secondary and/or "hard" emotions (e.g., anger) frequently changes one person's assumptions about who their partner is (e.g., "He is a loving individual who becomes overwhelmed and sad sometimes" versus "He is an angry jerk, and I have to walk on eggshells around him"). The overall premise is that cognitive restructuring can occur not only by intervening with cognitions directly (i.e., guided discovery interventions) but also as a secondary benefit from interventions primarily focused on emotional and/or behavioural change.

Concluding comments

As described previously, it is important to help couples differentiate distorted cognitions from negative ones. Reporting a negative experience with a partner does not necessarily indicate that a distortion is occurring. Therefore, the couple needs to realize that therapy will involve exploring the reality of their relationship, which might not always be comfortable. Indeed, cognitive work might lead individuals to reveal thoughts that have not previously been shared, possibly because they are painful to voice (e.g., "I have thought about leaving this relationship"; "I am not sure whether I love you anymore"). Couples need to realize that uncomfortable cognitions and feelings are likely to be experienced and expressed during the process of therapy and that their presence might indicate an area of realistic concern that needs to be addressed.

As noted in this chapter, therapists have the potential to draw on a wide range of interventions to support couples in achieving cognitive change when it is indicated. Some of these interventions, such as the "downward arrow" technique and behavioural experiments, have been well documented in the CBT literature more broadly. Others strategies, such as Socratic dialogue focused on the couple and helping couples enhance their ability for RSP, are more specific to CBCT and the ways in which therapists can work effectively with couple phenomena.

Regardless of the avenue pursued, all the interventions described in this chapter are used with the ultimate intention of helping couples have experiences that can enable new understandings of themselves (e.g., the impact of their own interpretations and subsequent reactions on their partner), each other (understanding the partner's perspective and what informs their reactions), and the relationship (how a couple can navigate two independent cognitive worlds in ways that enhance their relationship satisfaction).

Main points

- Individuals bring specific cognitive lenses to their relationships that shape how they see and feel about themselves, their partner, and their relationship. These cognitive lenses include experiences acquired through the partners' culture and personal histories.
- In addition to prior personal and relationship history, experiences that individuals have with their current partner also can give rise to distorted cognitions that have not been prominent before the relationship.

- In facilitating cognitive change, therapists use guided discovery in ways that create opportunities for the couple to have new experiences and enable the couple to experience the relationship in new ways. Cognitive restructuring in the form of logical disputation is rarely used in CBCT as individuals often are reluctant to revise their worldviews in front of a critical and blaming partner.
- It is important to help couples understand the difference between negative cognitions and distorted cognitions. Negative cognitions might be reasonable, drawing attention to aspects of a situation that need to change. Similarly, positive cognitions can be distorted if they prevent the couple from arriving at a balanced understanding of each other and the relationship. The aim is not to eliminate negative thinking and promote positive thinking but rather to help the couple modify distorted cognitions.
- For some couples, it is preferable to modify cross-situational, or macro-level, themes, rather than target individual cognitions.
- Change in the cognitive domain can be facilitated through a variety of cognitive, behavioural, and emotional strategies.

Note

1 The current focus is on searching for macro-level themes that might indicate an important relationship standard. However, identifying macro-level themes can be important in addressing all types of cognitions.

Chapter 6

Emotional factors

At the core, humans are inherently social beings. From an evolutionary perspective, the ability to form enduring social bonds, including couple relationships, is essential for human survival. To this day, individuals are healthier, live longer, and accomplish more when in adaptive relationships (Beckes & Coan, 2011; Holt-Lunstad, Birmingham, & Jones, 2008; Holt-Lunstad et al., 2010; Kiecolt-Glaser & Wilson, 2017). Yet, emotions in intimate relationships are about much more than survival and efficiency. Many adults want to connect in special ways with another person, and romantic relationships are the source of enough happiness, joy, anguish, and sorrow to fill centuries' worth of music and literature.

Strong positive emotions when interacting with a potential romantic partner can be highly rewarding or even experienced as intoxicating, motivating each individual to seek out the other person (Fredrickson, 1998). As someone might say early in a relationship, "Just thinking about her makes me feel wonderful!" Thus, emotions are a motivating force in the formation of meaningful relationships. Positive emotions also play a central role in maintaining relationships long term, with many relationships remaining healthy and fulfilling for a lifetime (Levenson, Carstensen, & Gottman, 1993; Palmer & Baucom, 1997). In long-term relationships, the emotional atmosphere might be less about excitement and more about a profound, enduring sense of closeness and security; emotions help to maintain relationships even in the context of complex, demanding lives. Indeed, in a study of couples who had been together for 30–60 years, some reported feeling that they had married "that special someone" for whom they had continued to feel great respect, admiration, and love for decades (Palmer & Baucom, 1998).

More broadly, good relationships can be a source of joy, deep emotional connection, and security; bolster individual well-being in good times; and support partners against life's challenges in bad times. For example, research has shown that the subjective sense of connecting emotionally with a partner even extends to the physiological aspects of emotions. Partners' emotional responses become linked, such that each person's responses impact the other's on an ongoing basis (Butler, 2011). Couples can experience being "in sync" emotionally, and their emotions can become closely coordinated in many interactions. These emotional connections are thought to be central to the long-term health benefits of stable relationships (Ditzen, Hoppmann, & Klumb, 2008; Sbarra & Hazan, 2008). Thus, emotions can both be the "magnet" for two people seeking a relationship with each other and the "glue" that holds them together once they have become close.

Just as emotions play an immensely important role in the formation and maintenance of relationships, relationship distress also is closely tied to emotions. Yet, not all discord is created equal: "I'm so miserable" might indicate either the absence of positive emotional experiences ("We used to have so much fun; now he's such a bore!") or the presence of negative emotions ("You are always so angry at me, no matter what I do!"). For many distressed couples, there is an absence of positive emotions and an abundance of negative emotions, along with chaotic emotional displays and emotional turmoil leading to arguments. Given their importance in relationship adjustment and distress, emotions are a central topic in most forms of couple therapy, such as emotionally focused couple therapy (EFT; Johnson & Greenberg, 1995). In early forms of behaviourally based couple therapies, emotions were primarily considered as a consequence of cognitions and behaviours and, therefore, were not the direct focus of intervention (D. H. Baucom & Epstein, 1990; Weiss, 1980); however, it is now known that the associations between emotions, cognitions, and behaviours are multidirectional and often recursive (Epstein & Baucom, 2002). Given the focus of the current chapter, the impact of emotions on these other domains is emphasized here.

Associations of emotions with behaviours and cognitions

One important function of emotions is to motivate behaviour in all areas of life. For example, a fear response quickly leads to stepping out of the way of a car speeding toward a pedestrian, or empathically feeling someone else's sadness can motivate offers of support. Within relationships, strong emotions (e.g., fear, resentment) often arise when important needs are unmet. In healthy relationships, such negative emotional responses often motivate adaptive behaviours to address those needs, such as initiating a problem-solving conversation with one's partner. Similarly, feeling positive emotions like love or joy can motivate joining behaviours, such as support and affection. On the other hand, emotions can motivate an individual to behave in unhelpful ways (e.g., to blame or criticize). Thus, the emotion itself might be quite adaptive, but the related behaviour might be ineffective or damaging for the relationship.

Emotions also influence cognitive processing, producing what is called "affect-driven cognition" (Planalp, Fitness, & Fehr, 2018). Research shows that emotions and overall mood can colour cognitions and memories in important ways. For example, negative memories are more easily recalled while in a negative mood state (Matt, Vázquez, & Campbell, 1992). In a related manner, negative mood often contributes to selective attention toward ongoing negative aspects of the relationship or a partner's behaviour, along with negative interpretations of those events (see Chapter 5). Such associations contribute to the development and maintenance of relationship distress.

In addition to the impact of emotions on cognitive processing, the overlap between emotions and cognitive experiences matters as well. Often, internal experiences that include both strong emotional *and* closely related cognitive components have the most wide-ranging impact, while merely "knowing" something on a purely cognitive level can fall short ("I *know* I can trust that she loves me, and all of this worry comes from my bad experiences while growing up. But I can't shake this fear that she's going to walk out one day"). An even more global, cognitive-affective experience of the partner and the relationship can take the form of "sentiment override" (Weiss, 1980). Sentiment override involves having a stable view and emotional experience of one's partner and the relationship, with an individual seemingly immune to new information to alter their view of their partner. For example, as Peggy noted about Mark, "At this point, all he has to do is walk into the room, and I already feel disgusted. He hasn't cared about me or the kids in years, so why should I care now?" In the presence of well-entrenched negative sentiment override, even strong positive efforts from the partner might go unnoticed, minimized, or even resented (Notarius, Benson, Sloane, & Vanzetti, 1989), thus confirming the overall negative experience of the relationship and the partner.

In summary, emotions are central in most intimate relationships and are not only the result of behaviours and cognitions. Instead, emotions have powerful impacts on both cognitions and behaviours as well. Given the centrality of emotions in relationships, this chapter presents a conceptual framework that emphasizes the role of emotions in relationships, along with interventions that target emotions directly.

Conceptualizing Emotions in Relationships

While research and theory suggest a variety of emotion-related constructs and processes central to relationships, here we focus on elements that are most important to the conceptualization and treatment of relationship distress within a CBCT framework. Given the complex interplay of emotional factors within the couple, it is useful to distinguish between factors related to (a) emotions within each person as an individual, and (b) the interdependence and interaction patterns of emotions that emerge between the two members of the couple. Figure 6.1 provides an overview of the factors that are discussed in more detail below. The first focus emphasizes within-person emotional experiences, and the second focus discusses the interdependence of emotions between partners and related adaptive and maladaptive interaction processes.

Individual emotional experience and expression

Three aspects of emotions within an individual merit discussion because of their impact on the relationship and individual well-being: (a) the type of emotion, (b) its intensity, and (c) its variability and regulation over time. Within each aspect, both the experience of emotions and the expression of emotions are important. In some instances, difficulties arise

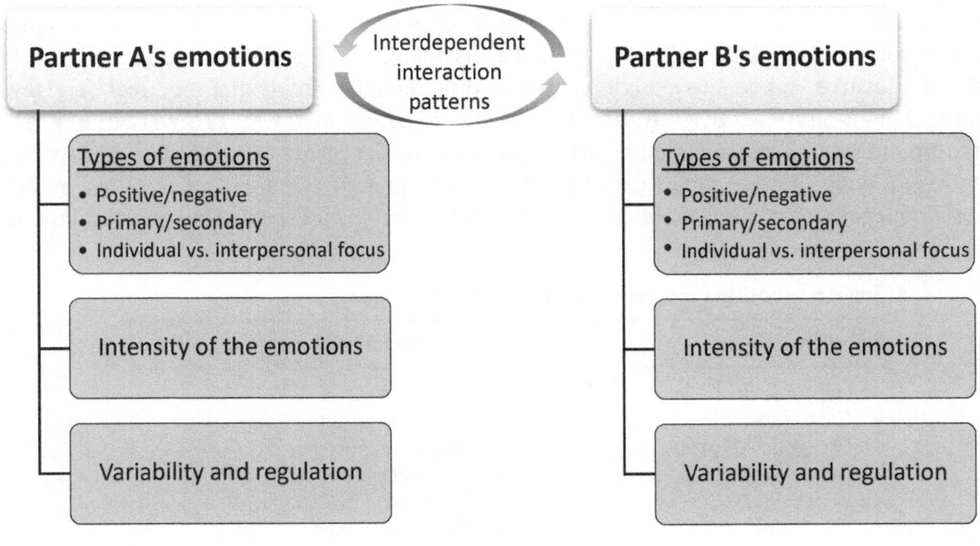

Figure 6.1 Conceptualizing the experience and expression of emotions in relationships

primarily from the experience of the emotions (for example, experiencing emotions very intensely). In other instances, the expression of the emotions is the main issue (e.g., even though emotions are experienced internally, they are not expressed, leaving the partner confused about what the person is experiencing). At other times, both the experience and the expression of emotion are problematic.

Types of emotions

Emotions have been discussed from a variety of theoretical perspectives, including theories of basic emotions (Ekman, 1992) and theories that refer to dynamic processes rather than distinct categories of emotions (Scherer, 2009). Without attempting to provide a comprehensive theoretical framework of emotions, several dimensions of emotional experience and expression are highlighted and discussed below as they relate to understanding relationship functioning (Epstein & Baucom, 2002).

POSITIVE AND NEGATIVE EMOTIONS

One of the broadest distinctions is between positive and negative emotions. In the current context, the terms "positive" and "negative" do not mean "good" and "bad" but rather imply the subjective experience that most people have relative to the emotion. That is, the terms imply that the emotional experience or expression is in some way pleasant or desirable versus unpleasant or undesirable. As such, negative emotions are not necessarily maladaptive, and as noted above, they can signal to the couple that something is amiss and needs to be addressed.

Whereas many individuals intuitively think of positive and negative emotions as opposite ends of one continuum, thinking of them as two separate dimensions is more useful (Epstein & Baucom, 2002). Experiencing positive emotions does not necessarily imply the absence of negative emotions, and vice versa. Instead, individuals (and couples) might experience and express high or low levels of both positive and negative emotions, similar to the various combinations of positive and negative behaviours described in Chapter 4. For example, some couples report that "we've always had a passionate relationship" including high levels of both positive and negative emotions, while other couples report that they feel very few positive emotions (e.g., love, joy, happiness) in the relationship as well as high rates of negative emotions (e.g., anger and hurt). While experiencing the gamut of emotions is normative, distressed couples often report experiencing high frequencies of negative emotions and/or low frequencies of positive emotions overall in their relationship. Table 6.1 shows additional

Table 6.1 Positive and negative emotions in relationships

Positive emotions	*Negative emotions*
• Happy–joyful	• Sad–depressed
• Close–warm	• Anxious–afraid
• Energetic–vigorous	• Angry–frustrated
• Relaxed–calm	• Contemptuous
	• Fatigued
	• Guilty–ashamed
	• Jealous

distinctions within positive and negative emotions; couples might vary in the degree to which they experience and are comfortable with a whole range of emotions and the degree to which each individual is able to make nuanced distinctions among these emotions.

PRIMARY AND SECONDARY EMOTIONS

The distinction between primary and secondary emotions made by Johnson and Greenberg (1995) is helpful in understanding difficulties that some couples experience in addressing emotions that are uncomfortable to them. In describing primary emotions, Johnson and Greenberg elaborate, "In this categorization, the primary emotions are viewed as essentially biologically adaptive, orienting the organism to the personal significance of outside events in relationship to needs and goals" (p. 126). That is, primary emotions play an important role in helping a person notice and address challenges, such as avoiding threats when feeling fear or reaching out to one's partner when feeling lonely. However, primary emotions might feel too difficult or threatening to experience or express (e.g., feeling weak or fearing the loss of one's partner). As a result, they might be concealed or replaced by secondary emotions which in some manner are experienced as "safer" (e.g., feeling angry). At times, difficulties with primary emotions are due to past experiences, such as punishment or criticism that someone received when they cried as a child. Likewise, punishing or unrewarding interactions during the couple's current relationship can result in a focus on secondary emotions rather than experiencing or expressing what the person "really feels."

Frequently, secondary emotions take the form of "hard" emotions that typically involve less vulnerability, such as anger, frustration, and resentment. Primary emotions that often are concealed tend to be "soft," more vulnerable emotions, such as sadness, fear, loneliness, or disappointment (Christensen, Jacobson, & Babcock, 1995). However, hard emotions such as anger also can be primary. For example, in some contexts, certain cultural groups (e.g., women, some religious groups) have been taught that it is not appropriate to experience or express anger ("If you don't have anything nice to say, don't say anything at all" or "Feeling anger is sinful"). In such instances, secondary emotions such as guilt might follow the primary emotion of anger. More generally, there are cultural differences in beliefs about emotions, such as which emotions are appropriate to experience or express and acceptable ways of expressing emotions, and therapists should familiarize themselves with these differences (Sue & Sue, 2012).

INDIVIDUAL VS. INTERPERSONAL ORIENTATION

Both positive and negative emotions can be individually oriented (emotions that do not reflect upon the partner or the relationship) or interpersonally oriented (emotions that are about the partner or relationship). At times, individuals focus on expressing individually oriented emotions which can limit the opportunity for emotional closeness. For example, when Lizzy described her experience of organizing her son's bar mitzvah with her husband Sam, she focused on the event itself: "Everything went well, and I'm so relieved." The therapist encouraged her to explore how she felt about Sam and their work together as well. In response, Sam was moved when she expressed how proud she felt raising a wonderful son together and how close she felt to Sam while preparing for this special event. Although it might seem that partners would want to share positive interpersonal emotions, such expressions can at times feel vulnerable, unfamiliar, or awkward. For example, telling someone that you adore being with them is risky if you do not know whether they will reciprocate the feeling. In addition, many individuals might simply miss opportunities for the expression of positive feelings even if they are not being avoided. Many couples report that they are "too busy" to stop and speak with each other in this way, and some believe that "he knows I love him; I don't have to tell him," or they simply are not accustomed to expressing a great deal of love and affection. Thus, interpersonal emotions can be an important type of primary emotion that is central to relationship functioning, but expressing positive interpersonal emotions might be rare in distressed relationships, even when they are experienced.

In summary, difficulties in relationships related to the type of emotion can arise if too little or too much emotion is experienced or expressed by one or both partners, or if primary emotions are frequently masked by secondary emotions. In addition to the type of emotions, how strongly emotions are experienced and expressed play an important role in relationship functioning.

Intensity of emotions

Difficulties can arise both at the individual and the couple level as a result of the intensity of emotions that partners experience and express. For example, couples might struggle if one or both partners frequently experience and express intense emotions (which can feel unpleasant to both partners and interfere with processes such as effective problem-solving), if one or both partners are fairly "unemotional" and emphasize intellectual domains instead (which contributes to the couple feeling distant), or if the partners are mismatched in how intensely they experience and express emotions (such that one partner experiences the other person as "cold" or "overly dramatic"). Additionally, the internal experience of emotion within one person does not always match that person's expression of emotion. For example, an individual who is experiencing strong negative emotions might attempt to withdraw, suppress, or "numb out" to express little emotion verbally and non-verbally to their partner, often leaving both partners confused and dissatisfied.

On an individual level, experiencing a high intensity of emotions can be challenging, as it places greater demands on the individual to regulate their emotions and prevent ineffective behaviours stemming from strong emotional experiences ("Honey, I bought us a llama; it was so adorable, I couldn't resist!"). In particular, high levels of negative emotions can interfere with constructive decision-making (Lerner, Li, Valdesolo, & Kassam, 2015) and have even been shown to interfere with communication skills acquisition during a premarital relationship education programme (B. R. Baucom, Weusthoff, Atkins, & Hahlweg, 2012).

Likewise, often there are interpersonal implications related to the intensity of emotions that are expressed, whether the intensity is high or low. For example, strong, unfiltered emotional expression can cause difficulties when it occurs at inappropriate times (e.g., at a family gathering) or in ways that are persistently overwhelming or hurtful to the partner. For other couples, the intensity of emotions experienced might not match a partner's expected expression of those emotions. For instance, Charlotte (who was Western European Caucasian) was surprised when she realized how saddened her husband Ji-Yeong (who was South Korean) had been since they learned shortly after their wedding that Charlotte was unable to conceive. As the couple explored this disappointment further in therapy, they became more aware that while Ji-Yeong assumed that Charlotte would know how he felt without explicitly verbalizing it, Charlotte's own cultural norms involved a more overt expression of emotions, such that she interpreted his more muted expression of sadness as a lack of caring.

As implied above, frequently an emotion must be expressed for a partner to know how to respond, and the intensity of emotional expression can help to convey the magnitude of the person's experience. Consistent with this notion, Cutrona and Suhr (1994) described the interpersonal process of letting a partner know that one person is seeking support. Within healthy relationships, such expression often leads to the partner responding with emotional or instrumental support as appropriate. Similarly, Cordova and Scott (2001) posit that emotional intimacy develops through a process of vulnerable self-disclosure from one person and caring responsiveness by the partner. Under these circumstances, expressing intense emotions in a vulnerable way can be healthy and can contribute to emotional closeness and a social support process (Fischer, Baucom, et al., 2015). Thus, there is no universally "adaptive" level of intensity of emotional experience or expression; rather, what is adaptive is highly dependent on the context and goals. The impact of the type of emotion and its intensity also will vary greatly depending on how stable the emotion is over time.

Variability and regulation of emotions over time

Individual and interpersonal well-being rely on (a) the ability to regulate emotions to optimize emotional stability and (b) the flexibility to adapt to changing demands of various situations (Butler, 2011; Gross, 2013). While individuals differ in overall temperament and the degree to which emotions tend to be stable versus volatile, emotion regulation—the ability to impact the occurrence, intensity, and experience of emotions (Gross, 2013)—is central to well-being. More specifically, effective emotion regulation is linked to psychological and physical health and better interpersonal relationships (Gross, 2013). On the other hand, excessive or uncontrolled variability in emotions (i.e., poor emotion regulation) tends to be exhausting and difficult to cope with, both for the individual and for the partner.

Even for individuals with effective emotion regulation skills, relationship distress and high conflict can be emotionally dysregulating. As Sachi told the therapist, "I promise I'm not usually like this. I'm usually pretty laid back, but in this relationship at the moment, I'm 0 to a 100 in no time and I can't help it!" Such an effect tends to be particularly pronounced following major relationship traumas such as infidelity, when emotional responses can mimic those of posttraumatic distress (D. H. Baucom et al., 2009). In other instances, individuals have poor overall emotion regulation, and their difficulties become greatly amplified in the presence of relationship distress. These couples might benefit from couple therapy with interventions focused on emotion regulation added to the treatment plan (see Chapter 13). Thus, it might not be immediately apparent whether an individual is struggling with emotion dysregulation broadly in life, or whether the emotion dysregulation is secondary to relationship distress. In any case, for therapy to be productive and for the couple's long-term well-being, it is important that both partners be able to regulate their emotions to provide a sense of stability within the relationship.

Interdependence and interaction of emotions between partners

The above factors refer to processes that occur within each partner in the relationship. However, emotions do not occur in isolation. Instead, the type, intensity, and variability of each person's emotional experiences and expression are closely associated with the other partner's emotional responses. In many instances, this interdependence can lead partners to feel that they are "in sync," with each person impacting the other on a moment-by-moment basis. Under optimal circumstances, this bidirectional linkage can serve important functions for helping an individual regulate emotions ("You give me a hug, and all of a sudden it feels like everything is going to be okay!"). Helping a partner regulate their emotions through interpersonal interactions can be thought of as interpersonal emotion regulation or "coregulation" (Butler, 2011). However, this interpersonal emotional process also can go awry. Closely linked emotions or stress responses between partners can backfire, for example, when they lead to further negative escalation or interfere with adaptive individual regulation (Fischer et al., 2017; Timmons, Margolin, & Saxbe, 2015). Consistent with this notion, research has shown that the bidirectional linkage in emotions between partners (including indicators linked to stress responses such as cortisol output and heart rate) can indeed have either positive or negative effects, depending on the context (Mercado & Hibel, 2017; Timmons et al., 2015).

Thus, linkage of emotions between partners can contribute to difficulties with emotions in relationships. As a result, it can be important for partners to learn either (a) to avoid being too reactive to each other or (b) to react in a compensatory manner. For example, one partner can provide a calming presence as the other person becomes more distressed. At the other extreme, a lack of reactivity, responsiveness, or interdependence of emotions between partners also can contribute to relationship distress. For example, one person can feel disappointed if a partner appears to be nonresponsive to positive emotions and seems disengaged when an individual wants to share exciting news. Likewise, some individuals escalate in expressing negative emotions if the partner does not seem to "get it," contributing to a demand-withdraw pattern. In conclusion, difficulties related to emotions can arise as a function of not only what each partner experiences or expresses, but also how the two partners interact. The centrality of emotions in intimate relationships calls for an understanding of how to address emotions in treatment to alleviate distress and help couples reach their full potential.

Interventions focused on emotions

Whereas cognitive and behavioural interventions often impact partners' emotions, strategies that focus more directly on emotional processes increase the flexibility and applicability of the treatment for a wide range of couple concerns. EFT places a primary focus on emotions in relationships, particularly helping couples access and express primary emotions (Johnson & Greenberg, 1995). The current CBCT perspective incorporates many interventions developed within an EFT framework, while emphasizing a variety of additional considerations to help address emotion-related difficulties that couples might experience.

In CBCT, emotions are addressed for two primary purposes. First, setting an appropriate emotional tone is important to conduct a successful couple therapy session, regardless of the primary goals of the session. That is, even if the main goal is to address cognitions or behaviours, this goal is difficult to achieve if one or both partners are emotionally dysregulated. Similarly, if the couple seems "flat" emotionally, it can be hard to engage them in the tasks of therapy. Thus, it is important to create an emotional tone in the session that facilitates couple engagement with appropriate control.

Second, when focusing on emotions per se, a major goal is to help individuals and the couple experience and express emotions that are *adaptive for a given context*, that correspond to events in a *balanced* manner (e.g., are not overly extreme or inconsistent with the person's cognitions and behaviours), and that are facilitative of the couple's *immediate and long-term goals*. That is, while emotions need to address the immediate context, couples also need to be mindful of the long-term effects, such that they are not (always) reacting only to the present moment. For example, as Suzie stated, "I realize now that always stuffing down my frustration means that Joe doesn't have a clue when I'm unhappy, and that doesn't give him a chance to do anything differently. My being a martyr really doesn't work well long term." Thus, at times, tolerating negative emotions in the moment might be unpleasant but important for long-term relationship or individual functioning. Across all emotion-focused interventions, the ability to express and describe emotions verbally in a manner that is appropriate to the context is central. Communication skills for sharing thoughts and feelings, as described in Chapter 4, can be a useful tool to combine with the intervention principles outlined below.

The remainder of this chapter addresses how the factors described above can be targeted in treatment, using a variety of strategies. Specific intervention techniques are discussed first, followed by general intervention principles for the therapist to consider when employing these techniques.

Intervention targets when addressing emotions

Interventions focused on emotions can target three aspects, each applicable to the experience and/or expression of emotions: (a) the type of emotion; (b) the intensity of emotion, including both increasing and decreasing the emotion or variability, and (c) the emotional responsiveness of the two partners to each other, either increasing or decreasing the reactivity between partners. Additionally, interventions might be focused on the couple as a unit (e.g., the couple is withdrawn and shut down) or on one partner (e.g., one partner quickly becomes highly emotionally distressed when the other partner raises minor concerns). While difficulties related to the intensity and type of emotions might be an issue for each individual, responsiveness involves an interpersonal experience. Nevertheless, a therapist might still intervene with one person at a time in the service of facilitating a more adaptive couple process.

As noted above, emotions might be the explicit, main focus of interventions for a given session; however, many of the interventions described below can be "infused" into interventions focused on behaviours or cognitions in order to create a more optimal emotional climate for behavioural or cognitive change. Whether to shift, contain, or heighten partners' emotions and reactivity to each other should always depend on the goal of the particular session, the nature of the interactions, and overall treatment goals. Often, therapists simultaneously target multiple processes (e.g., attempt to shift and heighten more vulnerable emotions in order to decrease the intensity of anger and hostility). For didactic purposes, we present the interventions separately by the primary goal or purpose under consideration, recognizing that most interventions have multiple impacts. Because intervening on the intensity of emotions often involves shifting the type of emotion as well (e.g., shifting from secondary to primary emotions in order to decrease the intensity of anger expressed), these two foci of intervention are considered together in the following sections.

Many of the strategies below involve the therapeutic process and how to manage emotions effectively in the session with a great deal of direct therapist involvement. This approach can seem quite different from the more skills-based communication interventions discussed in the chapter on behavioural factors and communication. Because the emotional climate in the session and the relationship evolves as a result of each person's emotional experience and expression, at times the therapist will focus on one partner's emotions if that individual is experiencing notable difficulties in this domain. Therefore, a single session might progress from addressing the couple as a unit, to focusing next on one person's emotions, then to reintroducing the other partner back into the interaction to reinstitute a couple focus in the session. Likewise, the therapist often employs their own verbal and nonverbal expression to alter emotions. This process aspect of couple therapy as it unfolds within and between sessions is a central part of successful treatment, similar to the factors discussed in Chapter 3 on conducting CBCT sessions.

Differentiating, identifying, and expressing more nuanced emotions

Attempting to alter the intensity of emotions and reactivity between partners, along with shifting emotions, can be more difficult if one or both partners have difficulty identifying what their emotions are. In addition, research suggests that labelling emotions helps individuals regulate emotions (Linehan, 1993). In an interpersonal context, accurate and nuanced labelling facilitates communication, promotes mutual understanding, and prevents misinterpretations of what one person is experiencing. Chapter 4 describes communication skills training for conversations focused on sharing thoughts and feelings, but it also emphasizes the importance of articulating clear descriptions of emotional experiences. In order for couples to express emotions clearly, first the emotions must be experienced and labelled.

Often, couple therapists draw on interventions commonly used in individual therapy for individuals struggling with identifying and labelling emotions. Thus, a CBCT therapist might help a partner relate emotions to cognitions or behaviours, if the latter are more easily accessible (see Chapter 5). For example, an individual might say, "I started to feel really bad when I thought about all the time that my partner is spending with his colleagues after work, when I get to see him so little. That seems unfair; this is not what we agreed on." Unfairness often is related to an experience of anger, so once the unfairness is identified, the therapist might help the individual relate it to an emotion of anger or a similar emotion. The therapist might provide psychoeducation to help the couple understand how different emotions typically are related to different thoughts or interpretations of a situation. That is, anger is typically associated with a sense of something being unfair; sadness is often tied to a sense of loss; anxiety to uncertainty and danger; shame to beliefs about having violated one's own values, and so on. Urges to act in certain ways can indicate emotions as well, such as yelling (anger), staying in bed (sadness), or asking for reassurance (anxiety). In addition to the individual benefits of labelling emotions in a nuanced way, doing so often facilitates more adaptive management of emotions interpersonally. That is, if emotions are not clarified, partners might respond to nonverbal, diffuse expressions, which leaves room for interpersonal misunderstandings. Handouts and visual aids that group emotions into categories can be helpful for individuals to label and describe their emotions more accurately as well. Appendix 3 provides a list of emotion words that can be shared with couples. Given that the appendix is intended as a handout for use by couples, the use of the term "emotions" is broadly defined to conform to what couples experience rather than being a scholarly delineation of emotions.

Heightening the experience and expression of emotions

As previously discussed, individuals and couples might experience emotions only to a minimal extent, experience emotions more fully but avoid expressing them, or express some emotions but avoid expressing others (e.g., express anger but not sadness).

In-session interventions for heightening emotions

Therapists might need to intervene in a variety of ways to heighten emotions selectively that facilitate the therapeutic process, or increase the overall intensity of emotions if they are minimized in a way that is problematic.

BALANCING POSITIVE AND NEGATIVE EMOTIONS

Individuals might present with varying experiences of positive and negative emotions in their daily lives and during a session. At times, negative emotions might be primary and essential to helping the couple address difficult issues. In such instances, the therapist might focus on teaching the couple to share their experiences effectively with each other while keeping the intensity of the emotions at a manageable level (see below). In many cases, however, negative emotions such as anger tend to dominate a session once they have arisen, and distressed couples have difficulty accessing positive emotions even when such emotions are present. In order to support the couple in maintaining hope and motivation, a therapist can encourage the couple to notice and experience positive aspects of a situation. For example, when Luis and Ana reported that their first attempt at a date night after many years had not been much fun, the therapist first explored what the challenges had been and then searched for positive aspects of their evening, even if they were minor:

Therapist: So this first attempt wasn't as enjoyable as we had hoped. It sounds like there are a few things we need to think about before your next date night. Before we do that, is there anything good that came from your experience?

Ana: To be honest, I'm not really sure. It seems like we can't do anything anymore without it going down the tubes.

Therapist: I understand your disappointment. You were looking forward to this time together, and it's a let-down when it doesn't go the way you were hoping. It can feel hard to keep trying when that happens. Is there anything, though, any aspects of this first attempt you made after many years that you appreciated?

Luis: Well, I actually was a bit surprised that we even went out! I don't want to do it again if it keeps going like this, but in the past we would make vague plans and then never even try to spend time together. So I guess just going out is some progress, and that feels good.

If a couple has been struggling severely and few positive aspects of the relationship remain, using behavioural interventions to increase positive behaviours first is likely to be appropriate. When helping the couple balance positive and negative perspectives and emotions, the therapist is not trying to elicit emotions that are not based in reality. Instead, the goals are to examine what is present, avoid selective attention that leads to missed opportunities for positive emotional experiences, shift toward and heighten positive emotions that are present but have been avoided, and otherwise change the couple's behaviour in ways that will contribute to a better balance of positive and negative emotions.

ACCESSING AND EXPRESSING A GREATER RANGE OF EMOTIONS

At times, one or both partners might avoid expressing a given emotion or set of emotions (e.g., vulnerable emotions) and instead express only a few secondary emotions (e.g., anger). A primary goal in such circumstances is to help both partners experience and express a wider range of emotions, including primary emotions.

Creating a safe environment Therapists need to ensure that the environment of the session is safe for individuals to experience and express difficult emotions. Often, the therapist needs to help one person express vulnerable emotions, while also helping the partner respond to this new emotional expression in ways that are validating rather than punishing. For instance, when Silvana opened up about the guilt and self-loathing she had harboured regarding her son's behavioural problems (believing she was to blame), the therapist asked her partner Trinity to summarize what she understood about Silvana's experience. In addition, the therapist reminded Trinity of her role and how difficult it might be, "Trinity, I know you see this very differently, and you've expressed many times that you don't think Silvana is to blame at all. But Silvana has just shared with you for the first time how deeply she experiences this excruciating guilt. Let her know that you value whatever feelings she has, even if you see the situation differently. So before you share your own perspective, what did you hear about her emotional experience; what is this like for *her*?" Such a statement is intended to help shape and focus the partner's response in a way that is validating, rather than focusing on differences in perspective.

Psychoeducation and "permission giving" If emotions are avoided because they are believed to be wrong ("As a mother, I should never feel angry toward my baby"), shameful ("Crying means I'm weak and worthless"), dangerous ("Bad things happen when I show strong emotion"), etc., providing information to validate the importance and validity of all emotions can be freeing for many clients. For example, the therapist might normalize a client's experience ("I can understand how you would have these moments of frustration and anger after being up every hour for many nights in a row, even if you know your baby is not doing that on purpose. Most new parents experience feelings like that. It's actually very common because frustration typically results from not being able to make things work or proceed smoothly, regardless of the reason"). Alternatively, the therapist might explore the client's beliefs directly ("You've mentioned that at times you're quite fearful of expressing much of any emotion because of all the criticism and punishment you received for expressing emotions when you were growing up. Can you tell us more about what that was like and how it has changed how you deal with emotions now?" . . . "I can really see how any child would learn to avoid expressing their emotions under those circumstances, and that was really the only option you had back then. What do you think that means for you now? Is it possible that the relationship you are in now might be different and safer?"). Such an approach will primarily be applicable if the individual's beliefs about the current relationship are not well founded. If concerns regarding emotional safety in the current relationship seem realistic, interventions to increase safety will take priority, such as improving communication and especially developing effective listening skills.

Modelling and drawing on the social context to heighten avoided emotions Across all interventions, the social context of having both the other partner and the therapist present provides powerful inroads to emotions, using both the other partner's and the therapist's emotional tone to help an individual address their emotional experience. If one partner is more skilled or in the moment is more open to expressing emotions, that individual can be asked to express their feelings first, both modelling openness and creating an emotional climate to facilitate sharing by the other person. For example, if a couple has experienced a tragic loss but one partner is avoiding experiencing their sadness, helping the avoidant partner listen and reflect while the other partner shares their experience might elicit feelings of sadness in the avoidant partner as well. Similarly, the therapist's own emotional tone and expression can set the overall atmosphere for the session and help with accessing avoided emotions by validating them both in words and in tone (e.g., in a sombre, sincere tone: "Listening to your description of what you have been going through is really striking. I imagine I would feel very sad if this happened to me").

HEIGHTENING MINIMIZED EMOTIONS

For many individuals and couples, the issue might not be the avoidance of certain emotions, but rather the minimization of experiencing or expressing emotions more generally. If this pattern has been identified as an important treatment target—for example, if the couple experiences their relationship as devitalized or distant—the therapist can incorporate common strategies used in individual therapy and applied to couples, as in EFT. These strategies include but are not limited to:

- Recounting the details of an event: Asking an individual to describe a past event in greater detail often evokes the associated emotions.
- Avoiding diversions: Once individuals begin experiencing unfamiliar emotions or emotions that are typically avoided, the inclination to try and "escape" from that emotional experience is understandable. Thus, therapists might need to help the individual "stay in" the emotion and experience new learning. Therapists can accomplish this by supportively "blocking the exits" (Johnson, 1996), that is, encouraging continued focus on the emotion or redirecting back to an emotional issue if the client has switched topics.
- Using metaphors, images: Various individuals access and experience emotions in different ways. If expressing emotions in words is difficult for someone, they might be more successful using metaphors or images to convey their emotional experience to a partner.
- Mindful observation of bodily cues: "Turning inward" to notice and then describe bodily sensation such as sweaty hands, a tight chest, tense shoulders, or tears can help individuals to "cue in" to what they might be feeling.

For various reasons, such as feeling unsafe or angry with the other person, one partner might have difficulty directly expressing their emotions to their partner but can do so with the therapist's assistance. In such instances, the therapist might "start where the client is" and then build toward emotional expression between the partners. Often, the therapist begins by speaking to one partner directly to help them access their emotions and express those emotions in an effective manner to the therapist. Once they are able to do so, then the therapist asks that person to express those emotions to their partner directly ("Okay, so you aren't just a little bit worried sometimes; it sounds like you are terrified of losing her to cancer, and it can be overwhelming. Can you tell her directly what that feels like to you, that the most important person in your life is seriously ill?").

In summary, therapists use interventions to heighten emotions at times when doing so serves therapeutic goals, and the session provides a "safe" context to do so. Because many in-session interventions on heightening emotions are highly dependent upon the structure provided by the therapist, especially in the beginning, additional considerations are important for continued progress outside of the sessions.

Outside-of-session interventions for heightening emotions

In addition to being able to experience and express heightened emotions during a session, in order for the couple to benefit long term, it is essential that they be able to express emotions in their everyday lives as well.

INTERVENTIONS FOCUSED ON THE INDIVIDUAL OUTSIDE OF THE SESSION

If one of the two partners struggles to access, experience, or express their emotions, helping this person to increase the frequency and range of such emotions outside of the session can facilitate better couple functioning. First, if one or both partners broadly experience restricted emotions or have extensively avoided certain emotional experiences, a variety of interventions can help them focus on emotions and "make them part of life," so that the person is able to bring these emotional experiences to the relationship as well. These interventions might include, for example, mindfulness interventions, guided imagery exercises, and self-monitoring to identify the type and intensity of emotions throughout the day. Second, many relationships also benefit from the two partners' awareness and experience of interpersonal emotions. In this realm, exercises might include instructions to focus on feelings toward the partner and the relationship specifically. For example, clients might be instructed to notice one positive action their partner performs each day and how that feels, or to note one attribute about their partner that they are grateful for each day.

INTERVENTIONS FOCUSED ON THE COUPLE OUTSIDE OF THE SESSION

Many behavioural interventions serve to shift or heighten emotions and can be employed with this explicit focus and purpose. For example, caring days (see Chapter 4) are used to increase positive experiences for the couple; intimacy-enhancing activities (e.g., increased physical affection, conversations about important topics) serve a similar purpose with greater emphasis on close, warm feelings. However, increasing emotions is not always about positives. Some couples are conflict avoidant and might need to practise accessing and adaptively expressing negative emotions; conversations focused on sharing thoughts and feelings will be useful to many couples for this purpose.

Thus, helping individual partners and the couple access and heighten emotions can be a therapeutic challenge, but such sessions rarely get out of control. For many therapists, the greater challenge involves helping the couple contain excess emotions.

Managing or decreasing intense emotions

Whether the members of a couple broadly experience frequent, intense, and prolonged emotions in all areas of their lives or whether it is a more isolated experience based on relationship distress, many therapists find themselves challenged to contain or decrease anger and hostility both inside and outside of the therapy room, particularly early in treatment.

In-session interventions for managing or decreasing intense emotions

Many couple therapists remark that maintaining control of a session as negative emotions rise is one of the most difficult aspects of conducing couple therapy. Several strategies and principles can be useful to therapists in containing high levels of emotion.

INCREASING THERAPIST INFLUENCE OVER THE EMOTIONAL PROCESS

As a general principle, those couples who are *less* able to manage their own emotions are also *more* likely to benefit from increased structure and therapist guidance. Thus, therapists can adjust how directive they are in guiding the couple as a function of the couple's emotional level. Strategies to increase therapist influence include asking partners to talk directly to the therapist rather than to each other (see discussion below on "who talks to whom"), asking specific rather than open-ended questions (thus providing less opportunity for partners to drift onto unhelpful topics not focal to the current discussion), and explicitly instructing partners to resist interrupting each other. Giving the couple a focal point, such as notes on a whiteboard, can add further structure.

SLOWING THE PACE OF THE INTERACTION

Ingrained patterns of negative reciprocity can surface very rapidly. That is, one person might make a backhanded comment that upsets the partner before the therapist is aware of what happened. In order to disrupt such patterns of rapid negative reciprocity, the therapist can teach guidelines for sharing thoughts and feelings, aimed at helping the couple learn to prevent escalation (see Chapter 4). Initially, therapists might need to offer a great deal of guidance to help partners remain in the speaker and listener roles. Assuring that the interaction includes time for the listener to summarize what the speaker has said contributes to a slower pace, less emotion escalation, and avoidance of misunderstandings. If speaking directly to each other is too difficult for the partners, the therapist can ask each partner to speak directly to the therapist, while using the same principles (asking one partner to speak at a time, then asking the other partner to summarize, potentially with some modelling or scaffolding by the therapist).

USING A COGNITIVE, LESS EMOTIONAL THERAPEUTIC STYLE AND TONE

Therapist responses play a critical role in heightening, containing, or having the couple "pull out" of an intense interaction. As a general principle, a more cognitive, "intellectual" style, often combined with asking the couple to observe the process rather than discuss the content of the interaction, can lead to a reduction in the intensity of emotions in the moment. For example, when Eryka reported a recent argument to the therapist at the beginning of the session, her husband Shawn immediately responded in an angry tone, "Oh, I see where this is going; now you're going to make me look like an idiot again!" Before the couple could get into a back-and-forth volley and instead of asking each partner to say more about what the argument was about (i.e., focus on content, which would heighten emotions), the therapist responded, "This is interesting, isn't it? When you came into the session, you seemed calm. But I wonder if the two of you noticed that the pattern we've been discussing happened just now: One of you says something negative, and then the two of you get into a lightning-fast back-and-forth. Did you notice that just now?" Eryka replied, "Well, it happens so fast that often I don't even notice until it is too late!" Then, the therapist commented and asked the couple, "That really is a strong pattern, isn't it? Is this what it looks like at home as well?"

By focusing the couple on the process and promoting an observer perspective on their interaction pattern, the therapist effectively helped the couple to gain distance from the content they were discussing, "pulling them out" of their emotions in the moment. A more cognitive perspective might also include brief psychoeducation. In this instance, information could be offered about the process of negative reciprocity. In essence, if the partners are becoming too emotionally aroused, the therapist can steer them in a more cognitive direction. Conversely, if the couple is becoming too intellectual in addressing their concerns, the therapist can direct them toward their emotions.

FOCUSING ON THE PROCESS

Included in the point above is the distinction between discussing the content of an issue versus the interaction process. Any given couple therapy session typically includes both (a) helping couples deal with substantive issues they are struggling with (content) and (b) helping couples become more aware of their interaction patterns and individual contributions to maladaptive patterns (process). Typically, when couples present for therapy, most of their attention focuses on the content of their concerns (e.g., "You spend too much money") with little insight into the interaction process other than recognizing that communication is not going well. As a general principle, conversations about the content tend to be more emotionally evocative (e.g., "You are late every time we plan to go someplace; it drives me nuts!"). Thus, another strategy to contain excessive affect is to (re)focus the couple on a discussion of the interaction process, which the therapist steers. If couples develop adaptive patterns of interaction when negative emotions are high, often these interaction patterns can be employed regardless of specific areas of concern that arise in the future. Chapter 4 provides more detail on addressing interaction patterns.

FOCUSING ON LESS EMOTIONALLY INTENSE ISSUES

Several strategies can be employed to shift the focus to less intense issues with lower levels of emotion attached. For example, if a broad topic becomes too overwhelming for the couple, the therapist might guide them to focus on a particular aspect of the broader topic. If a sensitive topic seems too difficult for a couple to begin to discuss, the therapist might ask them to discuss *why* it is difficult for them to address this topic rather than discussing the content of the issue. For example, if a couple has never discussed their sexual difficulties and does not seem ready to open up about this sensitive area, a more manageable entry point might include having the partners share their concerns about discussing this topic with each other.

NORMALIZING EMOTIONS

Frequently, if one or both partners believe that their own or their partner's emotions are unreasonable, abnormal, or wrong, their own emotional reaction might be greatly intensified. Normalizing each partner's emotional experience by providing brief psychoeducation about emotions can help to lessen the level of distress about the other person's reaction.

VALIDATING EMOTIONS THAT A PARTNER CANNOT VALIDATE

For some individuals, feeling unheard, criticized, or invalidated leads to withdrawal; others become more distressed and express their perspective with increasing intensity. As a result, couples presenting for therapy with heightened emotional distress and ineffective communication often struggle to contain escalating emotions in the presence of frequent invalidation between the two partners. If the therapist is able to validate the emotional response of one person that the partner seems unable to validate due to their own reactions, emotional arousal can be decreased. This is not to suggest that the therapist should reinforce maladaptive and ineffective behaviours (such as yelling at one's partner) or take one person's side in a disagreement. Rather, therapists can work to "validate the valid, not the invalid" (Linehan, 1993) or, in other words, find the "kernel of truth" in each person's experience that can be more effectively addressed in the session. For example, one person might be so angry about a depressed partner's failure to fulfil parenting responsibilities that they cannot empathize with the depressed person's debilitating sense of being overwhelmed. However, if the therapist empathizes with both the sense of being overwhelmed by the depressed person, along with the anger of the partner because the child's needs are being neglected, at times it can allow the couple to join together around their shared concern for their child and problem-solve around their parenting roles. Although it is crucial that partners learn to provide this emotional validation for each other over the course of therapy, at times the therapist might serve this important role to move the session forward.

RELATING CURRENT EXPERIENCES TO BROADER THERAPEUTIC GOALS

In many instances, decreasing intense negative emotions during a session is an important treatment goal that is unlikely to be accomplished immediately. While it is important to contain destructive expression of emotions as quickly as possible, early sessions might still be difficult to manage. Relating the couple's unpleasant experience in the moment to broader therapeutic goals and to the stage of therapy can help the couple take a broader perspective and view the current distress as part of the continuing effort of therapy. For example, near the close of a very difficult session, a therapist might state, "This was a really tough session, wasn't it? I know you both were trying, but it was really difficult to stop things from escalating. We've said that one of the main things we need to work on is your communication, and we're still early in the process. So we'll keep focusing on it, and I have a couple of thoughts about what each of you might try to keep things calmer when discussing difficult issues in the future. Does that sound okay to you?"

Outside-of-session interventions for managing or decreasing intense emotions

Couples also must learn to contain strong negative emotions outside of the sessions when the therapist cannot intervene. Helping couples to improve their own self-monitoring of emotions early in therapy and increasingly turning the control of this process over to the couple during the sessions can facilitate generalization. For example, couples might use the communication skills for sharing thoughts and feelings outside of the session during a particularly distressing time, as they share what they are experiencing in that moment (without escalating to discuss related issues), provide reflective listening, and decide what to do next to help manage the emotions. Additionally, the following strategies can assist couples to address negative emotions outside of the session.

SCHEDULING TIMES TO DISCUSS EMOTIONS, RELATED THOUGHTS, AND PROBLEMS

For many distressed couples who frequently experience strong, protracted negative feelings about their relationship, it can be difficult to engage fully in other aspects of life that would otherwise be enjoyable. Often, arguments spark quickly at inopportune times or intrude into other activities, such as family gatherings. Scheduling regular opportunities for the couple to address individual or shared difficulties with each other can help "contain" negative feelings or rumination about the relationship. The knowledge that there is a designated time and place for the couple to share can free the two partners to focus their attention on other domains without ongoing lingering negative feelings or arguments.

HEALTHY COMPARTMENTALIZATION

Often, strong negative feelings about some domain of the relationship that is at the core of the couple's distress (e.g., parenting difficulties, infidelity) are not contained within that one domain. Instead, relationship difficulties tend to spread, and couples might begin to struggle in multiple domains. They begin to bicker and fight about minor issues, based on their overall level of distress and frustration ("How could I sit down and have a meal with you when you just told me yesterday that I am useless as a father!"). While such tendencies are understandable, they contribute to worsening distress and pose a challenge in therapy when working on difficulties that cannot be resolved immediately. Therefore, a therapist might teach the couple the principle of "healthy compartmentalization." That is, the couple learns to begin improving areas of the relationship that are amenable to short-term changes in order to stabilize daily life and the relationship, while they continue to work on the larger issues that will take time to resolve. In order to help the couple do so, therapists might acknowledge the severity of the distress and disruptions in the relationship and make explicit that enjoying a meal together does not imply that all difficulties are swept aside or that hurtful behaviours are forgiven. Healthy compartmentalization means focusing on the present moment and not allowing it to be dominated by other areas of concern. Given the strength of "sentiment override" in distressed couples, this practice has the potential to be a valuable resource for some individuals.

TIME OUT

Particularly early in therapy, many couples need strategies to disrupt escalating interactions when effective conflict resolution is no longer possible. Helping the couple problem-solve in the session to develop a "time-out" plan can be beneficial; typical components include: (a) some form of respectful signal/key statement that either partner can use to express that they need to take a break from the interaction to avoid further escalation; (b) a plan for how long a time out will last and what each partner will do during this time to de-escalate (e.g., engage in individual coping strategies to calm down); and (c) when and how they will resume the interaction or revisit the topic in a more adaptive fashion. It is important that such time-out strategies be agreed upon in a manner that feels respectful to both partners, so that neither person feels dismissed (e.g., "I've had it; I'm done talking with you until you get your act together!").

ALTERNATIVE MEANS OF SEEKING SUPPORT

In addition to strategies focused on the couple, some partners might also benefit from dealing with their emotions individually or seeking appropriate support from other individuals. Strategies might include, for example, journaling, self-care strategies, seeking social support from friends and family (with attention to boundaries and what both partners find acceptable to disclose to others), or seeking additional professional support from a therapist.

In addition to altering the experience and expression of specific emotions, it also is essential to address the interdependence of emotions that occurs between partners, including both decreasing and increasing emotional reactivity between partners.

Decreasing reactivity/responsiveness

Decreasing emotional reactivity between partners might be needed if negative reciprocity is a prominent issue for the couple, or one or both partners are excessively sensitive to the other person's emotional expression. Thus, even in healthy relationships, one partner might have high emotional empathy and experience the other person's distress. At times, this ability can be adaptive, but at other times it can heighten the emotional ambience in the relationship to an unhelpful level, resulting in emotional overinvolvement (Hooley, 2007). Therefore, for a variety of reasons, it is sometimes helpful to focus on how each partner responds to the other partner's emotions.

In-session interventions for decreasing reactivity

Many of the interventions used to contain heightened emotions will be useful in the current context as well. For example, slowing the pace of the conversation and increasing structure (e.g., with the use of guidelines for sharing thoughts and feelings), targeting cognitions that lead to hypersensitivity to the emotional expression of the other partner (e.g., "If he gets mad at me, that means he's going to leave me"), and psychoeducation (e.g., focusing on negative reciprocity and the importance of "exiting the negative loop") can be used to target excessive reactivity between partners. Such strategies might allow the therapist to decrease emotional reactivity in the moment; moreover, couples might need to develop better self-monitoring skills so they can perform this function on their own. Thus, therapists might prompt individuals to identify their current intensity of emotions and trace possible causes that precipitated a quick response from the other person (e.g., catastrophizing thoughts about the other partner's expression of frustration). Additionally, therapists might explore factors that contribute to heightened reactivity in one partner (e.g., difficulty tolerating anger due to past experiences of abuse) or teach distress tolerance skills to help partners stay engaged in emotional interactions without escalating (see Chapter 13). While the therapist strives to provide a dyadic perspective when addressing such issues, at times the focus is primarily on assisting one partner who struggles to avoid reacting quickly to the other person's emotional expression. This step might be preceded with acknowledgment from the therapist that often one person has a stronger and more reactive "emotion system" than the other, which requires more effort to manage.

OUTSIDE-OF-SESSION INTERVENTIONS FOR DECREASING REACTIVITY

As with other interventions discussed thus far, one goal of in-session interventions is for the couple to generalize and take charge of addressing emotions in their daily life. Strategies might focus on slowing the pace of interactions between partners (e.g., with the use of communication guidelines and practising self-monitoring of emotions in the moment). Outside-of-session interventions for containing negative emotions often apply to emotional reactivity as well, such as time-out strategies and scheduled times to discuss negative topics. Similarly, strategies focused on one or both partners as individuals can help them decrease their own vulnerability to responding quickly and strongly to their partner's emotional expressions. These strategies might include a focus on various forms of self-care to put oneself in a good position while interacting with the partner. Thus, it can be beneficial to help each person recognize what they need as an individual to be in an optimal state for difficult interactions with a partner (see, for example, DBT skills for reducing emotional vulnerability; Kirby & Baucom, 2007a; Linehan, 1993).

Heightening reactivity/responsiveness

Increasing reactivity might be needed for disengaged couples who experience little emotional closeness, or if one partner generally has minimized their emotions and is unresponsive to the other person. That is, increased reactivity can help increase the overall intensity of emotions because it sustains the emotional focus that is present and perhaps accelerates it as well.

In-session interventions for heightening reactivity

Many of the interventions described to heighten emotions will also be of assistance in increasing mutual reactivity and responsiveness (i.e., responsiveness to each other often will be easier if emotions are more intense and more clearly expressed). For example, using communication guidelines for sharing thoughts and feelings and emphasizing emotional expression can be helpful strategies to increase mutual emotional responsiveness. "Blocking the exits" might be used, if one partner seems to distract or avoid when the other partner is expressing emotions. The following interventions can be effective as well.

Making physical contact can increase emotional arousal within each person (see Chapter 11 for a brief discussion of working with the physical aspects of couple relationships). Furthermore, research on emotion coregulation suggests that close proximity, physical contact (e.g., holding hands), and eye contact can increase the bidirectional linkage of emotional and physiological responses between partners (Helm, Sbarra, & Ferrer, 2012; Sbarra & Hazan, 2008). During a session (as far as is comfortable and appropriate), therapists might ask the couple to hold hands or sit close while having a conversation with each other, or discuss possible ways to increase physical contact for the purpose of increased connection and responsiveness outside of the session.

In a related vein, Carson and colleagues (Carson, Carson, Gil, & Baucom, 2004, 2006) developed and evaluated a couple-based mindfulness intervention for relationship improvement. The intervention included a variety of exercises to help couples learn to attend to each other mindfully and/or focus on themselves as a couple, at times systematically including physical touch. The structure of this intervention can provide avoidant and withdrawn couples with a platform to reconnect and increase their responsiveness to each other's emotions.

In addition to focusing on the couple's physical proximity and contact, other activities can help to heighten emotional expression and responsiveness between partners. For example, gratitude exercises can be helpful, such as having partners take turns telling each other something about the other person that they are grateful for (Algoe & Zhaoyang, 2016). Additionally, exercises to increase empathic accuracy can be beneficial, such as having one partner express, in their own words, their understanding of how the other person is feeling.

Outside-of-session interventions for heightening reactivity

In addition to applying in-session strategies to couples' daily lives, therapists can work with couples to establish routines that provide a context for emotional exchanges. For example, a couple might decide on a daily check-in time (such as after the children are in bed) when the partners can focus on each other and share their experiences during the day. The couple might be encouraged to eliminate distractions by turning off telephones, computers, and televisions during these interactions. Additionally, couples might benefit from activities which allow them to experience shared emotions and which are interactive (e.g., having a date night that includes dinner in a quiet setting rather than going to a movie).

Stylistic and session-management strategies

The interventions described above are most effective with a variety of stylistic and session management strategies in mind. While these strategies are particularly important with regard to emotions, they are frequently beneficial when taken into account for behavioural and cognitive interventions as well (see Chapter 3 for a broader discussion).

Directing who talks to whom

Effective CBCT therapists are able to direct the in-session process in the service of therapeutic change by remaining alert not only to the type of intervention they want to employ but also to the type of tone and context they want to create. The added complexity of having two clients in the room can pose challenges for session management, and one major way of managing the session is by directing who speaks to whom at any given point in the session. If the therapist directs the partners to speak directly to each other, increased emotional intensity and reactivity often result. That is, especially early in therapy, couples who experience high levels of anger and hostility might be unable to communicate effectively about evocative topics without quickly escalating when talking to each other directly. On the other hand, partners who have generally been distant and disengaged might be able to experience more caring and warmth toward each other when they speak to each other directly about a positive topic.

If the therapist directs the partners to talk to the therapist rather than to each other, this approach increases the direct influence that the therapist has over the communication process. Generally, having one partner talk directly to the therapist will help to decrease or manage the intensity of emotions, given that the therapist is less likely to amplify negative emotions without intending to do so. However, in some instances, the therapist might also have an interaction directly with one or both partners to help them access minimized emotions. Often after one partner speaks to the therapist and can express their emotions in an adaptive fashion, the therapist then encourages that person to express those feelings to the partner: "Excellent, now express those feelings to her." Over time, the goal is to shift more interactions to being directly between the partners, as they hone their ability to express emotions effectively without therapist intervention.

Using the therapist's own emotions and style as a therapeutic tool

As discussed in Chapter 3, therapists themselves are powerful "social stimuli," who can influence the intensity and range of emotions experienced and expressed during a session. This tool can be used to affect the overall emotional tone of the session, or it might be directed toward the couple as a unit or to one of the individuals to help them access, heighten, or contain emotion in the moment. Thus, the interventions described above will be most effective if the therapists attend to their own style, body language, choice of words, and emotional expression in light of the goal at hand, which requires them to be aware of their own emotional reactions and to be able to modulate them as well.

Emphasizing interventions that target multiple domains of functioning

As discussed in previous chapters, interventions that target other domains along with emotion (e.g., cognitions along with emotion, or the overlap of emotions and cognitions) are likely to be the most impactful on the couple. Often, changes in emotion during a session are opportunities for learning and for creating cognitive shifts as well. For example, when they first practised the guidelines for sharing thoughts and feelings, Zack and Toby were able to shift away from their typical highly critical, angry interaction style to a softer, more vulnerable discussion of their feelings. Once the therapist had helped the couple shift the focus away from the anger, she chose to heighten the couple's sadness and fears about their future instead, which helped the partners feel closer to each other. After the conversation, the therapist inquired directly about any cognitive shifts, in order to enhance change in multiple domains. Both Zack and Toby noted that the conversation was very different from what would have typically occurred at home. In response, the therapist commented, "That is quite striking, isn't it? I remember just a few sessions ago when you told me that you had given up on trying to talk to each other because of all the anger, and yet now you are interacting in such a different and effective way. What do you make of this shift?" Toby responded, "Well, we'll have to see how this goes at home without you, but it makes me realize that there's a lot going on with Zack other than the anger that I usually see, and that makes me think that we might have a chance after all."

Concluding comments

Emotions are central to relationships, serving both as "magnets" during relationship development and the "glue" that helps maintain relationships over time. Over the course of a relationship, emotions become closely intertwined and interdependent between partners, which serves important functions for the emotional and physical health of both partners as well as shared experiences of closeness and security. However, such interdependence can also be a challenge for escalating negative emotions between the partners. Thus, a variety of difficulties can arise regarding the types of emotions experienced and expressed, their intensity, and the interdependence of emotions between partners. Emotions often are one of the "ultimate" targets in couple therapy via behavioural and cognitive interventions, with the goal of increasing positive feelings between the partners or helping them address negative emotions adaptively. A variety of strategies can be used to help couples express emotions more effectively. Many of these interventions are effective in their own right, but often they also are infused into interventions focused on cognitions and behaviours in order to optimize those interventions.

Main points

- Humans are social beings, and emotions are central to both the formation and maintenance of relationships. Close, lasting bonds have positive effects on mental and physical health, which have been partially credited to adaptive interpersonal emotion processes.
- Both the presence of distressing emotions and the absence of positive, joyful, loving emotions are hallmark features of relationship distress.
- Traditionally, cognitive-behavioural models have focused on emotions as a consequence of cognitions and behaviours; however, emotions impact cognitions and behaviours in many ways. In CBCT, there is an explicit focus on emotions per se.

- Important factors related to emotions in relationships include the type, intensity, and variability of emotions within each individual and the couple as a unit, as well as the responsiveness or reactivity between the two members of the couple. This chapter describes a variety of adaptive and maladaptive processes in each of these domains.
- Interventions focused on emotions are used (a) to facilitate effective session management even when the main goal of a session is on cognitions or behaviours, and (b) to address emotion-related difficulties when these issues need to be the main focus.
- In-session and out-of-session interventions are described for each of the domains (i.e., shifting the types of emotions, heightening or containing the intensity of emotions, and increasing or decreasing the interdependence of emotions between partners).
- Session management and stylistic strategies are relevant for all CBCT interventions but are particularly central for interventions on emotions. Consideration is given to the direction of communication in the room (who talks to whom), the therapist's own emotional expression and style, and interventions that concurrently target multiple domains.

Part III

The contextual framework of CBCT—attending to the individual, couple, and environment

This book is about individual and relationship well-being and distress. In order to understand an individual's functioning, it is crucial to explore the relationships that are a part of their day-to-day experience and the broader environment in which they operate. Likewise, no two couples are the same, and to understand how a specific couple functions as a unit, it is essential to understand the two individual partners who comprise the couple and how the couple interacts with the environment. This concept is not merely an intellectual perspective; a voluminous amount of data confirms that these three contextual domains are integrally interconnected. Given the dual emphasis of this book on treating relationship distress and individual psychopathology, this contextual perspective unites these two goals and provides a single framework to guide treatment.

Chapters 7–9 address the individual, the couple, and the environment separately, recognizing and discussing the reciprocal associations among them. Volumes have been written about each of these domains from multiple perspectives over many years. The current book focuses on the aspects of each domain that are most central within a CBCT framework and that can be of value in treatment. Most importantly, this contextual framework is integrated with the behavioural, cognitive, and emotional factors discussed in Chapters 4–6 to provide an overarching model for understanding and treating relationship distress and psychopathology. In some cases, one partner might have cognitions about all three contextual factors—one's partner, the couple as a unit, and how they should interact with their environment. For example, the way that a couple has divided roles and responsibilities might result in one person working endlessly and seeking help from family members in order to keep their head above water. Thus, decisions made by the couple impact both partners as individuals and how they relate to their environment, and then the environmental response will impact the two partners and their relationship. The reciprocal nature of these interactions is ongoing.

Chapter 7

The individual

No two relationships are the same because each includes two unique individuals with their own learning histories, personalities, values, needs, and styles. As discussed in Chapter 2, a healthy, thriving relationship is one in which both partners are valued as individuals, and the relationship contributes to each partner's personal growth and well-being. For most people, it feels wonderful to be affirmed by a partner and either explicitly or implicitly receive the message that "I think you're a great person; I'm so lucky to have you in my life!" When life goes well, both the couple and the two partners thrive simultaneously. Thus, this chapter is focused on understanding how individual factors impact relationship functioning and how the relationship influences individual well-being. When couples struggle to accommodate these individual differences, CBCT addresses the interplay between individual and relationship functioning, the focus of the latter part of this chapter.

Negotiating individuals' motives, needs, and personality

Every individual has their own personal characteristics that help to define who they are. A variety of terms is used in describing these unique characteristics of the person, such as personality, personal style, character, and other labels. In this book, we use the term "personality" to refer to the enduring dispositions that involve an individual's tendency to behave, think, and feel in consistent ways across time and in various situations (Allport, 1937). In part, these enduring dispositions arise from efforts to meet important needs or motives. As described in Chapter 2, a motive is defined as a "learned, affectively charged anticipatory state aroused by various cues" (McClelland, 1987, p. 132). That is, people value certain types of interactions with specific people or particular experiences, and they seek out those opportunities that they find to be rewarding. Each individual does this in their own way, perhaps with an outgoing, cheerful style or perhaps with more hesitancy and in a low-key manner. What becomes complicated in committed relationships is that each person often includes the other partner in this process, and the partner responds with their own style as well, attempting to meet their needs at the same time. When both partners experience that their needs are met to a large degree and that their partner finds their personal style to be appealing, both partners are likely to feel satisfied as individuals. If the couple embraces the uniqueness of each person in a way that also allows the couple to meet the demands of daily life, the relationship is likely to thrive as well. Yet, meeting the needs of two people and accomplishing various daily tasks and long-term goals is not simple, and many couples struggle in their efforts. Indeed, although they might not label their discontent in this way, a primary source of relationship conflict often involves one or both partners experiencing that their needs are being disregarded or that their personality is being criticized: "I think you really don't like who I am or care about what I want in life."

In considering each individual's uniqueness, a number of issues need to be taken into account. Rather than being present or absent, various needs and personality characteristics exist on a continuum from very low to very high (e.g., a need for a great deal of intimacy versus a need for a moderate amount of intimacy; a person who is somewhat agreeable versus very agreeable). Also, the strength of one motive or personality characteristic does not dictate the strength of another (e.g., a person can simultaneously have a strong need for intimacy alongside a strong need for autonomy). Thus, numerous needs and traits at various strengths and combinations exist within each individual, which then must be accommodated within the relationship. Furthermore, the strength of needs and a person's individual style can change over time based on the developmental stage of the individual or relationship, as well as in response to changing environmental contexts. For example, after the onset of a serious illness, one or both partners might find that their need for achievement in a professional realm has decreased dramatically as they attempt to cope with this new challenge, which may more generally change their perspective on what is important in life. Likewise, how outgoing a person is might vary across time, "You might not believe it, but I used to be a very quiet, shy person. I've just become more comfortable in my own skin over time, so now I say and do what I want." Additionally, there is no inherently right or wrong, healthy or unhealthy strength of any of these needs and traits, and many combinations of need and personality style can serve the couple well. Of note, while some research suggests that similarities between partners' personality styles can be beneficial, overall evidence for this conclusion is weak and inconsistent (Weidmann, Ledermann, & Grob, 2016). In other words, the degree to which partners are similar is not inherently an asset or liability for the relationship; how they handle these similarities and differences is likely to be much more important.

Motives or needs

Two primary categories of motives are particularly relevant for relationship functioning: communal motives (those primarily oriented to relating to others) and individual motives (those oriented toward the person prospering as an individual). Healthy relationships ideally help each individual thrive by helping each partner to have their most important needs met, either within the relationship or by providing a context in which individual need fulfilment can occur individually or in relation to the environment, including other people.

Communal motives

Humans are social creatures, and they are motived to interact and be in relationships with others. As discussed in Chapter 1, successful intimate relationships appear to be one of the most important aspects of many adults' lives. In discussing the variety of ways that adults attempt to develop and maintain these relationships, Epstein and Baucom (2002) highlight four key communal motives relevant to relationship functioning based on what they want from those relationships: affiliation, intimacy, altruism, and succorance. *Affiliation* refers to the need to experience togetherness with others. A person with strong affiliation needs has a desire to be a part of a couple and/or group and wants to be with others a great deal of the time. If partners differ strongly regarding this motive and they have not been able to navigate this difference well, one person can feel isolated when affiliation needs are not met, while the other person can feel pulled into interactions with others that feel unfulfilling or exhausting ("Do we really have to get together with your cousins on Saturday evening? I would much rather stay at home and relax"). Difficulties also can arise when partners are similar (e.g., affiliating with others at the expense of spending time needed to address individual goals) or when one partner attempts to meet their needs in destructive ways (e.g., one person pursues a social life that excludes their partner).

Intimacy refers to the need for closeness within a relationship. When each person experiences that they are close and connected with their partner, they typically are secure and at peace. Yet, this picture can be complicated because individuals vary in how much closeness they desire along with the types of activities that fulfil their need for intimacy, such as having deep conversations, engaging in sex or other acts of affection, or sharing meaningful activities with their partner. Although some might view a need for affiliation and intimacy as identical, there is a notable difference. It is quite possible for someone to have a strong need for affiliation and to desire spending time with their partner, but not necessarily to be open and close to their partner (i.e., experience a high need for affiliation but low need for intimacy). This person might feel fulfilled, for example, when spending time in the same room with their partner without much interaction. For someone who greatly values both affiliation and intimacy, this dynamic can be confusing: "If you loved me, you'd want to be as close to me as possible. Something is wrong." To the degree that partners differ on the dimension of intimacy, one partner might feel suffocated while the other feels rejected as they attempt to navigate this difference. This difference can also be the basis for a demand-withdraw pattern of interaction in which the person wanting more intimacy pulls for greater closeness from the partner, and the partner withdraws or pushes the person away in an attempt to keep a comfortable level of closeness (Christensen, Eldridge, Catta-Preta, Lim, & Santagata, 2006). On the other hand, if both partners have a high need for intimacy, they might focus on their relationship to the exclusion of building relationships with others, or if they have a low need for intimacy, they might neglect important relationship-building activities, such as sex and affection.

While affiliation and intimacy involve the couple as a unit, altruism and succorance focus more on how one person takes care of and is taken care of by the other partner. *Altruism* refers to a sincere desire to be responsive to another individual, to meet their needs and bring them happiness. For many individuals, being altruistic to their partner is a source of pleasure: "Seeing you happy makes me happy, and it is wonderful to know that I can give that to you." However, if the other partner values self-sufficiency or does not want people "to make a fuss over me," that person might not want the other to "take care" of them or might not express appreciation when the other person goes out of their way to be helpful. In such instances, an altruistic partner can feel deprived of the joy of giving. Other individuals, even if not "selfish," are less motivated by altruism. They simply do not experience as much satisfaction from being responsive to their partner's needs and, therefore, are not attuned to looking for opportunities to do so. As a result, the relationship can start to feel imbalanced if one person is highly attentive to the other but the other person does not reciprocate.

Complementary to altruism, *succorance* involves a desire to feel cared for and attended to by another person, often one's partner. A person with a moderate to high need for succorance experiences pleasure or satisfaction when their partner engages in caring acts toward them (e.g., providing care during times of illness). Although this motive, as with any of the other motives, can be at an extreme or maladaptive level of "neediness," it also can be adaptive, especially when one is struggling or is overwhelmed by life's demands. Knowing that another person is "in your corner" can result in a strong sense of feeling supported, an awareness that one does not have to navigate life on one's own, and an overall sense of security within the relationship. Coming home to a cup of tea and a partner's smile might be just what is needed after a stressful day at work. Similarly, being celebrated or championed by one's partner when something goes well also can be seen as a way of demonstrating care and affirmation. As noted above, difficulties often arise when there is not a good match between partners' needs for altruism and succorance.

Individually oriented motives

Unlike communal needs, individually oriented needs involve experiencing oneself as a separate and effective entity, even while being a part of a couple. Individuals want to feel good about themselves as a person, and different motives contribute to that sense of being the "kind of person I want to be." There are three primary individually oriented motives that contribute to individual well-being and that are crucial to consider when trying to optimize relationship functioning. As introduced in Chapter 2 and discussed in Epstein and Baucom (2002), these needs are autonomy, power/control, and achievement.

Autonomy refers to the desire to operate independently in some way, separate from others including one's partner (e.g., the desire to engage in activities on one's own or complete tasks without the partner's involvement). If time is extremely limited, an individual might find it difficult to fulfil this motive, particularly if they also have a strong desire for affiliation and/or intimacy. Additionally, a couple can struggle if one person needs a great deal of autonomy and the other does not, often resulting in the latter partner feeling unloved or unwanted. Alternatively, if both partners have a strong need for autonomy, they might spend a great deal of time engaged in individual pursuits and run the risk of feeling distant from each other over time. On the other hand, both partners might have little need for autonomy, resulting in spending most of their time with each other. Such couples can start to feel enmeshed or become distanced from friends and relatives as they spend most of their time with each other. Despite these potential challenges, needs for autonomy and intimacy need not be viewed as incompatible. Indeed, the most satisfied couples in one study were those who reported that their partners contributed to both a sense of intimacy and autonomy (Rankin-Esquer, Burnett, Baucom, & Epstein, 1997). What appears to be important is that couples find ways to move flexibly back and forth between feeling close as a unit and functioning autonomously as two separate individuals (e.g., being autonomous from each other in their professional lives but coming home and feeling close as a couple).

Another individually oriented motive is the need for *control*; that is, the need to experience a sense of agency and the ability to help create a preferred environment for oneself and others. Such a sense of control is important in optimizing what is potentially good and altering what is unjust, maladaptive, or unrewarding. As discussed in Chapter 11, a lack of control can be a major basis for people becoming depressed. Yet, partners often vary regarding the strength of their need for control and the ways in which they attempt to meet that need. Some individuals engage in planning and attending to detail, as described below. Other individuals might be much more comfortable "playing it by ear" with the confidence that they can address whatever evolves. Navigating these two approaches can be difficult for a couple. In addition, how one attempts to meet a need for control also can be maladaptive. For example, if one individual attempts to gain control by taking away the other partner's control (e.g., telling the other person what to do frequently), the outcome can be that the first partner is experienced as "controlling." However, many individuals find healthy, adaptive ways to experience a sense of control in their lives without impinging on their partner's well-being.

Finally, individuals vary in their motive for *achievement*, which refers to a sense of accomplishment, recognition, or competence. Most individuals delight in experiencing some sense of mastery and accomplishment in domains that are important to them. Having a partner who rejoices in one's accomplishments and encourages them can help a person feel quite supported and affirmed: "I feel good about myself, and it is clear that you feel good about me as well. Thank you for supporting me in this endeavour." At the same time, achievement does not come without a cost. Regardless of the domain (e.g., work, school, a hobby, caring for one's home), high levels of achievement typically require a great deal of time, energy, and focus. The challenge involves determining how to pursue such achievement while balancing other needs at the same time. It might be difficult, for example, to balance a high need for achievement with a high need for intimacy, both within and across partners. Likewise, differences in the need for achievement between partners can be complicated for couples to manage, leading to comments such as, "It seems like you're really married to your work. Why am I always second priority?" Similarly, a person who is achievement-oriented can start to lose respect for or be less attracted to a partner who is much less ambitious.

Navigating needs and motives

Many couples are successful at meeting the needs of both partners and doing so in a way that also facilitates a thriving relationship. Conversely, there are numerous ways in which couples might have difficulties negotiating partners' needs. These difficulties can result from (a) differences between the two partners, (b) conflicting needs within one individual (e.g., a strong need for achievement interfering with a strong need for intimacy), (c) similarities between the two partners which skews the relationship, and/or (d) maladaptive strategies for meeting one's needs. Poorly negotiated differences between partners or unmet needs can lead to heated discussions in which each person attempts to convince the other to adopt their approach, presents the other person's position as extreme and unreasonable, or acts in ways to meet their own needs at the expense of the partner's. In addition, difficulties can arise when one individual experiences problems balancing their own motives and desires, often due to restricted time or energy. For example, an individual might value both autonomy and affiliation, desiring time to spend alone as well as with others. However, competing demands can make it difficult to achieve both goals, and the individual might resent giving up alone time in order to spend time with the partner, children, extended family, and friends.

Relationship difficulties result not only from conflicting needs within one person or differences between the two partners but also might develop when the partners are similar on some notable dimension. Such similarities between partners sometimes result in important aspects of life being inadequately addressed. For example, if both partners prioritize having fun, they might have plenty of quality time together but neglect the pragmatics of life, such as performing household chores or paying their bills. Furthermore, complications can arise when an important need is met in ways that are detrimental to the relationship. For example, if a partner who desires more closeness than the other person turns to someone else to meet their need for intimacy, that partner might violate the couple's boundaries, focus undue energy on the outside individual, or initiate an affair with that person. Thus, negotiating individual needs and styles can be challenging for couples in many ways. As mentioned below, many of the interventions described in Chapters 4–6 can be employed to address these difficulties when they surface.

Personality and other individual factors

In addition to partners' needs, there is a wide variety of other individual factors that can influence relationship functioning, contributing either to relationship satisfaction or to conflict and difficulties if couples have not found a way to navigate them adaptively. Because it is not feasible to discuss all such individual factors, the current focus is on dimensions that often contribute to relationship distress in couples presenting for therapy (see Winterheld and Simpson, 2018, for an in-depth discussion of personality in close relationships).

One such dimension involves a *task versus pleasure* orientation to life. Some individuals have a strong desire to complete tasks prior to engaging in play, while others prefer to orient their time toward leisure activities, incorporating tasks as needed. Although both perspectives can be adaptive, differences in this dimension can lead to an array of arguments, such as how to spend time on the weekends and whether certain tasks are important to complete at all. Similarities across partners also can become problematic as two highly task-oriented individuals miss opportunities for joy, pleasure, and connection, while two highly pleasure-oriented individuals might neglect important responsibilities, such as paying bills or cleaning the house.

Beyond a general orientation to tasks versus pleasure, individuals vary in how conscientious they are when approaching tasks and responsibilities. Conscientiousness includes qualities such as being organized, planful, reliable, and efficient (McCrae & John, 1992). Higher levels of conscientiousness, in general, are associated with higher relationship satisfaction for both partners (Dyrenforth, Kashy, Donnellan, & Lucas, 2010; Weidmann et al., 2016). Even so, at times individuals might perceive partners high in conscientiousness as being rigid, controlling, or stifling of personal creativity.

In terms of fun and pleasure, individuals also can differ in the degree to which they prefer *spontaneity versus careful planning*, and *novelty versus sameness*. Some individuals prefer "seizing the moment," spontaneously engaging in intimacy or taking an unplanned day trip. Other individuals might prefer planning when and how to engage in these activities ("What hotel will we stay in? What's our budget?"). Their view often is that careful planning maximizes the enjoyment of the adventure, and not knowing what to anticipate feels aversive. However, for the more spontaneous individual, planning at this level of detail diminishes the sense of adventure. Even if two individuals both enjoy spontaneity, they might differ in the degree to which they like to engage in novel activities ("Let's try skydiving!") versus more known activities ("I loved the restaurant we went to last week; let's go again!"). A person who has a strong desire for novelty might find that they are frequently coaxing or urging the other to try something new, often without success. A person who prefers familiarity can experience frequent change and novelty as unsettling. As with many individual differences, these personality traits might be part of what attracted the partners to each other initially ("She was so spontaneous and got me to try lots of new things"; "He keeps me grounded and much more organized"), although these same traits might be experienced much more negatively as the couple continually confronts these differences.

Another dimension that can greatly influence relationship functioning is the degree to which partners are "*agreeable*," meaning tending to be warm, kind, sympathetic, forgiving, and appreciative (McCrae & John, 1992). Unsurprisingly, in general both partners tend to be more satisfied in their relationship to the degree that they and/or their partners are perceived as agreeable (Dyrenforth et al., 2010; Weidmann et al., 2016). Indeed, the quality of agreeableness is associated with a variety of positive behaviours, such as greater perspective-taking as well as more positive interpersonal behaviours in the context of conflict resolution (Vater & Schröder-Abé, 2015). Two partners who are high in agreeableness often can function quite well in the absence of significant stressors. However, high agreeableness in both partners can be difficult in the context of major stressors because such couples can be somewhat conflict avoidant. Consistent with the notion that partners might be "nice" at the expense of the relationship, subgroups of women were observed within the context of relationship education programmes for nondistressed couples in the United States and Germany, who appeared to be extremely positive while interacting with their partners to discuss relationship concerns. This pattern of being extremely positive while minimizing concerns actually predicted relationship distress in subsequent years (D. H. Baucom et al., 2006; Schilling et al., 2003). On the other hand, differences in this dimension can lead to perceptions of partners as being either rude or thoughtless.

Finally, although individuals' thoughts and feelings can vary across situations, everyone also has a general tendency to think and feel in certain consistent ways. As described in Chapter 2, *positive affectivity* and *negative affectivity* (also known as neuroticism) are terms used to describe a dispositional tendency toward negative or positive emotions. That is, some people seem to experience negative emotions frequently and without strong provocation whereas other people tend to be happier and more upbeat on an ongoing basis, regardless of the current circumstance. It is important to note that negative affectivity does not refer to psychopathology but rather a dimension on which all individuals exist at some level. Particularly high levels of negative affectivity tend to be associated with lower dyadic adjustment (Daspe, Sabourin, Péloquin, Lussier, & Wright, 2013) and with more negative communication behaviours such as yelling, criticizing, and expressing blame (Caughlin, Huston, & Houts, 2000; McNulty, 2008; Vater & Schröder-Abé, 2015). On the other hand, very low levels of negative affectivity can result in a lack of attention to existing problems; as noted in Chapter 6, negative emotions can serve as a cue that problems need to be addressed.

More generally, people vary in the extent to which they live in an "affective world," meaning how much they experience emotion and put effort into understanding and expressing emotional content. Those who frequently feel and express emotions can overwhelm and exhaust those who naturally experience or express fewer or less intense emotions. On the other hand, more emotional individuals might find it difficult to understand or connect with their less emotional partner or experience a lack of emotional empathy from their partner.

Summary

Regardless of the extent to which two partners are similar or different from each other, a major task for couples is to meet the needs of both persons, affirming and hopefully celebrating each person as a valued individual with unique strengths and a distinctive personality. This emphasis on meeting the needs of each individual must be considered while also assuring that the couple as a unit is functioning well and the couple is operating effectively within their environment. For a variety of reasons, many couples struggle when attempting to meet these simultaneous goals. The section that follows highlights ways to assist the couple when an individual's well-being is not being optimized within the relationship or when conflicting needs or personality traits interfere with couple functioning.

Intervention

The interventions discussed below have already been described in Chapters 4–6, and there are no "new" intervention techniques for individual differences per se. Rather, the goal is to apply the interventions described earlier in a manner that is appropriate to the couple based on the individual factors described above.

Goals pertaining to individual factors

When helping couples address individual factors or differences, therapists consider several overarching goals. These goals are to:

- Normalize the idea of individual differences between partners and assist the couple in conceptualizing difficulties from a dyadic perspective.
- Assist the couple in increasing their awareness of both their own and their partners' needs and personal styles.
- Help to "depathologize" each partner (to the degree appropriate) and increase empathy that each person has for the other partner and for themselves.
- Determine whether behaviour changes might be necessary.
- Help couples make decisions regarding behavioural shifts that will better accommodate both partners' needs and styles and ensure that ways of meeting needs are constructive.
- If all efforts at behavioural changes to better accommodate individual differences have failed, help the couple determine whether they can accept the difference and "make it work" without needs being fully met, or whether their differences are a "deal breaker" for the relationship.

The discussion below includes ways in which a therapist can address these goals.

Dyadic conceptualization and the role of psychoeducation

At the outset of treatment, partners rarely have thought of their conflicts in terms of unmet needs or difficulty negotiating needs and styles in the way described above. Rather, they often view difficulties as being the result of a problematic partner and identify goals related to changing their partner (e.g., "He's so needy. He needs to learn to stand on his own two feet, and then we'd be fine!"). A crucial first step in assisting partners in this domain is to provide psychoeducation and feedback in a way that helps the couple reframe their concerns in a manner that can lead to constructive treatment goals (i.e., facilitate a dyadic conceptualization of issues). This discussion can include any or all of the relevant theory and research discussed above, provided it is presented in a way that highlights the couple's concerns as examples. The goal is to provide information that sets the stage for later work and begins to normalize partners' differences. Although this discussion will typically begin during the assessment feedback and treatment planning phase, psychoeducation will likely be interwoven into treatment as indicated. Psychoeducation might be included in sessions focused directly on addressing individual factors, as well as during sessions focused on other topics where individual differences appear to play a role.

For example, a therapist was helping Linda and Matthew negotiate a trip to Matthew's parents' home, and the couple began to argue about whether it was okay for Linda to visit some museums on her own, which she really wanted to do. Matthew viewed this idea as rude and concluded that Linda did not care for his family. In this situation, the therapist referred back to psychoeducation provided earlier in treatment and noted, "We discussed earlier in treatment how the two of you differ in how much 'alone time' you need to rejuvenate, and I'm wondering if that difference is playing out here. Is it possible that these differences are leading to the argument you are having now?" In response, Linda clarified that although she enjoyed Matthew's family, a visit with any larger group of people tended to be quite exhausting for her, and a chance to refuel on her own would allow her to be more present when around the family. Linda's comment ultimately changed Matthew's understanding of, or attributions for, her preference for alone time and allowed the couple to reframe the issue in terms of individual differences, prompting improved decision-making. Thus, while treatment often includes one or more sessions focused directly on intervening around individual differences (see below), it is also important to keep individual needs and styles in mind when addressing other issues in treatment.

Increasing awareness of motives and styles

At the point in treatment in which individual needs and personality styles are being considered, often therapists will have already taught the skills for sharing thoughts and feelings (see Chapter 4). These skills can be used to address a wide variety of topics, including individual differences. For example, after providing feedback and psychoeducation related to needs, a therapist might spend a session facilitating a conversation focused on sharing thoughts and feelings about questions such as the strength of various needs for each partner, how they prefer for their needs to be met, what needs they feel are or are not currently being met, etc. The goal of this discussion is for each partner to reflect on their own needs and styles (e.g., needs regarding intimacy and what makes a partner feel close) and to learn more about their partner's needs, while discussing these issues in a constructive and supportive manner.

Depathologizing differences and increasing empathy

At times, differences in personality styles and motives lead partners to have negative thoughts and feelings about each other or the relationship that hinder the couple from moving forward. Partners often "pathologize" their partner (i.e., hold negative assumptions about their partner and make global, stable, negative attributions about their behaviour) when their needs and personality styles conflict. For example, a laid-back partner might be considered *lazy*, an organized partner is labelled as *controlling*, and one with a high need for succorance is regarded as *needy*. Additionally, when someone's needs are not being met, that person might make an attribution such as, "My partner is/is not doing this because they do not love me or value our relationship," "There's something wrong with them," or "They're selfish." Also, when one does not perceive one's own needs as being considered or addressed, or when one's own personal style is criticized, an individual can experience strong negative emotions such as hurt, anger, loneliness, resentment, and disappointment. Over time, negative beliefs and emotions related to individual differences can become more extreme as relationship distress increases and the couple's capacity to find solutions jointly erodes.

In the context of these strong negative cognitions and emotions, considering behavioural changes can be difficult for both partners. In this case an important step in addressing individual differences includes assisting partners in shifting their attributions and assumptions (i.e., to "depathologize") and increasing empathy regarding the partner's personality and needs. Psychoeducation and sharing thoughts and feelings, as described above, can serve an important role in increasing understanding and empathy and in shifting cognitions. However, at times, additional cognitive interventions might need to be incorporated into treatment to address some of the cognitions described above more directly.

For example, while discussing the couple's transition from work to home life at the end of the day, Malek protested, "I know you are just asking me to come home straight from work to control me; you love to keep me under your thumb!" The therapist responded by asking Malek to rephrase this statement, expressing his opinion subjectively and including his emotions while not "mind reading" why Amber behaved in the way that she did. After several attempts, Malek was able to say, "Amber, when you ask me to come home straight from work, I feel resentful and like I have little control over my own time." Next, thinking that guided discovery might be helpful, the therapist turned to Amber and asked, "It sounds like Malek believes that the reason you want him to come straight home after work is because you want to control him. Can you let him know why it is important to you that he comes home straight from work?" Amber responded, "It's because I'm hoping you'll have time with the children before bedtime; they feel so let down when they do not get to see you." After some additional exploration and discussion, Malek no longer viewed Amber's request as being related to control and had a better understanding of her perspective. Of note, this does not necessarily mean that Malek and Amber would later decide on a solution in which Malek comes home straight from work; rather, by addressing cognitions and increasing empathy, the couple is in a better position to be open and flexible in decision-making.

In addition to attributions that one partner might make for the other partner's behaviour related to personality factors, standards that do not take individual differences into account also can create difficulties for the couple. Each partner might have empathy for the other person while also still wanting the partner to adopt more of their own style, convinced that their personal approach is the road to personal and relationship fulfilment. Strategies for intervening when a difference in relationship standards is interfering with needed behavioural changes are discussed in Chapter 5 and can be an important preparatory step for behaviour change to address individual difference factors. For example, the standard that "the family and the children come first" can seem quite appropriate and adaptive. Yet, such a standard can be complicated to carry out when one partner has high achievement needs and is in the early stages of developing a career. If the negotiation is not handled carefully, the partner with high needs for achievement can experience a great deal of internal conflict as well as arguments with a partner who pushes for more family time at the expense of professional development. Thus, discussions regarding various standards for how to conduct the relationship must include a consideration of the two partners and what each person needs in order to be fulfilled individually as well.

Deciding whether behaviour change is indicated

Changes in cognitions and/or emotions can be a valued outcome in treatment, and, at times, no behavioural changes are needed. For example, Declan and Maeve both preferred to engage in sex approximately 1–2 per month and often favoured having their needs for intimacy met in other ways (e.g., deep conversations). At the outset of treatment, Maeve stated that she would like to engage in sex more frequently and would like Declan to initiate more often. In discussing their desires for intimacy, Maeve noted that the reason she requested sex more often was because of her belief that "men who care about their partners want sex very often." She concluded that Declan's low frequency of initiation must be reflective of him not being attracted to her. Maeve's feelings of rejection were what motivated her to ask for more sex rather than her own desire for increased sexual intimacy.

Through sharing thoughts and feelings and guided discovery, Declan explained that he was very attracted to Maeve but was a person who simply desired a lower frequency of sexual intimacy. Additionally, the therapist provided psychoeducation about the frequency with which couples tend to engage in sex, noting that there is a wide variety of frequencies of sexual intimacy that seem adaptive. Thus, the combination of sharing thoughts and feelings, guided discovery, and psychoeducation shifted Maeve's assumptions about sexual relationships in general and her attributions about Declan, and she then felt comfortable with the level of sexual intimacy between herself and Declan. Therefore, no behavioural changes were needed.

In many instances, however, gaining greater understanding and empathy toward one's partner are not enough, and behavioural changes are necessary. For example, Sanjay had a high need for altruism, and Ethan had a high need for succorance and relished being taken care of. In the past, this combination of needs worked well for the couple, with Sanjay engaging in many supportive acts toward Ethan including helping him in unexpected ways. However, over time, Sanjay began to feel underappreciated and exhausted, and his own needs to be taken care of had gone unmet. At the same time, Ethan experienced the onset of depression in the context of losing his job, and his self-confidence and energy drastically decreased. At the outset of treatment, Sanjay noted that he had started to think of Ethan as being inconsiderate as well as overly dependent on him. Ethan noted that he thought of himself as a "loser" who was incapable of doing anything meaningful with his life. Helping Sanjay and Ethan shift their interactions such that Ethan was giving more to Sanjay (e.g., cooking dinner, taking on some of Sanjay's household tasks, giving a massage) had multiple benefits. Sanjay began to feel more appreciated and supported as well as less exhausted. Ethan's sense of self-efficacy and self-esteem increased as he experienced that he had much to give, and his depressed mood decreased. Additionally, both partners reported higher relationship satisfaction when there was more balanced giving and support between them. This example highlights that individual differences between partners can gradually become more extreme over time and become problematic, particularly when changing circumstances pose additional challenges. In this case, helping both partners change their behaviours without asking them to become different people was central to improving their relationship.

The above examples demonstrate that when considering individual differences, behavioural changes are sometimes needed, while at other times, increasing understanding and empathy might be sufficient. Thus, a crucial task for the couple and the therapist is to discuss together what they have learned from their discussions of individual needs and styles, and then to decide together what, if any, behavioural changes are indicated. If the presence or lack of a behaviour from one partner is distressing primarily because of what it means to the other person, a more detailed understanding of the behaviour (and subsequent shift in cognitions) might be needed. However, when the behavioural excess or absence is important because the other partner does or does not like the behaviour per se, then behaviour change often is appropriate.

Making behavioural changes

If the couple has decided that behavioural change is important in areas that involve needs or personality-related issues for one or both partners, the next step is to engage in decision-making conversations aimed at deciding what changes are needed and how those changes will be accomplished. Some changes are easy to make over the short term but are hard to sustain as the couple's focus on the issue diminishes; essentially, each person reverts back to their preferred style which requires little effort to sustain. Thus, it is important for couples to address what they can do to sustain changes over time when there is less therapeutic focus on the issue.

The goal of these decision-making conversations is to find a way to honour both partners' styles, personalities, and central motives. At times, that goal might be attained by "meeting in the middle" or agreeing on a direct compromise. For example, a couple might agree to adopt a careful planning approach during the work week but create a more spontaneous, "take-life-as it-comes" approach on the weekends. However, sometimes direct compromises are neither possible nor particularly satisfying for either partner. Additionally, there might be certain domains in which one partner cares a great deal more about an issue than the other person; thus a "meet-in-the-middle" approach would likely not satisfy the former partner or be important to the latter partner. For example, Isabella had a high need for achievement and as part of this need, she preferred a clean house and wanted her children to attend "top-notch" schools. Mateo did not care about how the house looked, and he believed that the children would be fine regardless of what school they attended. In this case, keeping the house "moderately clean" and signing the children up for a "middle-of-the-road" school might be quite dissatisfying for Isabella, and Mateo might still not care much one way or the other. One outcome might be for Mateo to agree to Isabella's desires in this domain, knowing that he is satisfying her need for achievement. Likewise, in some other domain that is more important to Mateo than to Isabella, Isabella might agree to Mateo's preferences. In essence, the couple maintains respect for both partners' needs across time and domains, rather than attempting to make each domain balanced as they reach decisions, a form of long-term reciprocity.

Deciding whether to remain with one's partner

All the above interventions are intended to maximize a couple's understanding and empathizing with one another and to ensure that the relationship is contributing to the growth and well-being of both partners. These interventions might stretch and shape each partner's behaviour in ways that increase the couple's satisfaction in the relationship; yet, there are limits to how much partners can and will change for the well-being of the other person or the relationship. No relationships meet all needs for each partner; such standards would be viewed as unrealistic. However, there are instances when even after significant effort in therapy, one or both partners start to consider whether the two of them are "just too different" to make the relationship satisfying. As Robin noted:

> Everything seems like such an effort. We both really love each other, which makes this incredibly sad, but it doesn't seem like we're the right people for each other. I think Logan could be so much happier if he had someone who wasn't always asking him to change who he is. I hate doing that, but he doesn't seem to be able to meet my needs.

When such sentiment from one or both partners appears to be well-considered and based on important, central needs that are difficult to accommodate within the relationship, then a careful discussion about whether to continue the relationship is appropriate.

On the other hand, addressing individual needs and personality styles can contribute to personal growth by improving one's understanding of oneself. Furthermore, many couples make considerable effort in treatment and either make behavioural changes or alter important cognitions that allow them to experience the other person and their relationship in a more rewarding manner. Indeed, many couples find that after working to address individual factors, they can not only survive but thrive in a way that both partners experience as rewarding and worthy of continued investment.

Main points

- All individuals have personal needs/motives and personality styles that affect their behaviour, regardless of whether they are in a relationship.
- Needs/motives exist within two broad domains: communal motives, which refer to relationally oriented motives (e.g., intimacy) and individual motives, which are concerned with prospering as an individual (e.g., achievement).
- Various combinations of partners' needs and styles can be handled effectively within relationships, but difficulties can result from (a) differences between the two partners, (b) need conflicts within one individual, (c) similarities between the two partners, and (d) maladaptive strategies for meeting one's needs.
- The goals of treatment might include (a) assisting the couple to conceptualize their difficulties dyadically, (b) helping each partner increase awareness of their own and their partner's needs and styles, (c) "depathologizing" and increasing empathy, (d) deciding whether behaviour change is necessary, (e) making behavioural changes if appropriate, and (f) deciding whether to remain in the relationship given the changes that were or were not made.
- No new interventions are presented in this chapter; rather, interventions already presented in Chapters 4–6 are utilized as a way of addressing this contextual domain.

Chapter 8

The couple

When partners commit to one another, they are choosing to become something greater than themselves as two individuals. They are becoming a unit, which can take many different forms and serve a variety of purposes. They also are becoming a system, a whole that is greater than the sum of its parts. That is, the two partners influence each other while working toward common goals that help them operate well as a couple, while also meeting individual needs. But what is necessary to become a couple "system"[1] with the capacity to be fulfilling in the present as well as successful over time, as the two partners age and experience new challenges and opportunities? In this chapter, we discuss the essentials of an effective system pertinent to long-term couple functioning, including: (a) defining the couple with a set of boundaries, (b) investing in the relationship so that it has energy and vitality, along with finding a way to meet the emotional and practical needs of the couple, (c) balancing a need for stability with the need for growth and change, and (d) adapting over time as the couple progresses through various stages of relationship development.

These system-level elements are common among all effective couples, although the specifics of how the couple approaches them vary, depending on individual differences and personal preferences, identity, cultural background, and external influences. To provide assistance to struggling couples, it is essential for therapists to understand these common qualities of successful systems, in conjunction with the many unique ways that couples experience their lives together. Some couples experience difficulties because the two partners are not functioning well as a system. However, other couples function well in terms of the broad factors that define a system, yet they struggle for other reasons, such as the particular, differing needs of each individual (see Chapter 7). Additionally, many other factors are discussed throughout this book that impact the couple, such as communication interaction patterns (see Chapter 4) and the ways in which needs for control are expressed between partners (see Chapter 7).

Many of the interventions discussed in Chapters 4–6 can be applied to assist couples who need to address system-level issues, such as learning to set boundaries with other people using behavioural techniques, along with exploring the couple's standards regarding boundaries. This chapter addresses what is required for a couple to be an effective system overall and explores the wide range of ways that various couples enact system-level constructs to bring their uniqueness to life. The challenges and issues discussed in this chapter also exemplify the macro-level themes in couple relationships that might underlie a range of more specific, micro-level concerns.

Common system-level elements of couple functioning

Defining the couple at a given point in time

Establishing and maintaining a sense of joint identity as a couple can sound like a vague, amorphous process, and on that broad level, couples likely have few or no conversations where they explicitly discuss "our couple identity." Even without their awareness, this "coupleness" becomes manifest in various ways, such as in their communication through pronoun use, referring to themselves as "we" rather than two individuals (Williams-Baucom, Atkins, Sevier, Eldridge, & Christensen, 2010). In addition, the details of what helps to define the couple as a separate unit at times often are discussed (e.g., "What do we think is okay to tell our parents about our financial difficulties and what information is only for us?"), even if the couple does not realize or label these discussions as identity or boundary discussions. Two broad sets of processes define the couple: (a) how they differentiate themselves from the outside world (e.g., "This is us, and then there is everyone and everything else") and (b) how they interact with each other to meet relational and individual needs (e.g., "Now we have to figure out what the 'us' looks like; how we do this relationship").

Relating to the outside world: Establishing couple boundaries

Most basic to creating a system and a sense of "coupleness," every couple must establish a set of boundaries that helps to define what is unique to them and what is shared with others (e.g., Is it acceptable to hug other people? What personal information is appropriate to share and what is kept private within the relationship?). Differentiating the couple from others around them involves relating to the couple's environment, which is discussed in Chapter 9. In the current chapter, the focus is on how the couple manages themselves and the environment to define themselves as a unit.

Many couples develop an implicit or explicit set of information and behaviour that is not to be shared with others; such matters are beyond the couple's boundary. For example, whether the couple hopes to have children or whether to disclose that one of them has cancer might be something they agree to keep just between the two of them. At times, the two partners might differ regarding preferences for what is to be shared with other family members, friends, or co-workers. Likewise, they might differ regarding what level of affection between them is appropriate to display in public or what types of physical interaction and emotional closeness with other people are acceptable. There is great variability in how couples define and live out these boundaries; for example, while sexual monogamy is paramount for many couples, other couples in a consensual, non-monogamous relationship might define different boundaries for their emotional intimacy and investment. Of note, male same-sex couples are more likely to have a consensual non-monogamy agreement compared to different-sex or female same-sex couples (Gotta et al., 2011; Whitton, Weitbrecht, & Kuryluk, 2015).

Couples can experience distress if they differ in preferences regarding boundaries because boundaries are central in defining "who we are, what is special between us, and what makes our relationship different from all others." Experiencing that "you don't want to keep that special something just between us" can lead a partner to feel devalued or betrayed. Committed relationships are important for many reasons, and one of the unique aspects of such relationships is that "you are my special person, and I am yours. No one is to touch or intrude upon that." A clear sense of boundaries and shared couple identity helps foster trust and intimacy. In a world increasingly marked by instant contact with many people and events both locally and globally, knowing that there is someone and a relationship that is unique and cherished can be very comforting.

In addition, even if both people subscribe to and honour the same boundaries, the couple can experience difficulties if those boundaries skew other aspects of their lives. For example, if the couple sets very tight or rigid boundaries regarding what they share with others or the extent to which they allow others into their system on a temporary basis, they might feel close to each other yet isolated from family or friends since they rarely share information with other people beyond a superficial level:

> I keep getting this vibe from my mother that she's so sad. When we're alone, she literally says things like, "I don't feel like I know you anymore. I'm delighted that you're married, but it feels so different." She is going to have to come to terms with it; you're my main person now; she isn't, and she won't be.

Likewise, if one partner knowingly violates important shared couple boundaries, for example, through an affair, it can have devastating effects on the couple: "I thought you cared about us. I can't believe you betrayed me and us in that way. Our relationship has just been a fantasy in my head. I don't know you; I don't know us anymore!" Because boundaries help to define what is special and unique about the couple, violation of aspects of those boundaries can be experienced as a major relationship trauma (D. H. Baucom et al., 2009; Snyder et al., 2007).

The above examples illustrate how couples create and employ boundaries as a way of making their relationship special, optimizing positives. In addition, individuals and couples also create boundaries to provide safety from what is experienced as a dangerous or hostile world, that is, to minimize negatives. Therefore, if one partner experiences certain aspects of the world as unsafe for a variety of reasons such as earlier trauma, being taught by parents that the world is a dangerous place, living in a neighbourhood with high rates of violence, or experiencing ongoing discrimination, then stronger boundaries might be preferred by the couple. To the degree that such safety measures are warranted, the goal of therapy becomes supporting the couple in determining how to create safety without establishing excessive boundaries. One of the potential negative consequences of strong boundaries is implied above; boundaries can create safety but also "shrink one's world" by providing a reduced safe space in which to operate. Thus, if one or both partners create boundaries that keep others or aspects of their environment out of their experience, they likewise reduce opportunities for what those people or their environment might offer that is positive. Therefore, the challenge becomes maintaining appropriate boundaries to create safety and trust while minimizing excessive boundaries.

Overall, boundaries are essential and can serve a variety of functions. Thus, it can be important to recognize each partner's sense of boundaries and whether those preferences are based on a desire for specialness, to minimize danger, or both. It also is important to navigate boundaries as a couple, given that these boundaries can have implications for each partner, their relationship, and their environment.

Partners relating to each other

While boundaries help to establish what is and is not shared between the couple and their environment, much relationship success involves what happens between the two partners.

A number of system-level considerations are integral to who the couple is and how they function. First, each partner needs to invest in the relationship; second, the couple needs to establish roles and meet responsibilities; and, third, they have to navigate an ever-changing set of demands and adapt over time.

INVESTING IN THE RELATIONSHIP

In order for the couple to thrive, each partner needs to invest in the relationship, which can be defined as the amount and type of time, energy, and effort that each individual contributes. Such investment varies notably by individual and by couple. Investments can be experienced subjectively and internally within the individual, such as spending time thinking about the other partner and how to bring them happiness. Likewise, investment can include strong behavioural manifestations, such as attending a sporting event primarily because it is important to the other person, or taking a less desirable job in a new location in order to support the other person's career. These investments can take many specific forms, largely categorized as emotional or instrumental.

Emotional investment Emotional investment involves allowing oneself to feel affection or love for the other person and the relationship, as well as allowing oneself to receive this love from the partner. This kind of investment can involve internal experiences such as having caring feelings for the partner and also can involve behaving in a manner to demonstrate these subjective experiences. Fundamentally, emotionally focused behaviours are intended to affirm the other person and to demonstrate caring for one's partner without attempting to accomplish a particular task. For example, a partner might send a "thinking about you" message while at work or greet the other person with a warm hug at the end of the day. Emotional investment also might involve a willingness to work through one's own hurt feelings or frustrations, such as when a partner has behaved badly and the couple needs to have difficult conversations in order to get back on track.

Individuals vary greatly in their desire both to provide and receive these caring, loving acts. For some people, such acts are paramount: "I just need you to love me; let me experience it, and let me love you. That is what is vital for me; it really is what gives my life meaning." Other people need and value such demonstrations much less, and frequent or intense demonstrations can feel uncomfortable, forced, or even aversive, even though the person cares deeply about their partner. These differences in investing by demonstrating care and love through emotionally expressive behaviours derive from a range of factors including family of origin, culture, and personal experiences in earlier relationships. In many instances, these individual differences are normal and healthy (see Chapter 7), and the couple must learn to navigate them without giving them excess meaning (e.g., "My not being very affectionate doesn't mean that I don't care about you. I'm just not a very physical person. I know it's a problem because you want that from me, but I show you that you are important to me in so many other ways"). On other occasions, a person's current preferences might result from aversive experiences which contribute to an avoidance response in terms of experiencing or expressing affection ("I can't help it; I was abused when I was young, and I can't handle it when somebody touches me; it's just automatic. I recoil immediately"). Or such responses might be part of a current psychological disturbance, such as emotional withdrawal as a part of depression. Any of these instances might become targets for change because it can be extremely disturbing to one person if their partner is unable to give to the relationship in an emotionally expressive manner. On the other hand, many couples maintain a strong level of mutually satisfying emotional investment over many years together. Dan and Sybil, who had been married for over 40 years, remarked, "We were walking across a parking lot the other day holding hands, and a total stranger said, 'You two look so happy together. You keep doing it; you show those young people!'" When couples are able to maintain a high level of emotional investment in the face of competing demands in their lives, they often report that they benefit greatly, and it helps to protect them from various daily stressors.

Instrumental investment Partners also invest in the relationship by accomplishing tasks that are instrumental or goal oriented. As discussed in Chapter 4, such actions are vital for a successful relationship, given that tasks need to be accomplished in order for the relationship to proceed smoothly, both in terms of day-to-day actions such as cooking meals, as well as major life domains such as moving for a new job. Many individuals define themselves as "a doer," and accomplishing tasks is their major way of demonstrating the importance of their relationship. Investing in a relationship in instrumental ways is driven in part by individual differences in overall personal style; people who generally find it rewarding to accomplish tasks, solve problems, and cross items off a list often invest instrumentally in the relationship.

Just as couples can experience difficulties when they differ on emotional investment, they can become distressed when there are notable differences in the extent to which they invest in the relationship in task-oriented ways. For example, one person might become frustrated by doing most of the work, or the other might become exasperated that "you always seem to put work first." Moreover, distress can arise when each partner invests in the relationship by providing what they themselves value, assuming it will meet the needs of the other person because it is what they would want to receive themselves. Thus, a person who greatly values emotional expression might provide much verbal affection, although such experiences might not be as valuable to the partner. As a result, it can be important for each person to balance providing what they want and value with what the other partner wants to receive with regard to investment of time and energy. Hence, the golden rule of "do unto others as you would have them do unto you" can be problematic if taken too literally or simplistically.

The above discussion highlights how relationship distress can result from the manner in which each partner gives or does not give to the relationship. Likewise, couples can struggle when one partner overall seems much more invested in the relationship than the other partner. For example, when Sprecher, Schmeeckle, and Felmlee (2006) studied dating couples, they found that couples were more satisfied and viewed their relationship as more stable when there was more equal emotional involvement by both partners. When emotional involvement varies notably between the two partners, frequently the more invested person makes even further efforts to secure more involvement from the partner, enacting a mindset that "I just need to try harder or do more, and then you will value me and our relationship." Such efforts might be unsuccessful because they inadvertently convey a message to the partner that even less is demanded of them since the other person is willing to put unceasing effort into the relationship. Accelerating a maladaptive interaction pattern rarely solves a problem. The person wanting more investment from the other might make those desires known explicitly and clearly, in a constructive manner. Alternatively, if a partner continually feels frustrated that tasks are not getting accomplished, they might begin complaining or demanding more. These efforts also are often unsuccessful and can serve as a basis for a demand–withdraw interaction pattern, as described in Chapter 4.

In summary, couples need to give effectively to the relationship. While couples and individuals differ in their abilities and desires to give in certain ways, most relationships require that both partners invest in the relationship both emotionally and instrumentally to some degree. How each partner invests and how those investments intersect with each partner's needs (see Chapter 7) can have a notable effect on the couple's satisfaction and effectiveness in proceeding through life.

Attending to the relationship over time: consistency and change

Just as with individual functioning, relationship well-being involves adaptation across time in response to a wide variety of demands from each partner, the relationship, and the environment. This adaptation includes a balance between consistency and change to respond to new demands and opportunities. Consistency provides a couple with predictability so that every task or decision does not need to be negotiated on a regular basis. This predictability also can contribute to efficiency as each person goes about meeting expected roles and develops expertise in certain areas of responsibility, such as one person keeping up with financial matters. At the same time, some couples who have been together for many years might complain that their relationship has become stale. Thus, they desire some level of novelty or change to keep the relationship fresh. In addition, different stages of life call for investing effort in different ways, and couples need to be aware of and adapt to these demands for change (e.g., recognizing the need for some time alone as a couple when raising young children). While the need for balancing consistency and change plays out in multiple ways, there are fundamental principles that contribute to these processes, as discussed below.

Roles and responsibilities across time

For most couples, each partner assumes numerous roles and responsibilities, which often persist for long periods of time. Some roles might be shared with the couple engaging in the task together (e.g., grocery shopping), or the partners might alternate in accomplishing the same task. In many instances, each partner takes on specific roles for which they are solely or largely responsible; for example, one person might take care of automobile maintenance and the other handles the monthly budget.

For some couples, their delineation of roles and responsibilities works well; yet, others struggle for a variety of reasons. In some instances, the sheer number of tasks each person assumes at home is skewed, with one person undertaking many more couple and family responsibilities than the other. In different-sex couples, on average, women assume much more of household and childcare responsibilities than males. For example, recent findings in the United Kingdom indicate that on average, women carry out 60% more unpaid work at home than men, and gender differences are found in every age group (Office for National Statistics, 2016). At times, this imbalance can lead to resentment resulting from role overload or a sense of unfairness from the person assuming the bulk of the responsibilities. This skewed distribution also can result in the overburdened person becoming depressed, feeling exhausted, experiencing life as filled with meaningless and trivial chores, and feeling hopeless about the situation. Such a distribution might even occur among couples who initially endorsed egalitarian values and an intention to share responsibilities equitably, until the responsibilities of one person's job increases dramatically. That is, couples can struggle to keep their relationship operating in a manner that is consistent with their own values: "Sometimes life just takes over. We have to divide and conquer to get things done, whether it seems like we're giving in to stereotypes or not." In other instances, both partners might agree on the distribution of roles and responsibilities, but the arrangement does not work well for the couple or one individual. For example, Freda and Samuel had traditional views of role responsibilities and agreed that a wife should make decisions about the home décor. Yet, Samuel had much stronger opinions about style than Freda and believed he had better taste than Freda did. The couple had frequent arguments about the house, based on the shared belief that Freda "should" be in charge of decorating with only minimal input from Samuel, yet he continually expressed his preferences in both direct and indirect ways, which made Freda believe that she wasn't "doing her job properly."

Accomplishing tasks not only involves a distribution of the workload, but for many couples, one person assumes the role of "family manager," that is, the person who oversees family life and makes certain that everything is happening as needed (Epstein & Baucom, 2002). Such a role does not necessarily mean that this individual carries out all the tasks, but rather that this person assumes a broader responsibility for coordinating tasks and family members' roles. Many couples never have conversations about the establishment of such a role, but rather it seems to evolve over time. Again, with different-sex couples, females seem much more likely than males to adopt this role. As life continues, it is not unusual for the family manager to become increasingly frustrated with the partner, who is perceived as neglecting their share of the family workload, until the family manager finally comments, "Why do I always have to remind you of what needs to be done? Why can't you see it and just do it?" The response from the other partner often is in one of two directions, "I am happy to do what you want me to do. Just tell me, and I'll do it," or "I wish you would stop nagging me. I know what needs to be done, and I will do it. Just back off!" It is important for the couple to recognize that this overseeing role requires time and energy, even if the person is not undertaking the tasks themselves.

While the distribution of roles and responsibilities between partners might work well at a given point in the relationship, a variety of factors can call for change over time. The need for change can result from changes in one partner, the couple as a unit, or the environment. For example, as an individual ages, they might find that they do not have the same stamina and level of energy that they had in earlier years. Therefore, the combination of working hard in a full-time position outside the home, moonlighting to earn extra income for the family, and contributing heavily to household tasks might work for some time but not be sustainable over decades.

Rituals

Distributing roles and responsibilities can provide much-needed predictability and efficiency, but such routines typically do not lead to a sense of closeness or specialness between partners. However, routines in the form of rituals can serve this function if they are carried out in a way that the couple experiences as meaningful. Thus, couples might have "our special restaurant," pet names for each other, holiday traditions, or a yearly viewing of their wedding video on each anniversary. Often, these special activities involve boundaries as well ("We don't use our pet names when other people are around"), creating a sense of uniqueness that only the couple can appreciate. At the same time, if activities that rely upon spontaneity or momentary feelings for their meaning become ritualized, those same behaviours can lose their meaning or even become negative. For example, the same good-bye kiss every morning for years might no longer be experienced as a statement of affection but rather just something the couple does in departing the house, similar to locking the door. Thus, couples benefit and feel close when rituals create a sense of specialness, but if too much of life or the wrong activities become ritualized, life can become boring. This balancing act suggests that couples must also find ways to continue to grow and to integrate novelty into their lives.

Novelty, growth, and keeping the relationship alive

For many couples, the early stages of their relationship are exciting as they get to know each other, engage in enjoyable activities together, and contemplate what might lie ahead in their future. Because this novelty results naturally from the newness of the relationship, it likewise decreases as the couple continues on their journey through life, and daily demands and routines come to dominate their experience. Not surprisingly, distressed couples who have been together many years sometimes seek couple therapy because life has become boring and devoid of meaning for them. In such instances, their distress results from a lack of positives rather than from the presence of excessive negatives. How then might couples keep their relationship alive and growing over time?

First, growth for the couple can result from one or both partners continuing to grow as individuals, as well as explicitly growing as a unit (C. L. Gordon & Baucom, 2004). Such growth can result from pursuing ongoing interests in more depth or by engaging in novel activities. From an individual perspective, such a pursuit could be learning more about a long-standing passion, or conversely, developing new hobbies or leisure activities. These strategies not only might have the general effect of keeping the individual engaged and fostering a positive overall mood, but also might provide an opportunity to bring something new to the relationship to share with the other person. In essence, this approach stems from the notion that in order to have an interesting, thriving relationship, it helps to be an interesting individual with whom other people want to spend time.

Likewise, the couple can create more in-depth or novel experiences for the two partners as a unit. Thus, they might build on their shared interest in nature and explore new outdoor activities, such as hiking. On the other hand, the couple might continue to grow by engaging in a whole new domain of activity, deciding to take dance lessons to counterbalance their outdoor passion. For each couple, the need to maintain domains of consistency while also continuing to grow in new ways will vary according to each person's individual needs and motives as described in Chapter 7 (e.g., a need for novelty and stimulation), environmental constraints (e.g., the couple might not easily explore nature due to living in a large city with few financial resources), and the developmental phase of the couple's relationship, which will be described below.

Changing patterns of commitment and marriage

Before turning to a discussion of the developmental stages of relationships, it is important to recognize the changing trends and patterns of long-term relationships and marriage and to explore the dynamics of commitment. The developmental sequence to be described below is based on the notion of two people getting married, or making some other form of public or private commitment, with the intention of remaining in the relationship for life. However, patterns of cohabitation, marriage, divorce, and remarriage continue to change over time, and many individuals have several committed relationships of varying lengths in their lifetime. In the United States, cohabitation rates currently are the highest that they have been in the past 20 years, including both young and older couples (Dush, Arocho, Mernitz, & Rhoades, 2019). In fact, almost two-thirds of American women cohabit at some point in their lives (Manning & Stykes, 2015). Despite this trend, the great majority of adults continue to marry or make a similar commitment at some point in life, within the context of first marriages occurring at later ages. In the United States, the median age of first marriage is now 27 for women and 29 for men (U.S. Census Bureau, 2018b). However, many individuals do not continue in that same relationship for life; among divorcing couples, the average length of their first marriage is 12 years in the United States (Spangler & Payne, 2012). In addition, divorce occurs across the age span: Approximately 25% of all divorces in the United States now involve people over the age of 50 (Brown & Lin, 2012). Furthermore, many divorcees are entering into a second (or third) committed relationship. For example, in the United States, only about one-half of women and men have been married only once: therefore, even though the majority of recent marriages (58%) are first marriages for both spouses, a substantial share of recent marriages (21%) involve both spouses marrying for at least the second time (Lewis & Kreider, 2015). Less data are available regarding long-term marriages among same-sex couples, given that marriage equality has been established in some countries fairly recently and, in other countries, not at all. Therefore, "typical" developmental trajectories vary dramatically, as societal standards and constraints regarding marriage and commitment evolve and couples are able to make increasingly diverse choices regarding how to live. Regardless of the specific trajectory of a relationship, one important aspect across couples is *how* they decide what form they would like their relationship to take over time, including choices regarding commitment.

The impact of "sliding versus deciding"

One intriguing set of findings regarding relationship development involves how couples early in their relationship either explicitly decide to commit to each other or seem to move forward in their relationship with somewhat less awareness, and how this approach predicts long-term relationship stability (Rhoades, Stanley, & Markman, 2012). This issue has become highlighted based on findings from the United States that suggest, overall, that different-sex couples who live together prior to marriage have a higher divorce rate than couples who do not live together (Kline et al., 2004). This finding might seem counterintuitive because one might anticipate that living together provides an opportunity to "try out" the relationship before making a formal commitment. However, upon further investigation, Stanley, Rhoades, and Markman (2006) found that there are two groups of different-sex couples who live together prior to marriage, who have quite different long-term relationship trajectories. They have termed the process that typifies these two groups as "sliding versus deciding." Couples who "slide" into marriage or a committed relationship seem to move forward from one step of relationship commitment to another without thinking about the issues carefully or mindfully deciding where they would like the relationship to be headed. As Ben recalled:

> Well, my lease was up and I needed to move. She needed a roommate to help pay the rent, so I just moved in. And the next year, I finished school and got a job in another state. So we moved in together and have been together ever since.

On the other hand, couples who "decide" seem to be aware of the decisions they are making about their relationship, typically discuss the issues and implications, and knowingly make various commitments to each other. As Rehaan stated:

> When she finished college and got a job, we talked a lot about what was next for us. We had been together for two years, and we didn't want to be boyfriend/girlfriend indefinitely. We agreed that if we were going to move together, we were making a long-term commitment to each other. We weren't ready to say the word "marriage," but we were clear that if we moved together, we were planning to stay together.

Research on different-sex relationships has shown that couples who live together and move forward by "sliding" have higher divorce rates, whereas couples who cohabit and approach their relationship through "deciding" have lower divorce rates (Stanley et al., 2006). Increased commitment behaviours (even without being recognized as increasing commitment) such as signing a lease together also increase the barriers to separation, even when that might be the most adaptive course of action for a couple. Of note, environmental factors (see Chapter 9) might make some couples more vulnerable to "sliding" than others, such as financial hardships that make it difficult to continue paying rent separately.

The concept of sliding versus deciding is important not only in terms of early relationship commitment but also throughout a couple's developmental stages across the life span, with ongoing implications for relationship well-being. As a couple moves from one developmental stage to another, there are new challenges and opportunities that they need to address. Often these adaptations and changes involve the relative balance of time and energy focused on each partner as an individual, the couple as a unit, and the social and physical aspects of their environment. At these various change points, many couples seem to be aware of the need for change and respond accordingly, but other couples are less attentive to new challenges and continue behaving as they did before. For example, if a couple has their first child, a major shift needs to occur in most relationships. Prior to having a baby, the couple might have devoted considerable time and effort to pursuing individual interests and enjoying activities together. However, the entry of a child into their family means that they have to reorganize, often with much less time for themselves as a couple and for each person individually. That is, it typically works best if couples do not mindlessly continue behaving and devoting energy as before when they add a child into the mix. Frequent late nights out and partying with other couples likely will not serve them well as a young family. This transition to parenthood with a wide variety of new demands is a time when an unequal distribution of chores can evolve unintentionally and when the family manager role becomes more demanding.

On the other hand, being mindful of the change at a given stage does not necessarily mean that the couple adapts optimally. An awareness that adaptations are necessary does not mean that the couple knows what will work best for them or is able to implement their plans. Thus, a couple might knowingly spend almost all of their time focusing on their children, with almost no time for them as a couple. Such neglect of their own relationship can lead to significant relationship discord, although both partners care about each other and greatly value their relationship. As discussed below, different stages pull for differential foci on the individual, the couple, and their environment, yet couples must be cautious to avoid responding too extremely because when they do, the neglected areas are likely to suffer (e.g., "Ever since we had our first child, I've quit going to the gym, put on 20 pounds, and am exhausted all the time. I'm starting to feel like I don't exist as a person anymore").

Developmental stages of couples' relationships

Many couples experience somewhat predictable developmental changes over the course of their years together that result from individual, relationship, and environmental shifts (Carter & McGoldrick, 1999; Nichols & Schwartz, 2001). A full discussion of developmental stages of relationships is beyond the scope of this book (see Friese, 2019, for a detailed discussion of couples and families across the life span). The current focus is on general principles along with specific examples, and the implications of these changes for relationship and individual well-being. Although couples experience different types of challenges across the decades of life together, including job changes, health complications, and the death of important people in their lives, the current discussion addresses the somewhat normative shifts that couples in long-term committed relationships commonly experience, with the awareness that many couples also experience other unique circumstances or stressors that require navigation and management. Also as noted earlier, the increased diversity among couples in today's societies means that many couples do not follow the path described below.

The start-up phase

Although couples are entering into their first committed relationship at later ages and a significant number of couples are in second or subsequent relationships, for simplicity, the current discussion is based on couples who are in their first marriage or committed relationship, which often begins in their 20s or 30s. However, many challenges also apply to couples in other circumstances, such as second or third marriages or committed relationships.

This early phase of relationships is what might be termed the "start-up" phase, during which the partners are learning how to function as a couple through establishing routines, delineating roles and responsibilities, setting boundaries with families of origin, etc. For many couples, this start-up phase coincides with the start-up of other aspects of life as well. Many individuals are finishing their education and starting their careers, and couples are trying to establish themselves financially. Starting almost any kind of meaningful endeavour requires considerable time, effort, and energy. Thus, couples often can be extremely busy, attempting to establish their relationship on a firm footing while also focusing on work pressures and facing significant increases in financial responsibility.

If couples have children during this start-up phase, the demands increase considerably, not only requiring additional time and energy, but also necessitating a reorganization of couple functioning during which the infant becomes a major focus of life. Although having a child is regarded in most societies as a cause for celebration, many couples experience a decrease in relationship satisfaction during the transition to parenthood (Doss, Rhoades, Stanley, & Markman, 2009), and approximately 19% of women experience postpartum depression in the first three months after giving birth (Gavin et al., 2005). Challenges for each partner can include operating on very little sleep, learning to soothe a colicky baby, feeling inadequate as a parent, or worrying about the health of the infant. For same-sex couples, additional challenges arise prior to having their first child, including learning about and navigating available routes to parenthood, at times with few role models that apply to their circumstances or limited guidance from family and friends.

Taking on the new role of parent also typically requires a fundamental shift in the way individuals and couples operate, although couples frequently do not anticipate the degree to which old patterns need to shift. Often the changes that do occur are not explicitly decided upon and can be detrimental to the relationship. For example, most households in Western cultures tend to be largely egalitarian prior to this transition; however, for different-sex couples, divisions of labour and psychological investment in roles shift to become more in line with traditional gender roles after the birth of the first child, often without explicit agreement (Glade, Bean, & Vira, 2005; Lawrence, Rothman, Cobb, & Bradbury, 2010). This shift can be associated with resentment and withdrawal (Glade et al., 2005).

The childhood years

This focus on the family as a broader unit with children continues as infants reach childhood. The family focuses on schooling, how their children spend their free time, and providing the children with opportunities to flourish. At times, this phase can include just trying "to get by" with financial and work obligations. While many couples experience the childhood years as extremely rewarding, most simultaneously describe this period as challenging in many ways, with the parents often feeling "spread too thin." It is crucial that the couple does not neglect their own relationship or individual growth during this stage. Focusing solely on being parents to the exclusion of also being a couple can sow the seeds of relationship or individual distress such as depression. This de-emphasis on the couple's relationship can manifest itself in a number of ways, all of which signify decreased contact, time together, or intimacy. For example, couples might indicate that they rarely talk to each other, and when they do, often it is to coordinate schedules to make certain that no child is left stranded at the curb.

The maintenance phase

As the couple moves into their 40s or 50s, they are likely to progress into a "maintenance phase" in multiple ways. For many individuals, their careers or jobs are on a stable path; many couples have established routines, roles, and responsibilities; and children are reaching adolescence and moving toward having more autonomy with less daily involvement with their parents. Therefore, this stage often is a time when couples might reassess where they are in their lives and whether they are satisfied with what they find—not necessarily a midlife crisis but at least a "midterm review." Often, this time of life is rewarding because all the effort associated with the start-up phase has ended. However, for other couples this time can introduce a difficult transition. If one partner has focused primarily on being the family manager and attending to other people's needs, they can start to feel uncertain about their role, as children need them less. As Milana commented, responding to her therapist:

> You asked me what I'd like for myself in this next phase of life. I have no idea; what I want personally has not been part of my life for so many years. I have been taking care of the children, taking care of Jacek; my life hasn't been about me. In fact, I don't even know if there is a "me" anymore.

On the other hand, some couples have looked forward to "launching" their children and the freedom it can bring. However, some of them find that they are attending to ageing parents, who might have increased emotional and pragmatic needs, negating the freedom that the couple anticipated. Moreover, some couples find themselves in the "sandwich generation," attending to their children's needs and the needs of their ageing parents at the same time. Thus, rather than experiencing a sense of maintenance in life, these couples actually might be facing increased demands. Because of the need to "divide and conquer," often one partner attends to their own biological ageing parent while the other partner tends to their children, leaving the couple with little time as a unit.

Even without such complexities, many individuals foresee their work and family trajectory and are not pleased about where they might be headed. For individuals who are dispirited about their family or professional roles and their future, this stage can be a time of dejection and can perhaps precipitate depression. For the couple as a unit, many report that they are getting along with each other without a high level of negatives. Yet, they have lost the vitality which they want for their relationship. In such instances, these couples might seek intervention because they want more from life than they are currently experiencing, such as a desire for more fun, excitement, or a renewed sense of closeness which has been lost as other priorities have prevailed.

The empty nest phase for couples with children

As children are launched from home to higher education or employment, couples have more opportunity to refocus on themselves as individuals and as a couple. If they have maintained a strong relationship, this stage can be a time of renewal with a re-emphasis on their relationship, particularly if they have maintained their health. However, if they have grown apart and no longer know how to talk to each other once the children are gone, voids in the relationship surface. The task then becomes finding new ways to build their relationship, either by reincorporating meaningful ways of relating from the past or by developing new patterns for the present and future:

> We've really looked forward to this time of the children being on their own, ready to face the world as young adults. But I'm also a little worried; our whole lives have been focused on the children and what they are doing. I literally don't know what to talk about now. We can go to the movies or do other things for fun, but if it comes down to talking to each other, I'm at a bit of a loss.

Ageing and the retirement phase

Regardless of whether one or both partners "retire" from the work and roles which they have pursued for most of their adult lives, individuals and couples need to continue to adapt as they become older, entering into a broad age group that many societies refer to as the "elderly." This phase is ill defined, yet, many people view it as being consistent with a society's typical or required retirement age. Regardless of the exact definitions employed, it is clear that this stage is an increasingly long time period as life expectancies increase. As a result, some gerontologists have divided this phase of life into several stages, using such terms as young-old (65–74), middle-old (75–84), and oldest-old (85+) (Zizza, Ellison, & Wernette, 2009). Although these stages provide differentiation based on age and possible changes occurring at these ages, individual trajectories at any given age in the elderly years vary widely. For example, some couples entering their 60s and 70s are in prime health, have ample resources, and enjoy strong support systems. Under such circumstances, these couples might experience this time as a "golden age" when they experience increased freedoms and opportunities to explore new aspects of life with fewer responsibilities. Other couples with fewer resources, ongoing obligations, or health concerns might find this phase of life to be much more stressful.

Among a wide range of issues that couples will confront, a major task at some point is to renegotiate roles and responsibilities and decide how to spend their time, given that they might be at home together much more now than before. This change can pose multiple challenges not only because one partner might now find the other person in "my territory," but also because ageing eventually brings physical limitations and health concerns, often with one partner declining before the other. Therefore, the couple dynamics can shift as one partner begins to take on a caregiver role. While the process of ageing varies widely among couples, it is important that all couples are mindful of ongoing changes they will confront and address these changes together, rather than sliding into this important phase of couple life.

Summary of developmental stages within the couple's system

Overall, the major message is that couples undergo a series of developmental changes over the years, and each of these stages presents challenges, needs for change, and opportunities to grow. Some couples might make appropriate adaptations intuitively, but for most couples, it is important to be aware of the needed changes so that they can thoughtfully consider how they want to adapt. As described in Chapter 2, these adaptations involve a degree of balance in attending to the individual, the couple, and their environment. While particular stages tend to pull for attending to one or more of these three areas, it is important that the couple does not overemphasize one domain at the expense of the others to a detrimental degree. Either on their own, or with the help of a therapist, the couple must negotiate these ongoing needs for stability and change.

Intervening on system-level issues

One of the hallmarks of cognitive-behavioural interventions is specificity, so it is important to understand how a consideration of broad system-level constructs such as boundaries can assist in case conceptualization and treatment planning. Together, the therapist and couple develop a comprehensive conceptualization of the couple's functioning (see Chapter 14). Within that context, it is valuable to consider whether the couple is functioning well or experiencing difficulties as a system, attending to the various factors discussed in this chapter. For example, treatment planning might revolve around the couple's difficulties with boundaries, investment in the relationship (types or balance), lack of rituals or overreliance on them, lack of novelty, or complications of moving from one developmental stage to another. In this way, the treatment can have coherence and address important patterns that make up the rich fabric of fulfilling relationships. Consistent with this approach, system-level concerns would be viewed as macro-level issues, meaning that they are broad thematic concerns that exist across domains of couple functioning and help to tie together specific concerns that couples might describe.

How then does a therapist proceed when part of the couple's difficulties appears to involve these broader system-level issues? The key to addressing system-level concerns is that in almost all instances, these broad patterns are addressed in therapy at a detailed, concrete level as they are manifest across specific aspects of the couple's relationship. Below are brief examples of ways that system-level issues related to (a) differential investment in the relationship by the two partners, (b) loss of vitality in the relationship over many years together, and (c) boundary issues might be manifested and addressed.

Suneyra and Mahir married while Suneyra was studying full time for her advanced academic degree. Mahir was committed to supporting Suneyra's education and long-term career goals. He was established in his own job (although not entirely fulfilled), which allowed him to dedicate substantial effort to their daily life as a couple. Given the extensive time demand of Suneyra's studies, he willingly took on most of the household tasks, their social life revolved around Suneyra's needs and preferences, and most of their conversations focused on her daily experiences at the university. However, two years after Suneyra had completed her education, the couple was still continuing with their same patterns of interaction without considering how they needed to adapt their system to a new stage of life. Mahir continued to take on most of the instrumental tasks needed to help them function day-to-day, while Suneyra pursued her career. Although Mahir was proud of her, he began to resent this imbalance. To make matters worse, his siblings were teasing him about the nontraditional roles that he and Suneyra had chosen. At the same time, Mahir told himself that if he "was truly committed to Suneyra and women's advancement more broadly," he *should* do all he could to support Suneyra's success. Suneyra was not selfish, yet they had developed these well-established roles over several years and continued them, without her awareness of his resentment or their lack of attention to Mahir's own personal needs and goals. Once this theme became clear, the therapist provided brief psychoeducation about the different stages of relationship development, how partners often trade off roles and for a time de-emphasize one person's needs for the well-being of the other person, and the importance of recognizing the need to re-evaluate their patterns when their circumstances change. This new information ushered in a series of conversations (targeting both cognitions and emotions) in which the couple discussed their beliefs about fostering professional development for both of them and how roles might shift over time as a result. The therapist also helped Mahir express his resentment for the continued imbalanced investment in household responsibilities and explore his guilt for feeling this way, given his belief that "women are well overdue to have their turn, and I should do everything I can." Suneyra was open to hearing his reactions and felt guilty that she had not realized the need to step back and re-evaluate. Using guided behaviour change and structured decision-making interventions, the therapist then helped the couple make changes in a number of domains to reflect their new awareness, including smaller day-to-day changes such as redistributing daily responsibilities, as well as larger long-term plans such as a possible career shift that Mahir wanted to consider.

Another couple, Simon and Andre, confronted a different set of system-level issues. Over decades of being together, they had worked out their respective roles and responsibilities, and each performed them effectively in what they described as "a well-oiled machine." There were few negatives in their relationship as each went about their daily routine, watched television together most week nights, and cooked dinner with a group of friends every Saturday. Their well-developed routines and rituals resulted in a somewhat dull, monotonous experience, leading them to ask, "Is this what you get after so many years of hard work and trying to get along? We can keep doing it, but more zest would be nice!" In this instance, the therapist talked with the couple about the need to balance stability with change and novelty across time. They had mastered the stability and predictability aspects of life with which many couples struggle; perhaps now they needed to think about change, growth, and novelty. Simon and Andre both responded with skepticism, given that each of them had grown up in a somewhat tumultuous family with limited resources. Thus, they had agreed from the beginning of their relationship that they would not continue this pattern. They wanted to prove to those who questioned the longevity of same-sex relationships that they were wrong, and as a couple, they valued being "good, solid citizens and partners," providing stability for each other and their community. The therapist had them explore the notion that they did not need to consider their situation as an "either–or" but perhaps a "both–and" approach (e.g., using conversations focused on sharing thoughts and feelings as a guided discovery tool). Thus, the therapists posed questions to the couple such as, "Within your general desire to provide stability, are there small changes you might make to create more of a sense of vitality in life for you individually and as a couple, and is it acceptable to pursue some of these changes alone as separate individuals?" They agreed that "we think we did what we said we'd do on the stability front" and explored the idea of "changing things up a bit." Through guided behaviour changes and structured decision-making, they began in small ways, taking a walk one night a week and playing board games once a week, rather than engaging in a steady stream of post-dinner television. Experiencing these smaller changes as rewarding, they progressed to taking dance classes (something they never thought they would try). Eventually, they decided that they were now financially stable enough that they could take a holiday away with just the two of them, even if it meant missing their weekend rituals with their group of friends, who seemed to delight in seeing the couple venturing forth in the world as if they were courting again. After extensive conversation, Simon and Andre both agreed that neither of them wanted much alone time or time with friends without including their partner; they felt renewed and more alive in the time they had with each other.

On the other hand, Sonny had no difficulties being on his own without Noreen and including other people in his life. As she described it, "I know I can trust him, but the man has no boundaries, and it makes me uncomfortable. He grew up in a kind of hippy family with parents from the 60s where almost anything seemed to go. They were good people, just 'flexible,' shall we say." Thus, Sonny's friends knew that his door was always open and that they were free to "crash" and stay overnight whenever they wished. He would do the same, at times calling Noreen at the last minute to say that he was staying over with a friend. In his generous manner, he was explicit in proclaiming, "If I have something you need, it's yours!" Thus, tools often seemed to disappear, or a friend might borrow the car on short notice. He talked with friends about his and Noreen's finances and the details of their most recent argument. When Noreen found out that he had widely discussed their difficulty conceiving a child, that was the last straw for her. The therapist raised the concept of "boundaries" with the couple and explained that they must decide both (a) what information or behaviours are to be shared with others and what is to be kept private, just for the two of them, and (b) where to set limits with others to help life run smoothly. Noreen and Sonny discussed their different experiences while growing up, and how those early experiences had shaped their beliefs about giving to and including others, versus making their relationship feel unique and special by setting boundaries. They struggled during these discussions because each understood the other but also held strong values that seemed incompatible with the other's. For Sonny, setting the boundaries that Noreen desired (not talking about their personal matters with other people, not having people spend the night unannounced) meant keeping people out, not being a good friend. For Noreen, the "chaos" created when people stayed in their home without warning, tools disappeared, or the car was unexpectedly gone made it difficult to plan. Moreover, Sonny's sharing of their "personal, couple information" with his friends was embarrassing to her and made her feel devalued. Making changes that cause each partner to feel as if they are compromising their values is challenging, and Noreen and Sonny had difficulty arriving at compromises that were acceptable to both of them. Thus, much of their time in therapy was spent in conversation between the therapist and the couple as well as between the partners, carefully exploring where common ground was possible, what the compromises would look like, how both partners felt about the compromises, and what the limits or potential "deal breakers" were for each partner.

As can be seen in the above examples, broad macro-level themes involving the couple as a system are sometimes a prime basis of relationship distress. These broad themes are incorporated into the case conceptualization, and they typically are addressed as they emerge in specific domains of functioning, employing a variety of cognitive, behavioural, and emotional interventions described in Chapters 4–6. In addition, and as alluded to earlier in this chapter, the couple as a system also exists in a broader environmental context that impacts and is impacted by the couple; this environmental context is the focus of the next chapter.

Main points

- All couples operate as a system in addition to each partner having their own unique qualities. Some relationship distress results from difficulties at a system level, with the couple struggling to define themselves and adapt as a unit over time.
- One important factor that is central to system functioning is where the couple sets boundaries between themselves and others, keeping some aspects of their lives reserved only for each other. Couples can struggle when the two partners differ in terms of where to set boundaries, or even if they agree, extreme boundaries can leave them isolated from or too involved with others.
- Couples' relationships also are defined by how partners invest in their relationship, giving to each other in both emotional and task-oriented ways. Distress can develop when what is given by one person does not match what is desired by the partner.
- Couples need to be able to maintain some level of consistency while also adapting to various demands for change over the course of their relationship.
- Consistency is created in numerous ways including (a) deciding on each partner's roles and responsibilities and (b) creating rituals which can make life special.
- Consistency must be balanced by continued growth and development, often accomplished though novel or more in-depth experiences.
- Couples must adapt to both (a) atypical and unexpected stressors and (b) more typical stressors that are part of the developmental life cycle of the couple.
- Various developmental stages require a redistribution of how couples devote energy to each partner as an individual, themselves as a couple, and their environment (including the needs of other family members such as children and the couple's parents).
- Behavioural, cognitive, and emotional interventions described throughout the book can be employed to address these system-level concerns as well as more specific, delimited problems for the couple.

Note

1 The term "system" is used in many ways in describing couples, many of which have some overlap with the current use of the term. At the same time, it is important not to confuse current usage with other applications of the term. For example, family systems scholars have developed entire theories of family and couple functioning emanating from this concept. The current concept of system is not part of those theoretical models, although the family systems concept of "boundaries" is important in current considerations. Similarly, a "dynamic systems" approach to understanding couple functioning is consistent with the current perspective in emphasizing that couples must be viewed as changing dynamically in response to a wide variety of factors, yet with some consistency and movement back to resting or set points. Dynamic systems modelling places an emphasis on the mathematical modelling of these patterns which can help to elucidate couple functioning but is not the focus of the current chapter.

Chapter 9

The environment

Throughout this book, we emphasize the importance of the interpersonal context for individual functioning and vice versa. In addition, couples and individuals do not exist in isolation. Instead, they are embedded within multiple layers of social and physical environments that include children, extended family, friends, their home, their neighbourhood, the local community, the work environment, and the current political and economic climate (Bronfenbrenner, 1989). These multiple environmental layers often are central to a couple's life and afford innumerable challenges and opportunities over time. For example, whether or not the couple's extended family lives close by, how closely knit the couple wishes to be with the family, and whether interactions with family members are a source of joy and support versus conflict and chaos can greatly influence the couple's relationship. The broader cultural and political environment in a given country or region, including dynamics of privilege and oppression, also shapes what daily life might be like for different couples. Thus, a comprehensive understanding of a couple's lived experiences takes into account the broader context of their well-being and distress.

Some aspects of the environmental context will likely function as stressors for the couple, such as financial strain, an ailing parent, or discrimination. Environmental stressors such as these can make it more difficult for the couple to meet each partner's needs. Furthermore, environmental stressors can impair couple-level processes, such as diminishing the quality of communication (Williamson, Karney, & Bradbury, 2013) or decreasing sexual intimacy (Bodenmann, Atkins, Schär, & Poffet, 2010). Thus, environmental stressors can place couples at risk if they are unable to navigate these demands in an effective manner.

The environmental context also might include important resources that support adaptive couple functioning, such as community resources providing financial assistance, childcare, or a sense of belonging. Indeed, most couples find that their environment encompasses a complex mix of stressors and resources. Of note, couples are not simply passive recipients of environmental influences; rather, couples are active agents in choosing and contributing to their environmental context as well, even within the constraints of their circumstances. Although at times these choices can be detrimental to the relationship (e.g., choosing friends who do not support a couple's values related to monogamy), the couple's interactions with the environment can facilitate individual well-being, couple functioning, and their broader community.

Thus, in addition to addressing each person's needs and personality styles (Chapter 7) and supporting the couple in functioning effectively as a united team (Chapter 8), well-functioning relationships also involve interacting effectively with the couple's social and physical environment. This chapter discusses this third contextual domain and addresses (a) how environmental demands can negatively impact relationship functioning, (b) the potential benefits of environmental resources when they are utilized, and (c) interventions to help couples interact with the environment in a way that meets individual needs, sustains and enhances couple functioning, and contributes more broadly to the environmental context.

Furthermore, this chapter considers a couple's cultural context, including how to adapt treatment to consider issues of diversity. Of note, diversity and cultural factors are not considered solely part of the environmental context, but rather are integral to individual and couple factors and reflected in emotions, cognitions, and behaviours as well. However, if one or both partners hold a minority cultural identity, they might have decreased access to environmental resources as well as additional systematic stressors (e.g., racism). Consistent with a minority stress model (e.g., Meyer, 2003), although minority stress can impact a couple's functioning at any level (e.g., individual, couple, or environmental level) or in any domain (e.g., cognitions, behaviours, or emotions), the *source* of minority stress is at the environmental level. That is, to a large extent, society is not set up to systematically affirm, represent, and provide resources to people with a minority identity. Thus, one focus in this chapter is to highlight examples of how environmental demands and resources might differ depending on the cultural identities of a couple.

Environmental demands and stressors

Many aspects of the environmental context can function as stressors on couples. Chronic stress from a variety of sources is associated with lower relationship satisfaction, steeper declines in relationship satisfaction, and less relationship stability (Barton, Futris, & Nielsen, 2015; Karney & Bradbury, 2005; Neff & Karney, 2007). What follows is a discussion of the types of environmental demands couples can experience and ways these demands can negatively impact the relationship.

Types of stressor

Couples might confront multiple types of environmental stressors, such as living in a disadvantaged neighbourhood, caring for elderly or disabled relatives, and institutionalized discrimination. Rather than discussing each of these individually, several dimensions of demands are highlighted briefly as a way to classify types of stressors (Boss, 1988; Epstein & Baucom, 2002). After describing this classification system, we address how they appear to impact relationships.

First, environmental stressors can either *directly* impact both members of a couple or *indirectly* impact the couple via the impact on one partner (Falconier et al., 2015). For example, the couple might together confront challenges related to parenting a child with behavioural problems. On the other hand, in a different area of life, one partner might experience external demands which indirectly impact the couple. For instance, research has shown that experiencing negative social interactions at work is associated with broad increases in anger expressions and withdrawal for both men and women; similarly, a heavy workload is associated with anger and withdrawal for women (Story & Repetti, 2006).

Second, stressors can be classified as *major* or *minor*, both of which can have a negative impact on the relationship. Major stressors might include tending to a relative after a significant accident, one partner losing their job, or a child's diagnosis of cancer. Often, couples and therapists are acutely aware of the impact of such major stresses on the relationship, but they might overlook the impact of chronic minor stressors. Yet, ongoing minor stressors such as a high workload and difficult interactions with friends are associated with couple arguments. This tendency toward arguments, in turn, is associated with decreased relationship satisfaction for both partners (Falconier et al., 2015).

Additional dimensions of external stressors to consider include *positive versus negative*, *normative versus non-normative*, and *volitional versus non-volitional*. Positive demands might include a job promotion or involvement in a hobby. These experiences can be desirable and often are of great value to the individual and the couple. However, these demands also consume time and energy, which can make it more difficult for individuals to meet other needs of each partner and the relationship. Similarly, while demands that are normative and/or volitional (e.g., getting married or buying a house) might appear easier to contend with than stressors that are non-normative and/or non-volitional (e.g., an unexpected major illness), each of these categories can have a significant negative impact. For example, a couple might have chosen to live a military life, yet there are numerous stressors that can accompany this choice. As a result, considerable effort has been given to developing couple-based interventions to address the effects of this broad environmental factor (Monson & Snyder, 2012; Sayers, 2011).

Transition to parenthood as a normative stressor

As noted in Chapter 8, the transition to parenthood (TTP) can be very stressful for one or both parents, even though it might be viewed as normative, volitional, and positive. Given its great impact on most couples who have children, additional consideration to this stage is provided here as an example of a normative stressor that still is quite challenging for many couples. Indeed, for many, the TTP is accompanied by increases in individual distress and relationship discord. Taking on the new role of "parent" typically requires a fundamental shift in the way individuals and couples operate, although couples frequently do not anticipate the full extent of such changes.

For instance, prior to having a child, Aliyah and Ernesto typically spent the first couple of hours after work each night on their own or with their own friends before coming home for dinner and spending time together. This ritual was an important way in which they met individual needs for autonomy and affiliation. Ernesto attempted to continue this pattern even after the birth of their son, Jerome. As a result, Aliyah would come home from work and care for Jerome on her own, while Ernesto continued to spend time with his friends after work. Aliyah began to feel resentful, overwhelmed, and alone, and when Ernesto came home, Aliyah would typically raise her concerns, which quickly turned into a heated argument. Ernesto started to feel that coming home was aversive and started staying out later, leading to additional arguments. Thus, a pattern of behaviour that worked effectively for the couple prior to the TTP contributed to relationship decline for the couple after having a child.

More generally, how individuals experience their roles, including the parental role, can have a profound impact on individual and couple well-being. Role overload (also known as work-family strain)—the feeling of being overwhelmed by multiple roles, or experiencing multiple roles as incompatible—is associated with relationship conflict during the TTP (Perry-Jenkins, Goldberg, Pierce, & Sayer, 2007). For women, work-family strain is also associated with postpartum distress (Boeding, Baucom, Cohen, Meltzer-Brody, & Brandon, 2017). Additionally, men's view of their new parental roles as being unacceptable to the men in some way is associated with poorer relationship adjustment for both men and women as well as greater postpartum distress for men (Boeding et al., 2017). Thus, even a "normative," "volitional," and "positive" demand such as the TTP can be challenging, placing high demand on the couple to adapt in a thoughtful and explicit way. As noted in this example of TTP, a stressor can have its impact on the couple in multiple ways which can be helpful to understand in order to develop effective interventions.

Ways in which environmental stressors can affect relationship functioning

Environmental stressors can impact relationship functioning in many ways. First, environmental demands can interfere with individual need fulfilment. Rituals (e.g., Friday night date night or weekend religious services) are ways that a couple can ensure that they are spending time together and meeting partners' needs for affiliation and intimacy. However, new environmental demands can impact the couple's ability to sustain prior rituals. Couples might no longer have sufficient time for meaningful activities or might have the time but not the energy or mental resources to focus on meeting their own and their partner's needs. Moreover, couples might fully understand *why* there is a disruption in having their needs met, but if they do not find alternative ways of meeting these needs, individuals can feel unfulfilled in the relationship.

Stress also can significantly interrupt couple-level processes such as communication and intimacy. Financial strain and other stressors are associated with more negative communication behaviour, such as the expression of contempt or hostility (Williamson et al., 2013) and the occurrence of demand–withdraw interaction patterns in couple interactions (Barton et al., 2015). Furthermore, higher levels of stress from a variety of sources (e.g., work, health concerns) are associated with increased conflict overall, and this outcome is especially likely when *both* partners report an increased experience of stress (Timmons, Arbel, & Margolin, 2017). Higher daily stress levels are also associated with decreased sexual activity and satisfaction for women (Bodenmann et al., 2010). Additionally, stress is associated with increased rumination and withdrawal (King & DeLongis, 2014). Thus, while communication, joint activities, and physical intimacy can increase feelings of closeness and connection to one's partner, stress can undermine all of these processes.

Environmental factors also can disrupt a couple's boundaries. As discussed in Chapter 8, couples differ regarding the boundaries they set between themselves and others, and partners within a given relationship might differ in their preferences, based on their own backgrounds and values. Often boundary issues are not discussed until one or both partners experience what they consider to be an infringement. For example, after their mother died, Raj invited his developmentally disabled brother, Naveen, to live with him and his wife, Jackie. Although extending this invitation was consistent with Raj's Indian values around caring for one's family, Jackie, who was Caucasian American, experienced it as a boundary violation, leading to arguments about whether it was acceptable for extended family to live with them. Thus, couples do not always have well-defined, mutually agreed-upon boundaries, and in the face of new demands, partners might unwittingly violate one person's assumptions concerning the "appropriate" way to act. Alternatively, couples might have an agreement regarding boundaries, but some aspect of the environment might intrude unexpectedly (e.g., a partner's boss might expect employees to respond to email throughout the evening, leading to frequent interruptions of family time).

Although much of the above discussion highlights changes the couple might experience under stress, at times environmental demands do not alter the relationship per se; rather, new environmental demands can bring to light incompatibilities between partners that they were previously unaware of, or that otherwise had little impact. For example, Mariana and

Alejandro both had always enjoyed high-paying jobs, but after several financial setbacks during a difficult time in the economy, the couple had to adjust their budget. In doing so, the couple learned that they had quite discrepant views on "what is really important to spend money on," an issue they had not had to contend with before, given their previous financial status.

In sum, environmental demands can negatively impact relationship satisfaction and stability via several routes, such as making it more difficult to meet individual needs, negatively impacting key dyadic processes such as communication, and bringing to light previously unrecognized incompatibilities between partners. Additionally, this impact can occur even for demands that are considered "normative," "minor," or even "positive." In addition to conferring stress, the environment can also contain resources that benefit the couple.

Environmental resources

Although the environmental context can place a variety of demands on the couple, it also might be rich with potential resources, including those provided by friends, family, community agencies, and broader communities and institutions. Being embedded in a community of family, friends, and co-workers who affirm the couple provides opportunities for enjoyment and meaningful experiences. In addition, as couples confront various demands, they might find themselves in need of support. First, they might need instrumental support, such as financial assistance, legal protection from discriminatory hiring practices, or care facilities for family members. Second, couples might need informational support, such as medical advice or information on how others have managed similar stressful circumstances. Finally, couples might need emotional support, including receiving messages of care and concern. These resources can not only help the couple to address demands and alleviate stress but also provide opportunities for the growth of each partner and the couple as a unit. Increased family and friend support predicts better individual well-being for those in same-sex and different-sex relationships; also, family support carries particular importance in predicting relationship quality for different-sex couples although not for same-sex couples (Graham & Barnow, 2013). For couples in which one or both partners are members of gender or sexual minorities, their families of choice (i.e., close-knit networks of friends who are central in the couple's life) tend to be particularly important when the partners' own families of origin are unsupportive or have rejected them as a couple.

Environmental resources are not only important for helping the couple confront demands; they also contribute to meeting individuals' needs, strengthening relationship processes, and contributing to the couple's environment in a positive manner. Interacting with others is an important way that people fulfil their personal needs (e.g., for affiliation by interacting with colleagues), which can be valuable in alleviating pressure for the relationship to meet all the needs of each partner. Additionally, the environmental context often is rich with opportunities that support the initiation and maintenance of rituals (e.g., spending holidays with family). Furthermore, couples have the potential to be a resource to the world around them, enhancing the well-being of others and improving the quality of their own environment. For instance, couples might volunteer at the local food bank or other community organizations dedicated to causes they value. In addition to positively impacting the world around the couple, these types of interactions can reaffirm the couple's values and strengthen their bond (e.g., "This is what we do; this is what we believe in and how we give back"). An added benefit is that these prosocial interactions can broaden the couple's view beyond themselves, which can be particularly important for distressed couples who are arguing frequently and losing sight of the bigger picture. Likewise, such acts that focus on the needs of others can shift the focus of attention for an individual who is struggling personally, such as a depressed person who has become self-focused.

Although resources are imperative for optimally functioning relationships, there often are barriers to their use. First, certain resources might not actually be available to a given couple (e.g., couples might not have the financial resources to hire someone to help them around the home). In other instances, resources might be available, but the couple is unaware of them (e.g., a couple might not know about resources available to parents of children with autism, or a non-English-speaking couple might be unaware of community resources because the pertinent outreach materials are provided only in English). Finally, one or both partners might have beliefs that represent barriers, such as "Seeking help means that I am weak." Thus, there can be several barriers to the use of potential resources. The above discussion emphasizes how a couple responds to stressors and resources in their environment once they are in that environment. In addition, it is important to understand the extent to which the couple might have the ability to select and create their own environment.

Couples creating and influencing their environment

Couples' environments might naturally carry with them certain demands or resources; however, rather than being passive recipients, couples also actively choose, create, and influence their environments (e.g., changing jobs, asserting their needs within particular relationships, or attempting to influence or change policies or laws). Thus, the relationship between the couple and the environment is bidirectional. For example, in some countries a same-sex couple might choose to move to an area that is more supportive of same-sex relationships. This new community could ultimately carry with it more job opportunities, friends who support the couple, and physical or psychological safety.

The ways in which couples shape their environment might be intentional or unintentional, and these interactions can have a positive, negative, or mixed impact. For example, a couple might decide to change their place of worship because their beliefs do not align with those of their local religious leader; however, the couple might then lose or become less connected to important friends from their previous religious community. Additionally, if couples interact with the environment to the extent that little time remains for individual or couple time, they might find that in fulfilling certain needs, others are left unmet. Thus, it is important for couples to consider the impacts that a given interaction with the environment might have and to find a balance between focusing on the self, the couple, and their environment.

While couples sometimes choose to interact with the environment in certain ways to meet individual needs or enhance their relationship, at other times the goal might be prosocial in nature, focused on improving some aspect of the environment, such as championing the cause of a local charity. These types of interactions might not be equally feasible across the developmental life span, with younger couples often having neither the time nor the money to pursue these avenues, even if they have the desire. Nonetheless, to the extent that couples can engage in these types of activities, couples might find that their own bond is strengthened amid improving the broader environment.

While all couples experience a mix of demands and supports in their environment and the specifics vary greatly depending on the couple, the two partners' cultural backgrounds and identities can increase the likelihood of experiencing certain stressors or being able to access particular resources.

Culture and diversity: demands and resources

Aspects of diversity and culture can result in different demands (e.g., minority stress) and/or access to resources (e.g., legal protections) for different couples. The following section highlights selected research related to additional demands that couples might experience if they are a member of a minority group based on some aspect(s) of their background or identity, recognizing that there are inherent strengths and unique resources associated with various identities as well. Given that a full discussion of this topic is well beyond the scope of this book, the current focus is on clinical issues and research findings to consider when working with couples.

One of the aspects that likely impacts how the social environment will respond to the couple is how visible a given aspect of their identity is, and/or what others assume about their identities based on the partners' or the couple's appearance. For example, couples in which a visible or readily identifiable aspect of their identity signifies cultural minority status or difference from a societal norm (e.g., same-sex couples, interracial couples, partners with notable age differences, a partner with a visible physical disability) often report experiencing stigma and discrimination. This discrimination might be directed not only toward the partners as individuals, but also toward the relationship per se. Same-sex relationships might be particularly impacted by this process, as one study found even higher rates of relationship stigma from family and the public for same-sex relationships compared to interracial relationships (Rosenthal & Starks, 2015), although the nature of this stigma likely varies greatly across specific regions and countries. Even so, relationship stigma from friends is associated with a variety of negative relationship outcomes for both same-sex couples and interracial couples, including lower love, trust, and commitment between partners, as well as greater rates of interpersonal violence (Rosenthal & Starks, 2015).

Related to the issue of visibility, couples may face difficulties if their particular background or identity, or the intersection of multiple aspects of their identities, makes it more difficult to find social circles where they feel fully embraced. Consequences might include decreased recognition, acceptance, and support. For example, Black Latino/Latina individuals in the United States might describe experiences of not feeling fully accepted in either African American or Latino/Latina communities, with each community perceiving the individual to be a member of the "other" group. Such experiences might be heightened based on their physical appearance (e.g., others assuming a Black individual is not Latino/Latina) and if their partner belongs to only one of the two groups (e.g., partner is Black and not Latino/Latina). Similarly, bisexual individuals experience even higher health disparities compared to those who identify as gay or lesbian. This disparity has been attributed to experiences of "bi-erasure" or bisexual invisibility. For example, when a bisexual man is seen in a relationship with a woman, others may not know, believe, or affirm his identity, instead perceiving him as heterosexual. Bisexual individuals also report lack of acceptance and discrimination in lesbian/gay communities (e.g., being accepted as gay when in a same-sex relationship but not receiving the same affirmation as bisexual). In general, research findings among LGBT individuals demonstrate that non-affirming environments are associated with adverse mental health outcomes, including suicide (Liu & Mustanski, 2012; Rood, Puckett, Pantalone, & Bradford, 2015; Skerrett, Kõlves, & De Leo, 2016). Thus, in many ways, the degree to which a couple's diverse aspects are easily "visible" to others can result in different types of pressure and support.

Other common difficulties couples might face in terms of environmental factors are unrelated to the issue of visibility or difference between the two partners. For example, low-income couples and families tend to face a range of unique stressors and challenges. Low-income populations are more prone to divorce than higher income populations (Karney & Bradbury, 2005). In general, the impact of stress on relationship quality is stronger for low-income couples, possibly due to more demands and less access to resources (Maisel & Karney, 2012). For example, for couples experiencing fertility issues, methods of becoming parents such as artificial insemination or adoption are less available to lower income couples due to financial costs (Cao, Mills-Koonce, Wood, & Fine, 2016). Additionally, lower income couples often cannot afford to hire someone to help with child care, home cleaning, or other needs around the home; thus, resources that can strengthen more affluent couples or buffer them from stress often are not as available to lower income couples. Not only does stress have a greater impact on low-income couples, but they often are exposed to a greater number and more severe stressors as well. For example, partners may need to have more than one job, accept less flexible work hours or work evening shifts, or have irregular income. In addition, challenges such as housing insecurity, living in disadvantaged neighbourhoods, limited access to high-quality education, and worries about their children's future, often without much experience to guide them (e.g., regarding access to higher education if the couple did not attend college themselves), create both long- and short-term consequences that make life more difficult and stressful. Research about psychological impacts of financial strain continues to expand. For example, individuals growing up in poverty have been shown to prioritize short-term over long-term rewards, likely based on lifelong experiences that working toward long-term goals (e.g., saving money to buy a newer car) might be impeded by the energy and effort needed to ensure short-term well-being (having to pay for expensive repairs to get an older car to work) (Griskevicius, Tybur, Delton, & Robertson, 2011).

In summary, there are many intersecting ways in which individuals and couples might experience unique stressors and environmental demands, based on their individual and joint identities and background. Below, we provide a more in-depth discussion of same-sex couples.

Sexual minority couples

Research has consistently shown that overall, many aspects of relationship functioning are not particularly different for same-sex versus different-sex couples (Green & Mitchell, 2015; Rostosky & Riggle, 2017). Same-sex couples typically report comparable levels of relationship satisfaction (Kurdek, 2005) and potentially even less decline in relationship quality over time (Kurdek, 2008). Same-sex couples typically argue about similar concerns, and the predictors of relationship quality and satisfaction are comparable to those for different-sex couples (Kurdek, 2005; Rostosky & Riggle, 2017). Furthermore, same-sex couples demonstrate multiple strengths, such as, on average, more equal divisions of household labour and child care, higher perceived intimacy, and better conflict resolution skills (Kurdek, 2005; Rostosky & Riggle, 2017).

Despite these similarities and strengths, sexual minority couples (whether in a same-sex or different-sex relationship) experience demands on their relationship that heterosexual couples do not. First, they can experience minority stress in multiple ways, including discrimination and homonegativity (i.e., negative attitudes about sexual minority individuals). Not only can couples experience homonegativity from those outside their relationship (including family, communities, and institutions), but one or both partners might also experience some degree of internalized homonegativity, that is, devaluing themselves due to their sexual identity. Increased internalized homonegativity has been associated with lower self-esteem, higher rates of depression and suicide, more relationship problems, and lower relationship satisfaction (Frost & Meyer, 2009; Green & Mitchell, 2015; Lavner, 2017). Furthermore, sexual minority groups do not, in many countries, have legal protections against discrimination. As a result, being "out" can carry with it economic risks, such as loss of employment. "Outness" also can result in increased risk of physical harm or exposure to prejudice (Green & Mitchell, 2015). Thus, the decision of whether to be out and to whom is complicated. Partners might disagree on the degree to which they disclose their relationship status to others, which can become a major source of distress for couples.

In many countries, same-sex marriage continues to be illegal. In the United Kingdom, The Marriage (Same Sex Couples) Act 2013 came into force in 2014, allowing same-sex marriages in England and Wales. The Scottish Parliament also has passed a Marriage and Civil Partnership (Scotland) Act 2014, with same-sex marriages becoming legal in Scotland in 2014. Within the United States, same-sex marriage became legal across all states in 2015 (Rostosky & Riggle, 2017). The continued lack of legal recognition in other countries can have widespread implications, such as affecting couples' financial opportunities, access to healthcare, and ability to adopt. On the other hand, a legal relationship status, such as a civil union or marriage, is associated with less psychological distress for partners in same-sex relationships (Rostosky & Riggle, 2017).

Another demand that affects all couples but can be especially complex for same-sex couples is that of role divisions (e.g., providing child care, earning money, taking initiative in resolving conflict; Green & Mitchell, 2015). Most same-sex couples were raised in different-sex households and, therefore, do not have a relational template which is representative of their gender makeup in the way that is typical for different-sex couples. This experience carries both advantages and disadvantages. For same-sex couples, there is greater opportunity for and valuing of equality; yet, there is also greater ambiguity regarding roles and a tendency to have a longer period of sorting out role divisions in relationships (Green & Mitchell, 2015).

Role ambiguity is challenging regardless of whether the couple has children, but it can become especially salient during the transition to parenthood. More generally, becoming parents carries additional demands for same-sex couples as they navigate challenges such as how to establish both partners' identities as parents when (a) only one partner is biologically related to the child and (b) they are likely to encounter negative views about the legitimacy of their family unit (Cao et al., 2016). Indeed, same-sex couples might feel the need to hide relationship or parental concerns for fear they will not come across as "good" or "adequate" parents, even though research does not support the idea that children of same-sex parents experience negative outcomes due to parental sexual orientation (Cao et al., 2016).

Finally, same-sex couples often find that they receive less support from their families of origin than different-sex couples do (Green & Mitchell, 2015). Instead, as mentioned above, families of choice (i.e., cohesive friend networks) often become primary sources of support for same-sex couples. Bisexual individuals can experience even less support overall than gay or lesbian individuals, as they receive less support both from their families and gay and lesbian communities (Green & Mitchell, 2015).

Summary

In summary, couples do not exist in isolation but instead interact with countless other individuals and systems; this environmental context includes a mixture of demands and resources for all couples, which might vary depending on aspects of diversity and culture. Interactions with the environment are bidirectional and can meet individual needs, enhance relationship processes, and improve the broader environment. Yet, at times, the couple might not have the ability to navigate demands on their own, might experience barriers to much-needed resources, or might interact with the environment in ways that are detrimental for one or both partners and/or the relationship. In the sections that follow, interventions focused on assisting the couple in interacting with the environment in an effective manner are discussed. Of note, no new interventions are introduced, since addressing this domain involves the same cognitive, behavioural, and emotional interventions discussed earlier in this book. Rather, the following sections illustrate ways in which these interventions can be applied to address this particular domain.

Interventions to cope with environmental stressors and access resources

As discussed previously, environmental demands can affect the couple either directly as a unit or indirectly via the impact on one partner. Below are discussions of how the therapist might address both indirect and direct demands on the couple, as well as considerations for addressing diversity-related issues in treatment.

Indirect stressors on the couple via one partner

At times, one or both partners might be contending with a specific stressor in their individual life, such as feeling burned out from work or resolving a conflict with a friend. Although the given issue might not directly involve the couple's relationship, it frequently happens that one partner's stress indirectly impacts the relationship (e.g., feeling too exhausted at the end of the day to engage in sexual intimacy). Contending with a partner's stress can be difficult, and even when a partner is well intentioned, there often is a limit to the amount of support they can provide. If a given stressor persists or the individual appears to experience one stressor after another, the other partner can begin to feel resentful or withdraw from the person coping with the demand.

There are multiple goals in couple therapy when a demand is negatively impacting at least one individual and is indirectly impacting the relationship, including: (a) increasing partners' empathy for one another and the situation they are encountering individually and as a couple, (b) increasing individual coping strategies, (c) decreasing negative responses of the partner (e.g., withdrawal, criticism), (d) increasing support, and (e) problem-solving together to address the demand. Numerous strategies can be utilized to this end, such as facilitating sharing thoughts and feelings and decision-making conversations. Ultimately, any of the strategies discussed in the cognitive, behavioural, and emotional chapters (see Chapters 4–6) can be utilized to accomplish these goals.

For example, when Colin first started having disagreements with his father about how to manage the family pub, Emma was quite supportive. When at home, Colin frequently raised the issues he had with his father and ruminated about the lack of forward progress. Although initially supportive, over time Emma started to feel overwhelmed by Colin's distress and hurt that her needs to feel close were not being addressed because of his absorption regarding his difficulty with his father. Therefore, when Colin arrived home, she greeted him but then withdrew to spend time alone. Over time, Colin and Emma became increasingly disconnected, with each of them feeling that they were confronting a difficult situation on their own rather than as a team.

As illustrated in the above example, people often do not understand the ways in which their individual stress is impacting the relationship, and over time the other partner might be less empathetic than when the demand began. Therefore, an initial goal might be for both partners to understand more about how the stressor and its management is impacting each other. Thus, in this case, the therapist presented feedback to the couple about the way in which Colin's disagreement with his father appeared to be impacting their relationship. Then the couple had a conversation focused on sharing thoughts and feelings, in which Emma expressed to Colin how his self-absorption had impacted her, including how uncared for she had felt recently. Colin also explained that his current fear of talking to his father came from many frightening experiences he had as a child, when he was belittled and blamed when anything went wrong. These conversations were invaluable to the couple as they developed greater mutual empathy.

In addition to increasing empathy and understanding, the therapist helped Colin increase his individual coping and emotion regulation skills (see Chapter 13 for specific strategies) as well as helping Emma to decrease her withdrawal in response to Colin. Emma was able to provide more support as Colin improved in his ability to regulate his emotions. In a situation such as Colin and Emma's, an important goal is to ensure that the nonstressed partner's needs also are considered. To accomplish this goal in this case, the therapist provided psychoeducation about the importance of maintaining some sense of balance in giving and receiving support and how that approach might assist both partners. Additionally, the therapist used guided behaviour change to help both partners determine ways they could increase and otherwise improve their provision of support to one another. Finally, even if both partners and the couple are coping with a demand effectively, often it is valuable to problem-solve around the stressor itself, exploring whether there are ways to minimize or alleviate the demand when appropriate. Thus, the therapist led the couple in a decision-making conversation in which multiple ideas were considered for addressing the underlying issue (e.g., selling the business or directly expressing Colin's concerns to his father). Given that the couple had developed more effective ways to cope with the existing stress themselves, they were in a better position to problem-solve as a team. Overall, the therapist helped Colin and Emma address this indirect demand with a number of strategies described in Chapters 4–6 and 13, including: (a) increasing their understanding and empathy for one another, (b) increasing their individual coping strategies, (c) increasing their support for one another, and (d) problem-solving around the issue together as a unit.

Direct demands affecting both partners or the couple directly

At times, a given environmental demand affects the couple directly, such as when a couple realizes that they have not saved enough money for retirement and will need to adjust their spending, or when a couple fears for their family's safety because of an increase in neighbourhood crime. Sometimes couples underestimate the impact that these types of demands have on their relationship and instead present for treatment identifying more proximal and perhaps secondary concerns (e.g., increased arguing). In other instances, couples present with a high degree of hopelessness regarding the stressor and overestimate its effects.

Thus, one goal for couple therapy when a couple is jointly managing an environmental stressor is to assist the couple in realistically appraising the stressor and instilling hope to the degree appropriate. Other goals include (a) increasing the couple's awareness and understanding of the impact of the stressor on each partner and the relationship and (b) collaboratively identifying strategies and resources for its management. For example, a conversation focused on sharing thoughts and feelings can help couples more realistically appraise a given demand and help the couple to feel like a team again, what Christensen, Doss, and Jacobson (2014) refer to as "empathic joining." Then, decision-making conversations can help the couple identify ways to address that stressor. Of note, therapists might provide psychoeducation at key points during these sessions regarding typical ways in which various demands (e.g., miscarriage, "empty nest syndrome," retirement, diagnosis of a serious illness) affect couples and suggest strategies based on this knowledge. This information can be particularly valuable among couples who seem to arrive at decisions that the therapist believes might be counterproductive (e.g., deciding that it is fine for a depressed person to stay in bed routinely while the other individual takes over all household chores).

Helping couples access resources

As noted previously, couples can face numerous barriers to utilizing available resources, such as a lack of awareness or beliefs that impede their use. Thus, it is helpful if therapists are well-versed with local support groups and organizations, transportation, and child care services. It is impossible to remain informed about all available resources; thus, being able to assist the couple in researching these resources can be an important intervention in its own right. Furthermore, it can be helpful for the therapist to adopt an open and creative stance, adapting interventions according to what resources are available in the wider environment. For example, if a therapist is utilizing behavioural activation as a way of treating depression, it can be helpful for the therapist and couple to determine options that are free of charge or inexpensive for couples living on low incomes. Furthermore, to the extent that particular cognitions represent barriers to the use of community supports or to asking family members for help when appropriate, the therapist might utilize a variety of cognitive interventions, as discussed in Chapter 5.

Adapting treatment strategies based on diversity/cultural factors

Research on couple therapy in general, including CBCT, has traditionally focused on Caucasian, middle or upper class, heterosexual couples; thus, there is a dearth of empirical data to guide decisions of whether and how to adapt treatment to various cultural subgroups (Kelly, Bhagwat, Maynigo, & Moses, 2014). Indeed, it is possible that CBCT will not be equally effective with all cultural subgroups. However, a CBCT-based relationship education programme that originated in the United States—the Prevention and Relationship Education Program (PREP)—has been shown to be effective in studies of Army couples, African American couples, and prison inmates, which lends some support to the notion that CBCT can be used with diverse couples (Beach et al., 2011; Einhorn et al., 2008; Owen et al., 2012; Stanley et al., 2014). Building on the promising findings regarding relationship education, Whitton et al. (2017) have created a relationship education program for same sex female couples, and the initial findings are promising. Likewise, meta-analytic studies comparing the outcomes of behaviourally oriented couple interventions in the United States (e.g., D. H. Baucom, Sayers, & Sher, 1990), Europe (e.g., Hahlweg, Schindler, Revenstorf, & Brengelmann, 1984), and Australia (e.g., Halford, Sanders, & Behrens, 1993) have found those interventions to be equally effective, recognizing that across those continents, the samples have typically consisted of middle-class couples (D. H. Baucom, Hahlweg, &

Kuschel, 2003). However, a study on behaviourally based couple therapies with military veterans in the US showed that African American couples benefited *more* from the intervention than Caucasian couples (Doss et al., 2012). Furthermore, the emphasis in CBCT on collaboration, building on strengths, adapting to individual needs, and hypothesis testing are all particularly well-suited to treating couples from a variety of cultures (Kelly et al., 2014; Kelly & Iwamasa, 2005). That is, CBCT does not take a "one-size-fits-all" approach but instead values and emphasizes adapting treatment to each couple based on broad intervention principles. Therefore, there is reason to believe that broad CBCT intervention strategies can be utilized cross-culturally if they are adapted to address the specific needs of particular couples (e.g., dealing with different extended family norms if the couple has become acculturated into another culture over time).

Ultimately, treatment should proceed by utilizing the overarching framework and underlying principles outlined throughout this book, while being sensitive to issues relevant to couples from a given cultural group. If a given partner or couple experiences internalized homonegativity, for example, cognitive interventions aimed at modifying these beliefs and helping partners to see oppression as the issue rather than sexual orientation might be helpful (Green & Mitchell, 2015). Also, if a given couple is experiencing high levels of homonegativity from their environment, decision-making might focus on considering changing the environmental context (e.g., moving).

At times, therapists might adapt their style or select particular interventions, based on the culture of the couple. For example, in Chinese culture, there is less use of direct confrontation and more emphasis on indirect communication to help the other person "save face" (Epstein et al., 2012; Epstein, Curtis, Edwards, Young, & Zheng, 2014). Additionally, some Chinese families are more likely to express love via actions rather than through direct expression of emotions. Furthermore, Chinese culture emphasizes loyalty and putting the collective good over individual good (Epstein et al., 2012). Much of CBCT fits well with Chinese culture, such as the therapist being directive (given the emphasis on hierarchy) and providing psychoeducation, skills training, and homework (Epstein et al., 2012). However, communication with an emphasis on direct expression of emotions might not be appropriate (Epstein et al., 2012). Additionally, Chinese couples might be less likely to give feedback to their therapist (again, given the emphasis on respecting authority). Thus, it might be helpful to ask Chinese couples regularly for their feedback about treatment (giving them permission to voice concerns), to work with the couple to utilize communication guidelines but to adapt the guidelines to their own style, to recognize action-based expressions of love (versus verbal expression), and to consider individual sessions for addressing cognitions (Epstein et al., 2012).

While being aware of culturally specific factors that couples might encounter, couple therapists also need to be aware of within-group diversity as with any client, and avoid under- or overestimating a particular couple's problems and strengths and the effects of their identity and cultural background. More extensive resources for clinicians to increase their knowledge and competence in working with culturally diverse clients focused on individual therapy are available and applicable to CBCT as well (e.g., Hays, 2016; Sue & Sue, 2012), including considerations related to the clinician's own identities and cultural values. As discussed in Chapter 3, the therapist becomes an important aspect of the couple's environment during treatment, with a variety of implications for cultural considerations. In addition to issues that can arise in individual therapy, further complexities can occur in couple therapy depending on the real and perceived similarities and differences between each partner's and the therapist's identities (e.g., couple perceives the therapist to be more similar to one but not the other partner). In general, we encourage CBCT therapists to initiate open conversation about such issues in treatment (for additional resources in approaching such topics, see Sue and Sue, 2012; Hays, 2016).

In summary, in most instances, culturally sensitive CBCT does not involve new therapeutic interventions per se; rather, it is essential that the therapist has the knowledge and comfort level needed to discuss and address diversity-related concerns openly, applying the same types of intervention to the specific content that is relevant for that couple. At the same time, it is possible that new approaches will be needed to be of maximum value to the diverse range of couples who seek assistance. Likewise, the currently discussed, overarching CBCT approach integrated with new intervention strategies might be optimal. At present, it is crucial that theoreticians, researchers, and clinicians maintain an open, flexible perspective in addressing these complex issues.

Main points

- Couples are embedded in layers of social and physical environments, including their home, children, extended family, neighbourhood, work environment, and the current social and political climate.
- The bidirectional interactions that couples have with their environment can either sustain and enhance their relationship or contribute to its deterioration.
- That is, the environmental context often affords both stressors or demands for change, as well as resources to assist the couple. Stressors can inhibit the couple's ability to meet individual needs and can impede dyadic processes (e.g., communication); resources can help the couple cope with various stressors, meet individual needs, enhance couple processes (e.g., intimacy), and contribute to others' well-being.
- Couples are not passive recipients of their environment; instead, to some extent, they choose, help to create, and influence their environmental context.
- The types of stressors that couples experience and the resources available to them depend on the couple's culture. All aspects of the model discussed in this book can be impacted by culture (e.g., ways of thinking, emotional expression, individual styles).
- Helping couples navigate stressors and access resources, as well as addressing the couple's cultural context, involves utilizing the cognitive, emotional, and behavioural interventions that were discussed previously. Rarely are new types of interventions needed to address environmental factors.
- Goals aimed at addressing indirect demands include: (a) increasing partners' empathy for one another, (b) increasing individual coping strategies, (c) increasing support, and (d) problem-solving together to address environmental factors.
- Goals aimed at addressing direct demands include: (a) assisting the couple in realistically appraising the demand and instilling hope, (b) increasing the couple's understanding of the impact that the demand has on each partner and the relationship, and (c) collaboratively identifying strategies and resources for managing the demand.
- In treating diverse couples, it is appropriate to utilize the overarching framework and principles discussed throughout this book, adapting to a given culture; that is, certain interventions might be differentially emphasized or adapted to address the specific needs of each unique couple.

Part IV

Addressing psychopathology in a relationship context

Individuals become depressed, develop anxiety disorders, or misuse substances, so it is understandable that the standard of care has been individual therapy for various types of adult psychopathology. At the same time, both empirical findings and clinical observation make it clear that these disorders do not exist in a vacuum. Instead, psychological disorders impact and are impacted by the person's partner, their relationship, and their broader social and physical environment. Therefore, taking into account these various layers of our contextual framework has the potential to broaden treatment options and improve response rates, even for disorders for which there are existing empirically supported treatments. Across disorders, a significant proportion of patients does not respond optimally to treatment, drops out prematurely, or relapses after initially successful treatment, suggesting that there is still much to learn in the field of psychotherapy.

Including the partner in treatment is one viable option for addressing the limitations in our current intervention efforts, with unique opportunities for effecting profound changes. A distressed relationship is a chronic stressor with the potential to precipitate, maintain, or exacerbate a disorder. Even within satisfied relationships, partners often do not know how to help and can inadvertently respond in ways that are counterproductive in the long run. On the other hand, partners and couples' relationships can be invaluable resources in assisting with a wide range of psychological disorders.

While including a partner in treatment can sound reasonable, that broad assertion does not clarify specific ways that a partner can be of assistance during therapy sessions or in the couple's daily life. Chapters 10–13 provide an overall perspective, along with detailed recommendations for specific disorders. Chapter 10 describes our conceptual framework for understanding psychopathology in a couple context, along with an overview of treatment principles and clinical guidelines applicable across disorders. Because depression and anxiety disorders are seen so commonly in routine outpatient settings, Chapters 11 and 12 are devoted to these two groups of disorders, respectively. Chapter 12 also addresses two additional disorders—OCD and PTSD—that are closely related to anxiety disorders and are frequently seen in outpatient settings. Chapter 13 presents a consideration of a variety of other disorders that can be approached from a couple-based perspective as well.

Couple-based treatment outcome research for some disorders is well developed and convincing. For other disorders, couple-based intervention outcome research is still at an early stage, and thus far the findings are quite promising. This broad conclusion is not surprising given that in every instance, the interventions described in these chapters incorporate principles from empirically supported individual treatments into the couple-based interventions. These individual treatment principles are then integrated with empirically supported strategies for promoting healthy changes in couples from CBCT and other couple therapy models, for the purpose of alleviating psychopathology in one or both partners.

Chapter 10

Treating psychopathology with couple-based interventions

Chapters 1–9 describe the CBCT model and interventions to treat relationship difficulties, while attending to factors related to each individual as a person, the couple as a unit, and how the couple relates to their broader environment. In addition to normative differences such as unique personality characteristics and differing needs, many people in committed relationships also experience "non-normative" issues such as trauma or psychopathology. Although psychopathology in adults is often framed as an individual problem, psychological disorders have a wide-ranging impact on relationship functioning (Whisman & Baucom, 2012). In addition, relationship factors can greatly impede or facilitate symptom improvement. In this chapter, we provide an overall framework for conceptualizing psychopathology in couples from a cognitive-behavioural perspective, along with our approach to treating psychopathology by intervening with the couple (see Snyder & Whisman, 2003, and Hahlweg & Baucom, 2008, for additional discussion of how to work with couples when one or both partners have a psychological disorder).

The goal of these interventions, which we call *couple-based treatments* for psychopathology, is to treat the individual disorder, whereas the primary goal of *couple therapy* is to treat relationship distress. Rather than creating entirely new interventions, however, the couple-based treatments integrate evidence-based principles from both CBCT and individual CBT in order to address a given disorder. Therefore, CBT therapists can draw on familiar treatment strategies viewed through an interpersonal lens, utilizing the power of the relationship to assist with the disorder. Improving the relationship can be an important secondary goal of the treatment, given that a positive social environment facilitates the person's functioning. However, couple-based interventions do not assume the presence of relationship distress and can be indicated when the couple is satisfied with their relationship. Even caring, well-intentioned partners often inadvertently behave in ways that maintain or even exacerbate the disorder.

As noted in Chapter 1, ample research demonstrates the bidirectional relationship between psychopathology and relationship distress (e.g., Whisman, 2019; Whisman & Baucom, 2012). Although the symptoms and associated characteristics vary widely across disorders, most forms of psychopathology have in common that negative emotions are increased in frequency and intensity, positive emotions are diminished, and behavioural repertoires become more limited and rigid. Consequently, in the presence of psychopathology, there might be little space for positive experiences in relationships, and more frequent negative experiences might dominate the couple's interactions (i.e., the hallmark features of relationship distress). On the other hand, relationship distress creates a chronically negative, stressful environment that increases the risk of the development, maintenance, or exacerbation of symptoms.

Additionally, healthy relationships fulfil an important function in maintaining psychological and physiological balance (Sbarra & Hazan, 2008). Thus, in addition to overt social support, the "hidden" ways of being able to draw on a partner to deal with negative emotions are central to relationships, but relationship distress interferes with this important resource to support individual functioning.

In contrast, satisfying relationships can impact the course of a disorder positively with an overall caring atmosphere, ample social support, and interpersonal emotion regulation. Despite these positive effects, partners often do not know how to help their loved one and, at times, their well-intentioned responses inadvertently contribute to symptom maintenance over the longer term. To some degree, partners' behaviours vary in response to the specific disorder that the other person is experiencing. That is, different types of disorders "pull" for specific types of interaction patterns with close others, such as partners becoming very involved (e.g., providing excessive reassurance, accommodation) or being shut out (e.g., withdrawal, little self-disclosure, participating in avoidance) (Fischer et al., 2017). This principle (i.e., interaction patterns changing based on the symptoms) has been referred to as "symptom–system fit," with broad applicability to a range of disorders, and it is discussed further below (Shoham, Butler, Rohrbaugh, & Trost, 2007).

Some theories have posited that psychopathology is a family problem that is being manifested as psychopathology in one individual; however, most contemporary perspectives including cognitive-behavioural and systems theories do not make this assumption. Within the current CBCT framework, there is no assumption or evidence that partners or relationships are at fault in causing a disorder or that individual difficulties are an enactment of a broader family issue. Instead, the complex pattern of reciprocal associations between psychopathology and relationship functioning can inadvertently precipitate, maintain, or exacerbate an individual's symptoms and distress (Fischer & Baucom, 2018).

Understanding this interpersonal context and the bidirectional associations of psychological symptoms and relationship functioning has important treatment implications. Therefore, the current chapter first discusses how relationships can impact psychopathology in the context of both distressed and satisfied relationships, and how psychopathology impacts romantic relationships. Next, a conceptual framework for couple-based interventions and clinical guidelines for interventions are provided.

How relationships impact psychopathology

The precise association between relationship functioning and psychopathology depends on the nature of the disorder and relationship; however, there are several common dimensions to consider. The relationship context influences psychopathology on two levels—first, the *broad atmosphere* either can be facilitative of symptom improvement (in a well-functioning relationship that creates a positive environment for both partners) or can serve as a diffuse, chronic stressor that negatively impacts the disorder (in a distressed relationship). Second, *specific responses* to symptoms and interaction patterns resulting from characteristics of the disorder have an impact, regardless of the quality of the relationship. For example, partners of individuals with anxiety disorders, posttraumatic stress disorder (PTSD), or obsessive-compulsive disorder (OCD) frequently attempt to help the person avoid or reduce anxiety in the short term by providing reassurance or assisting with safety behaviours and avoidance of fear-provoking situations (Reuman & Abramowitz, 2018). These responses might be well intended or represent attempts to avoid arguments. However, these behaviours "make room" for the symptoms to continue. Due to the long-term negative impact on the course of the disorder, these partner behaviours are termed *symptom accommodation* (Calvocoressi et al., 1995; Shafran, Ralph, & Tallis, 1995), which is an important concept in understanding the interpersonal context of psychopathology and is discussed in more detail below. Although the term "symptom accommodation" (sometimes referred to as "family accommodation") has been used most frequently in the literature on anxiety, eating disorders, and substance use, most disorders "pull" for couple interactions that result in accommodation. Thus, partners of individuals with depression might take over family responsibilities that the patient[1] finds overwhelming, resulting in a decline in self-efficacy for the patient. Of note, these two levels of how relationships can influence psychopathology (broad atmosphere and specific responses) also apply to other domains of individual functioning, including medical illness (e.g., D. H. Baucom, Porter, et al., 2012).

Despite some overlaps, the ways in which relationships impact psychopathology at the broad and specific levels tend to vary as a function of relationship distress; thus, relationship functioning is another dimension to consider. For example, expressed emotion (discussed in more detail below) might manifest itself differently depending on relationship satisfaction, with greater tendencies for critical/hostile responses in distressed relationships and emotionally overinvolved responses in satisfied relationships.

Drawing a dichotomous distinction between distressed and satisfied relationships is an oversimplification, since relationship satisfaction exists on a continuum and many relationships function well in some domains while facing difficulties in others. However, an understanding of the role of (a) broad versus specific impacts and (b) distressed versus satisfied relationship and how they interact can help to inform case conceptualization and treatment planning for a variety of disorders within couples. As highlighted in Table 10.1, taking into account relationship satisfaction and its impact on psychopathology conceptually results in four categories that clinicians might consider and address. We discuss these pathways in more detail below.

How distressed relationships impact psychopathology

As mentioned previously, many people with relationship distress also experience psychopathology. Indeed, one study found that those in a distressed relationship who were not

Table 10.1 Relationship satisfaction and common broad versus specific influences of relationships on psychopathology

	Distressed relationship	*Satisfied relationship*
Broad level	• Overall negative, stressful atmosphere • Lack of positive, rewarding interactions	• Overall positive, supportive atmosphere • Few negative, stressful interactions
Specific level	• Expressed emotion: criticism and hostility regarding the disorder • Symptom accommodation to avoid conflict and arguments	• Expressed emotion: emotional overinvolvement/excessive self-sacrifice related to the disorder • Symptom accommodation out of care and concern, or not to "rock the boat"

currently depressed were 2.7 times more likely to develop depression in the following year, compared to people who were in a satisfied relationship (Whisman & Bruce, 1999), and were 3.7 times more likely to develop substance use disorders (Whisman, Uebelacker, & Bruce, 2006). Other findings support similar associations between various clinical presentations and relationship distress, with some indications that this association might be particularly strong for other internalizing disorders, such as anxiety disorders (Egan & Smith, 2017). This close association between relationship distress and the most common forms of psychopathology highlights the need to consider relationship distress as a broad, chronic, diffuse stressor. At this broad level, perceived stress increases with relationship difficulties (Bodenmann & Cina, 2006), and chronic stress of almost any nature tends to worsen individual functioning, including psychological disorders (Coyne & Downey, 1991). In this context, stress might result from a host of negative interactions, such as arguments, devaluing comments, or aggression. In the context of relationship distress, adaptive dyadic coping with daily stressors is diminished (Revenson, Kayser, & Bodenmann, 2005), important needs for intimacy and affiliation remain unmet (Epstein & Baucom, 2002), and loneliness is common, which in turn has adverse effects on personal functioning, mental health, and even mortality (Holt-Lunstad, Smith, Baker, Harris, & Stephenson, 2015).

In addition to a broad aversive atmosphere, interactions around specific symptoms also have the potential for adverse effects on the patient. For example, if a depressed individual struggles to get out of bed in the morning, a partner might become irritated and critical. A distressed but disengaged partner might be less likely to criticize the depressed person's inactivity overtly. Instead, they might ignore the behaviour and provide little incentive for the depressed partner to become active in the presence of low energy. In both cases (hostile or disengaged relationship), the patient might be less likely to be disclosing or seek (and receive) social support from their partner; both self-disclosure and social support are important interpersonal processes that can support healthy individual functioning yet have the potential to become undermined in this context. Moreover, patient behaviour that has the potential to alleviate depression (i.e., getting out of bed and engaging in activity) is not being encouraged or reinforced by the partner, and, instead, the patient's withdrawal is being accommodated. Thus, in distressed relationships, partners' reactions to psychopathology are more likely to be hostile or distant, or they might accommodate in order to avoid additional arguments. Both partners likely experience a host of unmet needs, which can create ongoing emotional distress with further negative impacts on emotional well-being for both people.

In addition to symptom accommodation, another aspect of partner responses to the disorder is referred to as *expressed emotion* (Hooley & Teasdale, 1989). In expressed emotion, partners exhibit two overall response styles relative to the patient: First, partners might respond with high levels of criticism and hostility, particularly if the partner attributes the symptoms to be within the patient's control (i.e., believes that the patient could just "snap out of it"). Second, partners can become emotionally overinvolved and excessively self-sacrificial (e.g., they might treat the patient as less capable than is needed, excessively take over responsibilities, and become highly distressed by signs of the patient's suffering). In distressed relationships, partners might be more likely to show criticism and hostility rather than emotional overinvolvement or excessive self-sacrifice. Expressed emotion has been extensively researched in family members of individuals with a variety of disorders such as schizophrenia, mood disorders, PTSD, and eating disorders, and robustly predicts negative outcomes such as relapses and worse treatment effects (e.g., Chambless, Floyd, Rodebaugh, & Steketee, 2007; Hooley, 2007; Hooley & Miklowitz, 2018; Szmukler, Eisler, Russell, & Dare, 1985).

How satisfied relationships impact psychopathology

A common misconception is that couple-based treatments are applicable only for people in distressed relationships. However, partners in satisfied relationships also can adversely impact psychopathology and its treatment, typically unintentionally. In satisfied relationships, the broad atmosphere is of less concern, as it tends to be more positive and adaptive. For example, among women who had recovered from anorexia a decade earlier (a disorder which can have a very long or even chronic course in adults), a supportive partner was one of the most frequently cited influences in their recovery (Tozzi, Sullivan, Fear, McKenzie, & Bulik, 2003). Yet at the specific level, the interaction between the partner and patient around the patient's symptoms can become problematic, even in happy relationships.

For many partners, it is painful to watch their loved ones struggle with distress, so they attempt to prevent or alleviate that distress on an immediate basis. A partner of an individual with a social anxiety disorder might therefore decline social invitations, inadvertently contributing to avoidance, which is one of the most central maintaining factors of social anxiety. By helping to alleviate the distress that comes from engaging with an uncomfortable situation, the partner inadvertently "makes room" for continued maladaptive behaviours that have short-term regulating benefits for the patient (e.g., avoidance, substance use, compulsive behaviours, disordered eating, medication nonadherence). In addition to preventing or alleviating the patients' distress out of care and concern, some loving partners also experience distress when they see the patient suffer, and accommodation can be an attempt to decrease their own distress (Fischer et al., 2017; Weber et al., 2018).

Within nondistressed relationships, expressed emotion might be less likely to be in the form of criticism or hostility; rather, emotional overinvolvement or excessive self-sacrifice might be more common. Sacrificing one's own daily activities beyond what is needed in order to assist the patient can carry the message that the patient is unable to cope without the partner, undermining the patient's sense of self-efficacy. Consistent with this broader perspective, Fredman, Baucom, Boeding, and Miklowitz (2015) found that if family members demonstrated high levels of emotional involvement in interacting with patients with bipolar disorder prior to treatment, then family therapy which addressed such interaction patterns was more effective than individual therapy.

In summary, both satisfied and distressed relationships have the potential to impact the symptoms and course of a variety of disorders, often in the context of both patients and partners making their best efforts to cope and responding in ways they think will be helpful. In order to understand how relationships have these impacts on the disorder, it is necessary to consider both the broad relationship atmosphere and the interactions around particular symptoms. Within this bidirectional linkage, psychopathology also can greatly impact the couple's relationship, which then can further limit patients' and partners' ability to respond adaptively to the disorder.

How psychopathology impacts relationships

Besides the effects of the interpersonal context on psychopathology, it is also important to consider the reverse—how psychopathology affects relationships. Even among couples who report high relationship satisfaction, the presence of a psychological disorder increases the risk of relationship satisfaction declining in the future (Whisman & Baucom, 2012). While research on the particular pathways that result in these adverse effects is still in its early stages, a number of insights can be drawn by integrating empirical and clinical observations.

Overall, psychopathology restricts what a person can do; in other words, psychopathology "shrinks one's world." Psychopathology often necessitates that the patient spend an inordinate amount of time and energy coping with negative emotions and behavioural symptoms and leaves little time for optimizing potentially positive aspects of life; as a result, overall, individual functioning in a range of contexts declines. Given that the partner and the relationship are part of the patient's world, the relationship often "shrinks" as well, in terms of the range of adaptive behaviours, emotional experiences, and ways the two partners are able to relate to each other.

The manner in which the relationship shifts depends on the particular disorder and the unique characteristics of the two people involved. As mentioned above, different clinical presentations tend to "pull" for particular interaction patterns and ways partners relate to each other, resulting in the relationship or a family system reorganizing itself in order to "make room" for the disorder (Fischer et al., 2017; Shoham et al., 2007). These resulting patterns can in turn affect the disorder long term and are, therefore, important treatment targets that can be uniquely addressed in couple-based treatments. Among other factors, the tendency to engage in approach versus withdrawal behaviours in response to the distress and the temporal course of the disorder greatly impacts the relationship as a system. As Sillars and Vangelista (2018) note, early research on communication assumed that approaching with openness and disclosure was constructive, and withdrawing along with a focus on individual privacy was maladaptive. Recent perspectives provide a more balanced view on the potential value of these two responses (see Sillars & Vangelista, 2018). In the context of psychopathology, however, both of these interpersonal strategies often are enacted in an extreme, maladaptive way.

Approach/withdrawal in response to distress

Most people have strategies and skills to cope with or lower emotional distress (i.e., emotion regulation strategies). Such strategies involve ways to modulate emotions on one's own (individual emotion regulation) and ways to incorporate close others, including partners, to help deal with distressing emotions (interpersonal emotion regulation). There appear to be systematic differences in the tendency to include or "bring in" versus "shut out" close others in addressing concerns as a function of specific disorders (Fischer et al., 2017). Depending on the context and frequency of engaging in these interpersonal strategies for emotion regulation, such tendencies can be maladaptive and part of the ways that the couple's relationship adapts to the patient's symptoms.

Some disorders are associated with a tendency to engage the partner in addressing the patient's disorder-related distress (such as anxiety and sadness). Although seeking social support or expressing distress to close others is generally adaptive, in the context of psychopathology such attempts can become excessive or ineffective, or can create a pattern that inadvertently maintains the symptoms over the longer term. Other disorders are associated with patients' tendencies to regulate their distress individually. In some instances, patients withdraw actively and even push their partners away. This tendency has been described in the literature on eating disorders, both in clinical studies (Fischer, Kirby, Raney, Baucom, & Bulik, 2015; Schmidt & Treasure, 2006) and in empirical investigations (e.g., Huke & Slade, 2006). How partners respond to patients' attempts to regulate emotions in solitude can also have a negative impact. For example, mutually avoidant interaction styles for both partners can lead to an overall "cloud of secrecy," within which eating disorders thrive

(Fischer, Kirby, et al., 2015). Avoidance and emotional numbing in PTSD can have similar negative effects on relationships, whereas increased self-disclosure is associated with more favourable outcomes (Monson & Fredman, 2012).

Importantly, the partner also needs to have healthy individual and interpersonal emotion regulation skills in responding to the patient. If a partner becomes overwhelmed by the patient's distress or is experiencing psychopathology themselves, they might be less able to interact with the patient in adaptive ways. Our recent work in England within the National Health Service confirms the widespread existence of this pattern. In our investigation of the effectiveness of couple-based interventions when one person was diagnosed with depression, approximately half of the partners also experienced clinically significant levels of depression or anxiety symptoms (D. H. Baucom et al., 2018). Such couples likely struggle for a variety of reasons. For example, they might have difficulty with either partner lacking the resources or focus to assist the other person in regulating emotions when they themselves are struggling to cope due to their own symptoms.

In other couples, partners might withdraw for a different reason. At times, partners describe their experience of "walking on eggshells" when the patient has a disorder that is associated with a high degree of emotional reactivity/lability, or severe difficulties regulating negative emotions. These disorders include borderline personality disorder, PTSD, some eating disorders, and in some cases depression with high levels of irritability or agitation. Partners become concerned that they will upset the patient, leading to an argument, or worsen the patient's distress; therefore, partners might self-censor what they say to the patient. When a patient has borderline personality disorder, the couple commonly experiences frequent intense emotional exchanges, and partners might be wary of engaging with the patient around potentially evocative topics, given that negative emotions might quickly escalate beyond the patient's control (Kirby & Baucom, 2007a).

Timing of the onset and the episodic nature of the disorder

The impact of the disorder on the relationship also can vary depending on the timing of the onset and course of the disorder relative to the relationship development. Although not all disorders are persistent, the fact that approximately half of all disorders begin by the mid-teens and three-quarters by the mid-20s (Kessler et al., 2007) suggests that many disorders are present by the time that many people marry or make similar commitments. For example, persistent low-level symptoms of anxiety that have been present since the beginning of the relationship could pose challenges, but the couple might have found a way to respond to the symptoms such that they do not impact the relationship in a major way. On the other hand, a couple in which both partners have generally been healthy might struggle more with the later onset of a disorder that imposes new restrictions on the relationship, leads to a shift in roles and responsibilities, or is confusing to the partner—for example, interpreting withdrawal in the context of PTSD as a sign of loss of interest in the partner rather than a mental health issue (Monson & Fredman, 2012). However, periods of healthy functioning also can help the couple to build an effective, resilient relationship that is then better equipped to respond to a new challenge in adaptive ways.

Once a disorder has begun, its impact on the relationship also depends on whether the disorder is episodic in nature. Bipolar and psychotic disorders tend to follow a cyclical pattern or are recurrent with better functioning between episodes. Individuals with other common disorders also experience recurrent episodes, although relapses might build more slowly and episodes might be less distinct (e.g., a slowly evolving major depressive episode or eating disorder relapse compared to a manic episode with a rapid onset). As a result, couples need to adapt their interactions, and partners need to respond differently depending on the patient's current status, which can be challenging. For example, partners might need to "take over" during a manic episode to ensure that the patient receives appropriate treatment when they are unable to recognize their own needs. However, if partners continue to behave in the same way after the manic episode has subsided, such a response likely is "excessive self-sacrifice," with negative impact on the relationship, partner, patient, and disorder (Fredman, Baucom, et al., 2015). Thus, any disorder that is recurrent or cyclical requires considerable flexibility to respond adaptively in different ways at various times, with partners potentially moving in and out of a caregiver role. While some couples might be quite effective in doing so, others experience difficulty and strain as a result (see Chapter 13 for a fuller discussion of this challenge).

Thus, there are many ways in which psychopathology impacts relationship functioning and relationships influence psychopathology. Clinicians can benefit greatly from understanding these complex reciprocal associations when planning treatment and intervening with both psychopathology and relationship concerns. We now turn to a consideration of how these factors can be taken into account during intervention.

Intervention strategies

As described above, the term "couple-based interventions" refers to a treatment approach that involves couples in which one or both partners experience psychopathology, and the primary goal of treatment is to treat the disorder. When relationship distress is present as well, the dual goals of attending to the disorder and relationship well-being become joint priorities. Cognitive-behavioural, couple-based interventions represent an integration of CBCT with evidence-based principles from established individual treatments for a given disorder (typically individual CBT). Thus, novel couple-based approaches do not aim to "reinvent the wheel" in treating psychopathology. Instead, couple-based interventions use what has been shown to be effective in individual therapy as a centrepiece and expand on these best practices by working with the couple. Thus, a couple-based intervention for anxiety disorders is likely to involve exposure exercises, and treatment for depression will involve behavioural activation. In addition, the partner's participation in treatment also provides the opportunity to address issues that would be difficult if not impossible to address adequately in individual settings, such as difficulties with physical intimacy in eating disorders, expressed emotion from partners, or symptom accommodation. Consistent evidence across disorders demonstrates that cognitive-behavioural, couple-based interventions are at least as effective, and in many instances more effective than individual therapy (Fischer et al., 2016). Furthermore, emerging evidence suggests that couple-based treatments might be equally effective even when the partner also experiences depression or anxiety, and partners who were not originally the focus of treatment also benefit notably in terms of their own symptom improvement (D. H. Baucom et al., 2018; Belus, Baucom, & Abramowitz, 2014).

In summary, there are compelling reasons to involve partners in treatment. However, this broad statement does not explain how the couple and partner can work together effectively during treatment. In order to delineate how partners might be included in treatment most effectively, D. H. Baucom, Shoham, Mueser, Daiuto, and Stickle (1998) have distinguished among (a) partner-assisted interventions, (b) disorder-specific interventions, and (c) couple therapy. Most comprehensive couple-based treatments combine all three types of intervention, often beginning with interventions specifically focused on the disorder and broadening later to include relationship factors less focal to the disorder. Below is a brief overview of the three approaches, again applicable to a range of disorders, incorporating an integration of CBCT principles with the particular individual, evidence-based interventions.

Partner-assisted interventions draw on the partner as a "coach" in helping the patient make needed individual changes; they do not attempt to change the relationship itself. In essence, such interventions rely on the partner to encourage and enable empirically supported interventions without attempting to change relationship patterns (e.g., encouraging a depressed person to go to work as a form of behavioural activation for depression). In this way, partner-assisted interventions are most closely focused on the disorder, can be indicated regardless of the level of relationship satisfaction, and have been used successfully among both distressed and non-distressed couples. Frequently, these interventions are used early in treatment. However, clinicians might consider the order of interventions when working with a highly distressed couple that is struggling to contain criticism and hostility, which might interfere with engaging in the intervention (see below for clinical guidelines regarding sequencing).

Disorder-specific interventions broaden the intervention to focus on altering aspects of the couple's relationship that are relevant to the maintenance and treatment of the disorder. These interventions attempt to change how the couple interacts in domains focal to the disorder (e.g., redistribution of partners' responsibilities such that a person with agoraphobia goes out of the house to shop, a central aspect of exposure treatment). Thus, disorder-specific interventions can play a central role in reducing symptom accommodation, expressed emotion, or other maladaptive interaction patterns. The couple's relationship and each person's behaviour within that relationship are being directly addressed, but only if they are directly relevant to the patient's symptoms. For example, if disagreements about in-laws are not related to the disorder, they would not be addressed. Given that both distressed and satisfied couples tend to display symptom accommodation and other interaction patterns that might maintain the disorder, again, there is no assumption that relationship distress is present when disorder-specific interventions are indicated.

Couple therapy is the broadest type of intervention and targets general relationship difficulties to decrease the negative impact of relationship distress as a chronic stressor on the person with psychopathology. It is important to note that couple therapy is the only one of the three types of interventions where relationship distress is assumed to be present. If the couple is in a satisfied relationship, couple therapy is not needed. If time permits, brief relationship enhancement to optimize relationship functioning among satisfied couples might be included.

Common elements in comprehensive couple-based treatments

While the particular treatment and content of the session will vary greatly depending on the disorder, some common elements are shared among many cognitive-behavioural, couple-based interventions. Some of these interventions have been manualized (i.e., presented in a manual, with specific goals and techniques for each session). However, if clinicians understand the overall rationale, framework, and sequence, they can tailor an intervention to the needs of a given couple. The following common elements are frequently employed in cognitive-behavioural, couple-based interventions, often in the following order unless other factors indicate that interventions should be sequenced differently (see clinical guidelines below).

Psychoeducation

After the initial assessment, treatment often begins with psychoeducation about the disorder, its etiology, common issues related to the interpersonal context (e.g., how both partners experience the disorder, how the disorder affects and is affected by the relationship), and the overall treatment principles. Psychoeducation also explains what each person's role will be and how the partners will work together as a team in therapy. In this process, clinicians also might gather information regarding the dimensions previously discussed to gain a more in-depth understanding of the couple (e.g., how they have adapted to past episodes of the disorder). Other important goals for psychoeducation are to counter possible misconceptions about the disorder and treatment, and to begin countering maladaptive attributions about both partners' behaviours relative to the disorder.

Communication skills training—sharing thoughts and feelings and problem-solving skills

Following psychoeducation, the treatment often moves to communication skills training (see Chapter 4), with a specific focus on using the communication skills to address the couple's experiences with the disorder. Frequently, over the course of treatment, content needs to be addressed that either the patient or the partner finds difficult to discuss. Additionally, treatment for most types of psychopathology requires a wide range of behaviour changes, which can be challenging for the patient and the couple to implement. Thus, couples benefit from a solid foundation in communication and joint problem-solving skills in preparation for the remainder of treatment, to equip them to navigate any upcoming emotional and practical challenges.

Partner-assisted and disorder-specific interventions

In many couple-based treatments, these two ways of intervening with couples represent the core of the treatment. For example, a couple-based intervention for depression includes behavioural activation, with support and/or participation from the partner, such as helping the patient identify available exercise programmes or engaging in more frequent joint pleasurable activities such as a walk together. Other treatments might include components of interventions for medication adherence, such as in bipolar disorder. Thus, the therapist might encourage each partner to express their concerns and struggles related to the medication. Depending on what was revealed, the therapist then selects an appropriate intervention, such as psychoeducation to rectify misconceptions about the medication, or problem-solving to identify ways the partner can help remind the patient to take the medication without causing tension between them (partner-assisted intervention) or to assist with developing different daily couple routines to minimize missed doses of medication (disorder-specific intervention).

Couple therapy/addressing broader relationship issues

As the intervention with the broadest focus and applicability to couples with relationship difficulties only, general CBCT interventions often are a useful component of treatment, particularly toward the end of therapy when issues relevant to the disorder have been resolved. Reducing chronic stress that results from relationship difficulties facilitates the maintenance of treatment gains and further symptom improvement. For some disorders such as depression, addressing relationship distress can be important for relapse prevention. Given that many couples have already built a variety of skills throughout treatment, and some might already have seen improvements in overall relationship satisfaction, these skills can now also be applied to broader issues unrelated to the disorder (e.g., arguments about finances). As discussed further below, for some couples it might be necessary to intervene on broader relationship issues first, if these issues seem to interfere with partner-assisted and disorder-specific interventions (e.g., the presence of very high levels of hostility).

Subsequent chapters will provide a more in-depth discussion of how the above elements have been adapted to treat particular disorders, with additional recommendations for clinical applications (see Chapters 11–13). However, some common, general clinical decisions are likely to be necessary regardless of the disorder, such as the determination of whether a couple-based approach is indicated. Below, we provide general guidelines relevant to optimal care.

Guidelines for clinical decision-making

In clinical practice, depending on the referral and prescreening system, the clinician needs to make a range of decisions regarding the appropriate treatment of a particular couple or patient. Questions to be addressed include whether a couple-based treatment is indicated, how the primary presenting concerns (relationship versus individual distress) and referral source might impact openness to a couple-based treatment, whether partners should be included in treatment on a more limited basis, how to sequence interventions within a couple-based approach, and considerations for treating couples in which both partners experience significant distress or psychopathology. While empirical evidence can inform some of these decisions, in many areas research is lacking regarding individualized decisions in routine clinical care. The recommendations provided below are based on empirical evidence where available, along with our collective clinical experience.

Individual versus couple-based treatment

First, a clinician must decide whether to use a couple-based intervention for the disorder, and if so, whether working with the couple will be the sole intervention. We are not proposing that all therapy for psychopathology should be couple-based. However, growing evidence suggests that couple-based interventions should be considered as an option for partnered patients. There is some indication that individual therapy tends to be less effective when relationship distress is present; therefore, when both individual psychopathology and relationship distress are present, a couple-based intervention should be given strong consideration.

In many instances, both partners experience psychopathology or a subclinical level of symptoms. For example, in our dissemination work with the National Health Service in England, therapists provided our couple-based treatment for depression in routine clinical settings in which one partner was referred for depression. Because not all partnered patients could be offered a couple-based intervention, therapists were encouraged to target relationally distressed couples, since couple-based interventions might have unique incremental benefits for such couples, compared to individual CBT. In the initial evaluation of treatment outcomes in these settings, approximately half of the couples included a "non-patient partner" who scored in the clinical range on depression or anxiety (D. H. Baucom et al.,

2018). Encouragingly, the couple-based intervention was effective in alleviating distress in both partners, without providing individual therapy for either partner. Additionally, the intervention was equally effective for patients with, and patients without, a partner who also experienced clinically significant depression or anxiety (D. H. Baucom et al., 2018). Thus, couple-based interventions might be appropriate when both partners experience distress along with relationship discord, leading to an efficient use of therapist effort by conjointly treating two patients at the same time.

However, there also are circumstances in which individual therapy (or individual therapy preceding a couple intervention) is indicated, which include but are not limited to the following three common contexts. First, a patient might need or desire to explore long-standing, unresolved issues that predate the current relationship within the privacy and freedom of individual therapy, such as the unaddressed repercussions of childhood sexual abuse or previous relationship trauma (e.g., intimate partner violence or partner affairs from a previous relationship). Although it might be important also to address aspects of such long-standing issues conjointly with a partner, sometimes it can be beneficial to help the person address a painful past experience individually before deciding how to approach it with a partner present.

Second, if it is necessary to address individual issues, some patients might wish to exclude the partner because of concerns about privacy or the partner's potential reactions to the issues. For example, if someone is grappling with their gender identity and experiences depressive symptoms during this exploration, such issues clearly have implications for their relationship. However, identity-related questions might first need to be examined independently. Concerns about how a partner might react and having to address the partner's own emotional responses can inhibit the patient's open exploration. If the couple is distressed as well, it might be appropriate for the patient to be in individual therapy while the couple continues to work together to cope with the ambiguous situation and ensure that they do not address it in a destructive manner.

Third, the nature of one or both partners' psychopathology might require individual therapy prior to or alongside a couple-based approach. The complexity of some disorders requires a multidisciplinary approach, with multiple providers contributing their area of expertise. Such approaches exist, for example, to treat anorexia nervosa, borderline personality disorder, and schizophrenia. We recommend collaboration and consultation among the treating providers to maximize consistency in the approaches being employed. Even when a multidisciplinary team is not needed, the nature of either partner's difficulties might severely interfere with conjoint sessions and result in imbalanced sessions focused mainly on the patient. In this case, one or both partners should be in individual therapy prior to or concurrent with the couple-based intervention. For example, although there is strong evidence for the effectiveness of conjoint therapy for PTSD (Monson et al., 2012), when a patient with PTSD is struggling to regulate anger and the couple is experiencing high relationship distress, conjoint sessions might be challenging if the relationship distress consistently triggers anger in the partner's presence. Similarly, individuals with borderline personality disorder might benefit from some initial training in emotion regulation and distress tolerance skills to equip them to engage effectively in couples work, given that relationship distress often has dysregulating effects even for people with no broader emotion regulation difficulties. Contraindications for general couple therapy for certain types of psychopathology apply to couple-based treatments for psychopathology as well, such as severe domestic violence or heavy substance abuse, if it is not the index disorder to be treated.

Finally, in some clinical settings, the above decisions might not be only case-by-case decisions; rather, clinic policies or the limited availability of therapists who are trained in couple-based approaches might require systematic triaging of patients to either individual or couple-based treatment. While there are no available research studies that have directly tested differential treatment effectiveness of individual and couple treatments when patients have been "matched" to a treatment modality, a number of factors are predictive of treatment outcome in general, with some evidence that they can be alleviated most effectively in a couple-based format. These factors include (a) relationship distress, as discussed above, (b) high levels of symptom accommodation particularly in anxiety disorders, OCD, and PTSD, and (c) high levels of expressed emotions (criticism/hostility) among partners across disorders.

Thus, a variety of characteristics of the presenting concerns, relationship dynamics, and characteristics of the clinic setting can guide decisions regarding which modality to recommend as the treatment of choice. Clinicians should keep in mind that individual and couple-based treatments are not mutually exclusive, and they might consider combining the two modalities with coordination between providers, or purposefully sequencing the two (e.g., begin with individual therapy to increase individual skills that will help the patient use the couple sessions well, then proceed to couple-based interventions). Typically, individual therapy and the couple-based treatment are delivered by two different providers in order to avoid complications with the therapeutic alliance. However, there might be some settings in which individual therapy is conducted and partners are brought into therapy sessions for a limited time. In such instances, the individual therapist likely works with the couple in a limited capacity, and the interventions are primarily partner-assisted interventions (e.g., psychoeducation, increasing support around particular interventions).

CONSIDERATIONS FOR TREATMENT SETTING, REFERRAL SOURCE, AND PATIENT PREFERENCES

Given that couple-based approaches are still uncommon and likely unfamiliar to most laypersons, therapists will rarely encounter patients who specifically request a couple-based treatment of their disorder. Thus, clinicians will find themselves in the position of raising this possibility and should consider how the context might impact the patient's receptiveness to the recommendation. Depending on how the individual or couple entered therapy, different challenges arise. For example, if a couple presents for couple therapy focused on relationship distress and it becomes clear that one partner has notable psychopathology that warrants treatment prior to addressing the relationship difficulties, this partner might feel blamed for the relationship difficulties if the therapist suggests treatment for their disorder. Alternatively, a different set of concerns might arise for patients presenting for individual therapy for a particular disorder and the clinician suggests bringing the partner into treatment. However, in our experience with couple-based treatment studies for eating disorders, OCD, anxiety disorders, and depression, partners rarely refuse participation in treatment if patients are willing. In fact, many partners appear relieved to be involved with the opportunity to share their concerns and frustrations and learn how to be helpful.

Considering the high rates of comorbidity of relationship distress and psychopathology, couple therapists should expect to encounter a range of psychological disorders on a routine basis even when the primary presenting concern is relationship distress. If it becomes evident that one partner is experiencing psychopathology and the clinician has determined that a couple-based treatment to address the disorder is optimal, providing psychoeducation about the available treatment options will support the couple in making an informed choice. For example, a clinician might recommend that one or both partners seek treatment focused on their psychopathology and that this could either occur in a couple-based format, or via referrals for individual therapy while the couple focuses on their relationship distress. For couples in which only one person has a disorder that warrants treatment, it is critical to approach this conversation in a way that does not inadvertently suggest that this person is "the problem" or the person to blame for the relationship difficulties; likewise, some partners might be concerned that they have caused the other person's disorder. Clinicians can help avoid such misunderstandings in two ways. They can explicitly state that the recommendation to focus on the disorder first is not to suggest that the disorder/patient is the root cause of the couple's difficulties, and that the relationship and partner are not to blame for the disorder. In addition, they can provide a rationale for the recommendation. For example:

> You are very likely to benefit from couple therapy, and I highly recommend that you focus on your relationship. However, if we can make some progress on the OCD symptoms first, that will give you much more time and freedom to focus on your relationship and might also reduce the frequent arguments you have, particularly when you're with family and the OCD-related anxiety intensifies.

As with this example, language that "externalizes" the disorder as a problem separate from the patient (e.g., "OCD limits what both of you can do" rather than "You (the patient) limit what both of you can do") facilitates a non-blaming discussion on how best to approach the task of achieving change.

If the couple chooses to pursue individual treatment while also beginning couple therapy, it is important for the therapist to coordinate with the individual providers to ensure that the treatments are consistent and compatible. Thus, if one patient needs to complete time-intensive exposure outings for agoraphobia over the weekend, the couple therapist should be aware and could, if needed, help the couple use problem-solving guidelines to plan their schedule to allow the patient sufficient time while also addressing other family needs. Similarly, even if the disorder is not the primary focus of treatment, the couple therapy might still need to be adapted to account for this important factor. For example, joint activities that are enjoyable for couples might be impacted by the disorder, such as dinner outings in the presence of an eating disorder.

INCLUDING PARTNERS IN TREATMENT ON A MORE LIMITED BASIS

At times, it is not possible to conduct a comprehensive couple-based treatment in which both partners attend all sessions; for example, scheduling issues, limited availability of trained clinicians working with couples, or concerns regarding insurance coverage can create constraints. Alternatively, a therapist might conclude that individual therapy is most appropriate, but integrating the partner in treatment in limited ways would still be beneficial. Although systematic clinical trials are yet to be conducted for most disorders in terms of the best ways to incorporate partners on a limited basis, there are reasonable starting points for maximizing the benefit of a smaller number of couple-based sessions along with routine individual therapy. In these circumstances, the main goals of such an approach are (a) to ensure that the partner has accurate information about the patient's symptoms and behaviours and to counter potentially hostile attributions regarding the disorder, and (b) to ensure that the partner does not inadvertently interfere with treatment or engage in excessive symptom accommodation. Partners also might benefit from having a clearer sense of how they can help, as reports of feeling helpless or concerned about making things worse are common among partners (Huke & Slade, 2006).

To help a partner understand the disorder and learn how to assist the patient, psychoeducation sessions explaining the disorder and the general therapeutic principles are a useful starting point. If the patient has already received psychoeducation, they can participate in presenting and discussing this information with the partner. Additionally, the partner might have their own observations regarding the patient's symptoms or their consequences that the patient is unable to identify on their own. Psychoeducation might start with general, open questions about what the partner knows about the disorder, what they have noticed in the patient, and what they believe to be the cause of the disorder. Simple handouts listing the main symptoms can provide a useful structure and basis for discussion.

The discussion also might include some instructions for what the partner should avoid (e.g., high levels of criticism, overinvolvement) as well as concrete ways to be helpful (e.g., increasing joint positive activities as part of depression treatment). If the couple struggles to discuss the disorder, communication skills training, particularly for sharing thoughts and feelings, can help the couple be more open about the disorder and its impact on their lives so that each does not endure the difficult situation in isolation.

Sequencing interventions in couple-based treatments

If a comprehensive couple-based treatment is chosen, various ways of sequencing the interventions can be considered. As discussed above, a common sequence of assessment, psychoeducation, communication training, partner-assisted/disorder-specific interventions, and couple therapy interventions works well for a wide range of couples. However, if the patient sought treatment for a psychological disorder and agreed to a couple-based treatment, we recommend beginning with a focus on the individual disorder as the primary presenting concern when plausible and when the partner has agreed. On the other hand, there are at least two circumstances which call for an increased focus on the couple's distressed relationship early in treatment. First, when the couple's relationship distress is characterized by high levels of negatives, it can be difficult to focus on the disorder because the couple's negative interactions become the focus of attention. Such couples might struggle to engage in disorder-focused discussions in a helpful manner, and therapists can find themselves frequently interrupting hostile interactions. When there is a great deal of negative interaction between the two members of the couple or the partner is ambivalent about supporting the patient, then improving the relationship becomes a high priority so that the couple can work together effectively to address the psychopathology. Other types of distressed couples bring a different set of challenges. For example, disengaged couples often do not experience much negative interaction but rather, they are distant and deflated. For these couples, the joint task of approaching the individual's disorder provides a forum for them to work together and allows for an early focus on the psychopathology. In fact, such an approach is consistent with interventions that would commonly be used to treat the relationship distress as well (i.e., finding joint goals and activities that help the couple reconnect).

Second, the relationship distress sometimes is a significant precipitating and maintaining factor in the patient's psychopathology, such as when one partner became depressed in the context of the deteriorating relationship. In such instances, the relationship distress might require significant attention early in treatment in order to facilitate improvement of the disorder. In general, it is rare that either individual psychopathology or relationship distress is completely addressed in isolation. Fortunately, many interventions impact both; for example, behavioural activation serves as a treatment component for depression as well as increasing pleasurable time the couple spends together. If the relationship functions well, the clinician can quickly turn to partner-assisted and disorder-specific interventions and employ the couple's relationship and the partner as important resources in treatment.

Considerations when both partners experience significant psychopathology

For many couples, both partners experience psychopathology, at times each with multiple comorbidities. Thus, clinicians frequently encounter situations in which they need to determine the appropriate treatment plan that takes these complexities into account. Options might involve (a) jointly treating both partners' disorders at the same time, (b) focusing on one partner first and then turning to the other within the context of working with the couple conjointly, or (c) referring one partner for individual therapy while treating the other partner's disorder by working with the couple. Clinicians might be more successful treating both partners jointly if (a) the symptoms are primarily depressive (possibly combined with generalized anxiety) and likely to improve if relationship distress improves, (b) evidence-based individual treatments for the two disorders share common principles (e.g., behavioural activation for depression and exposure outings for agoraphobia), and/or (c) it is possible to sequence the treatment such that one partner's disorder can be treated first, requiring the other person to de-emphasize their own individual difficulties for a while. In the latter scenario, careful consideration should be given to the individual well-being of the partner who initially takes a "back seat." This approach might be recommended in cases in which one partner has been experiencing long-standing but mild symptoms or is unsure whether they are willing to be the focus of therapy at this time. Additionally, if the partner's symptoms (e.g., anxiety, depression) are secondary to their own caregiver distress, focusing on the index patient's disorder first could be helpful for the partner's symptoms, and the partner might indeed prefer to begin in this manner.

On the other hand, difficulties might arise if both partners are so distressed individually that they are unable to devote energy and attention to the other person's difficulties, or if the symptoms of the disorders "interlock" in a way that would pose challenges for the treatment. For example, while it might be possible to do a couple-based treatment for one partner's anorexia nervosa when the other partner has OCD, a couple-based treatment requiring a wide range of behavioural changes from both partners will be much more challenging if the other partner's OCD is focused on contamination fears with a wide range of rigid rules and rituals around food preparation.

Thus, clinicians need to assess each individual's symptoms, current functioning, and preferences for treatment, and consider what will be needed to treat each disorder and how the treatment might need to be integrated, sequenced, or supplemented with additional professional help.

Concluding comments

This chapter has provided an overall conceptual framework for the understanding of psychopathology in a relationship context, along with a resulting perspective regarding the treatment of psychopathology with couple-based approaches. While this approach to intervention is in its early stages given the pervasive emphasis on individual therapy for psychopathology, rapidly expanding research continues to encourage clinicians to consider couple-based intervention principles in clinical practice. Understanding the conceptual underpinnings of the interpersonal context for psychopathology and the framework for couple-based interventions allows clinicians to adapt interventions for a large number of disorders and tailor them to patients' unique needs. The next three chapters provide more detail on common disorders that can be treated in outpatient settings with a couple-based intervention.

Main points

- Although psychopathology in adults is often framed as an individual problem, psychological difficulties have wide-ranging impact on relationship functioning, and relationship factors can greatly impede or facilitate symptom improvement in the individual.
- While couple-based treatments draw heavily from CBCT interventions to treat relationship distress, the primary goal of couple-based treatments for psychopathology is to treat the disorder.
- Couple-based treatments can be indicated both in the presence of relationship distress and when such distress is absent.
- Relationships impact psychopathology both on a broad level (e.g., overall atmosphere in the relationship; relationship distress serves as diffuse chronic stressor) and on a specific level in terms of partners' responses to and couple interaction patterns around symptoms (e.g., expressed emotion, symptom accommodation).
- Psychopathology impacts relationships in a multitude of ways; for example, it contributes to an increase in negative interactions, a decrease in positive interactions, shifts in roles and responsibilities, and distress resulting from misattributing disorder-related behaviours (e.g., avoidance) as relationship behaviours (e.g., disinterest in the partner).
- Three different types of intervention strategies are partner-assisted interventions, disorder-specific interventions, and couple therapy.
- The common elements of couple-based treatment include psychoeducation, communication skills training, partner-assisted/couple-based interventions (integrating individual evidence-based interventions), and couple therapy.
- Guidelines for clinical decision-making regarding the indication for individual versus couple-based treatments include clinical guidelines for sequencing interventions, limited partner involvement, and psychopathology in both partners.

Note

1 In couple therapy, both partners are considered the "client." In order to distinguish the individual with the disorder that is the focus of intervention in couple-based treatments from the other partner, we use the term "patient" to refer to the individual with the disorder and the term "partner" to refer to the other partner.

Chapter 11

Depression in couples

Depression has been ranked by the World Health Organization as the single largest contributor to global disability (World Health Organization, 2017). Depression also is one of the most economically and socially "costly" of the individual disorders (Layard & CEP Mental Health Policy Group, 2006). In 2015, the proportion of the global population experiencing depression was estimated at 4.4%. This percentage equates to an estimated total number of people currently living with depression of 322 million worldwide (World Health Organization, 2017), with wide-ranging impacts on the lives of the depressed individuals as well as their families and communities.

Of all the individual disorders, depression has attracted the most empirical research demonstrating its complex reciprocal association with relationship distress, both concurrently and over time (Whisman & Baucom, 2012). Treatment outcome research strongly suggests that targeting depression in its interpersonal context can facilitate more effective treatment (D. H. Baucom, Whisman, & Paprocki, 2012). Couple-based interventions for depression address a range of interpersonal factors that might be implicated in the development and maintenance of the disorder as well as in relapses after successful treatment, including relationship distress. However, even among relationally satisfied couples, treatment can be enhanced if the couple understands the interpersonal context and the ways in which well-intended partner responses can inadvertently contribute to the maintenance of depression.

Although many couples present with a clear diagnosis of depression, or depression in the context of relationship discord, they often are not the only persons affected. In many couples, the partner also experiences depression or another disorder such as anxiety or substance misuse. For example, the rates of comorbidity between depression and anxiety disorders have been estimated at up to 50% (Hirschfield, 2001). Thus, the clinical picture can be complex, with a variety of comorbidities between both members of a couple.

While depressed mood occurs in a variety of disorders, this chapter focuses on major depressive disorder, as defined in the DSM-5, as well as closely related disorders (e.g., persistent depressive disorder and adjustment disorder with depressed mood). Bipolar disorder is discussed in Chapter 13. In the current chapter, the key features of depression in an interpersonal context are discussed, as well as guidelines for intervening with the couple. This discussion is guided by the overall framework for couple-based interventions for individual disorders, as described in Chapter 10. In many circumstances, clinicians also draw on principles and interventions described in other chapters when comorbidities are notable (such as principles and interventions for working with anxiety disorders) and consider how best to integrate and sequence those interventions.

Brief overview of clinical features of depression and the cognitive-behavioural model

Major depressive disorder (MDD) is defined by prolonged disturbance in mood (dysphoria and/or anhedonia) as well as alterations of cognition and behaviour that result in interference in day-to-day life (American Psychiatric Association, 2013). Somatic symptoms such as sleep disturbances, decreased libido, and changes in appetite or weight are common as well. Suicidal ideation and suicide attempts are among the most concerning aspects of depression. The World Health Organization (2017) reports that there are approximately 800,000 suicides per year worldwide, with depression being identified as the major contributing factor to those deaths.

There are also important variations in the way depression presents clinically. These include some cultural variations; for example, it has been found that individuals from non-Western cultural backgrounds tend to present with a greater focus on somatic complaints and less on the cognitive and emotional aspects (Vittengl & Jarrett, 2014). Gender differences also have been noted. Some research suggests that particularly among men (Salk, Hyde, & Abramson, 2017), the primary mood disturbance can be irritability rather than dysphoric mood. Additionally, there is a significant difference between men and women in the frequency of diagnosis of depression, with rates among women reported to be between 1.5 to 3 times higher (Byers, Yaffe, Covinsky, Friedman, & Bruce, 2010). Numerous theories have been offered to account for this gender difference, including those that emphasize biological, societal, and cultural factors, with no clear conclusion regarding the relative weight and influence of these factors (Salk et al., 2017). Likewise, the course of depression is variable. Most of those who experience depression eventually recover to normal or near normal mood with or without treatment; however, 15–25% of individuals develop a more chronic form of the disorder (Eaton et al., 2008).

Individual CBT can often be effective in treating depression (Vittengl & Jarrett, 2017). Beck's seminal work on depression (A. T. Beck et al., 1979) notably informs the CBCT approach to working with depression in an interpersonal context, along with behaviourally focused interventions such as behavioural activation (Martell, Dimidijian, & Herman-Dunn, 2013). In brief, Beck and his associates theorized that a person who is vulnerable to depression often, although not in all cases, has had early experiences that led to negative core beliefs and depressogenic schemata. These thoughts can include core beliefs such as, "I am unlovable" and "others will reject and ignore my needs." The individual, in order to cope, also develops assumptions and "rules for living." For example, a person with the core belief of "I am defective" might develop the rule, "As long as I work hard and show self-control, others won't realize I'm defective." In cases in which an individual subsequently encounters stressors such as losing a job, a relationship breakdown, or a health problem, the rule no longer functions well, and the core belief is activated. This sequence then results in negative automatic thoughts, images, and memories coming into consciousness, resulting in negative emotions. In turn, the individual often employs a range of maladaptive coping strategies such as rumination, social withdrawal, and behavioural avoidance, which exacerbate negative mood. Often, this vicious cycle takes on a life of its own regardless of the original causes of the depression, with both cognitions and behaviours acting as central maintenance factors. As described below, the CBCT model substantially expands this individually focused perspective by clarifying a range of couple-based processes at the behavioural, cognitive, emotional, and environmental levels that intersect with depressive symptoms, thus illuminating the development and maintenance of depression in its interpersonal context.

Understanding the bidirectional associations between depression and relationship distress

Depression, along with substance misuse, has been the most frequently studied of all disorders within the context of romantic relationships, revealing consistent associations between relationship distress and depression (D. H. Baucom, Whisman, & Paprocki, 2012; Whisman & Bruce, 1999). When examined both cross-sectionally and longitudinally, relationship distress and depression frequently co-occur and are predictive of each other (D. H. Baucom, Whisman, & Paprocki, 2012). Approximately 50% of committed partnerships that include a depressed partner are also relationally distressed. Longitudinally, relationship distress is a significant risk factor for the development of depression, with various studies finding that the onset of depression occurs from one year (Whisman & Bruce, 1999) to three years (Overbeek et al., 2006) after noting relationship distress. In addition, the reverse is true as well, with depression predicting subsequent relationship distress over a two year period (Whisman & Uebelacker, 2009). Relationship distress and depression also are associated among couples seeking treatment for relationship distress; 50% of these couples have either one or both partners experiencing clinically significant levels of depressed mood (Whisman & Baucom, 2012). Thus, depression has a clear negative impact on relationship functioning, and relationship difficulties can contribute to the development and maintenance of depression.

Furthermore, the presence of relationship distress can complicate the treatment of depression. The norm in almost all countries is to treat depression with individual psychotherapy. However, when patients[1] are in a distressed relationship, individual therapy for depression is less effective, and the chances for a depressive relapse after treatment increase (Fischer et al., 2016). Additionally, it appears that even when individual therapy is successful in treating depression, it does little to reduce relationship distress, which is a risk factor for future depression. Thus, it appears that individual therapy for depression is compromised when the patient is in a distressed relationship.

By contrast, couple-based treatments for depression seem to provide significant advantages when the person's relationship also is distressed. A meta-analytic review found that couple therapy for relationship distress was as effective as individual therapy in reducing depression and, importantly, also significantly improved relationship distress, thus addressing a notable risk factor for depressive relapse (Barbato & D'Avanzo, 2008). Thus, a couple-based approach to treating depression might be the treatment of choice for depressed individuals when relationship distress also is present. As mentioned above, however, even in happy relationships, couple interaction patterns that inadvertently contribute to the maintenance of depression can uniquely be addressed in a couple-based format.

Given that couple-based interventions for depression are valuable for couples with varying degrees of relationship distress, it is important to recognize how depression might present differently as a function of relationship satisfaction.

The impact of relationships on depression

As discussed in more detail in Chapter 10, relationships impact individual psychopathology on both (a) a broad level, and (b) a specific level in terms of responses to particular symptoms. A distressed relationship functions as a diffuse, chronic stressor that can lower the threshold for the development of depression as well as act to maintain depressive symptoms over time. In satisfied relationships, by contrast, the relationship might be a key source of support. Thus, at the broad level, the presence or absence of relationship distress affects the overall atmosphere in which the patient exists. A depressed individual in a distressed relationship might find themselves exposed to frequent hostility, as well as the withdrawal of positive social support. In contrast, a depressed person in a satisfied relationship often lives in a caring, supportive environment that might minimize stress on the individual or at least does not produce additional stress due to a distressed relationship.

In addition to impacts on the overall atmosphere of the relationship, there can be a range of responses to the symptoms of depression that maintain and exacerbate the disorder in both satisfied and distressed relationships, as noted below.

Accommodation

As discussed in Chapter 10, individual disorders such as depression and anxiety can "pull" the partner into the disorder, with the result that partners behave in ways that unwittingly maintain symptoms (Fischer et al., 2016). That is, the relationship adapts to the disorder such that there is more "room" for the disorder to become part of daily life, and the individual's and couple's world "shrinks" at the same time. The concept of symptom accommodation has been most extensively studied in the area of anxiety disorders (see Chapter 12) but also operates in couples dealing with depression. More specifically, one of the most common behavioural features of depression is withdrawal from pleasurable activities as well as avoidance of tasks and responsibilities inside and outside of the home. A partner might accommodate behavioural withdrawal, for example, by shielding the patient from phone calls from employers or other relatives, by taking over roles and responsibilities from the patient, or by agreeing to cancel joint activities so the patient can "rest." Thus, by facilitating the couple's withdrawal from demands and activities, the partner might attempt to lessen the burdens on the depressed person in the short term. However, doing so also negatively reinforces depressive withdrawal and avoidance in the longer term, which is a key process in the maintenance of depression over time.

Symptom accommodation occurs in both distressed and nondistressed relationships. In a distressed relationship, symptom accommodation might take the form of mutual disengagement between the two partners, with the nondepressed partner having "checked out" because the depressed person and the relationship are both aversive. In this context, the partner might place few demands on the patient, perhaps having attributed the symptoms of depression as being part of the patient's lack of interest in the relationship rather than being expressions of an identifiable, and treatable, disorder. Alternatively, with a highly conflictual couple, the partner might begrudgingly accommodate, while at the same time complaining about the patient's behaviour, such as not following through on tasks and responsibilities. These highly critical comments can further damage and maintain the patient's low self-esteem and low self-efficacy.

Additionally, depressed individuals frequently ruminate over past experiences. The process of rumination, which is both a behaviour and a cognitive process, maintains and exacerbates depressed mood. A partner might respond to rumination by providing frequent reassurance and efforts at problem-solving (e.g., trying to convince the patient that they are not a disappointment to the family). Such efforts might be an attempt to provide emotional support to their depressed partner. However, these efforts to "help" often are ineffective or only effective in the short term and act to reinforce the process of rumination and excessive reliance on the partner's reassurance.

Expressed emotion

As discussed in Chapter 10, *expressed emotion* (EE) refers to the tendency (a) to express criticism of a patient's behaviours and hostility toward them and/or (b) to become emotionally overinvolved and excessively self-sacrificing. EE can exacerbate depressive symptoms and undermine treatment efforts. For example, Carl and Rebecca had a very unhappy relationship, and Carl had become depressed. Rebecca attributed Carl's low motivation to "his laziness"; as a result, she frequently criticized his inactivity ("I have one child to deal with; I don't need another one to look after!"). So, when Carl struggled to get out of bed on the weekend, Rebecca shouted at him from another room before leaving the house with their child. In response, Carl felt even more discouraged and spent most of the day isolated and inactive. Over time, Rebecca concluded that Carl could do nothing on his own and begrudgingly concluded that she needed to be with him all the time, stopped going out with friends, cancelled her gym membership, and excessively sacrificed her own well-being while continuing to complain. Engagement in this form of EE (i.e., excessive self-sacrifice) carried the message that Carl was incapable of doing anything on his own, thus undermining his sense of self-efficacy, while also complaining about him and criticizing him.

The impact of depression on relationships

Not only does the relationship impact depression, but also depression often has negative impacts on relationship functioning as well. As mentioned above, compared with people without depression, individuals who are depressed are more likely to report relationship distress (D. H. Baucom, Whisman, & Paprocki, 2012). Additionally, couples with a depressed partner engage in less positive or constructive communication and more negative and avoidant communication compared to couples without a depressed partner (Byrne, Carr, & Clark, 2004). Clinically, when depression and relationship distress are present, it can be difficult to tease apart those factors attributable to depression and those more attributable to relationship distress. Nevertheless, it is possible to differentiate a range of domains in which depression might negatively impact relationships.

Change in the emotional milieu

Given the low mood and lack of interest or pleasure experienced by the patient, the overall emotional climate in the relationship can become more negative or lacklustre. The patient might frequently express a range of negative emotions and thoughts to the partner in addition to engaging in rumination and behavioural avoidance; this increase in negatives and lack of positives from the patient can become draining, such that the relationship itself might present as devoid of positive emotion and engagement. Also, as they try to make sense of these changes in the patient, many partners make inaccurate attributions that negatively impact the relationship (e.g., "She hasn't been coming to church with me for ages; she knows how important this is to me, so she must not care about our family anymore!"). These types of attributions can further worsen the emotional climate of the relationship. Overall, being around a patient's overall negative perspective and related behaviours can be depressing to the partner and their relationship.

Decrease in positive behaviours

Depression often results in decreased positive behaviours and emotions for the couple. Withdrawal and isolation limit what the couple can do as well. Many patients experience sleep difficulties, which can result in a loss of family routines if the patient naps during the day. Depression, and certain antidepressant medications, can contribute to poor libido, leading to a loss of intimacy in the partnership. Thus, partners are likely to experience the depressed individual as less caring and loving, and less engaged in the relationship. In addition, depressed individuals might no longer meet their daily responsibilities, such as contributing to the management of the household, caring for children, or managing finances. Communication tends to be affected as well; for example, the patient might avoid expressing how they feel because they believe that they should not feel as they do, they want to spare their partner, or they have learned that their partner typically responds in unhelpful ways. Overall, the partner might experience a significant loss, reflected in statements such as, "I feel like I've lost my partner; the vitality and fun that we used to share has just vanished. It's like someone blew out your flame, and everything feels so lifeless. I want you back!"

Increase in negative behaviours

In addition to a decrease in positive behaviours, depression in an interpersonal context often includes an increase in negative behaviours as well. For example, in more severe cases of depression, there can be self-harm as well as suicide attempts, and substance misuse is frequently comorbid with depression. At a relational level, depression has been found to be related to poor communication and problem-solving, poor support, negative relationship events, and insecurity (see Davila, Stroud, and Starr, 2014, and Davila, Starr, Stroud, and Li, 2019, for in-depth reviews).

Attributions

The types of causal attributions made by individuals experiencing depression have been found to be remarkably similar to the types of attributions associated with relationship distress. That is, individuals who are depressed often attribute negative events to stable, internal, negative aspects of themselves (e.g., "I failed this job interview because I have always been a loser, and I will never be able to succeed"). Similarly, partners often attribute manifestations of depression to assumed negative qualities of the patient or the relationship (e.g., "You are no longer interested in any affection; clearly you have no desire to be close to me or to keep our relationship alive"). Thus, in many instances, both partners blame the patient when things go poorly, increasing the patient's sense of failure and hopelessness. Alternatively, partners might blame themselves (e.g., "Why can't I make you happy? I must be missing something"). More hostile negative misattributions can contribute to increased EE as well (e.g., "I know you're feeling down, but also you just aren't trying. I don't get the luxury to just sit around; why do you?").

Depression, relationship distress, and behavioural interaction patterns

As stated above, the manner in which depression impacts a relationship likely is affected by the degree of relationship distress. Thus, it is important to understand how depression and the level of relationship satisfaction/distress result in various couple interaction patterns. As discussed in Chapter 4, there are several patterns that couples develop based upon each partner's approach or withdrawal (see Figure 4.1). Because a variety of factors contribute to a given couple's interaction patterns, there is no single "depression interaction pattern," yet there are frequent patterns that reflect the reciprocal associations between depression and relationship satisfaction.

DEPRESSION AND COUPLE INTERACTION PATTERNS IN A NON-DISTRESSED RELATIONSHIP

In an otherwise well-functioning relationship, many depressed individuals either (a) withdraw from the partner, based on depressive symptoms per se, or in an attempt to avoid burdening the other partner; or (b) approach the partner, for example by becoming overly dependent, expressing uncertainty about day-to-day decisions, and engaging in reassurance-seeking. Depending on how a partner responds to the patient's approach or withdraw behaviours, multiple patterns can emerge.

First, if patients withdraw from their partners, some partners withdraw as well, perhaps in an effort to give the patient quiet time and not cause additional stress: "She has been so tired and exhausted lately, I decided the best thing would be to give her time to rest." Conversely, a partner might initially assume a very different role and reach out to the patient, providing reassurance that things will "get better if you can just look at the bright side." They might try to be as upbeat as possible in an effort to shift the patient's negative mind-set. In many cases, if depression persists, partners might not indefinitely continue to approach in a positive manner, either losing hope and reducing their efforts, or experiencing role strain. Additionally, the partner might feel more isolated and alone as a result of the patient's withdrawal. It is highly likely that their own relational needs are not being met and their own risk for developing an individual disorder such as depression might be increased.

Second, instead of withdrawing, the patient might approach their partner. This behaviour might take the form of appropriate requests for social support. However, reaching out also might take the form of seeking excessive reassurance and becoming dependent on the partner when the patient feels incapable of making decisions or completing tasks. Again, partners might respond either by reciprocating the approach strategy, or by withdrawing. In situations where the partner also approaches, the result might be adaptive social support. However, although unintended, loving partners might respond in ways that ultimately function as accommodation or excessive self-sacrifice. Similarly, providing frequent reassurance regarding everyday decisions reinforces reassurance-seeking as a coping strategy and can inadvertently confirm the patient's beliefs that they are unable to cope on their own.

DEPRESSION AND COUPLE INTERACTION PATTERNS IN A DISTRESSED RELATIONSHIP

The patterns described above often occur more negatively in the context of a distressed relationship. When a patient approaches their partner, they might express criticism and complaints about their partner and the relationship; indeed, this displeasure with the relationship can be a precipitating factor in depression. If the partner responds with an approach strategy, they might defend themselves and express their own complaints and criticisms. For example, Frank was depressed, and complained that Lawrence was unavailable and disinterested in him. Lawrence responded with equally negative comments such as "Why did I marry a child? Why can't you be a man and stop being dependent on your husband to sort your life out for you?" While unpleasant for both members of the couple, such a pattern can be particularly toxic for depressed individuals, who are less likely to recover when experiencing hostility and criticism on a frequent basis (Hooley & Miklowitz, 2018).

Alternatively, instead of responding to approach/attack by the patient, the partner might not want to "deal with" the patient and withdraw. If the patient continues to attempt to engage the partner, a demand–withdraw pattern is likely to ensue, with negative impacts on both members of the couple and the relationship, as discussed in Chapter 4. Given the limited success of the patient's attempts at engagement, the patient might give up on such efforts and withdraw, further entrenching a pattern of isolation.

In summary, couples experiencing the impact of depression might interact in a variety of ways as a function of their level of relationship distress. The various patterns of interaction described above highlight processes that might place the couple at risk of (exacerbated) relationship distress and worsening depression, as well as provide fruitful targets for intervention in therapy. While not all couples "fit" neatly into one of the above categories, most couples presenting with depression typically demonstrate some or all of the above patterns of interaction. Thus, identifying and addressing these dynamics often becomes a part of treatment.

Interventions

Chapter 10 introduced the major intervention principles common to cognitive-behavioural, couple-based interventions for psychopathology. Similar to couple-based treatment for other disorders, couple-based interventions for depression have the primary goal of treating the disorder. Thus, a couple-based approach to treating depression includes integrating principles and techniques from both CBCT broadly (the approach described throughout this book) and individual CBT for depression. The three types of couple-based interventions described in Chapter 10 are relevant in treating depression: *partner-assisted interventions* (partner acts as a "coach" to support patient-led changes), *disorder-specific interventions* (a broadened focus to address aspects of the relationship that are relevant for the disorder), and *couple therapy* (addressing aspects of the couple's relationship beyond the disorder) (D. H. Baucom et al., 1998).

In addition to the interventions themselves, stylistic and session management strategies can optimize treatment effects. Individual CBT for depression often features a high degree of structure provided by the therapist. The same principle holds here, particularly for cases involving severe depression. Whisman and Beach (2015) suggest that the structured nature of sessions can provide a model for couples regarding a more "action-focused" approach where the goal is to assist the couple in working together as a team against the depression. Once some improvement in depression severity has been achieved, the therapist can gradually reduce the level of structure in order to allow the couple to take greater "ownership" of the content and direction of therapeutic work. While a couple's treatment plan flows from the unique case conceptualization for each couple, most couple-based interventions for depression address a number of the following goals:

- increasing knowledge about depression, its maintenance, and the interaction between depression and relationship functioning;
- enhancing emotional and physical safety in the relationship;
- reducing negative communication and increasing appropriate emotional expressiveness relative to depression;
- identifying and decreasing partner accommodation to depressive behaviour;
- directly addressing depressed mood and avoidance behaviour;
- dealing with distorted cognitions;
- working with emotions in the context of depression;
- addressing the couple's physical relationship;
- addressing depressogenic environments; and
- ameliorating broader relationship distress and/or enhancing relationship satisfaction.

These goals are addressed through a variety of interventions strategies described throughout this book, including psychoeducation, guided behaviour change, and communication interventions. Often, as is outlined below, an intervention can be employed to address more than one of these treatment goals simultaneously. The following section outlines strategies for focusing various interventions to achieve these goals, as appropriate.

Increasing knowledge about depression, its maintenance, and the interaction between depression and relationship functioning

Many couples enter treatment with a variety of inaccurate and unhelpful "theories" about the nature of depression such as, "Depression is a character flaw." Some of these attributions lower motivation and might also be implicated in dysfunctional couple interaction patterns. Providing both partners with psychoeducation is often a direct and effective way of beginning to address these beliefs.

Psychoeducation regarding depression, relationship functioning, and the aims and interventions of CBCT should occur at the beginning of therapy and be used throughout treatment as needed. At the start of therapy, this discussion can be used to elicit each partner's knowledge and attributions regarding depression and its treatment. Topics for psychoeducation might include: (a) the nature of depression, its symptoms, and effects of depression on couples' relationships; (b) the CBCT model of depression and the structure and process of therapy; (c) the impact of relationships on depression, including symptom accommodation and expressed emotion; and (d) if applicable, the role of medication and common side effects. A key goal when implementing psychoeducation is to present a rationale for the couple addressing depression as a team. Rather than continuing to locate the disorder solely "inside" one of the partners, successful psychoeducation supports the couple in taking an active stance of "pushing against" depressed mood and clarifying each partner's role in this endeavour (i.e., the therapist works to "externalize" the disorder from the couple). Understanding the rationale for the interventions is crucial; otherwise, some interventions might seem counterintuitive or uncaring (e.g., encouraging a tired depressed person to get out of bed). Thus, both partners need to understand why a partner engaging in accommodation behaviours is not helpful in the long term, although it might alleviate some distress immediately.

Enhancing emotional and physical safety in the relationship

A key priority in the early stages of treatment is to facilitate both partners feeling safe to address difficult issues. This goal might pertain to matters of physical safety, such as managing suicide risk, and/or emotional safety, such as reducing hostility (see Chapters 4 and 6 for relevant interventions). When the risk of suicide is high, safety planning procedures include a discussion of how best to involve the partner. This discussion typically includes signs that the partner can look for that might indicate increased risk, as well as behaviours that both the patient and the partner might engage in to manage and reduce the risk. Thus, the couple might agree to engage in mutual positive activities as a temporary distraction from suicidal ideation, as well as to contact relevant professionals when needed.

The manner in which suicide risk is addressed will vary in part based on the stage of treatment in which it is encountered. When suicidal ideation and risk have been identified before any couple-based interventions have been used, the therapist might take a more directive role in putting risk management plans in place. On other occasions, the issue of suicidal ideation might be addressed within the context of the main therapeutic work, drawing on the couple's communication skills. Within a guided conversation focused on sharing thoughts and feelings, the therapist might assist the patient in speaking more openly to their partner about some of their more difficult emotions and thoughts associated with the depression to counter feelings of isolation, an important risk factor for suicide. This discussion might include addressing the patient's suicidal ideation. The couple is encouraged to work together to clarify signs that suicidal ideation is becoming more severe and to identify behavioural plans that can be put in place to manage this concern.

In contrast to many CBCT interventions in which a goal is to encourage equality for each person's perspective, some cases of immediate risk of suicide might be more appropriately addressed by advocating for some temporary, targeted inequality, with the nondepressed partner taking the lead. That is, through psychoeducation, the therapist might make the case that, when highly depressed and suicidal, the patient's ability to make good decisions becomes impaired. As such, in instances when the partner is significantly concerned about a critically elevated risk, this partner's perspective should be given more weight in deciding on appropriate responses, even if the patient disagrees. Thus, the couple might agree to contact the therapist at such times, so that an assessment can be made of how best to respond. While this strategy carries the risk of more frequent "false positives" (i.e., acting when it was not needed), the couple can be encouraged to view it as an acceptable consequence when compared to the potentially irreversible and tragic consequences of a "false negative" (not acting when it was needed). Decisions regarding what the couple can manage themselves versus when they might benefit from consulting with the therapist or other professionals must also take into account the partner's judgment and well-being in such complex situations.

Reducing negative communication and increasing appropriate emotional expressiveness relative to depression

Problems in communication are likely to interfere with couples' ability to respond to the challenges of depression. Use of communication-focused interventions can improve mutual understanding and restore greater intimacy and cohesion, while also reducing maladaptive interaction patterns.

Sharing thoughts and feelings

Conversations focused on sharing thoughts and feelings can be used in a targeted way to address several of the problematic interaction patterns associated with depression as described above (see Chapter 4 for details regarding communication skills training). One impact of depression can be a loss of intimacy and connection in the relationship, often associated with withdrawal by both partners. In such instances, the therapist might use interventions focused on sharing thoughts and feelings to create more connection between withdrawn partners. For patterns of approach–approach and approach–withdraw that involve the unhelpful expression of negative emotions and hostility, communication-focused interventions are useful in supporting partners to express both negative and positive emotions more appropriately.

When the patient has withdrawn, the therapist might assist them in speaking with greater depth regarding their experience of depression. This strategy might at times increase the emotional distress experienced by both the patient and the partner, although they often will benefit from the increased awareness of each other's experience and feel closer and less alone as a result. That is, going through a difficult time with a loved one can promote a sense of intimacy and hope. Therapists need to monitor whether the discussion diverges into "co-rumination," which might leave both partners feeling stuck and hopeless. When the emotions expressed during these conversations become dysregulated, the therapist can use their own body language, tone of voice, and "presence" to assist the individual to make contact with and appropriately express a range of underlying, more vulnerable, softer emotions that have a greater likelihood of being beneficial for the couple's communication (see Chapter 6). Emphasizing mutual understanding as a basis for joint coping also can be useful.

In addition to the patient speaking about their experience of depression, the partner will in turn be encouraged to disclose their experience of the impact of the patient's depression on them. This aspect is important as it encourages the partner to express their frustrations, sadness, and fatigue that might have resulted from caring for the patient, including a loss of couple activities and a shift in roles. This disclosure can help the patient to better understand the experience of their partner and to provide emotional support; additionally, it can serve as a motivator for the patient to engage in needed interventions. Consistent with the guidelines outlined in Chapter 4, the therapist also encourages the expression of underlying positives for both persons. For example, the couple might discuss how the partner misses and desires the return of the many positive aspects of the relationship that existed prior to the depression.

When either the patient or the partner, or both, engage in ineffective approach strategies such as attacking or becoming excessively dependent, sharing thoughts and feelings can assist the partners to communicate their concerns more effectively. This approach has the added benefit of reducing hostility and criticism that might be both an expression of, and a maintenance factor for, depression and couple distress. When working with couples who have a greater degree of hostility or negative approach patterns, the therapist might use increased structure to reduce the overall negative emotional tone and improve partners' sense of emotional safety (see Chapters 3, 4, and 6 for more in-depth discussions of moderating structure and managing high levels of negative emotions).

Decision-making or problem-solving conversations

Assisting couples to make decisions and solve problems can be highly relevant when one partner is depressed. Often, there is a shift in roles and responsibilities (at times functioning as accommodation) when one partner is depressed, and a build-up of practical problems and unmade decisions contributes to both partners feeling overwhelmed. Engaging *both* partners in decision-making reduces a variety of stressors. Moreover, decision-making conversations can function as behavioural experiments (testing beliefs such as "I'm incapable"); as problems are solved more effectively, the patient often experiences an increase in self-efficacy. When a patient has "checked out" of important decisions, this communication format can be valuable in encouraging them to state more clearly their preferences, needs, and values. That is, structured decision-making has the antidepressant effect of encouraging the patient to be more involved. The additional involvement is often then positively reinforced when decisions result in positive consequences for both individuals.

Identifying and decreasing partner accommodation to depressive behaviour

Interventions to reduce partner accommodation to symptoms of depression are essential. A typical pattern of partner accommodation is when a partner has taken over a range of practical tasks from the patient. A range of interventions might be used to focus on this form of partner accommodation. These interventions include:

- Psychoeducation for both partners regarding common patterns of symptom accommodation and how they arise from an understandable effort to cope with the depression but over time function to maintain it.
- Communication interventions to facilitate discussion between the partners about how they both have experienced the patterns of symptom accommodation (sharing thoughts and feelings) and how they might shift these patterns (decision-making). A patient might, for example, be encouraged to express how on the one hand they have valued the efforts that their partner has made to "take the load off my back," while at the same time acknowledging negative consequence of "increasingly feeling like I am not competent to do anything."
- Guided behaviour change interventions that encourage the patient to take on more frequent, less demanding household tasks, based on the severity and pervasiveness of depressed mood and levels of psychomotor retardation.

An alternative and common form of partner accommodation occurs when the patient frequently approaches their partner to express emotional distress but in a highly ruminative and ineffectual manner. In a nondistressed relationship, a partner might provide excessive reassurance, which ultimately maintains the behaviour of reassurance-seeking at the expense of more effective strategies. Over time, this sequence can evolve into a pattern in which the non-depressed partner responds with either hostility or withdrawal (as the reassurance-seeking becomes more repetitive and more aversive), interspersed with periods of engagement and reassurance-giving. When this pattern of symptom accommodation is present, the therapist might intervene by providing:

- psychoeducation about the role of rumination in depression and how it can manifest itself interpersonally in a way that maintains the disorder;
- guided behaviour change, including determining activities the patient can engage in to distract themselves and disengage from reassurance-seeking;
- communication exercises for both partners to enable the patient to communicate their experience of depression and feel heard by their partner, along with the partner having the same opportunity (i.e., engaging in balanced, non-rumination-based conversations);
- behavioural activation interventions for both partners that can help with co-rumination along with other aspects of depression; or
- interventions described in Chapter 4 to address demand–withdraw communication patterns, if relevant.

Directly addressing depressed mood and behavioural withdrawal

Behavioural activation (BA) is a class of interventions that directly targets depressed mood and restricted behavioural repertoires that are both a symptom of, and a maintenance factor for, depression. CBCT, consistent with individual CBT, emphasizes that while behavioural withdrawal and avoidance are part of depression, they also maintain and exacerbate it. Moreover, withdrawal and avoidance tend to increase the risk for couple distress. Individual BA is a key treatment strategy for depression with an impressive evidence base (Martell et al., 2013). CBCT for depression includes BA at an individual level as well as BA at a couple level as outlined below. In both cases, BA likely involves changes for both the patient and partner. Here, we choose the terms *individual* and *couple-level* BA to identify whose behaviour is the focus of activation in alleviating the depression. That is, if the goal is for the patient to exercise, this behaviour would be called individual BA if the patient exercises alone while the partner encourages the patient to do so; it would be viewed as couple-level BA if they exercise together. For both types of BA, therapists employ guided behaviour change and structured decision-making conversations to develop appropriate plans.

The dual emphasis on individual and couple-level BA is adapted to a variety of factors depending upon the couple. Yet, overall, individual BA is emphasized when the patient has become too dependent on the partner, while couple-level BA is emphasized when the patient has withdrawn into a more isolated existence. A combination can be helpful when both are true; that is, if the patient is very dependent on the partner related to tasks *and* the couple engages in few pleasant activities together, then both forms of BA are likely to be beneficial. The current discussion focuses on aspects of BA employed when working with the couple in therapy; if needed, clinicians should familiarize themselves with general BA intervention skills (Martell et al., 2013) as the foundation for this intervention in a couple context.

Individual behavioural activation

Individual BA focuses on behaviours the patient can (re-)engage with separate from their partner which involve increasing the frequency and range of behaviours that create experiences focused on mastery, pleasure, and key personal values. From a couple perspective, relating BA tasks to important values (e.g., sharing equally in the household) can have the added benefit of reducing role strain on the nondepressed partner and allowing them time to return to previously meaningful activities that they gave up while caring for the patient.

It is important to discuss with the couple what role the nondepressed partner might take with regard to the patient's individual BA. When the patient has been highly withdrawn and inactive, a partner might assist by helping the patient plan and set up new activities, such as discussing a suitable running route that the patient will then run on their own, or reinforcing the patient's efforts when the behaviour has been completed. The therapist has a key role in facilitating conversations to help the couple reach agreement on what level of support from the partner would be appropriate, as well as using guided behaviour change to encourage a reduction of partner involvement when autonomy and self-efficacy are important goals. Similarly, a partner might assist in BA by creating an environmental context that appropriately facilities the patient's activation (e.g., caring for the children while the patient goes to the gym).

The content and balance of individual BA vary greatly depending upon factors such as the severity of depression, the nature of the couple's current environment (demands and resources), and the developmental factors impacting the couple's relationship. For example, Alice and Li Cheng needed to contend with Alice's suicidal ideation and behavioural withdrawal that had lasted more than a year. Alice had lost touch with most of her friends and had stopped engaging in her hobbies. Li Cheng was highly anxious about Alice doing anything on her own, due to his fears regarding her safety. Individual BA for this couple proceeded in a highly structured manner, such that the therapist worked to break down what each partner might do over a 24-hour period, with particular attention toward helping Alice rebuild valued aspects of life, such as recontacting friends. The therapist concluded that the current risk of suicide from Alice was low and individual activities would not pose significant risk; thus, part of the intervention was to help manage Li Cheng's fears regarding Alice's safety. This intervention involved an attempt at reducing symptom accommodation from Li Qiang (e.g., accompanying her everywhere). As such, it was also a behavioural experiment for Li Cheng (i.e., testing the belief that Alice could not stay safe if he was not there) with the goal of reducing his anxiety. Thus, BA is designed according to the particular needs of both partners and the couple.

As noted earlier, living with someone suffering from depression frequently creates role strain and a risk of burnout for the nondepressed partner. Thus, increased activity for the patient can provide some respite for the partner, and the discussion with the couple might involve behaviour changes for the partner as well.

Couple-level behavioural activation

Couple-level BA serves a range of purposes. Behaviours to be activated can include joint activities that are directed toward fun and recreation as well as joint projects, such as time spent gardening, that have an additional instrumental role in maintaining the couple's environment. These types of activities can be of dual value, activating the patient and helping the couple engage in actions that will likely improve relationship distress. Couple-level BA also has other benefits. Involving the partner in planned activities might improve the likelihood that they will be carried out due to the higher energy and motivation of the nondepressed partner. Moreover, the partner will be able to provide observations on the patient's behaviour and mood, not to "tell tales" to the therapist but instead to provide a second set of eyes when the patient struggles to self-monitor. Occasionally, couple-level BA activities require the therapist and couple to explore new ways of broadening the couple's repertoire of behaviour. This need can be particularly acute when depression, and possibly relationship distress, have arisen during a new phase in the couple's life, such as following the birth of a child. Here the couple might need to find new ways of interacting or new activities that they can share as a couple that reflect their changed circumstances but that still embody their values.

Strategies for implementing behavioural activation

In both individual and couple-level BA, the therapist typically begins by discussing the rationale for this intervention. The therapist focuses on returning to important domains of individual or couple-level behaviours that were present before the depression or finding new domains in cases in which greater flexibility or adaptation to changed circumstances is needed. As in other interventions described throughout this book, the therapist first clarifies the principle underlying its use. In this instance, the important link between decreased behaviour and depression is emphasized. The couple is then guided to decide on the particular behaviours that would be targeted and activated in their situation to counteract depression. The therapist maintains an active stance in encouraging the couple to consider the degree of structure necessary as well as the importance of being clear about agreed-upon BA tasks, such as the timing and duration of activities, and ensuring that selected activities are broadly consistent with the goals of therapy. For example, if a couple decided to sit on the couch and watch television for five hours on a weekend as couple-level BA, the therapist would re-emphasize the notion of joint *activation*. The therapist might then assist the couple to define potentially more goal-consistent tasks to counter inactivity, such as going for a walk together or visiting relatives.

BA as an intervention can be both simple in design (although not necessarily easy to carry out) yet profound in effects. It can be simple in the sense that the intention is to support the couple to work together as a team to push against the passivity of depression. It also can be profound, as the focus of BA evolves over time to engage important and central aspects of individual and relationship functioning. BA might start with relatively simple tasks that counteract behavioural withdrawal and the inertia of depression. This emphasis might then evolve to include more central life goals, such as studying for an entrance exam to pursue higher education. In all instances, CBCT requires the therapist to be flexible and to sequence and integrate interventions creatively so that the couple is supported to focus on highly specific behavioural changes when they are indicated. These behavioural changes can be more difficult to achieve if the depressed person has pervasive distorted cognitions that decrease motivation to pursue these activities.

Dealing with distorted cognitions as a part of depression

Working directly with cognitions is often important as negative automatic thoughts, selective attention, and memory for negative events and negative globalized attributions and assumptions can all be central in the maintenance of depression. Thus, a goal for couple-based interventions can be to work toward more balanced and flexible ways of thinking. In contrast to individual forms of CBT, however, CBCT therapists rarely directly challenge cognitions or ask the partner to do so (see Chapter 5 for a discussion of CBCT principles for addressing cognitions). Instead, the therapist can flexibly use both guided behaviour change and communication interventions to facilitate a guided discovery process and encourage cognitive flexibility, in essence providing experiences that will lead to thinking about the partner and relationship differently. In addition to the core CBCT intervention principles for cognitions, the therapist also uses psychoeducation to highlight typical patterns of depressed cognitions (such as selective attention); thus, the idea is neither presented nor experienced by the patient as a message of "your thinking is all wrong."

Additionally, when working with the nondepressed partner, it becomes possible to assist them to shape their communications with the patient in a way that both validates the patient's perspective while also stating that the partner sees the situation in a different, more hopeful light. For example, when responding to Lydia, rather than trying to "reason her out of her depression," Walter was able to say, "I can really see that you have been feeling very depressed and empty and you believe that you are not being a good partner to me. I know that must be terrible. I also want you to know that in my eyes, you are a wonderful partner. I know you are struggling, and I believe that we can get through this together. I really want us to try to do that." This type of communication is intended to assist Lydia in accepting Walter's perspective, while still experiencing that her own perspectives are respected. Such an approach might lightly challenge Lydia's cognition, without making her feel invalidated, defensive, or dismissed.

Overall, given the negativity often experienced between partners, it is usually more effective to create behavioural changes that lead to a different way of experiencing the partner and relationship rather than directly calling one person's thinking into question. In addition, it is not useful for the partner to play the role of a cognitive therapist, helping the patient recognize the errors in their reasoning. Typically, the patient either will defend themselves or take the partner's message to heart and feel even worse.

Working with emotions in the context of depression

Chapter 6 provides detailed guidelines for addressing the emotional aspects of couple distress as well as managing emotions during sessions. Attending to the emotional domain is essential when working with depression due to the profound impact of depression on emotional experience and expression. It might be particularly challenging when depression and couple distress are both present. A key task for the therapist is to manage the emotional tone of a session so that the depression does not overtake the atmosphere and prevent productive work. Therapists need to self-monitor their own emotional reactions; frequently ending a session with the therapist feeling drained and low might be an indication that the therapist needs to bring added structure and energy to the session to counteract the "pull" of depressed mood that can permeate a session.

At times, depression has a general emotional blunting effect and interferes with an individual's ability to identify and express a range of more nuanced emotions. In such instances, the therapist might need to assist the patient in differentiating among various emotions and allow themselves to experience and express a fuller range of emotions. Therefore, rather than "I am feeling down and depressed," a patient might be asked to give greater detail regarding what this experience of feeling down is like. This inquiry might reveal a range of emotions such as guilt and anger along with depressed mood. Having this greater richness of emotional expression also is likely to inform related cognitive and behavioural interventions, given that emotions, cognitions, and behaviour are interrelated.

Additionally, during communication interventions as well as BA, the therapist remains alert to and focuses on emotional shifts that a patient demonstrates in a positive direction. At such times, the therapist typically slows the conversation in order to accentuate and build on the positive feelings, both assisting the depressed person and often leading the couple to join around the positive experience. For example, as Jason was discussing his experience of depression with Renata, he gave a brief smile. The therapist asked, "What were you feeling just then?" Jason responded that he had experienced a memory of a more positive and joyful time earlier in his relationship with Renata. Jason quickly responded with a series of negative cognitions regarding the loss of this aspect of the relationship. Rather than focusing directly on these negative cognitions, the therapist instead asked Jason to elaborate on his mental image of the past, describing in more depth some of the emotions that arose during his memory, then relating these emotions to their current discussions of how they would like their relationship to include the possibility of greater intimacy and fun. Given the tendency of depressed individuals to be drawn to negative emotions and thoughts, helping the couple regain a balance of both positive and negative emotions and related cognitions and behaviours is a crucial aspect of addressing depression.

Addressing the couple's physical relationship

For many couples, their physical relationship is an important source of comfort, and intimacy, and a way to reconnect when feeling distant. In fact, in a meta-analysis of factors that predict long-term relationship stability and satisfaction, Karney and Bradbury (1995) found that sexual satisfaction was one of the strongest predictors of both outcomes. Given that both depression and some antidepressants can interfere with the patient's libido, focusing on the couple's physical interaction and sexual relationship can be an important domain in working with depression. Difficulties in the physical relationship can predate and be a trigger for both relationship distress and depression, and equally they can be a symptom of depression or a consequence of relationship distress. Some couples might present with a diagnosable sexual dysfunction, such as premature or delayed ejaculation or vaginismus. Treatment of these sexual dysfunctions is beyond the scope of the interventions described in this text, and in such instances, therapists often refer the couple for specialist assessment and treatment if the therapist is not trained to treat sexual dysfunctions.

On many occasions, however, a couple's concerns about their physical relationship are not about a sexual dysfunction per se. Instead, they might differ in their sex drives, which might become more accentuated with depression, have disagreements over who initiates physical interaction, or differ in what they enjoy. Many couples—distressed, depressed, and even happy couples—struggle in this domain and have difficulty knowing how to improve this aspect of their lives. In fact, even acknowledging physical and sexual concerns is difficult for many couples in therapy. Therefore, it is important for the therapist to create a comfortable, safe therapeutic environment for the couple when approaching these issues. As discussed below, the same interventions employed in other aspects of relationship functioning can be employed here as well. Given that the couple's physical relationship often is addressed after therapy is well under way, the couple will be accustomed to the broad therapeutic approaches that are employed which can decrease their awkwardness in addressing these issues.

Psychoeducation regarding the couple's physical relationship

An early step in addressing physical aspects of the couple's relationship is to provide psychoeducation. This approach can feel less threatening to a couple since it involves discussing the typical ways that partners relate to each other physically and inquires about how these domains are relevant to this couple, normalizing that couples vary greatly in their preferences and comfort with these domains. During the psychoeducation, three different forms of physical interaction in close relationships are discussed. The first form is *physical comfort*, which refers to behaviours that serve the purpose of reducing an unpleasant emotional state in the other person. That is, when one person is feeling down or distressed, a partner might respond with a hug or by taking the other person's hand in an attempt to decrease the negative emotions of the distressed person. Second, *affection* involves behaviours that express caring, tenderness, and a desire to be close to the other person, a form of "social bonding." In these instances, the goal is to increase special positive feelings. The behaviours might be the same as in comfort but with a different goal, namely increasing positive emotions rather than decreasing negative emotions. The third form involves sexual interaction, which serves a wide range of functions including experiences of intimacy, drive reduction, play, and procreation.

In addition to discussing each of these domains individually, the associations among the three are important to discuss as well. For example, when one or both partners have withdrawn from sexual interaction, often there is also a significant reduction in affection and comforting behaviour. Partners might avoid affection and comfort due to concerns that any such behaviours will be interpreted as an invitation to sexual interaction. Therefore, even though the couple might want more affection, it has been minimized due to low sexual desire.

As the therapist presents information on these three domains of physical interaction and the associations among them, the couple is encouraged to participate in a dialogue in which they address what their physical relationship was like prior to the depression, what each of them wants at present, and their long-term desires for their physical relationship. Such conversations typically do not include a discussion of who touches whom where or how, and many couples are relieved that the conversation is structured and focused on broad domains of functioning. Even when such conversations are difficult, with the therapist's assistance they can serve as an entrée into further discussions and launch subsequent interventions.

Communication regarding the couple's physical relationship

Once the therapist and couple have briefly discussed these three forms of physical interaction during psychoeducation, the therapist often helps the couple have more extensive conversations between the two of them regarding these domains. Typically, these conversations begin by having both partners share their thoughts and feelings about some domain such as affection. Rather than focusing primarily on how bad it is at present, the therapist might assist the couple in emphasizing what they have valued and enjoyed in the past, what is reasonable at the moment, and what each person would hope for the future, building in positives wherever realistic. Such conversations can set the stage for the couple to have decision-making conversations regarding how to proceed, with the therapist providing guidance regarding the importance of proceeding slowly, employing general principles of exposure and response prevention. It is important to stress that it might be helpful for the couple to push themselves a little beyond their current comfort zone to counteract avoidance, but neither partner should be asked to engage in physical or sexual activities that they find aversive or which are contrary to their values. In some instances in which the couple needs more guidance and structure, the behavioural interventions might take the form of guided behaviour change and BA.

Guided behaviour change and behavioural activation regarding the couple's physical relationship

It is often appropriate to assist the couple in increasing the frequency and range of physical interaction if they wish. Any or all of the three domains might be involved in these efforts. For example, if the physical relationship has greatly deteriorated, many couples choose to begin with affection or comfort so that they can feel more at ease with each other again before approaching sexual interaction. The therapist becomes increasingly involved in providing guidance when the couple has difficulty discussing the topics on their own, has limited knowledge or experience regarding physical interaction, struggles with ideas about how to gradually increase physical interaction, or generates decisions that are contrary to therapeutic guidelines.

The interventions discussed thus far focus largely on the depressed person as an individual and the couple as a unit. In addition, intervention for depression needs to take into account the environment in which the couple operates.

Addressing depressogenic environments

As discussed in Chapter 9, the impact of the environment can be understood in terms of potential environmental demands and stressors, as well as sources of support. In the current context, living in a stressful environment can contribute to or help maintain depression. For example, economic deprivation, racial prejudice, or homonegativity places additional demands on a couple's ability to cope and sends disparaging messages about the couple or the individual, perhaps contributing to the depressed person's sense of worthlessness. On the other hand, having caring people in one's environment can serve to counter self-doubt, assist with practical demands, and contribute to a sense of hopefulness. Thus, a full range of behavioural, cognitive, and emotional interventions can be considered in addressing the couple's environment. For example, for Nazanin, couple-level BA was central in helping her return to their mosque with Mohammed and test her negative predictions that other people there would ignore her. For couples who have moved to a new area, problem-solving might be needed to assist the couple in finding new sources of support. In other instances, couples might need to address whether the current environment is toxic and whether they need to protect themselves from the environment by moving to a new setting, perhaps one that is more affirming of their minority status. Overall, finding ways to address all aspects of the environment as a team is crucial, not only in ameliorating depression but also in preventing relapse.

Ameliorating broader relationship distress

In many instances, depression and relationship distress are comorbid and require interventions using the broad range of CBCT strategies for couple distress as outlined in this book. In some instances, treatment might reveal other aspects of the relationship that have made one or both individuals vulnerable to experiencing depression, even when the couple does not present with a high degree of couple distress. That is, the depression might be so strong that it dominates the clinical picture in spite of underlying relationship distress. Therefore, the therapist broadens the focus from depression and employs the full range of CBCT interventions to address relationship distress.

Guidelines for sequencing interventions

As noted throughout this chapter, depression and relationship distress frequently co-occur and influence each other, and depression often presents clinically quite differently in the absence versus the presence of relationship distress. It can be a challenge for the therapist to decide whether to focus first on reducing couple distress or targeting depressive symptoms. In addition, decisions need to be made regarding the sequencing of the various behavioural, cognitive, and emotion-focused interventions. General clinical guidelines for sequencing interventions are discussed below.

First, the therapist should assess factors that will make it difficult for the couple to work together as a team to address the depression. When the couple is broadly satisfied with their relationship and the couple is willing to focus on the depression, often the therapist can do so early in treatment. Distressed couples who are primarily disengaged (with low levels of both positives and negatives) can benefit from depression-focused interventions early on as well. Working together on the depression can be a positive, shared goal for partners who mainly feel disconnected from each other. However, if the couple presents with a high level of hostility, criticism, or other forms of aversive interaction, the therapist should consider addressing relationship distress first. Without the initial focus on relationship distress, efforts at focusing on the depression often are contaminated by frequent arguments or by one partner's withdrawal in the face of negative interactions. When relationship distress is addressed first, the couple is better able to tackle depression as a team; moreover, the alleviation of relationship distress through decreasing negatives such as hostility and criticism can assist with depression as well.

For all couples with depression, psychoeducation and BA are likely to be implemented as early as possible in therapy. BA is a key intervention, as it can improve both depression and couple distress simultaneously. The therapist needs to consider BA at an individual and couple level. If the patient is extremely dependent on the partner, then individual BA is used to accentuate autonomy. Likewise, if relationship distress needs to be focused upon first, the therapist can at times encourage individual BA for depression simultaneously with addressing the relationship distress, until the couple is able to pursue couple-level BA together. If the patient is withdrawn, couple-level BA helps the patient reengage interpersonally as well as become more active in general. As a general clinical guideline, BA interventions take priority over more cognitively focused interventions when the level of depression is more severe, since more severely depressed individuals often struggle with the level of concentration needed for cognitive interventions. More generally, for these patients, cognitive interventions are integrated lightly throughout treatment (rather than being the sole or primary focus for a given session), often in the context of communication interventions and guided discovery.

Following the initiation of BA (which is often continued to some extent throughout treatment), intervening on communication might assist in building intimacy and solving problems. Communication training and problem-solving also can be major vehicles for addressing suicidal ideation as well as the couple's physical relationship; usually these domains are introduced after BA and communication training for several reasons. First, when couples are better able to communicate, they are in a better position to address these domains in an open and fruitful manner. Additionally, BA often produces change in depressive symptoms fairly quickly, which can increase hope for the couple and thus help them to "stick with it" when discussing areas that take longer to change (e.g., sexual intimacy or suicidal ideation). On the other hand, if suicidal ideation is frequent, strong, and/or contributes to self-harm behaviours (whether they are suicidal or non-suicidal), then it should be addressed at the outset of treatment and revisited as frequently as is needed to keep both partners safe.

Empirical status of cognitive-behavioural couple-based interventions for depression

As previously mentioned, behaviourally based couple therapies have been shown to be effective in the treatment of depression across multiple studies, even when the treatment consists of couple therapy focused on relationship distress. In a meta-analytic review, Barbato and D'Avanzo (2008) found couple therapy to be as effective as individual therapy in reducing depression, with the added benefit of couple therapy significantly improving relationship distress, thereby addressing an important risk factor for relapse of depression. Although this meta-analysis also included investigations based on other theoretical orientations, the results of the five studies using behaviourally based treatments were consistent with the overall conclusions. More recently, behaviourally based couple therapies have been adapted to address depressive symptoms, again demonstrating improvements in both relationship distress and depression (D. H. Baucom et al., 2018; Bodenmann et al., 2008; Cohen, O'Leary, & Foran, 2010). The treatment model for depression described in this chapter has been investigated as part of a service evaluation in community clinics within the context of the "Improving Access to Psychological Therapies" (IAPT) programme in England. In an open trial of the currently described couple-based intervention for depression, 57% of clients in London with depression recovered, compared to 41% for all IAPT treatments for depression in the same geographic area. Additionally, approximately half of the "nonindex patient" partners experienced clinically significant depression or anxiety as well, and 48% of these partners recovered, even though their symptomology was not the focus of treatment (D. H. Baucom et al., 2018). Thus, among couples with two clinically distressed partners, the couple-based intervention effectively treated two patients with one treatment. Importantly, the treatment was as effective for the index patient even when the partner was depressed or anxious as well; that is, this more complicated clinical picture did not impact treatment success. Taking these findings along with evidence that depressed individuals in distressed relationships are most likely to experience the greatest added benefit of a couple-based versus individual treatment (Beach & Whisman, 2012), a couple-based approach to treating depression in relationally distressed individuals might be the treatment of choice. Overall, the findings are strong and based on multiple studies; they generally suggest that cognitive-behavioural, couple-based interventions are at least as effective and likely more effective compared to individual interventions, particularly when relationship distress is present.

Main points

- Depression and couple distress frequently co-occur and reinforce each other. Each is a risk factor for the other.
- Couple-based interventions for depression can be targeted to address depression, relationship distress, and their co-occurrence, as appropriate.
- Depression presents differently as a function of the degree of couple distress present. In order to intervene effectively, the therapist must assess and construct a conceptualization for the manner in which individual, couple, and environmental factors have interacted with depression over time.
- Depending upon the degree of couple distress, effective couple-based interventions for depression include (a) formal couple therapy which impacts the overall emotional atmosphere in which the patient lives, along with (b) partner-assisted and (c) disorder-specific interventions that target the depression. The last two strategies utilize what is known regarding individual, evidence-based interventions for depression and adapting them for an interpersonal context.
- Partner-assisted and disorder-specific interventions include guided behaviour change, communication interventions, behavioural activation at an individual and couple level, emotion- and cognition-focused interventions, and other strategies that assist the couple in addressing the depression.

Note

1 In couple therapy, both partners are considered the "client." In order to distinguish the individual with the disorder that is the focus of intervention in couple-based treatments from the other partner, we use the term "patient" to refer to the individual with the disorder and the term "partner" to refer to the other partner.

Chapter 12

Anxiety, OCD, and PTSD in couples

As discussed in Chapter 10, various forms of psychopathology, including anxiety disorders, obsessive-compulsive disorder (OCD), and posttraumatic stress disorder (PTSD), exist in an interpersonal context with symptoms impacting relationship functioning, and relationship functioning in turn impacting the disorder. A firm understanding of this dynamic, bidirectional process can greatly enhance treatment of such disorders by allowing a therapist to employ couple-based treatments effectively, improving both individual symptomology and relationship functioning simultaneously.

Although in the DSM-4 both OCD and PTSD were classified as anxiety disorders, in the DSM-5, OCD and PTSD were reclassified into two new categories, obsessive-compulsive and related disorders, and trauma- and stressor-related disorders, respectively (American Psychiatric Association, 2013). This reclassification resulted from the recognition that although there is significant overlap in the features (e.g., anxiety), maintenance mechanisms (e.g., avoidance behaviour), and treatment (e.g., exposure therapy) among the three, there are also elements of OCD and PTSD that warrant separate consideration. In terms of OCD, the argument for separating the diagnosis is that there are more similarities between OCD and disorders such as body dysmorphic disorder than between OCD and anxiety disorders, a proposition that has been contested (see Abramowitz, 2018). Regarding PTSD, the change was based on the fact that while individuals who experience traumatic events (e.g., military combat, a car accident, sexual assault) do experience anxiety symptoms, there are also other prominent emotions (e.g., anger, guilt), thoughts (e.g., "I'm to blame," "This means that people are untrustworthy"), and features (e.g., flashbacks, nightmares) which are qualitatively different from what is experienced in panic disorder, phobias, and other anxiety disorders. Even so, there remains significant overlap among all three forms of psychopathology in terms of clinical features, interaction with relationship functioning, and treatment approaches. Thus, this chapter discusses anxiety disorders along with OCD and PTSD, including how they are manifest in relationships and their treatment in a couple context.

Brief overview of clinical features and the cognitive-behavioural model

A full discussion of these disorders is beyond the scope of this chapter, but each will be reviewed briefly from a CBT perspective as a point of reference before discussing the interpersonal context of the disorders. Although almost everyone at times experiences anxiety, and anxiety can be adaptive (e.g., cueing people to a potentially dangerous situation), individuals with anxiety disorders experience excessive anxiety symptoms (i.e., frequent, intense anxiety that is out of proportion to the actual threat). The primary difference between each anxiety disorder is the source of threat/anxiety. For example, in panic disorder, physiological symptoms themselves (e.g., rapid heart rate) are the object of fear whereas a phobia involves a fear of a specific type of object or situation.

Regardless of the type of anxiety disorder, maintenance of the disorder includes both a cognitive component and a behavioural component (Antony & Swinson, 2000). Cognitively, individuals with anxiety disorders tend to predict that a feared outcome is both likely and catastrophic (e.g., "If I go into the supermarket, I'll have a panic attack, and I will die"; "If I speak in front of others, I'll humiliate myself and be rejected"), and these patterns of thinking produce frequent, intense anxiety symptoms. Behaviourally, individuals engage in a wide variety of avoidance strategies to prevent or alleviate anxiety. Avoidance might take the form of not approaching the situation at all, escaping the situation, or enduring the situation while using "safety behaviours." For example, Dima had a fear of driving over bridges and therefore either avoided bridges entirely or, in order to feel "safer" and "prevent driving off the bridge," would grip the steering wheel, drive slowly, and turn off the radio. While these behaviours produced short-term relief (and thus were negatively reinforced), they ultimately maintained the disorder by preventing new learning. For example, if Dima crossed the bridge without safety behaviours, he would learn that anxiety dissipates without the use of safety behaviours and that the feared outcome of driving off the bridge is highly unlikely.

OCD involves unwanted and distressing thoughts, images, impulses, or doubts (e.g., "If I touch this doorknob, I'll get AIDS"), and functionally related compulsions/rituals that the person uses to reduce the obsessional anxiety and/or prevent a feared consequence (e.g., handwashing). As with anxiety disorders, there are both cognitive and behavioural components to OCD symptom maintenance (Abramowitz, 2006). Of note, most people experience occasional intrusive thoughts, but for most people these thoughts do not cause debilitating anxiety. However, individuals with OCD tend to have beliefs about the intrusive thoughts that cause notable anxiety, including assigning excess meaning to otherwise common thoughts. For example, a person might overestimate the likelihood and severity of a potential negative outcome. Or a person might experience a sense of "excessive responsibility," believing that if they had a thought suggesting that something *might* happen to another person (e.g., image of a family member burning in a fire), then it is their responsibility to prevent that outcome from happening (e.g., repeatedly checking to be sure that all electric appliances are unplugged). Another common thinking pattern is "thought-action" fusion, in which a person either (a) believes that having a thought is as bad as the action itself (e.g., an intrusive image of stabbing one's partner is the moral equivalent of actually stabbing their partner), or (b) that having a thought means that they will act on it (e.g., "Because I had this image, it means I will actually stab my partner unless I take precautions"). These beliefs cause the anxiety rather than the intrusive thought itself. That is, if someone has an intrusive thought but recognizes that it is only a thought, they are less likely to feel anxious.

Behaviourally, a person with OCD often avoids or escapes situations that might provoke intrusive thoughts and related anxiety (e.g., a person with blasphemy concerns and intrusive images might avoid places of worship). Alternatively, they engage in compulsive rituals to reduce obsessional anxiety or prevent the feared outcome; rituals might be overt (e.g., checking locks) or covert/mental (e.g., counting, repeating specific phrases to "undo" a thought). As with other fear-based disorders, compulsions produce short-term relief and are maintained through negative reinforcement. However, in the long term, these compulsive behaviours maintain or exacerbate the disorder by reinforcing the individual's way of thinking and preventing new learning.

Finally, PTSD involves a set of symptoms that occur after experiencing a traumatic event (i.e., an event involving a life threat or sexual violence) existing in four clusters: (a) re-experiencing or intrusive symptoms (e.g., intrusive memories, flashbacks, nightmares); (b) changes in arousal/reactivity (e.g., irritable behaviours, hypervigilance, difficulties sleeping); (c) changes in mood and cognition (e.g., emotional numbing, feeling detached from others, believing that oneself is to blame for what happened); and (d) avoidance (e.g., of one's own thoughts, emotions, memories; of places or situations that feel unsafe). Experiencing a traumatic event can have a profound impact on an individual's beliefs about themselves, others, and the world more broadly, which can maintain the disorder if not addressed (e.g., "The world is entirely unsafe," "If I get close to someone again, I'll be hurt"). Also, avoiding thinking or talking about what happened and avoiding anxiety-provoking situations (e.g., avoiding men for someone who was raped by a man) might produce short-term relief, but avoidance ultimately maintains unhelpful beliefs and results in symptom maintenance. Thus, both distorted beliefs and avoidance contribute to symptom maintenance.

Understanding the bidirectional association between anxiety disorders, OCD, PTSD and relationship distress

Anxiety disorders, OCD, and PTSD each can have a profound impact not only on the patient[1] but the partner and relationship as well; relationship functioning also can have a significant impact on the development, maintenance, and/or alleviation of the disorder. Indeed, although much research has been cross-sectional in nature and thus cannot confirm causality, theory and longitudinal research support the notion that there is a bidirectional relationship between these disorders and relationship functioning.

Relationship impact on anxiety disorders, OCD, and PTSD

As discussed in Chapter 10, relationship functioning can impact psychopathology at both a broad and a specific level. At the broad level, relationship dysfunction serves as a chronic, diffuse stressor, and just as with any other stressor, can contribute to the onset or maintenance of a given disorder. Indeed, relationship discord is predictive of anxiety disorders both cross-sectionally and longitudinally (Whisman & Baucom, 2012). Notably, one OCD treatment study found that at pretreatment, close to 50% of OCD patients were also relationally distressed (Riggs, Hiss, & Foa, 1992). Similarly, PTSD symptoms are associated with relationship problems and discord (Monson, Taft, & Fredman, 2009; Taft, Watkins, Stafford, Street, & Monson, 2011).

On the other hand, in a strong, well-functioning relationship, a partner's support can be helpful in ameliorating or decreasing the negative impact of symptoms. For example, social support is one of the strongest predictors of fewer PTSD symptoms (Monson et al., 2009) and is associated with more disclosure of military and combat-related experiences (Balderrama-Durbin et al., 2013). More generally, patients often report that they are better able to engage in difficult tasks (e.g., sharing "unacceptable" OCD thoughts; confronting a fear of heights or enclosed spaces) when partners are supportive (e.g., expressing belief in the patient's ability to engage in difficult activities; expressing empathy in the context of emotional disclosures). However, given the bidirectional impact between couple functioning and individual functioning, social support can erode in the presence of sustained symptoms (Kaniasty & Norris, 2008). Partners might find it difficult to sustain support over time for a variety of reasons, including their own distress related to the disorder. Moreover, even in highly satisfied relationships with well-intended partners, certain types of responses to symptoms can unintentionally serve to maintain or exacerbate the disorder, i.e., relationships can impact the disorder at the specific level as well. One such response at the specific level is accommodation.

Accommodation

Anxiety, OCD, and PTSD symptoms can "pull" the partner into the disorder, and partners often respond in ways that are similar to the patient's own avoidance behaviours (Fischer et al., 2016). There are innumerable ways that partners accommodate, but essentially the term refers to the partner altering their behaviour in some way to either prevent or alleviate the patient's anxiety (or other negative feelings such as anger in PTSD). Partners might help the patient explicitly avoid anxiety-provoking situations, participate in the patient's "safety behaviours" or rituals, alter roles/responsibilities to help the patient avoid distress, or provide excessive reassurance. For example, Carol was outgoing and sociable but regularly declined invitations to parties, restaurants, and concerts because she knew that Stephen, who suffered from social anxiety, would feel uncomfortable (i.e., overt avoidance). As a different example, Tiana had OCD, including intrusive doubts about whether she had completed tasks in entirety. Multiple times each day, she read through a list of tasks she was unsure she had completed, and Xavier in turn said after each item, "Complete. It is 100% done" (i.e., participated in her compulsive ritual). Xavier also regularly reminded Tiana, "Don't worry. I'm sure you remembered everything you need to" (i.e., provided reassurance). Finally, Patrick had PTSD and was willing to go to restaurants but only if he could sit with his back to the wall, eat quickly, and scan the room repeatedly, looking for potential threats. His partner, Elaine, therefore asked the host for particular seating, allowed Patrick to choose his seat at the table first, and hurried the children as much as possible during dinner (i.e., participated in safety behaviours). Additionally, Patrick used to be the one to cook the meat in the house, but after his trauma, the smell of meat reminded him of burning flesh, so Elaine took over all cooking (i.e., changed roles/responsibilities). Although different in form, all these partners inadvertently acted in ways that contributed to maintenance of the disorders.

Accommodation exists with similar frequencies across anxiety disorders and OCD (Reuman & Abramowitz, 2018) and appears to be a fairly universal phenomenon. For instance, *all* participants in two studies of fear-based disorders (Reuman & Abramowitz, 2018) and OCD (Boeding et al., 2013) endorsed symptom accommodation occurring within the previous month. Accommodation is most likely when it occurs in response to behaviours that are more obvious to the partner; for example, accommodation is particularly associated with contamination-type OCD symptoms, which typically include overt versus covert (mental) rituals (Boeding et al., 2013).

Partners might engage in accommodation behaviours for numerous reasons, such as showing love, care, and concern or to avoid arguments (Calvocoressi et al., 1995, 1999). Indeed, one study found that empathic concern and expressed emotion (EE) marginally predicted accommodation across the gamut of anxiety disorders and OCD (Reuman & Abramowitz, 2018). This finding suggests that well-meaning, empathic partners who understand the patients' distress might engage in more accommodative behaviour, often believing they are "helping." Similarly, accommodation is significantly associated both with OCD patients' criticism toward their partners in relation to OCD matters and with patients' perception that their partners are critical of them regarding OCD (Boeding et al., 2013). Furthermore, accommodation to PTSD symptoms is associated with patient and partner anger (Fredman, Vorstenbosch, Wagner, Macdonald, & Monson, 2014). Thus, at least for some couples, accommodation exists in an atmosphere of criticism and anger from both individuals, suggesting that this strategy might be employed begrudgingly to avoid conflict. Accommodation also might serve as an attempt at interpersonal emotion regulation, with partners attempting to decrease patients' distress as well as their own (Fischer et al., 2017). That is, some partners might accommodate not only to assist the patient but because they alleviate their own distress by doing so (Fischer, Baucom, Abramowitz, & Baucom, 2018; Weber et al., 2018).

Consistent with patients' own avoidance strategies, accommodation prevents or alleviates anxiety in the short term but ultimately maintains symptoms and can undermine treatment because it contributes to patient avoidance and withdrawal (Boeding et al., 2013; Campbell, Renshaw, Kashdan, Curby, & Carter, 2017; Fredman et al., 2014). Interestingly, some partners might know that accommodation is not helpful in the long run but continue to engage in the behaviours anyway if they do not know what else to do.

Not only can accommodation maintain or exacerbate symptoms, but also it can be taxing for partners and impair relationship adjustment. For example, one study showed that on days in which women with anxiety disorders experience greater anxiety, male partners report feeling more anger, particularly those who accommodate more (Zaider, Heimberg, & Iida, 2010). Thus, not only anxiety itself but also the act of accommodating to the anxiety might be experienced by partners as frustrating or burdensome. Also, accommodation to OCD symptoms is associated with more relationship distress for partners but not patients (Boeding et al., 2013); that is, patients might be appreciative of the accommodation and not view it negatively whereas partners can find it to be challenging for themselves or the relationship. In contrast, accommodation to PTSD symptoms is associated with lower relationship satisfaction for both patients and partners (Fredman et al., 2014). One possibility for this difference is that while accommodation can be varied for something such as OCD (because OCD itself has a variety of presentations), with PTSD a common method of accommodation involves avoidance of public spaces. This method of accommodation can be detrimental to relationship satisfaction for both partners in that it often prevents shared activities and other opportunities for connection. Thus, accommodation, even if well-intended, undermines patient, partner, and relationship functioning and ultimately contributes to the maintenance of patient symptoms. In addition to accommodation, a further frequently cited set of partner reactions to psychopathology is that related to expressed emotion.

Expressed emotion

As discussed in Chapter 10, EE refers to three common aspects of relatives' (in this case partners') responses to patients with psychopathology, including criticism of the patient's behaviours, hostility toward the patient overall, or emotional overinvolvement (EOI; i.e., intrusiveness, excessive self-sacrifice, or exaggerated emotional response). EE behaviours can exacerbate symptoms by contributing to an overall negative atmosphere or by conveying messages that undermine patients' self-esteem and self-efficacy by suggesting that the patient's behaviours are intentional or controllable (in the case of hostility or criticism) or that patients are incapable of caring adequately for themselves (EOI). Although the effects of EE have been more extensively studied for disorders such as schizophrenia, there is some empirical evidence showing that high levels of EE predicts worse treatment outcomes for panic disorder, OCD, and PTSD (Chambless et al., 2017; Renshaw, Chambless, & Steketee, 2003; Tarrier, Sommerfield, & Pilgrim, 1999).

Attributions for symptoms rather than the symptoms themselves can contribute to EE. For instance, greater panic or OCD symptom severity is not associated with higher levels of EE (Chambless et al., 2017; Renshaw et al., 2003). On the other hand, partners' *perception* that the patient has control over their symptoms is associated with partner criticism for panic, OCD, and PTSD (Barrowclough, Gregg, & Tarrier, 2008; Renshaw et al., 2003). Notably, relatives are not always able to determine which behaviours are due to the disorder versus some other reason, such as the patient being a "difficult person" (Renshaw, Chambless, & Thorgusen, 2017). These findings are somewhat complex, but overall, they indicate that misattributions regarding patients' behaviours are common; these misattributions then contribute to partner EE, and in turn, EE undermines treatment success.

How anxiety, OCD, and PTSD can impact the relationship

Although the negative impact that anxiety disorders, OCD, and PTSD can have on patients is somewhat self-evident, these disorders also can have a profound, negative effects on partners and relationships. Caregiver burden or distress is common among partners (Lambert, Engh, Hasbun, & Holzer, 2012; Vikas, Avasthi, & Sharan, 2011), and partners might find that their own personal needs (e.g., intimacy or succorance) are left unmet in the context of caring for the patient. The extent of the negative impact is at least partially dependent on the partner's own coping strategies. For example, hope and positive coping strategies (e.g., seeking social support, reframing) in caregivers of OCD patients is related to less depressive symptoms in caregivers, whereas denial or disengagement is related to more depressive symptoms (Geffken et al., 2006). Therefore, when these disorders are present in one member of the relationship, it is crucial to consider how the partner copes with these demands as well.

Additionally, as noted previously, these disorders are all associated with worse relationship quality cross-sectionally, and there is at least some longitudinal research suggesting that symptoms predict relationship quality over time. For example, a daily diary study showed that on days in which women experienced more anxiety, both partners reported worsened relationship quality (Zaider et al., 2010). Additionally, PTSD symptoms are associated with declines in relationship adjustment and divorce (Meis et al., 2017; Monson et al., 2009). Relationship quality might be negatively impacted by these disorders in numerous ways, including a change in the emotional milieu in the relationship, an increase in negative behaviours (e.g., hostile comments), or a decrease in positive behaviours (e.g., sexual intimacy). These changes can be especially problematic when partners make misattributions about patients' behaviour. Each of these factors is described in detail below.

Change in the emotional milieu

Each of the disorders discussed inherently contributes to an increase in the frequency, intensity, and duration of negative emotions in patients. While anxiety is a core feature across disorders, other negative emotions are common as well, such as guilt or frustration with oneself or one's partner for how the disorder is being managed. Individuals with PTSD often feel negative emotions more easily and strongly than they did before experiencing the trauma and are less able to experience positive emotions; on the other hand, many also endorse emotional numbing. Partners can feel overwhelmed, frustrated, emotionally distant, or otherwise distressed by patients' symptoms. Furthermore, the emotional experiences between partner and patient might be interrelated. Research in this domain is new, but a preliminary study on coregulation in couples where one partner had OCD found that when discussing a concern related to OCD, patients' emotional arousal was unpredictable from moment to moment but distressing to partners if it increased; at the same time, the exchanges seemed counterproductive in helping patients regulate their emotions (Fischer et al., 2017). These types of changes in emotional milieu can be distressing and confusing to couples as they seek to navigate negative emotions related to the disorder and can contribute to an increase in negative behaviours and a decrease in positive behaviours between them.

Increase in negative behaviours

Navigating a relationship when anxiety, OCD, or PTSD is present can be difficult and can lead to significant breakdowns in communication and increases in negative, conflictual behaviours such as hostile or critical comments (Fredman et al., 2017). Indeed, couples in which one partner has PTSD exhibit higher levels of hostility, sulking, blaming, and controlling behaviour, and less "connection" behaviour during conflict discussions (Knobloch-Fedders, Caska-Wallace, Smith, & Renshaw, 2017). Moreover, PTSD, particularly hyperarousal symptoms, is associated with increased risk of perpetrating psychological and physical aggression (Monson et al., 2009).

These breakdowns in communication and increases in conflict are typically observed across all of these disorders, including in couples that traditionally have been supportive and constructive in their communication styles. Maria and Aileen, for instance, historically had a warm and supportive relationship. However, when Maria's mother died unexpectedly and she arranged to travel home for the funeral, Aileen, who had social anxiety as well as panic disorder with agoraphobia, felt unable to cope with the travel and social interactions and refused to go. While Maria understood Aileen's concerns, she also wanted her support. An argument ensued with Maria yelling, "You are the most selfish person I know! I let you off everything because of your anxiety, and you can't just this once get over yourself and be supportive. I can't believe you; my mother just died!" Aileen yelled back, "You need to back off. You don't know how hard this is for me! I'm not going." As in this example, opportunities to provide support or to connect can be lost (see discussion below), and negative reciprocity can become more frequent or intense in the context of navigating these various disorders. Thus, while hostility and criticism can contribute to symptom maintenance or exacerbation, symptoms and symptom management also can contribute to criticism, hostility, and conflict.

Decrease in positive behaviours

Anxiety disorders, OCD, and PTSD tend to "shrink a couple's world" primarily via behavioural avoidance symptoms. In turn, this more limited existence can interfere with meeting individual needs, maintaining couple processes, and preserving supportive relationships with the environment. Interactions with the "outside world" (e.g., travel for someone with a fear of flying; any social setting for someone with social anxiety) can be so anxiety provoking for the patient that couples begin to avoid the settings that trigger discomfort for the patient. Although this avoidance might begin with small actions (e.g., bypassing the park for someone with a fear of dogs), avoidance often increases in scope over time (e.g., avoidance of all public spaces in which someone *might* bring a dog). Places and activities that might have been a source of pleasure or meaning for the couple are no longer visited and for some couples, interactions with friends and family are no longer sought out. Thus, in an effort to prevent or alleviate anxiety, couples cease the very activities that serve as a foundation for couple functioning.

In addition to avoidance of external places or situations, avoidance within the relationship itself is common and can interfere with the couple's sense of closeness and connection. Indeed, intimate behaviours such as self-disclosure, emotional expression, or sexual intimacy, all of which require being open and vulnerable with one's partner, can be challenging for those with anxiety disorders or trauma histories. For instance, social anxiety is associated with a fear of intimacy, less self-disclosure and emotional expression, and lower sexual satisfaction (Sparrevohn & Rapee, 2009). These intimate behaviours can feel "too vulnerable" for individuals with social anxiety and given the potential for judgment, embarrassment, or rejection, patient avoidance is a frequent reaction. The impact of OCD on intimacy can vary by type of OCD. For instance, some patients with a contamination type of OCD either avoid sexual intimacy or have extensive, disruptive rituals related to sex (e.g., an elaborate cleaning routine). Or, if a patient with OCD experiences "unacceptable" thoughts, they might not disclose these to their partners due to shame. Often patients with PTSD report worrying about what their partner's reaction might be if they were to disclose the details of what happened to them (e.g., worry that the partner might no longer love them if they learned what they had to do in the context of war; worry that they might "damage" their partner). Avoidance of internal experiences (e.g., emotions, thoughts) and emotional numbing symptoms also interfere with the experience and expression of emotions for patients with PTSD. Of note, avoidance and numbing are the symptoms that are most strongly related to poorer relationship quality in couples with PTSD (Monson et al., 2009). That is, partners often can tolerate symptoms such as flashbacks or nightmares better than they can tolerate the lack of connection that comes from avoidance, low self-disclosure, or emotional expression (i.e., being "left out" of the patient's internal world). Thus, communication can be conflictual and highly negative at times, and at other times, relatively benign but not intimate.

Finally, these disorders interfere with important support processes for couples. For instance, on days in which women experience higher anxiety, male partners report a decrease in positive aspects of the relationship such as receipt of support (Zaider et al., 2010), perhaps because their female partners are focused on their own anxiety. Also, social support can be very helpful for those with PTSD, but PTSD tends to erode support over time (Kaniasty & Norris, 2008). Overall, this pattern points out that patients in distress who might most need support often neither receive nor provide that support optimally.

Attributions

Finally, partners frequently misunderstand what symptoms are part of a disorder or what they mean or why they exist. Partners might believe that symptoms are more easily controlled by the patient or more intentional than they actually are. Or, they might believe that a symptom (e.g., emotional numbing) means that their partner does not love or care for them. These patterns can vary by symptom type. For instance, partners tend to make external attributions for re-experiencing symptoms of PTSD (e.g., nightmares, flashbacks) but make internal attributions about the patient for numbing or withdraw symptoms (Renshaw, Allen, Carter, Markman, & Stanley, 2014). As noted above, numbing and avoidance symptoms in the context of PTSD are the strongest predictors of poorer relationship quality, and this finding in part might be due to partners' tendencies to assume that these symptoms are related to the patient (i.e., they are intentional and controllable—e.g., the patient is "cold/uncaring" as a person) rather than due to the disorder. Thus, partner distress and relationship satisfaction can be impacted not only by changes in emotions and behaviours but also by partner attributions about those changes.

Summary

Anxiety disorders, OCD, and PTSD can negatively impact relationship functioning, and, in turn, relationship functioning can contribute to the maintenance or alleviation of the disorder. Relationship functioning can impact patient symptoms at the broad level (i.e., contributing to an overall stressful or supportive atmosphere) or specific level (i.e., by responding to symptoms with accommodation or EE, both of which can exacerbate symptoms). These disorders can in turn impact relationships by changing the emotional milieu, increasing negative behaviours, and decreasing positive behaviours, all of which can be made worse by certain attributions (e.g., "This behaviour is purposeful"). Within this context, individual needs can go unmet, and support can decrease while conflict increases. Given the strong association between individual functioning and relationship functioning, couple-based interventions can be employed to address anxiety, OCD, and PTSD symptoms concurrently with strengthening relationship processes, as discussed next.

Interventions for couples in the context of anxiety disorders, PTSD, and OCD

Couple-based interventions for anxiety disorders, OCD, and/or PTSD all integrate CBCT (i.e., the principles and strategies discussed throughout this book) and individual evidence-based CBT treatments, with the overarching goal to treat the disorder while also enhancing the relationship as needed. Various CBCT-based "treatment packages" have been created to address some of these disorders, which will be described briefly later in this chapter. First, however, the common goals and treatment elements within these interventions are described so that the therapist can flexibly choose and order interventions based on an assessment and conceptualization of each unique couple.

Treatment goals generally involve factors discussed above that are present for the couple and which maintain the disorder and/or relationship distress. More specifically, goals often include:

- increasing knowledge of the disorder (e.g., symptoms, maintenance factors) and its interaction with relationship functioning;
- enhancing emotional and physical safety in the relationship;
- improving communication to decrease negatives and increase adaptive emotional expression relative to the disorder;
- decreasing misattributions for the disorder that are contributing to EE or relationship discord;
- identifying and undermining avoidance strategies and working toward approach strategies focal to the disorder;
- identifying and challenging distorted or unhelpful cognitions related to the disorder;
- identifying and decreasing partner accommodation; finding alternative ways of expressing care and concern not focal to the disorder; and
- ameliorating broader relationship distress when present or engaging in relationship enhancement for satisfied couples in order to optimize the patient's social environment.

Common intervention elements

The following section describes common elements for treating these disorders in a couple context. These interventions are described in the sequence in which they are often utilized, but a therapist can choose to alter the order (as well as omit interventions) depending on the conceptualization for a couple (see Chapter 10 for general sequencing guidelines). As discussed in Chapter 10, we distinguish three types of couple-based interventions for psychopathology: *partner-assisted interventions* (partner acts as a "coach" to support individual changes), *disorder-specific interventions* (a broadened focus to address aspects of the relationship that are relevant for the disorder), and *couple therapy* (addressing aspects of the couple's relationship beyond the disorder).

Psychoeducation

Patients and partners vary widely in their level of knowledge of these disorders including symptoms, course, maintenance factors, how the disorder interacts with couple functioning, and treatment. Some couples know very little, some believe they "know" but have significant misconceptions, and some have a nuanced understanding but still struggle to implement needed changes. Thus, some amount of psychoeducation is nearly always utilized in a couple-based intervention, but both the amount provided and the content emphasized vary. The goals of psychoeducation are to place symptoms and their effect in an understandable context, to challenge misconceptions, and to help the couple understand the rationale for different interventions, including each person's role in the treatment. Simultaneously, the therapist gains a more in-depth understanding of the couple as they discuss how the information applies to them.

A number of the interventions for anxiety disorders, OCD, and PTSD can sound counterintuitive if not cruel (e.g., exposure to situations that create intense distress) unless both partners understand the basis for their use. Likewise, important aspects of couple interaction patterns common to these disorders, such as symptom accommodation, need to be discussed. Psychoeducation typically is provided when giving feedback from the assessment (tailored according to the case conceptualization) as well as being incorporated throughout treatment as required.

Communication skills training

Communication skills training is often used in couple-based interventions for these disorders, utilizing the strategies discussed in Chapter 4. As described in this earlier chapter, the therapist likely begins by teaching the guidelines (initially working with sharing thoughts and feelings and in later sessions working on decision-making), followed by having the couple engage in practice conversations during the session, focused on the disorder. Topics might include how the disorder has impacted both partners and the relationship, or how to implement strategies that will address symptoms and strengthen the relationship.

There are multiple benefits to including a focus on communication skills training and using the skills to address the disorder early in treatment. Sharing thoughts and feelings can reduce criticism and hostility about the disorder (EE), increase empathy, enhance emotional safety (e.g., for couples with PTSD who experience escalating anger in conversations), change misattributions (about the person, disorder, or treatment), and help the couple feel and behave as a team in addressing the disorder. Additionally, in many instances, engaging in this type of conversation functions as a form of exposure in and of itself. For example, if someone with social anxiety avoids communicating about topics that they find embarrassing (e.g., sexual difficulties) for fear of being judged negatively, then talking about that topic and seeing their partner respond in a noncritical and supportive manner can counteract that belief. Or, in PTSD, cognitive and affective avoidance is common, and sharing thoughts and feelings can help counteract these forms of avoidance, allowing the patient to increase comfort with approaching their internal experience. Finally, learning decision-making skills can assist the couple in making decisions about how to execute the different aspects of the treatment (e.g., how can we together learn to approach instead of avoiding situations related to the disorder?).

Partner-assisted and disorder-specific interventions

Psychoeducation and communication skills training are the foundations upon which other elements of treatment are built, giving couples the information and skills needed to address the disorder as a team. Couple-based treatments also include a focus on empirically supported interventions for a given disorder (e.g., exposure), which are conducted in a partner-assisted manner, disorder-specific manner, or both. Overarching goals include building safety (as needed), counteracting avoidance (including safety behaviours, accommodation), addressing problematic thoughts, and providing the couple with adaptive ways to approach life more broadly without focusing on the disorder long term. That is, a goal is to have the disorder become a smaller part of the couple's existence, with increasing emphasis on maximizing joy and meaning rather than devoting so much time and energy to avoiding distress.

ENHANCING EMOTIONAL AND PHYSICAL SAFETY IN THE RELATIONSHIP

To the degree that one or both partners have difficulties regulating strong negative emotions (e.g., the PTSD patient experiencing dysregulated anger) and this difficulty results in behaviours such as yelling, hostile or critical comments, and/or physical aggression, a primary focus early in treatment likely is addressing emotional and physical safety in the relationship. This part of the treatment can include psychoeducation about the causes and effects of behaviours noted above, teaching strategies for recognizing and managing strong emotions in other ways, and time-out strategies. Other chapters in this book describe interventions that the therapist might employ to help couples regulate emotions and enhance emotional and physical safety. Most notably, Chapter 6 includes an in-depth discussion of helping couples regulate strong emotions both inside and outside of sessions, and Chapter 13 examines how to assist couples in which one or both partners experience broader, long-term emotion regulation difficulties. In this instance, these intervention strategies are targeted to emotion dysregulation focal to the disorder.

With regard to time-out strategies, ultimately the message to the couple is that if one or both partners are not able to engage effectively at the moment (i.e., emotions are strong and the urge to engage in actions such as yelling or physically harming the other is high), then it can be adaptive to take a break, cool off, and return to the conversation when able to do so effectively. The therapist helps both partners to identify "signs" that they might need a time-out (e.g., angry at level 7 or greater on a 10-point scale; pacing and having strong urges to yell). Additionally, the therapist can help the couple to identify a predetermined phrase or nonverbal indicator (e.g., "I need a break") that signifies that they are calling for a time-out.

Often, if time-out is not officially "called" and one partner simply walks away, the other partner tends to follow and continues to engage in the conversation. The goal is to call a time-out for oneself rather than for one's partner; in other words, it is similar to the strategy in a sports game and is not meant as a punishment for the other partner, avoiding a message of, "I've had enough of you; I'm not talking to you any further." Therapists can help the partners develop a plan for where they will go, how long their time-out will last, and what "cool-down" strategies each will use during the period spent apart. Finally, it is helpful to emphasize that the goal is to resume the conversation at some point; a frequent pitfall for couples is calling a time-out but then never reengaging. By using time-outs effectively, couples can ensure that they are engaging in conversations in a state in which they can use skills and reduce or eliminate behaviours such as hostile comments or physical aggression. Once the couple can maintain emotional and physical safety, treatment can begin to address other important issues related to the disorder.

COUNTERACTING AVOIDANCE

As discussed throughout this chapter, avoidance is a primary maintaining mechanism across all anxiety disorders, PTSD, and OCD. Consequently, individual empirically supported treatments for anxiety disorders, OCD, and one of the primary empirically supported treatments for PTSD (Prolonged Exposure; Foa, Hembree, and Rothbaum, 2007) all emphasize exposure to counteract avoidance. Within a couple-based treatment, at times the partner can serve as a "coach," helping the patient to engage in exposure practice (i.e., partner-assisted intervention) or the couple can engage in approach tasks that alter relationship functioning (i.e., disorder-specific approach). For example, if a patient with generalized anxiety disorder tends to express worrisome thoughts for hours rather than engaging in tasks related to the object of worry (e.g., paying bills) and the partner typically listens and offers a perspective on the worry thoughts, a change to the relationship dynamic might be needed in the service of exposure. The patient might be asked to engage in the set of avoided tasks (e.g., paying the bills) while the partner provides encouragement for this approach behaviour (e.g., "I know how anxious you are, and I'm so proud of you for paying the bills anyway!"). Or, for a couple in which a partner has PTSD and finds public settings anxiety provoking, assigning a date night in a public space can both alter a relationship dynamic and serve as exposure. Regardless of the form the intervention takes, counteracting avoidance and working toward approaching aspects of life that have been avoided is central to all of these treatments. This approach has numerous benefits including improving symptoms, increasing opportunities for positive interactions and joint activities with one's partner, increasing intimacy, and potentially decreasing conflict. Similar to the treatment for depression in a couple context which includes both individual and couple-based behavioural activation, often individual exposure is important to incorporate into treatment to help develop a sense of self-efficacy for the patient.

Partner-assisted exposure In individual exposure and response prevention (ERP), the first step is the creation of a hierarchy of situations that prompt distress or avoidance for the patient. The patient rates each item on a 0–100 scale based on how distressing it would be to approach this item and then engages in exposure practices, starting with items that prompt low to moderate distress (e.g., 30–50) and gradually working up to more difficult items. For example, a hierarchy for a patient with a bee phobia might include items such as looking at pictures or videos of bees, interacting with an artificial bee, sitting in an area around a hive, and allowing a bee to rest on their finger. Patients are asked to remain in the exposure until their distress level lowers to a mild or moderate level. Additionally, the therapist helps the patient identify and refrain from safety behaviours which would prevent the patient from experiencing the full level of distress resulting from exposure. Exposure might include interoceptive exposure (i.e., exposure to body sensations), in-vivo exposure (i.e., in real life, such as going to a store), or imaginal exposure (e.g., revisiting a traumatic memory). If a therapist is unfamiliar with ERP, it is highly recommended that they review disorder-specific materials providing additional detail and examples of exposures (Abramowitz, 2006; Antony & Swinson, 2000; Foa et al., 2007) prior to engaging in partner-assisted exposure.

Partner-assisted exposure emphasizes the overarching principles of individual ERP with the partner serving in a role of "coach" and encouraging the patient to proceed with the exposure, reminding the patient of important principles if needed. It is important that the partner not serve in the role of a safety signal such that the patient experiences that they can *only* confront distressing situations by being protected by the partner. Instead, the partner's role is to encourage the patient to confront the distress as explained below.

Guidelines for how to approach exposure for OCD as a couple are discussed by Abramowitz, Baucom, Wheaton, et al. (2013); the principles underlying this approach have applicability across couple-based interventions for disorders in which avoidance is central and can be adapted accordingly. First, prior to exposure, couples use communication skills to decide on what exposure they will engage in and how they will conduct the exposure, as well as share how they feel about the upcoming practice. These steps can help the couple feel like a team and provide an opportunity to offer emotional support to one another.

Second, during exposure, the patient is encouraged to share how they are feeling throughout the exposure, thus confronting rather than avoiding distressing feelings. The partner's role is to provide support and reinforcement for exposure without accommodating. For instance, if an OCD patient is engaging in an exposure to a door knob, a partner's inclination might be to provide reassurance such as, "I'm sure there are no germs, and you won't get sick," and they might not recognize that this response is accommodation. Thus, just as the therapist must help the patient to avoid engaging in safety behaviours, the therapist will also need to help the partner to avoid accommodating. It can be helpful to provide the partner with examples of statements that are supportive but not accommodating (e.g., "I can see how the doorknob is making you anxious; remember that anxiety is distressing but won't last forever; I'm so proud of you; hang in there!"). Even with instruction and the rationale for not accommodating, refraining from doing so can be hard for partners. Within a healthy relationship, watching one's loved one experience high levels of distress can be upsetting to the partner, and refraining from doing what is possible to lower that distress is difficult. In essence, this experience can be a form of exposure and response prevention for the partner as well, watching the patient in distress and not attempting to remove the distress. Therefore, the therapist must be attentive to how the partner experiences ERP and support the partner through this process as well. Partners who are more highly affected by the patient's distress (i.e., partners who quickly become distressed also) tend to have greater difficulty reducing accommodation and might require additional support such as teaching them additional emotion regulation skills (Fischer et al., 2018).

Third, at times, patients experience higher levels of distress than anticipated during exposure and want to stop the exercise. Patients are asked to express their feelings to their partner with partners doing their best to provide emotional support and encourage the patient to remain in the situation. In order to avoid power struggles between the patient and partner regarding whether to continue with the exposure, the therapist clarifies that the patient always maintains control and makes the final decision. Thus, if the patient insists on stopping, the couple stops the exposure for the moment. If the patient decides to take a break from the exposure, during this brief time-out, the couple uses their communication skills to share what they are feeling, provide support, and decide if, when, and how to return to the exposure. If the patient decides to discontinue the current exposure, the couple is encouraged to consider substituting a less distressing exposure so that the patient does not end the experience with an escape response.

Finally, after the exposure is complete, the couple discusses the exposure experience, including what the patient learned and what the partner did that was or was not helpful. In order to maximize a sense of self-efficacy during treatment, typically the partner is faded out of the exposure as therapy proceeds yet maintains the role of encouraging the patient, asking about the solo exposure experiences and troubleshooting with the patient about future exposure efforts.

Addressing accommodation In addition to avoiding accommodation during partner-assisted exposures, treatment includes a broader focus on identifying and decreasing accommodation that occurs during everyday life (i.e., a disorder-specific approach to overcoming avoidance). Often, partners will have decreased accommodation behaviours following psychoeducation and ERP. However, some accommodation is still likely to be present either because the behaviour is especially difficult to change or because the couple has not identified partner behaviour(s) that contribute to avoidance. For example, a couple might not question the partner doing all the cooking because "this is just how we have divided the roles in the household for years," even though an OCD patient with obsessions related to the dangers of handling raw meat might benefit from taking on some of the cooking tasks. Thus, utilizing decision-making skills for finding ways to change roles and otherwise reduce accommodation is crucial.

Additionally, the therapist can guide the couple to brainstorm ways to show love, care, and concern in a manner that is unrelated to the disorder so that undermining accommodation does not also unwittingly undermine relationship satisfaction. For example, if a major way a partner shows care and concern is by engaging in the patient's ritual (e.g., the partner checking all doors and windows every night to make certain they are locked and reassuring the patient about being safe), then eliminating this behaviour can leave the couple feeling disconnected. Working toward engaging in shared activities, providing emotional support more broadly, and increasing affectionate behaviours can help the couple to remain connected even while decreasing accommodation behaviours.

ALTERING MISATTRIBUTIONS/MALADAPTIVE COGNITIONS

As described above, patients with any of these disorders might overestimate the probability and severity of a feared outcome. Additionally, a variety of thinking errors (e.g., thoughts-action fusion) are common in OCD; similarly, PTSD patients frequently begin to have strong, negative beliefs in several domains (e.g., safety or trust). Moreover, partners frequently endorse misattributions for the patient's behaviours (e.g., "She won't have sex with me because she doesn't love me" versus "Sexual intimacy is difficult for her because of her sexual assault"). Frequently, psychoeducation, sharing thoughts and feelings, and approach tasks all undermine these distorted or maladaptive ways of thinking. However, if these thought patterns continue, treatment might benefit from the inclusion of guided discovery, as discussed in Chapter 5. For example, the couple might have a conversation focused on sharing thoughts and feelings in which the patient describes how being physically intimate evokes painful images, and explains that her discomfort results from her desire to avoid these aversive images rather than from her partner being unappealing.

Couple therapy/broader relationship issues

Couple-based interventions for anxiety, OCD, and PTSD can also incorporate a focus on more general CBCT to address issues that are either unrelated or secondary to the disorder. For example, a couple might have difficulties navigating interactions with their in-laws, which might be unrelated to the disorder. However, the couple's arguments surrounding this issue likely contribute to an overall stressful atmosphere, perhaps exacerbating underlying anxiety or other symptoms. Thus, problem-solving around in-law issues is likely to decrease arguments and might indirectly improve anxiety symptoms by decreasing the overall negative ambience of the relationship.

In addition, at times the anxiety is about the relationship itself. Some individuals experience unwarranted worries and concerns that their partner does not love them or will leave them, what Paprocki and Baucom (2017) have called relationship-based anxiety. Such concerns can lead to frequent requests for reassurance that the partner is not going to leave and that "everything is okay." Ongoing requests even after reassurance can actually contribute to relationship distress, an unfortunate self-fulfilling prophesy. A brief couple-based intervention to address such concerns shows initial promising results (Paprocki & Baucom, 2017).

Furthermore, at times the disorder affects those outside of the couple, such as the couple's children. For example, Dara insisted on having the house "just right." Home accessories needed to be symmetrical, pictures needed to be hung straight to the fraction of an inch, and everything had its "proper place." As a result, Dara frequently yelled at his six-year-old twin girls for making a mess and threw away their paintings because they did not fit with Dara's sense of the house being "just right." As his OCD symptoms abated, he and his partner worked to identify strategies to strengthen his damaged relationship with their twins, such as apologizing to them, increasing time spent playing with them, complimenting their artwork, and hanging up their newer pieces of art. Ultimately, the goals in addressing unrelated or secondary issues are to improve relationship functioning overall for its own sake, as well as to improve disorder-related symptoms indirectly by helping the relationship become less stressful and broadly supportive for both the patient and the partner.

Guidelines for clinical decision-making

When considering a couple-based approach for an anxiety disorder, OCD, or PTSD, clinicians need to make a number of decisions. Given that there are empirically supported individual interventions for these disorders, a first question is whether to utilize an individual or couple-based approach. As couple-based approaches can address individual and couple issues simultaneously, these interventions might well be considered when relationship distress is serving as a stressor on the individual, when levels of accommodation and/or EE are high, or in circumstances when the couple prefers to work together in approaching the disorder. Contraindications for a couple-based intervention for anxiety disorders, OCD, or PTSD are similar to contraindications for most outpatient couple-based interventions: an unwilling partner, psychosis, a current and severe substance use disorder, and current and severe intimate partner violence (IPV). If IPV is present but not severe, couple-based interventions can still be utilized, but addressing safety concerns should be emphasized early in treatment.

Another common question surrounds which interventions to choose and in what order. The therapist selects interventions based on the case conceptualization for each unique couple. For instance, if the patient and the partner can engage with each other in emotional and physically safe ways, time-outs might not be needed. Or, if a couple is highly distressed and conflictual, addressing broader relationship issues prior to partner-assisted interventions focusing on the disorder might be warranted. Similarly, a recent and significantly destabilizing couple-related issue (e.g., the discovery of an affair) can make engagement in a couple-based intervention focused on the patient's disorder extremely difficult; thus, an initial focus on such high-demand, distressing issues might be warranted prior to interventions that are more focal to the disorder. Chapter 10 provides a broader discussion of sequencing interventions and additional clinical considerations for couple-based interventions which apply to the disorders discussed here.

Empirical status of couple-based interventions for anxiety, OCD, and PTSD

Several CBCT-based protocols have been created and evaluated for the disorders discussed in this chapter with overall positive findings; yet, the field is still in an early stage with much to learn. Currently, in addition to the studies reviewed in this chapter so far, couple-based interventions for panic disorder with agoraphobia appear to be equally effective as individual CBT at treating the disorder while also leading to improved relationship functioning (Byrne et al., 2004; Daiuto, Baucom, Epstein, & Dutton, 1998). Although it is not yet clear due to a lack of follow-up data, if relationship distress turns out to be a risk factor for relapse as it is in depression, the improvement in relationship functioning is noteworthy. Several of the current authors have been part of a team that has developed a CBCT-based intervention for OCD (Abramowitz, Baucom, Boeding, et al., 2013; Abramowitz, Baucom, Wheaton, et al., 2013). This 16-session intervention includes assessment, psychoeducation, partner-assisted exposure, communication skills training, and strategies to decrease partner accommodation and increase appropriate ways of caring, along with addressing broader couple issues to ameliorate general relationship distress or enhance functioning in nondistressed relationships. This couple-based intervention was evaluated in an open trial for couples in which one partner had OCD. The magnitude of change in OCD symptoms following treatment was striking, along with strong one-year maintenance of gains. Also, overall relationship adjustment improved. In addition, benchmark comparisons with other published trials comparing the couple-based intervention to (a) individual exposure and response prevention or (b) individual cognitive therapy suggested stronger effects for the couple-based treatment for OCD (Abramowitz, Baucom, Boeding, et al., 2013). However, controlled trials that directly compare couple-based and individual treatments are yet to be conducted.

CBCT for PTSD was developed and evaluated by Monson, Fredman, and colleagues (2012). It includes 15 weekly sessions that incorporate psychoeducation, communication skills training, overcoming avoidance, challenging maladaptive cognitions (e.g., regarding self-blame and trust), and discussing posttraumatic growth. Three uncontrolled trials of CBCT for PTSD have been conducted, two with military veterans and their partners (Monson, Schnurr, Stevens, & Guthrie, 2004; Schumm, Fredman, Monson, & Chard, 2013) and one with a combined sample of civilians and veterans along with their partners (Monson et al., 2011).

A wait-list-controlled randomized controlled trial was completed as well (Monson et al., 2012). Across studies, the results indicate improvements in PTSD, comorbid symptoms, and relationship functioning. Given that some couples might find it difficult to attend 15 weekly sessions, Fredman and colleagues (Fredman et al., 2018) conducted an open trial to evaluate an intensive version of CBCT for PTSD delivered over a single weekend in a couple group format. At three-month follow-up, there were significant reductions in patients' PTSD and comorbid symptoms, and partners' psychological distress, as well as improvement in relationship satisfaction. Thus, several trials consistently point to the value of including partners in the treatment of PTSD from a CBCT perspective.

Overall, the findings thus far exploring CBCT for these disorders are favourable, generally suggesting that CBCT is at least as effective or more effective compared to individual interventions. This conclusion is not surprising, given that the couple interventions incorporate empirically supported principles from individual CBT, broadened to include the partner as a central part of the patient's immediate social environment.

Main points

- Anxiety disorders, OCD, and PTSD all have a bidirectional relationship with relationship functioning.
- Relationship functioning can impact patient symptoms at the broad level (e.g., by contributing to an overall stressful or supportive atmosphere) or specific level (e.g., by responding to symptoms with accommodation or EE).
- These disorders impact relationships by changing the emotional milieu, increasing negative behaviours, and decreasing positive relationship behaviours; the impact of these disorders also depends on attributions for the patient's symptoms and behaviours.
- In the context of these disorders and their management, individual needs can go unmet, and over time the environment can become less supportive while conflict increases, perpetuating the disorder.
- Couple-based interventions for these disorders typically include a variety of strategies such as:
    - psychoeducation;
    - communication skills training;
    - partner-assisted and/or disorder-specific interventions (i.e., interventions aimed at building safety, overcoming avoidance as a team, and addressing maladaptive ways of thinking); and
    - a broader focus on couple's issues beyond the disorder.
- Treatment protocols have been created to address some of these disorders. Although these protocols vary in detail, overall they emphasize the principles noted throughout this chapter.

Note

1 In couple therapy, both partners are considered the "client." In order to distinguish the individual with the disorder that is the focus of intervention in couple-based treatments from the other partner, we use the term "patient" to refer to the individual with the disorder and the term "partner" to refer to the other partner.

Chapter 13

Other disorders in couples

A detailed overview of the model and principles regarding how to intervene with couples in which one partner is experiencing psychopathology has been provided in Chapter 10. Moreover, because depression and anxiety-related disorders are so commonly encountered in couple therapy, separate chapters address how to adapt the model to these specific disorders. In the current chapter, we briefly discuss how to treat a number of additional psychological disorders and transdiagnostic concerns with couple-based interventions, including: (a) eating disorders, (b) bipolar disorder, (c) insomnia, (d) emotion regulation difficulties, and (e) substance use disorders. These disorders are included because they are likely to be encountered in outpatient settings and can reasonably be treated by many clinicians who have a good overall understanding of couples and psychopathology, by utilizing a cognitive-behavioural framework. Some disorders which require more specialized training, such as psychotic disorders and sexual dysfunctions, are not included. In determining whether to treat a given couple versus refer the couple elsewhere for treatment, clinicians always restrict their interventions to domains in which they have appropriate expertise and ensure that treatment is provided consistent with ethical and legal guidelines.

In each case, the overall cognitive-behavioural, couple-based treatment model applies and can be adapted to the specific disorder. Also, because relationship distress appears to have a similar exacerbating effect across disorders, we simply reiterate that relationship distress can be viewed as a broad, diffuse, chronic stressor which creates an overall negative environment with negative impact on the disorder. Therefore, relationship distress is not considered separately when addressing each disorder below. Instead, this chapter addresses aspects that are unique or central to the treatment of a given disorder within the context of the broader treatment model. As noted in Chapter 10, there are several common elements in the treatment, typically in the following order:

- initial assessment and feedback;
- psychoeducation about the disorder;
- communication training, including sharing thoughts and feelings and decision-making, applied to issues that are specific to the disorder;
- partner-assisted and disorder-specific interventions to address symptoms, with an emphasis on couple interaction patterns that can maintain or exacerbate the disorder; and
- couple therapy addressing broader relationship issues.

To a large extent, the uniqueness of each disorder lies in the specific symptoms, along with ways that each disorder "pulls" for interaction patterns or partner responses that might be maladaptive. The most common interaction patterns observed clinically for each disorder are the focus of this chapter, with the recognition that these patterns do not apply to all couples. In each instance, the couple-based approach draws from currently existing, empirically supported individual treatments (predominantly CBT). A detailed discussion of these individual interventions is well beyond the scope of this book; therefore, references are provided for basic readings on these treatments.

Eating disorders

Eating disorders involve unhealthy or maladaptive ways that individuals relate to food and their own weight and shape. The DSM-5 (American Psychiatric Association [APA], 2013) includes three main eating disorders: anorexia nervosa (AN), binge eating disorder (BED), and bulimia nervosa (BN). AN is characterized by a significantly low body weight along with an intense fear of gaining weight or becoming fat, or persistent behaviour that interferes with weight gain. This low weight often is accompanied by notable body image distortions in which the person believes that they are large and that body image has a major impact on their self-worth. Thus, individuals with AN typically feel highly distressed about their body, might attempt to hide it with loose clothing, and might be reluctant to exhibit their bodies even during intimate interactions. Although AN has the highest mortality rate associated with any psychiatric disorder, often the person with AN has little or no recognition of the disorder. In an effort to lower their weight, patients[1] frequently restrict their food intake or purge to lower their weight in secret, due to their own shame or their realization that if others know about their eating behaviours, they will likely object. Thus, as described in more detail below, the pattern of restricting food intake often generalizes to restricting what patients share with others more broadly, dealing with their notable emotional distress on their own and remaining emotionally distant from others, even their partners (Fischer, Kirby, et al., 2015; Schmidt & Treasure, 2006).

On the other hand, patients with BN and BED engage in discrete episodes of eating large quantities of food in a short period of time (binge eating), during which the person experiences a loss of control over their eating. Patients with BN engage in purging (e.g., vomiting, laxative use, excessive exercise) to compensate for binge eating, but individuals with BED do not. Severe body image distress and food restriction between binge episodes are typical as well. The impulse to eat and the related loss of control during eating episodes can be related to other impulsive behaviours, resulting in a less planful, organized lifestyle, along with stronger or more frequent expression of emotion than is typically seen in AN. Further complicating the clinical picture, psychiatric comorbidities are common with all eating disorders, including depression, anxiety disorders, and substance use disorders. Typically, the eating disorder needs to be targeted specifically in the context of these comorbidities and cannot be expected to remit in response to treatment aimed at lowering depression and anxiety, for example.

Both the empirical and clinical literatures provide strong justification for including a partner in the treatment of eating disorders. Individuals recovering from eating disorders describe supportive relationships as central to their recovery (Linville, Brown, Sturm, & McDougal, 2012; Tozzi et al., 2003). However, some couples struggle with maintaining healthy relationships in the midst of an eating disorder. More specifically, couples with eating disorders report significant relationship distress, fewer positive interactions, and more negative communication than couples without eating disorders (Van den Broucke, Vandereycken, &

Vertommen, 1995; Whisman, Dementyeva, Baucom, & Bulik, 2012; Woodside, Lackstrom, & Shekter-Wolfson, 2000). They also often report difficulties around sexual functioning and intimacy, likely in part due to body image distress and shame (Castellini et al., 2010; Pinheiro et al., 2010).

While there are many commonalities across eating disorders (such as body image distress), as alluded to above, there also are differences which have implications for couples' relationships and couple-based interventions. For example, because individuals with AN often are emotionally avoidant and struggle to express their feelings, they tend to have difficulty articulating their needs, tolerating distress in the relationship, or remaining close with others. On the other hand, individuals with BN also might lack constructive communication skills and tend to be more impulsive compared to individuals with AN (Cassin & von Ranson, 2005), which can contribute to negative interactions within the relationship. Many individuals with BED experience emotions intensely and have been described as having difficulties with setting boundaries in relationships, which might contribute to their experience of interpersonal relationships as stressful (Riener, Schindler, & Ludvik, 2006).

Not surprisingly in this context, partners often struggle as well. Partners commonly report difficulty understanding the eating disorder. Many find the patient's secrecy about their disordered eating challenging to live with (Huke & Slade, 2006), and they feel devalued or mistrusted because they have been shut out of such an important area. Many feel powerless and perceive that their well-intentioned attempts at supporting their loved one often backfire ("damned if I do, damned if I don't"). Some partners become fearful of saying or doing something hurtful or counterproductive and, thus, become avoidant, whereas others become critical or blaming. Overall, the challenges of the eating disorder create significant caregiver distress and burden (Zabala, Macdonald, & Treasure, 2009) and can contribute to escalating issues in the relationship. Thus, working with the couple to address the eating disorder is a plausible approach.

Anorexia nervosa

As noted above, and consistent with these patients' strong control regarding eating, individuals with AN often demonstrate rigid behavioural repertoires and withdrawal in their broader interactions with their partners, both around the AN per se and in their reluctance to communicate and share their emotions more generally. In addition, many patients are highly sensitive to the emotional expressions of others. In response to these challenges and the overall difficulties in treating adult AN and subsequent complications, Baucom, Kirby, Fischer, Baucom, Hamer, and Bulik (2017) created a couple-based intervention for adult AN, called Uniting Couples in the Treatment of Anorexia Nervosa (UCAN; D. H. Baucom et al., 2017; Bulik, Baucom, & Kirby, 2012b). UCAN is provided in conjunction with individual CBT, dietary counselling, and medical monitoring, consistent with best practices for a multidisciplinary treatment of AN. The couple-based intervention described below is drawn from the principles developed for UCAN (Bulik, Baucom, & Kirby, 2012a; Bulik et al., 2012b).

Addressing avoidant interaction patterns

Many adults with AN deal with broader distress and their eating disorder by avoidance and withdrawal, including attempts to "contain" anxiety and emotional distress by eating-disordered behaviour (e.g., restricting, excessive exercise). Often, patients are reluctant to discuss their disordered eating and their concerns about their body but instead withdraw, hide their eating disorder, and rarely turn to their partners to address the disorder; frequently, couples describe a "cloud of secrecy" that allows the AN to continue (Fischer, Kirby, et al., 2015). Therefore, a major goal of treatment is to bring the disorder into the open and help the couple address the problem together as a team. In doing so, the disorder ceases to function in its typical, elusive maintaining environment, which provides new ways to approach this complex disorder. This goal is integrated into each element of the treatment. Thus, in the feedback session following the initial assessment as well as the subsequent psychoeducation, the therapist discusses the nature of AN and the strong pull to withdraw and keep symptoms hidden. Both partners are encouraged to describe how they experience this secrecy and withdrawal, thereby beginning to alter the avoidance pattern even while discussing it. In the following therapy excerpt, the therapist encourages the patient to talk about her avoidance, bringing her typical pattern of responding into the session where it can be discussed and alternatives considered at some point in treatment.

Therapist: Anne, you have said that it is really hard for you to talk about your eating difficulties with Colin. When he does raise it, what goes through your mind; what are you thinking and feeling, and what do you typically do?

Anne: I just panic, and my mind goes blank. I want to run or go inside my head if I can't find a way to get out of the room. I don't want to say anything because that will just lead to more discussion, and I'm not comfortable talking about it with anyone.

Therapist: So what do you literally do, if you can't get up and leave?

Anne: Either I just sit there quietly, try to change the topic, or sometimes I cry.

Second, when teaching communication skills, a major emphasis is placed on sharing thoughts and feelings, and the therapist often needs to provide a great deal of support and encouragement for the patient, and often for the partner. After one couple discussed the patient's restricted eating in a manner that to an observer might have appeared to be brief and somewhat perfunctory, the patient responded, "That was really hard. We've been married for 20 years, and we have *never* had a conversation like that. I'm not so sure how I feel about doing this."

Moreover, the patient and partner often experience the disorder and related concerns differently, so the importance of accepting the other person's experience is essential as an emphasis in communication training. For example, the patient and partner frequently have vastly different perceptions of the patient's body size. Individuals with AN are often notably underweight yet perceive their bodies as obese. Understandably, partners find this notion hard to believe and attempt to convince the patient of their thinness. It is challenging for each person to accept that what seems like concrete reality is so discrepant from the other person's "facts." Therefore, the communication skills that are described in Chapter 4 are taught to the couple, with the therapist's awareness that certain aspects of communicating are likely to be particularly important and challenging for couples addressing AN.

Addressing AN symptoms and related features

AN symptoms are addressed with both partners together, which serves the dual purpose of continuing to remove the secrecy surrounding the disorder as well as helping the couple make good decisions and implement plans to normalize eating and associated behaviours. Because of the potential medical complications and the difficulty in cognitive processing that can accompany very low body weight, early efforts typically focus on weight restoration, followed by addressing other disorder-related concerns. Thus, the couple might have a number of decision-making conversations guided by the therapist, addressing such topics as purchasing foods, preparing meals, expanding the range of foods the patient eats, creating a positive meal environment, identifying high risk-times for purging, etc. Because of its social elements, couples frequently discuss how to manage eating with others. In addition, in many cases, couples need to discuss changes that might be needed in their couple and family routines, as well as symptoms frequently associated with AN such as anxiety, depression, and concerns about sexuality and body image.

A detailed discussion of how to address each of the above issues is beyond the scope of this chapter, and the reader is referred to Bulik, Baucom, and Kirby (2012a) for more information on how to address these goals within a couple-based context. Broadly speaking, the above topics are approached with conversations that emphasize sharing thoughts and feelings, followed by decision-making and guided behaviour change interventions, with the therapist making sure that all decisions are consistent with overall AN treatment goals and guidelines, derived from individual CBT for AN. While it might seem straightforward to encourage the couple to share their thoughts and feelings and make joint decisions on eating-related issues, often these interventions are not at all straightforward for the couple to experience because the idea of change is highly distressing to most patients, thus sowing the seeds for couple disagreements. The patient's ambivalence about change is reflected in the common statement, "I want to get better; I just don't want to eat." For example, increasing the range of foods the patient eats is central to recovery. However, consuming long-avoided foods can evoke significant anxiety. As a result, the patient might be extremely reluctant to do so, or after agreeing, might have difficulty following through. For the partner, it is difficult to know when to back off versus when to encourage the patient to go ahead in spite of distress. Extensive follow-up with the therapist is often required. Consequently, the therapist and couple frequently need to make multiple attempts as they troubleshoot and fine-tune to achieve desired changes. Given this slow pace of change and the time needed for weight restoration, our couple-based intervention for AN often continues for six months or longer.

Couple-based intervention for AN within a broader treatment context

Although many disorders such as anxiety and depression can be treated in a couple-based format as the sole form of intervention, the treatment of AN is almost always interdisciplinary, as recommended by current guidelines (NICE, 2017). For example, UCAN's treatment team includes a psychiatrist, an individual therapist, and a dietitian. A psychiatrist is needed for medical monitoring; although there are no proven efficacious medications for treating adult AN, medications might be appropriate to treat related symptoms such as anxiety. Individual therapy is an essential part of treatment as well. Many individuals have a number of psychological factors that contribute to the disorder, including notable distorted cognitions about their physical appearance or self-worth. The depth and breadth of these concerns often necessitate an individual focus; otherwise, the couple intervention can become individual therapy with a partner attending the session. Finally, most individuals with AN need extensive assistance developing a meal plan appropriate for weight restoration, which is beyond the expertise of most psychotherapists; hence, a dietitian's knowledge is also needed. Given that the treatment of AN is complex and multidisciplinary, it is important that all these professionals participate on the treatment team and that the treatment is coordinated among them.

Binge eating disorder and bulimia nervosa

Although all eating disorders typically involve secrecy regarding eating-disordered behaviours, individuals with BED and BN tend to be more outgoing and emotionally expressive than individuals with AN (particularly compared to the restricting subtype who greatly limit food intake). Indeed, emotional and behavioural impulsivity can become a salient part of the clinical picture, and emotions can be a major trigger for binge episodes. Particularly for BED, this dysregulation often is accompanied by a lack of structure in life, including inconsistent eating patterns, irregular sleep cycles, and a lack of regular daily routine. Partners often are unaware of the disordered eating, yet they are greatly affected by the inconsistent routines.

Addressing couple interaction patterns

In order to address relevant individual and relationship patterns, the same researchers who created UCAN adapted the treatment for BN and BED, creating a programme called Uniting Couples in the Treatment of Eating Disorders (UNITE; Kirby, Runfola, Fischer, Baucom, & Bulik, 2016; Runfola et al., 2018). Consistent with our overall couple-based approach, this intervention begins with assessment and feedback, then proceeds to address communication skills focused on the disorder. Sharing thoughts and feelings for this population often targets two somewhat opposite interaction patterns, depending on the couple's typical dynamics. For couples who avoid addressing the disorder, the focus is on helping the couple reduce secrecy surrounding the eating disorder, similar to the emphasis with AN. However, for couples who are struggling with emotional dysregulation, the focus is on helping the couple share their feelings in a more regulated fashion without maladaptive, negative escalation. Thus, in some instances, communication skills training can be sufficient to help the couple express emotions adaptively. However, when expressing emotions adaptively appears to be a core deficit for the patient, more explicit interventions might be needed, as described later in this chapter.

Addressing maladaptive eating and related features

Problem-solving skills focus on helping couples work together to develop a more consistent and nutritionally balanced eating schedule to reduce dietary restraint and urges to binge or purge. Often, individuals with BN and BED engage in a cycle in which they attempt to restrain eating, which increases the likelihood of binge eating, followed by purging in the case of BN. A major goal of treatment is to develop a regular pattern of balanced eating that avoids such cycles. Although couples cannot always eat meals together, they can develop strategies for the patient to have a regular eating schedule when they are apart, with the partner providing appropriate support in the process (e.g., helping to make certain that appropriate foods are available and that the daily schedule facilitates regular meal times). Importantly, the couple is encouraged to develop a positive eating experience for times when they are together. Couples also learn how to respond more effectively to urges to binge or purge by addressing major triggers. For example, when urges are strong, strategies such as joint activities for distraction can provide helpful structure for the patient to tolerate the urge until it subsides without engaging in the behaviour.

As the couple makes progress in the above domains focal to disordered eating, additional topics frequently encountered in BN/BED are addressed such as body image, sleep, weight and health concerns, weight stigma, emotion regulation, and intimacy or sexuality. In each instance, these substantive issues are addressed through a combination of psychoeducation, sharing thoughts and feelings, and problem-solving. Because some patients, particularly with BED, might be obese, issues such as weight stigma can be embarrassing for patients to address. Thus, it is essential that clinicians help partners respond to these concerns in caring and accepting ways. Moreover, it is important to help partners appropriately express their own concerns as well. This step can be complex given that some partners might have developed negative attitudes toward the patient. Partners might harbour criticism and hostility toward the patient for engaging in binge eating, believing that the patient needs to "simply eat like normal people do. Many people would enjoy lots of cakes; they just exercise some self-control!" Partners might also feel notable weight stigma toward the patient or find the patient unattractive, particularly in the context of weight gain. Hence, the therapist needs to balance openness and honesty with tact regarding what is shared between the partners. Our approach does not assume that partners always share everything they are thinking and feeling with each other. Instead, the immediate and long-term impact along with tact and kindness are central in deciding what to say to a partner, both in treating ED and in relationships in general.

Bipolar disorder

The DSM-5 distinguishes between two bipolar disorders: bipolar I (one or more manic episodes either with or without a major depressive episode) and bipolar II (at least one hypomanic episode and a major depressive episode). Because depression has been discussed in Chapter 11, the emphasis here is on the challenges that patients and partners experience resulting from a manic episode. Overall, a wide range of findings indicate that individuals with bipolar disorders struggle with intimate relationships; they are less likely to marry, experience notable levels of relationship distress, and have high divorce rates (Davila et al., 2019).

Bipolar disorder is a cyclical disorder, and one of the major complications for both partners is that life can change drastically when the patient experiences a manic episode and then returns to a premorbid level of functioning. For the partner, instead of being one of the two people who typically function as "equals," during a manic episode they become a caretaker who at times needs to "take over." Because the patient might have grandiose beliefs about their abilities and goals during a manic episode (e.g., a desire to invest substantial family funds in a very risky endeavour), the partner might attempt to take over decision-making. In some instances, the partner also attempts to undo actions already committed by the patient or minimize consequences of such actions (e.g., the patient disrupting important relationships during bouts of anger). Such variations in roles can be very unsettling, particularly when partners also experience that they are "losing" their mate during manic episodes. The patient can experience these shifts as vacillating between feeling respected during their stable states and feeling that the partner is being condescending and "treating me like a child" during manic episodes. Because the patient might lack insight into their manic symptoms combined with being agitated and irritable, intense disagreements might result.

Couples also often interact in other maladaptive ways during a manic episode, beyond the effects of irritability. The expressed emotion literature demonstrates that family members can significantly influence the course of a loved one's disorder as a function of how they understand the disorder and how they interact with the patient. Often a partner's responses to symptoms of mania involves expressing hostility and criticism toward the patient, which can interfere with the patient's recovery (Hooley & Miklowitz, 2018). Another detrimental aspect of expressed emotion that seems quite different from hostility involves emotional overinvolvement from the partner. For example, partners sometimes excessively sacrifice their own responsibilities and sources of enjoyment beyond what is needed in order to attend to the patient. Thus, some partners might curtail or change their jobs or discontinue going out with friends in order to stay with the patient, when such changes are not needed. Another form of family emotional overinvolvement involves giving unsolicited advice in domains where the patient is capable of functioning without such input (e.g., reminding the patient to dress warmly when going outdoors). Emotional overinvolvement predicts less favourable outcomes for patients, likely in part because such overinvolvement undermines a sense of self-efficacy as well as behaviourally restricts patients' interactions with their environment.

However, as research has shown (Fredman, Baucom, Miklowitz, & Stanton, 2008), there is an important distinction between appropriate involvement versus inappropriate overinvolvement. That is, during a manic episode, it might be important for the partner to be heavily involved in the patient's care and assume a greater role in decision-making; the difficult judgment involves deciding when and in what contexts high levels of partner involvement are beneficial versus detrimental. The importance of this judgment is demonstrated by the findings that when emotional overinvolvement is high, compared to individual therapy, patients benefit more from family-focused therapy which incorporates psychoeducation about bipolar disorder, communication training, and problem-solving around the patient's symptoms (Fredman, Baucom, et al., 2015).

Addressing couple interaction patterns

Because of impairments in the patient's cognitive processing during a manic episode, intervening with the couple is likely to be most productive when the patient is in a more stable state so that the couple can plan how to address issues both in the present and if/when the patient has a further manic episode. Therefore, psychoeducation is essential to help the couple understand bipolar disorder and how it affects each person and the relationship, both during stable times and during manic episodes, including a discussion of the strain it can place on couples to alternate between two very different ways of functioning. Another important focus involves the early detection of warning signs for an oncoming episode and preventative actions.

During communication training, the couple discusses what each person finds useful and difficult as they encounter the challenges related to mania, including the difficulties of distinguishing appropriate partner involvement from emotional overinvolvement. Similarly, the couple often discusses symptoms of agitation or irritability during the manic episode and the partner's typical responses. Partners' responses might vary from (a) responding with negativity, contributing to escalating negative reciprocity and destructive arguments to (b) withdrawing or "walking on eggshells" in order to avoid upsetting the patient. Thus, the therapist helps the couple clarify and articulate their adaptive and maladaptive interaction patterns, both during stable times and during manic episodes, before deciding together on more effective strategies that they will attempt to adopt in the future. Likewise, the couple and therapist discuss the couple's interaction patterns during depressive episodes if applicable, as described in Chapter 11.

Addressing manic symptoms and related features

Although couples might need to address a wide range of symptoms, many of these symptoms relate to what occurs during a manic episode, including symptoms that impact (a) both individuals, (b) their relationship, and (c) their interaction with the wider environment. First, in terms of symptoms that impact the patient, often the individual no longer engages in adaptive, self-care behaviours related to sleep, diet, or exercise. For example, the patient might become exhausted due to lack of sleep, eat excessively, and dramatically increase or decrease exercise, thus increasing their vulnerability to additional symptoms. Consequently, the couple might decide how to help the patient create regular, healthy approaches to daily living in these domains and others, consistent with principles also described in *interpersonal and social rhythm therapy* (Frank, 2007). Also, most individuals with bipolar disorder benefit significantly from appropriate psychotropic medications, yet some discontinue their medications because they enjoy mild versions of their symptoms (e.g., increased energy) or believe they no longer need the medication. Therefore, it is important for the couple to develop effective medication adherence strategies, which at times involve significant involvement from the partner.

Second, in addition to the maladaptive interaction patterns discussed above, behaviours that occur between the partners often need to be addressed. Some individuals experience a greatly increased sex drive during a manic phase, which is undesirable for the partner. Helping the couple negotiate these challenges can be crucial to maintaining a healthy sense of intimacy. Furthermore, some patients exhibit an increase in their verbal behaviour, which can include pressured speech with rapid and ongoing conversation. Partners can feel overwhelmed by the intensity of such interactions and either withdraw or become angry with the patient.

The above changes in various domains often are accompanied by more intense emotional reactions. While some patients are increasingly happy and joyous during manic states, others become agitated and are sometimes verbally or physically abusive. Thus, it is important to help the couple develop appropriate safety plans if the patient, partner, children, or others are placed at risk. These plans could include having the partner initiate involuntary hospitalization procedures if the patient becomes dangerous to self or others. For many couples, initiating a psychiatric hospitalization is an emotionally difficult and logistically complex decision, so advanced planning and empowering the partner to take needed action in consultation with care providers can be helpful. Often, considerable effort is needed to help the partner deal with the guilt arising from taking such action; psychoeducation can help clarify the importance of tolerating immediate distress to achieve long-term outcomes that benefit the patient, their family, and others in their environment. Ideally, the patient can give "advance permission" to the partner to take such actions as part of a joint plan developed when the patient is well, with the patient's instructions to the partner to ignore a change of mind while they are manic.

Third, the patient's behaviour during a manic episode can greatly disrupt or alter relationships outside of the couple, as well as creating other difficulties in the couple's wider environment. For example, because patients might behave in ways that damage relationships with other family members, friends, and co-workers, it can be valuable for the couple to discuss who should be told about the bipolar disorder. Also, because the patient might need to curtail or take leave from work, it is important that the couple discuss, while the patient is in a stable state, how to manage such work-related changes. Furthermore, the couple might need to decide how they will deal with the consequences of a variety of poor judgments made during manic episodes (e.g., poor financial decisions).

Given the complexity of these issues and the centrality of the partner in the patient's life, it is understandable that partners often experience considerable caregiver strain. Their own workload in accomplishing daily activities might increase during the manic episode; interactions with the patient can be strained, and dealing with complications resulting from the episode can be exhausting. Furthermore, the partner might curtail their own self-care while focusing efforts on the patient, thus leading to increased emotional and physical vulnerability for the partner. Finally, the couple often has to spend considerable effort after a manic episode discussing what occurred and how they can attempt to shift back into a more equitable couple relationship.

Couple-based intervention of bipolar disorder within a broader treatment context

The treatment of bipolar disorder most often includes psychotropic medication as an essential part of a comprehensive treatment plan. Therefore, ongoing collaboration between the therapist and a physician with expertise in bipolar disorder can be valuable. Not only do the health care professionals involved need a consistent, agreed-upon treatment plan, but also observations from another professional can be invaluable as an additional source of information, given that patient's own reporting might be skewed, especially during symptomatic episodes.

In summary, addressing bipolar disorder is complex for the couple, yet there are a number of guidelines and issues that the couple and the therapist can be sensitive to and address, as outlined above. Although a couple-based approach might not be essential in treatment for all partnered patients, the findings to date suggest that it might be the most efficacious intervention in instances where there are notable maladaptive couple/family interaction patterns (Fredman, Baucom, et al., 2015). Even when such interaction patterns are not present, a couple-based intervention appears to be as effective as individual therapy, and many couples prefer to work together to address this complex disorder.

Insomnia

Insomnia disorder involves difficulty falling asleep, difficulty maintaining sleep, or early morning awakening, and it is associated with substantial impairment in many domains, such as a lower overall quality of life than the general population (LeBlanc et al., 2007), a greater risk for accidents (Simon & VonKorff, 1997), and higher rates of psychiatric comorbidities (Ford & Kamerow, 1989). For many people, sleep takes place in an interpersonal context, with the majority of adults having bed partners. Most couples prefer to sleep in the same bed and report that their sleep is worse when they sleep alone, but objective findings point to negative sleep consequences from sleeping with a partner (Rogojanski, Carney, & Monson, 2013). Sleep difficulties also can contribute to relationship discord; patients with sleep-onset insomnia are more likely to report relationship problems as a result of their own or their partner's sleep problems (National Sleep Foundation, 2014). Finally, even when partners are attempting to be helpful regarding insomnia, they can perpetuate the problem. For example, a caring partner might encourage a patient to sleep later in the morning or take a nap after a bad night of sleep, actions that are contrary to effective treatment as described below. Therefore, including a partner in treatment for insomnia has the potential to enhance treatment effects by using the partner to enable challenging behavioural changes for the patient and ensuring that the partner does not inadvertently accommodate unhelpful patient behaviours.

Cognitive-behavioural therapy for insomnia (CBTI) is the psychosocial intervention of choice for treating insomnia (Morin et al., 1999). There are two components of CBTI that account for its efficacy: sleep restriction therapy and stimulus control therapy. Sleep hygiene (SH) is another strategy in CBTI, but it has been shown to provide little benefit as a single therapy (Morin et al., 2006) and therefore is not included in our discussion of couple-based approaches. A detailed description of how to conduct CBTI on an individual basis is beyond the scope of this book; see Perlis, Jungquist, Smith, and Posner (2005) for a more extensive description of CBTI. The effects of CBTI are seen in both primary insomnia and insomnia that is comorbid with other disorders (Manber et al., 2008). Furthermore, it appears that the relationship between insomnia and comorbid conditions is reciprocal, such that the two conditions can exacerbate and maintain each other (Sánchez-Ortuño & Edinger, 2012). These findings indicate that in addition to treating it as a primary concern, insomnia can be targeted for treatment in the context of other disorders.

Despite the efficacy of CBTI in controlled investigations, in routine clinical settings the effectiveness of treatment can be compromised by a lack of adherence to the complex, demanding treatment protocol, as well as by patients dropping out of treatment. Lack of adherence and attrition are understandable, given that CBTI requires significant behavioural and lifestyle changes that are uncomfortable for many patients. For example, sleep restriction therapy requires that the patient stay awake much later than usual and/or get out of bed much earlier, initially increasing fatigue. One potential way to address these concerns is to include the partner in treatment, applying our same broad framework. Jenkins, Baucom, Drummond, and Nappi (2016) developed partner-assisted CBTI (PA-CBTI), which involves seven sessions with the couple as described below.

Addressing couple interaction patterns

While insomnia can have broad effects as a result of fatigue, the disorder itself is defined by difficulties in sleeping. As a result, most of the couple's interaction patterns are focal to attempts to sleep, plus broader reactions to sleep disturbances (e.g., anger resulting from being awakened nightly by the patient). Therefore, these couple interaction patterns are discussed below along with ways the couple can deal with the symptoms of the disorder within a couple-based intervention.

Addressing symptoms of insomnia and related features

Sleep restriction therapy (SRT) focuses on the importance of efficient sleep, which is a ratio of total time asleep relative to total time in bed. That is, the goal of SRT is to have the individual be asleep almost all of the time they are in bed; however, people with insomnia typically spend many sleepless hours in bed. SRT involves having the patient stay up late or get up early so that they become sleep deprived or build up "sleep debt." Likewise, it is important that the patient not take naps during the day. As sleep debt increases, the patient is more likely to fall asleep quickly and have sustained, sound sleep, thus increasing sleep efficiency. SRT is highly effective, but it can seem counterintuitive to both the patient and the partner without a full explanation. For example, it can seem cruel to a partner to encourage the patient to stay up when the patient is so tired (e.g., "Honey, I know they said you just have to stay up even though you are exhausted. To be honest, I think you should do whatever makes sense to you"). Therefore, psychoeducation with both partners present is important to obtain their commitment to a potentially confusing intervention.

Most importantly, the couple needs to decide how the partner can appropriately assist in SRT. They might decide that the partner will stay up with the patient every night until bedtime, stay up some nights, or perhaps not stay up with the patient at all. If the partner will not be present while the patient stays up, the couple can still discuss what the patient will do to stay awake, with the partner often having insights into the patient's behaviour and what might be important to change. Also, the partner can help the patient find alternatives to napping during the day. Depending on their schedules and other demands, the couple might decide on alternative activities they can engage in together to counteract drowsiness, such as playing a game or going for a walk, which can also contribute to relationship well-being.

Another component of the treatment, stimulus control therapy (SCT), is based on classical conditioning principles in which the goal is to condition the bed as a place for sleeping (and sex if the couple prefers) and not for other activities. Thus, the following guidelines are provided to assist in conditioning the bed for sleeping:

- Lie down and try to go to sleep only when you are sleepy.
- Do not use the bed for anything except sleep.
- If you cannot fall asleep within about 15–20 minutes, get out of bed, go to another room, and do something relaxing with as little light as possible.
- If you cannot fall asleep after going back to bed, repeat the above steps. Also, follow these steps if you wake up in the middle of the night and cannot fall back to sleep.
- Get up at the same time every day (even weekends), regardless of how much you slept the night before.

The couple's goal is to work together to help the patient accomplish these stimulus control guidelines. Consistent with SCT, bringing their evening to a close together in a caring manner can be a positive experience for couples as well. For example, the couple might decide that they want to stop all chores at a certain time each night and wind down together.

Although partners might be a valuable resource in SCT, sleeping together also can complicate matters. The guideline to "lie down and try to go to sleep only when you are sleepy" can be difficult when two people have different bedtime preferences. The partner might want to get into bed and read with the light on or play on some digital device such as a phone, making it difficult for the patient to fall asleep. Or, the partner might want to sleep later on weekend mornings and might find that the patient's getting up disrupts their sleep. At times, then, the intervention can call for the partner to change their own bedtime routine, and it is important to be aware of their needs as well, in order to avoid creating agreements which the partner will later resent or fail to implement.

For some couples, the above complications also raise the issue of whether they would benefit from sleeping in separate rooms for the duration of the treatment. Because sharing a bed is an intimate experience, sleeping apart can be interpreted as a signal that something is wrong with the couple's relationship. The therapist can help the couple discuss the pros and cons of this strategy and try to ensure that such an option is not given excess relationship meaning beyond the importance of being able to sleep well and adhere to the treatment regimen. Such an option can be presented as a temporary intervention to facilitate improved sleep before integrating sleeping in the same room back into the couple's life.

As noted above, insomnia can be comorbid with other conditions. For example, a military veteran with PTSD might wake up during the night and walk the perimeter outside of the house to ensure that everything is in order. While exposure treatment might call for the patient to tolerate the distress and not check for intruders, such an approach is unlikely to contribute to a relaxed state in which the patient can resume sleep quickly. Thus, the order of attending to symptoms in complex cases must be planned, with the patient and partner understanding and aligning their behaviour with the treatment principles employed.

In summary, CBTI is an efficacious treatment for insomnia, and given that many adults sleep with a partner, even when individual treatment is employed, the CBTI intervention strategies are being implemented in an interpersonal context. Therefore, explicitly integrating the partner into treatment holds notable promise for helping individuals and couples have a more rewarding sleep experience.

Emotion regulation difficulties

Relationship distress is emotionally dysregulating for many people, even those who typically have good control over their emotional experience. Even so, some individuals frequently cry or get angry very quickly during couple sessions, often with seemingly little provocation. Very little is needed to set off a strong emotional reaction that often is reciprocated by the partner. This vulnerability to strong negative emotions seems to be a core aspect of relationship distress for numerous couples, and as the relationship improves, emotion regulation does also. In these instances, the therapist relies on their ability to manage the session, control emotional arousal, and slowly shape the couple to address emotions in a more productive fashion (see Chapter 6).

However, in some instances, one or both partners continue to struggle with regulating their emotions as the relationship shows signs of improvement, or significant emotion dysregulation seems to get in the way of improving the relationship. With further discussion, it might become clear that this person struggles with regulating emotions in other domains of life and other relationships and that this pattern has been consistent across time. In essence, one person might experience more enduring, broad-based emotion dysregulation, which needs to be addressed. At times, some patients might have a diagnosis of borderline personality disorder.

For some individuals, negative emotions are experienced as intense, draining, and difficult to change or reduce; both they and their partners can feel dominated by the person's emotional experiences. Linehan (1993) has described "emotional vulnerability" as being highly sensitive to emotional stimuli, having intense emotional responses, and returning slowly to an emotional baseline. Emotional vulnerability can be compounded if the person also lacks strategies to modulate emotion, including difficulty with: (a) inhibiting maladaptive behaviours driven by emotions, (b) engaging in behaviours to achieve positive goals independent of current mood, (c) increasing or decreasing physiological arousal as needed, (d) distracting attention from emotionally evocative stimuli, and (e) experiencing emotion without either immediately withdrawing or producing an extreme secondary negative emotion. The combination of emotional vulnerability with deficits in being able to modulate emotions when they arise is referred to as "pervasive emotion dysregulation" (Linehan, 1993). As might be expected, these difficulties can be detrimental to the individual's well-being, as well as to a partner and the couple's relationship. For example, in response to feeling anger, the patient might respond in a hostile manner, knowing that the behaviour will be counterproductive (e.g., "I know I should keep my mouth shut, but I just can't. At times when I get really upset, my mouth starts going before my brain engages. I tell myself, just don't overreact, and then it happens all over again").

Although patients might turn emotion-driven behaviours toward themselves in the form of self-destructive acts (including self-harm or suicidal behaviours), often the partner, children, or others are targets as well. Partners typically respond in one of two ways or perhaps vacillate between the two. Some respond by becoming distraught themselves and reciprocating negative responses, perhaps including verbal or physical aggression. Other partners have learned that responding is counterproductive; therefore, they withdraw when the patient displays strong emotions. They describe their lives as "walking on eggshells" as they stay hyperalert to the patient's emotional state. Others describe that for the most part, they avoid emotionally evocative interactions but at times "can't take it anymore" and then arguments ensue.

While pervasive emotion dysregulation is identified as a central characteristic of borderline personality disorder, emotion dysregulation can be comorbid with a variety of mental health disorders or might be a domain of difficulty for individuals who have no psychiatric diagnosis. Thus, our approach is to target pervasive emotion dysregulation as a transdiagnostic syndrome that involves an important skill deficit, which merits explicit attention. (See Fruzzetti and Payne, 2015, for a discussion of couple-based interventions targeted for couples including one partner diagnosed with borderline personality disorder.)

When such broad-based emotion regulation difficulties are present, treatment might need to be expanded beyond the typical CBCT interventions. Otherwise, the therapist might be asking the patient to engage in behaviours beyond their actual skill level. Given the importance of focusing explicitly on emotion regulation difficulties in an interpersonal context, Kirby and Baucom (2007b) developed a couple-based intervention to target emotion regulation difficulties exacerbated in the context of relationship distress. They integrated principles from CBCT with interventions from dialectical behaviour therapy (DBT; Linehan, 1993), which places a major emphasis on individual emotion regulation skills.

Addressing couple interaction patterns

Psychoeducation about emotion regulation difficulties is an essential part of the intervention. Although emotion dysregulation is comorbid with many disorders, such as depression, anxiety disorders, binge eating disorder, and various personality disorders (Kirby & Baucom, 2007b), it is not a defining characteristic of these disorders. Therefore, partners might view the difficulty as something the patient should be able to control (e.g., "Everyone gets upset and at times wants to yell or say whatever comes to mind. I know I feel that way, but I don't allow myself to do it. That is what it means to be an adult. You just need to stop being so dramatic!"). Consequently, providing information about individual differences in emotional vulnerability and emotion regulation ability can be helpful in giving both partners a new way to think about the patient's deficits without excusing maladaptive behaviours. It is important to supplement this type of discussion with an exploration of how these difficulties are manifest in the couple's relationship, including how both people experience the problem, what factors serve as a trigger or seem to increase the likelihood of such experiences, and how the partner responds to the patient's behaviours in an adaptive or maladaptive fashion. Over the course of therapy, the couple has an ongoing discussion about how to alter these interaction patterns, contingent upon the development of skills needed to make such changes.

Addressing features and consequences of emotion dysregulation

A variety of interventions from DBT can be adapted for use with couples, including: (a) mindfulness skills, (b) emotion regulation skills, and (c) distress tolerance skills. This content is drawn primarily from Linehan's DBT skills training curriculum (Linehan, 2015), with an emphasis given to couple-level experiences of these phenomena (Kirby & Baucom, 2007a). A detailed description of these DBT skills is beyond the scope of this book and can be found in Linehan's DBT texts and skills training manual (Linehan, 2015). What follows is a brief introduction to their application in a couple context, while acknowledging that a substantial emphasis is the development of individual skills that are then applied interpersonally. Although these skills typically are taught because one member of the couple experiences difficulties, teaching the skills to both persons together can be effective, and partners often remark that they benefit notably from focusing on the role of emotions in their own lives as well.

Mindfulness skills

The therapist can introduce mindfulness skills that are selected for a given couple, such as: (a) developing a "wise mind" by integrating one's reason and emotions, (b) observing one's own experiences, and (c) describing one's own experiences using words or labels. Regarding wise mind, the couple might discuss how the two partners have different tendencies to focus primarily on emotions versus reason, and how this difference might complicate the couple's ability to work together effectively, particularly when making decisions. Thus, a person who relies primarily on logic might invalidate the other person, who relies heavily on their emotional reactions (e.g., "But what you are saying isn't logical; you're just being emotional"). Helping each partner to integrate reasoning and emotion and doing so as a couple can result in a different, productive way of discussing issues and making decisions.

Mindfulness skills might also be taught to the couple. These skills consist of participating fully in the present moment, using a nonjudgmental approach when observing and describing experiences, and adopting the stance of doing what works rather than what is "right" versus "wrong." Developing these skills not only assists the individual but also has couple-level implications in terms of helping avoid debates about who is right and wrong when sharing experiences or making joint decisions.

Emotion regulation skills

Emotion regulation skills presented to a couple might include: (a) identifying and labelling emotions; (b) reducing emotional vulnerability through strategies such as caring for one's physical health, daily mastery, and pleasurable experiences; (c) mindfulness of one's current emotion; and (d) acting opposite to the behavioural urge that a challenging emotion creates (when this urge might be ineffective). As with the mindfulness skills, couples are asked to consider how they might incorporate these strategies as a unit. For example, the person struggling with emotion regulation might have an urge to leave the house after an argument and drive in a reckless fashion. In this instance, the couple could discuss how that person might act in a manner opposite to this urge, by either staying engaged with the partner or taking time out from the interaction in a more adaptive fashion. It is important to clarify the partner's role in facilitating this change as well.

Distress tolerance skills

The couple also is introduced to distress tolerance skills, including distracting, self-soothing, improving distress in the moment by building in positives, and radical acceptance. These skills might be relevant to a number of domains in each person's life and can be particularly beneficial if the couple is experiencing relationship distress. Thus, couples might think about ways for the patients to distract themselves at high-risk times following upsetting interactions with the partner. Likewise, couples might discuss how they can engage in "healthy compartmentalization" to avoid certain situations or conversations until they can be engaged with the issue more adaptively (e.g., avoiding difficult conversations after they turn off the light and get in bed at night).

CBCT interventions

As discussed above, many DBT-related skills can be taught in a couple context by employing the interventions discussed throughout this book. Thus, communication skills which assist the couple in expressing emotions adaptively and validating the other person's experience can be vital in this regard. There is no set order in which the DBT and CBCT interventions are used, and these interventions should be tailored to each couple's needs. To the degree that difficulties with emotion regulation interfere with overall couple progress, they should be addressed early in treatment. To the extent that relationship distress can be alleviated with typical CBCT interventions, such strategies can lower the frequency and intensity of emotional distress experienced by the patient, thus reducing the level of emotional dysregulation that needs to be modified.

Couple-based intervention for emotion dysregulation within a broader treatment context

Depending on the magnitude and pervasiveness of the emotion dysregulation, treatment might be solely couple-based or it might call for the involvement of an individual therapist as well. When pervasive emotion dysregulation has been identified previously, the patient might be currently involved in individual therapy. For example, Kirby and Baucom (2007a, 2007b) provided treatment to couples for whom emotion dysregulation had previously been identified as salient to patients who were currently in individual therapy and had received DBT for at least one year prior to the couple intervention. In other instances, the difficulties are less central, and the therapist might have the expertise and experience to address the deficits in a couple context. In large part, the decision regarding the need for individual therapy depends on the extent to which the patient requires additional assistance to put the skills in place in everyday life and the extent of risk of harm to the patient or others. Just as in the treatment of AN, the therapist might conclude that the complexity of the case is too great to manage in isolation, thus calling for other clinicians, each of whom assumes a specific and coordinated role in the overall treatment plan.

At times even with treatment, difficulties with emotion dysregulation persist, and some partners decide they cannot continue in the relationship. Terminating important relationships can exacerbate emotion dysregulation even further, and therapists might well decide with the couple if the therapist can be of assistance as they enter into this next potentially difficult phase of life. Lebow (2019) provides a thoughtful discussion of how to help couples who are experiencing complex divorces for a variety of reasons, including addressing strong ongoing negative emotions.

Substance use disorders

The DSM-5 defines substance use disorders as involving a pathological or maladaptive pattern of behaviours related to the use of a substance. The distinctions between abuse and dependence that were part of earlier diagnostic systems are no longer used. Instead, substance use disorders are classified as mild (two or three symptoms), moderate (four or five symptoms), or severe (six to 11 symptoms), based on how many of the 11 possible symptoms an individual exhibits. These 11 symptoms group into broader domains, including impaired control over using the substance, social impairment resulting from using the substance, risky use of the substance, and pharmacological criteria such as tolerance and withdrawal (APA, 2013).

An important question is whether a clinician without specialized training in substance use disorders should work with couples presenting with such concerns or under what circumstances it is appropriate to do so. There is no simple answer to this question, but our recommendation is that if the substance use disorder is in the severe range, the person has tried numerous times unsuccessfully to decrease or eliminate substance use, tolerance and withdrawal are present, or highly destructive behaviours such as physical violence are involved, a couple-based intervention should be delivered only by therapists highly trained to work in this area. When couple-based interventions are used with couples with more severe disturbances by highly trained therapists, these interventions can be highly effective. On the other hand, many couples present with mild to moderate substance use difficulties within the context of relationship distress or comorbid with other psychiatric conditions, and these concerns can be integrated into a broader treatment plan. In particular, when the mild to moderate substance use concerns include negative consequences for the couple's relationship (e.g., being withdrawn and noncommunicative at night after drinking several bottles of beer), addressing such concerns fits well with a couple-based approach. An alternative presentation within the context of relationship distress or psychopathology is when the substance use appears to be part of a broader pattern of behaviour that contributes to negative mood, lack of motivation, or difficulty following through with plans, even though other major concerns are not present (e.g., missing work).

Thus, one way of determining whether the couple therapist should work with or refer a couple with a substance use disorder is based on severity and the symptom profile. In discussing alcohol use disorders, McCrady (2014) suggests that the clinician think about alcohol problems as existing on a continuum and focus on the person's patterns of drinking, negative consequences of drinking, behavioural deficits and excesses in various aspects of life, and strengths in addressing the substance use. A similar approach can be used in addressing other substances as well. A major focus is on what factors are maintaining the current substance use, and consistent with the CBCT model, McCrady suggests that maintenance of substance use can result from individual, relationship, and environmental factors. As with the other disorders discussed throughout this text, the following analysis identifies how substance use fits into the individual's and couple's lives, followed by interventions targeted to these domains.

Addressing couple interaction patterns

As with eating disorders, many individuals with a substance use disorder deny to themselves and others that they have a problem. Thus, they might minimize or hide their use or be deceitful if confronted. As a result, partners might be unaware of the substance use and its extent, or they might believe that the person has stopped their earlier use. Alternatively, partners might see the signs of the substance misuse but deny or avoid acknowledging it to themselves or to the patient. This denial might occur for various reasons: They do not want to disrupt their positive view of their partner or their relationship; they generally are unassertive or conflict avoidant; they have experienced that raising their concerns results in arguments without changes in behaviour; or the partner enjoys the patient's substance of choice and wants to maintain the couple's joint use of it. In such instances, often the therapist's first step is to help the couple address this area of concern in a constructive manner, allowing either partner to express worry, concern, and care for the person with the substance problems without blaming and criticism, which are likely to evoke a defensive response.

In other instances, couples develop a variety of interaction patterns around the substance use. As with any maladaptive behaviour, partners can become highly critical and hostile toward the patient. At times, pushing the patient to confront the reality of the problem might be needed; however, a critical and hostile style toward almost any disorder predicts a negative outcome. In a related vein, partners might adopt the role of "monitor," in which they check frequently for hidden substances and confront the patient when they find such substances. Again, addressing reality is important but adopting the role of checking on one's partner is not a desirable or effective long-term strategy. Indeed, in the area of smoking cessation, researchers have found that nagging, complaining, and policing by a partner are ineffective strategies and at times predict increased smoking (Mermelstein, Lichtenstein, & McIntyre, 1983).

Rather than having a critical response, some partners might accommodate the substance use problem, either through denial as described above, or in other ways. Some partners "cover" for the patient when their behaviour would have negative consequences; for example, a partner might call the patient's workplace to say they are ill when in fact they are hungover. At times, partners take over the patient's responsibilities when the patient is intoxicated. Or, the couple might use substances together, such as drinking heavily on weekends or smoking marijuana after the children are in bed to "take the edge off." As with other disorders described thus far, the therapist's role is to provide psychoeducation regarding accommodation and the forms that it can take, help the couple explore how the partner might accommodate the substance use, evaluate the consequences of accommodating in particular circumstances, and discuss alternative responses.

Addressing the symptoms of substance use disorders and related features

The explicit goal of working with the couple is to decrease substance misuse, with a major emphasis on factors that maintain the problem in the present, including individual, relationship, and environmental factors.

Individual risk factors

On the individual level, some patients might have a biological vulnerability to overuse substances once they have started using substances. Although such vulnerabilities cannot be determined, the possibility of their existence does raise the issue of whether total abstinence or more limited, controlled substance use is the goal of treatment. As McCrady (2014) discusses, moderate use might be appropriate as a goal when: (a) the person has a history of successful moderate use; (b) the person does not have a family history of substance use problems; (c) moderate substance use would not complicate other medical or psychological problems; and (d) there are no signs of dependence or withdrawal. Helping couples navigate this decision can be difficult, but it is important to ensure that everyone is attempting to accomplish the same goals.

Beyond setting realistic goals for substance use related to presumed biological vulnerabilities, certain individual states can be high risk for substance misuse. Thus, some individuals cope with negative mood or physical symptoms of other disorders by taking substances as a form of self-medication. Recognizing these high-risk times can be helpful so that the couple can attempt to avoid these situations when possible (e.g., employing appropriate interventions to address chronic pain) or deal with their presence more effectively (e.g., responding to negative mood by doing something pleasurable together).

Couple risk factors

Likewise, the couple might have developed behavioural patterns in which substance use has become integral. They might regularly smoke marijuana together to relax at the end of the day or celebrate special occasions with cocaine. Effective strategies in many contexts involve stimulus-control procedures. If the goal is abstinence, it might mean not having the substance available in the home, or avoiding the broader context in which the substance use occurs. For example, the couple might decide to forego wine at dinner, or they might avoid social gatherings where illicit drugs are likely to be present and begin to establish a sober community.

The couple also can use these opportunities to build their relationship or individual functioning in a more positive fashion. Therefore, the interventions might be more successful and serve multiple purposes if the couple can discuss how they want to build their relationship and use their time together more constructively, while also decreasing substance use.

Environmental risk factors

Finally, substance use, like food consumption, often occurs in broader social contexts. Therefore, the couple needs to know how they will respond when they are with other people, ranging from being offered a glass of wine at a work gathering, to socializing with friends where substance use is a part of the fabric of getting together. With regard to alcohol, findings indicate that helping an individual develop drinking refusal skills (e.g., being clear and confident in saying "no" to alcohol when offered, requesting an alternative beverage, etc.) can be part of an effective treatment programme (Witkiewitz, Donovan, & Hartzler, 2012). In a couple context, the couple can decide and practise how to respond to such situations, including whether both or only the patient will refuse the substance.

In summary, the therapist and couple should conduct a functional, behavioural analysis to understand the individual, relational, and environmental contexts that contribute to the maintenance of the substance use problems and use problem-solving skills consistent with stimulus control, distraction and alternative behaviours, and interpersonal assertiveness skills to work together as a team in addressing the domains relevant to the disorders.

Empirical status

Couple-based interventions for most of the disorders discussed in the current chapter are at a similar early stage of development and evaluation. They also appear to be reaching broadly similar conclusions: These couple-based interventions appear to be at least comparable and possibly superior to individual interventions, although many findings are based on open trials which provide only initial indications of treatment utility. Below is a brief summary of relevant treatment outcome research to date.

Turning first to eating disorders, as noted earlier, a couple-based intervention called UCAN targets the treatment of AN. In an open trial, 20 participants and their partners received treatment over approximately 26 weeks, including: the couple-based intervention, individual CBT, psychiatric medication management, and nutritional counselling. The findings indicated that patients improved at posttest and three-month follow-up on a variety of AN-related measures, anxiety and depression, and relationship adjustment. Likewise, partners also improved on anxiety, depression, and relationship adjustment. In an exploratory analysis, the multi-component couple treatment intervention was benchmarked to well-conducted randomized controlled trials of individual therapy for AN; in this comparison, the couple intervention compared favourably on AN-related measures with a lower dropout rate than individual treatment (D. H. Baucom et al., 2017).

Also, as noted above, UCAN was adapted for the treatment of BED in a programme called Uniting Couples in the Treatment of Eating Disorders (UNITE; Kirby et al., 2016; Runfola et al., 2018). In an open trial, couples received 22 sessions of UNITE. At the end of treatment, 80% of the patients demonstrated objective binge episode abstinence, which is higher than the 50–60% rate reported in larger trials using individual treatments (e.g., Brownley, Berkman, Sedway, Lohr, & Bulik, 2007). In addition, patients improved on other eating disorder symptoms and measures of psychopathology. Thus, initial findings are encouraging for the utility of including a partner in the treatment of both AN and BED.

In treating bipolar disorder, Miklowitz and Goldstein (1997) developed family-focused therapy (FFT), consisting of psychoeducation about coping with bipolar disorder, along with communication training and problem-solving skills. FFT resulted in more rapid recovery from illness episodes and longer periods prior to recurrence over 1–2 years compared with patients who received medication plus brief psychoeducation (e.g., Miklowitz, George, Richards, Simoneau, & Suddath, 2003). In addition, Fredman, Baucom, et al. (2015) found that couple dynamics were important in predicting who responded well to FFT. More specifically, patients with family members who exhibited high rates of inappropriate emotional over-involvement benefitted more from FFT compared to an individual intervention, whereas there was no difference between the two interventions at low levels of inappropriate emotional involvement. Thus, when maladaptive family interaction patterns were present, a family-based intervention was the treatment of choice.

The couple-based intervention for insomnia, PA-CBTI, has had preliminary evaluation in an open trial of eight couples, with each couple receiving seven sessions. PA-CBTI produced large to very large effects on sleep outcomes, which were larger than the effects from individually administered CBTI. In addition PA-CBTI reduced symptoms of depression (Jenkins, Nappi, Cassidy, Khosa, & Drummond, 2015).

A couple-based approach to addressing emotion dysregulation is in a similar stage of early development, with promising results from a small open trial. In a couple treatment developed by Kirby and Baucom (2007a), which integrates DBT and CBCT, couples met in a group format and were taught emotion regulation, communication, and problem-solving skills. Couples were then led through an exploration of how strong feelings both affect and are affected by their relationship. Ten couples in which at least one partner had experienced chronic difficulties in emotion regulation received 16 group sessions, following a format based on DBT skills training groups (Linehan, 2015). At the end of treatment, patients demonstrated notable reductions in depressive symptoms and emotion dysregulation, and partners increased in relationship satisfaction and their confidence that the patient could regulate emotions (Kirby & Baucom, 2007b). Fruzzetti and Payne (2015) also have commented on findings from an initial pilot study of couples based on DBT, which similarly resulted in increased relationship satisfaction and improved communication for patients and lowered depression for partners.

Unlike the couple-based interventions for the above disorders which are at an early stage of evaluation, behaviourally oriented couple interventions for alcohol use disorders (AUD) are well-researched interventions. As noted earlier in the chapter, these interventions target couple interaction patterns to promote abstinence and sobriety by decreasing negative communication patterns and increasing positive interactions around sober behaviours (e.g., McCrady & Epstein, 2009). Behaviourally oriented couple interventions for AUDs have consistently been shown to be efficacious in improving alcohol consumption and relationship functioning (e.g., Walitzer & Dermen, 2004). They also have been shown to be superior to individual treatments on some alcohol and relationship outcomes and equal on others within each study (see Fischer et al., 2016, for a detailed review), including when a female rather than a male partner has the AUD (e.g., Schumm, O'Farrell, Kahler, Murphy, & Muchowski, 2014) or when both partners have a current AUD (Schumm, O'Farrell, & Andreas, 2012). Overall, behavioural-couple therapy for AUDs has consistently been at least as effective and often more effective than individual treatments, both in terms of substance-related outcomes and relationship adjustment.

In summary, when comparing across the disorders addressed in the current chapter, the amount of research varies greatly, ranging from initial open trials for most disorders to an established body of treatment outcome research for alcohol use disorders. Yet, the pattern in each case is consistent, demonstrating the promise of couple-based treatments that incorporate empirically supported individual treatment principles derived from CBT.

Concluding comments

The current chapter provides a brief overview of how to adapt couple-based interventions to several specific disorders and emotion regulation difficulties. Additionally, it provides a blueprint for how the same overall treatment approach can be adapted to other disorders, as the therapist learns about the couple's interaction patterns relative to the disorder and focuses on how they can work together as a team to address specific symptoms within an interpersonal context. We anticipate that the treatment strategies will continue to evolve as we learn more about specific disorders and how they are manifest in an interpersonal context. Given that many patients are in committed relationships, the disorder typically occurs in an interpersonal context; thus, explicitly taking that interpersonal context into account might notably enhance the effectiveness of the treatment delivered.

Main points

- Relationship functioning and psychopathology are intertwined, impacting each other in a reciprocal fashion. Therefore, integrating relationship factors into the treatment of psychopathology in a couple format has the potential to improve treatment effectiveness.
- A general couple-based treatment plan including the following elements can be individualized according to the needs of the couple and the disorder being considered: initial

assessment and feedback; psychoeducation about the disorder; communication training, with an emphasis on using these skills to address the disorder; partner-assisted and disorder-specific interventions to address specific symptoms or aspects of the disorder; and couple therapy to address relationship issues beyond the disorder.

- Adaptations to this general treatment plan focus primarily on the couple's interaction patterns relative to the disorder and how the couple can address specific symptoms.
- In order for these couple-based interventions to be optimally effective, the therapist needs knowledge of: the symptoms of the disorder and the individual interventions that are effective in treating it, ways of adapting those interventions to a couple context, and ways of broadening treatment to include domains that can best be explored with the couple present as opposed to the patient alone (e.g., interactions around physical intimacy).

Note

1 In couple therapy, both partners are considered the "client." In order to distinguish the individual with the disorder that is the focus of intervention in couple-based treatments from the other partner, we use the term "patient" to refer to the person with the disorder and the term "partner" to refer to the other partner.

Part V

Assessment, case conceptualization, and treatment planning to address relationship distress and psychopathology—pulling it all together

Conducting an initial assessment, conceptualizing the case, creating a treatment plan, and providing feedback to the couple typically are the starting points in working with a couple. These activities are described at the end of the book because it is helpful to be familiar with the CBCT model and available couple-based interventions when carrying out these initial activities with a couple. That is, the therapist needs to know what to assess and how to intervene on various domains of importance before undertaking this process—knowledge and perspectives that we have attempted to provide throughout this book.

As described in Chapter 14, the assessment proceeds through a number of specific steps using a variety of assessment strategies to gain a firm understanding of each partner, their relationship, and how they interact with their environment, both historically and in the present. Working collaboratively, the therapist and the couple create a shared understanding of the couple's current situation and the most central factors to address to improve individual and/or relationship functioning. Chapter 14 details how to take a vast amount of information from the initial assessment, integrate the relevant factors into a thoughtful and understandable conceptualization, and share feedback with the couple, including a proposed plan for moving forward with treatment. Of course, this initial conceptualization and treatment plan evolve as treatment proceeds. Just as with the couple's relationship, treatment is a dynamic process that incorporates consistent principles combined with change and unpredictability, which the therapist and couple approach in a flexible manner.

In Chapter 15, we summarize the potential challenges and rewards of including both partners when working with couples to treat their relationship distress and one partner's psychopathology. Finally, we present our closing thoughts about this most engaging process of helping two individuals grapple with their relationship and individual distress directly in the therapy room, as the therapist guides them and becomes an integral part of this intimate process.

Chapter 14

Assessment, case conceptualization, and treatment planning

CBCT begins with an assessment of the couple's presenting concerns, strengths, and goals for treatment, drawing on the underlying principles of the model as described in Chapter 2 and interventions elaborated on in subsequent chapters. Therefore, the current chapter is presented following the discussion of the model and treatment strategies, although initial assessment precedes treatment in clinical practice. This chapter examines the core components of CBCT assessment and provides a structure for organizing the assessment process, along with the subsequent case conceptualization, feedback to the couple, and treatment planning.

Aims and structure of the assessment

Aims

In CBCT, the assessment has multiple aims. One aim is to establish whether CBCT is appropriate for the couple at this time. In most instances when a couple requests assistance with relationship difficulties, couple therapy is appropriate. Similarly, a couple-based approach can be indicated for many couples in which the primary concern is a psychological disorder in one partner (or both), or when a disorder becomes evident during the assessment process. However, as noted throughout the previous chapters, often there are complicating factors that can indicate the need for alternative or collateral interventions. The most important contraindications are:

- If serious intimate partner violence (IPV) is present, individual treatment for the violent partner might be necessary instead of, or prior to, couple therapy. Past or current mild to moderate IPV is not necessarily a contraindication for treatment; however, depending on the recency and severity of the violence, increasing safety will typically be an immediate target in working with the couple.
- If one or both partners have significant unresolved psychological difficulties that are best addressed in an individual context (e.g., unresolved effects of childhood sexual abuse) or that require a higher level of care such as hospitalization (e.g., for severe anorexia nervosa or substance use disorders), then individual treatment might precede or be used concurrently with working with the couple. Specific considerations for recommending a couple-based versus individual treatment approach for psychopathology are discussed in Chapter 10.
- In some instances, it becomes clear that one partner is not interested in treatment but has been "dragged in," or one partner already has decided to end the relationship. In such instances, the couple and therapist must decide whether or how the therapist can be of assistance to the couple.

The second aim of the assessment is to develop a case conceptualization and tailored treatment plan, which will be shared with the couple during a feedback session. This explicit discussion is an important opportunity for the couple to decide whether they want to engage in couple therapy or a couple-based treatment approach to one partner's psychopathology, and whether the current therapist and the setting are a good fit for them. Alternatively, the therapist or the couple might decide that the format or setting is not optimal, or that couple work would be inappropriate without additional intervention, such as individual therapy for one of the partners.

In order to address the above issues, the therapist develops a thorough case conceptualization based on the CBCT model. This conceptualization incorporates important contextual factors, including the individual, dyadic, and environmental aspects of the couple's current functioning (see Figure 2.1 in Chapter 2). These contextual factors also incorporate each partner's emotions, cognitions, and behaviours relevant to the relationship, as well as the partners' reciprocal influences on each other. If present, psychopathology is integrated into the conceptualization as well, with particular emphasis on how the disorder unfolds in an interpersonal context. That is, the therapist will determine: (a) how the relationship has affected the disorder in terms of broad impacts (overall relationship atmosphere) and specific impacts (responses to symptoms), and (b) how the disorder has impacted the relationship and the other partner (e.g., caregiver burden).

A number of assessment strategies can be employed by the therapist within a flexible structure to achieve these goals, as described below.

Structure

With some notable exceptions (e.g., when a couple enters therapy in a state of crisis or in brief therapy settings where a condensed format is required), the assessment typically spans two or three sessions. If the setting allows, assessment sessions are one and a half to two hours long. The process itself (described in detail below) is facilitated through the use of: (a) joint interviews with the couple; (b) self-report questionnaires; (c) observations of patterns of couple interaction; and (d) individual interviews with each partner.

Assessment sessions differ from treatment sessions, particularly in terms of the greater amount of structure provided by the therapist, with the goal being to obtain useful information in a condensed period of time, while preventing overt conflict in the session and beginning to create a sense of hope, to the degree appropriate. During the assessment, the therapist structures the session in terms of who is talking to whom. At times, the therapist speaks to one person while the other partner listens, a strategy used primarily to obtain each person's perspectives while preventing the couple from arguing. During observations of the couple's communication, however, the partners speak to each other, and the therapist does not intervene, in order to provide a more naturalistic context for the therapist to assess the couple's interaction patterns. When the therapist obtains a history from each person, the partner is absent from the room so that each individual can speak without reacting to the partner and also to allow for open discussion with the therapist regarding historical information prior to the couple's relationship. Thus, structuring who talks to whom during different phases of the assessment can help to alleviate the experience of "things getting out of control" when highly emotional couples first present for treatment.

The process of assessment

In order to achieve the above aims, the assessment typically begins with a joint meeting to establish initial rapport with the couple and orient them to the assessment process. The assessment then progresses through the following stages, all with both persons present, except for the individual interviews:

- clarifying briefly why the couple is seeking assistance;
- conducting a history of the current relationship;
- obtaining a detailed assessment of current relationship functioning;
- conducting behavioural observations of the couple communicating with each other;
- conducting individual interviews with each partner regarding their personal history and functioning;
- providing feedback to the couple regarding the therapist's conceptualization of the couple's strengths, difficulties, and needs, obtaining the couple's feedback on the conceptualization, and discussing an appropriate treatment plan; and
- jointly agreeing whether to pursue couple therapy.

In most instances, the assessment begins with an overview of current concerns and how the relationship has evolved historically, and subsequent components can be conducted in any order. When the primary presenting concern is psychopathology and/or the couple explicitly presents for a couple-based treatment for this disorder, and in the absence of major relationship difficulties, the assessment might adopt a greater focus on the symptoms and maintaining factors. Therapists can choose to add disorder-specific assessment tools (such as self-report tools, structured interviews) as they see fit. Each of these stages is described in detail below.

Conjoint assessment session

Depending on the nature of the couple's reasons for seeking help as well as the amount of information that needs to be reviewed, the initial conjoint meetings are likely to span one or two sessions, in which the therapist seeks to achieve the following:

- orient the couple to the assessment and treatment;
- obtain a brief description from each partner regarding the presenting concerns and reasons for seeking therapy;
- conduct a review of the history of the relationship (and psychopathology, if applicable); and
- assess the couple's current relationship functioning in detail (including bidirectional influences between relationship functioning and psychopathology, if applicable).

Orienting the couple to the assessment and treatment

Along with the typical procedures of orienting new clients to the clinic setting and treatment (e.g., discussing limits of confidentiality), the therapist briefly explains the two distinct phases of (a) assessment and (b) treatment, and discusses the aims and expectations of the assessment phase. This information includes the aims discussed above and the expectation that both the therapist and the couple will make an informed decision about proceeding with couple therapy or a couple-based intervention at the feedback session. The therapist clarifies that couples should not expect improvement at this stage since no targeted interventions are employed during assessment, although many couples find the process to be beneficial. Therapists should also explain the structure of the assessment and how information provided to the therapist (e.g., during individual interviews and on questionnaires) will be managed.

Additionally, the therapist provides guidelines for the couple's behaviour during the sessions. Angry partners might feel drawn to provide a litany of complaints about each other and attempt to make the other person look like "the problem." Therefore, it can be helpful for the therapist to be proactive and highlight the futility of replicating the maladaptive patterns of communication that take place at home. Instead, the therapist clarifies that they are interested in hearing each person's perspectives, recognizing that such perspectives are subjective, and that little effort will be devoted to establishing "truth" or blame. A dyadic perspective is presented as the overriding orientation of the work together, based on the notion that each person contributes to the couple's current functioning in unique ways. This perspective is applicable even if the primary presenting concern is one person's disorder. The therapist should take care to emphasize that a disorder is seen as having an impact on both partners, and understanding how their relationship has responded to this issue is important. By asking each person to describe their experience and observations, the disorder is "externalized" in a way that leaves room for the two partners to join around their difficulties, rather than describing the person who has been diagnosed as "the problem." If partners enter the assessment with little prior knowledge, brief psychoeducation might be useful to further externalize the disorder and discuss it in a non-blaming manner.

Clarifying briefly why the couple is seeking assistance

A first aim of the initial session is for the therapist to obtain an overview of the main areas of concern experienced by each partner. Each person is invited to explain in approximately 5–10 minutes what they see as the major concerns. This brief overview is provided with one person speaking to the therapist while the partner is asked to listen, recognizing that the two partners likely have different perspectives. For some couples, this conversation might be the first opportunity they have had to express their concerns to a safe, interested, receptive third party. As a result, one or both partners might want to describe their concerns in considerable detail. If so, it is important for the therapist to clarify that what is sought at this stage is a "big picture" overview only. For example, the therapist might state, "I would like to hear from each of you individually regarding what you see as the main issues in your relationship. I realize that these might be issues that you have discussed with each other at length or only very little, and it is common that two partners have very different perspectives on what the issues are. My goal is not to figure out who is 'right,' but just to get an initial overview of each of your perspectives. We'll come back later to talk about these concerns in much more detail, so right now I am looking for an initial overview, with each of you taking a turn and the other person simply listening to what's being said."

In the absence of highly pressing concerns that require immediate interventions (e.g., IPV, a potentially life-changing decision with which the couple is confronted that cannot be delayed), the therapist then obtains a history of the couple's relationship.

The history of the current relationship

Assessing the history of the relationship places the couple's current concerns in a broader context and helps the therapist understand how the presenting difficulties and areas of strength have evolved. This history includes information on significant events and periods of transition and on how these events were managed (such as a major relocation for one partner's career, the transition to parenthood, or major family crises and losses), and individual and couple strengths and resources that the couple has used in their environment. The relationship history also allows the therapist to assess (a) how the couple has behaved in their relationship across time, (b) their cognitions about what has happened (e.g., blaming each other or themselves for any difficulties encountered), and (c) their emotional reactions to what has occurred over time as well as the overall emotional tone of the relationship at different times. Thus, the framework of considering the individual, couple, and environment while attending to relevant behaviours, cognitions, and emotions begins with the initial assessment and is maintained throughout treatment.

Even though the primary focus is on information gathering, the therapist also can work to capitalize upon the experiential and cognitive effects of the interview; that is, many couples find that remembering the early days of their relationship and reexperiencing some of the positive emotions associated with that time can evoke a sense of hope (e.g., "Sometimes we forget that we actually do like each other when we're not fighting!"). As the therapist begins to recognize important themes and provides brief summaries throughout, the couple can gain new perspectives on their experience. For example:

Therapist: It sounds like for quite some time, the two of you very easily agreed upon most things and never had to have long discussions when making decisions. It's almost as if that made it even harder when the first roadblocks came up in your relationship and you had to grapple with a difference in opinion on important decisions for the first time, without much prior practice.

Partner: I had never thought about it like that, but I think that makes a lot of sense.

Therapist: Got it. Tell me more about how the two of you interacted when you worked through those first difficulties.

If psychopathology is a significant aspect of the couple's main concerns, the relationship history can provide important information about the history of the disorder itself (e.g., how it has worsened or improved over time) as well as how it has evolved in the context of the relationship. This developmental perspective will be particularly useful in assessing the ways in which the relationship has impacted the disorder, and how the disorder has influenced the relationship, both of which have treatment implications as discussed in Chapter 10. If a disorder emerged or worsened notably when the couple was already in the relationship, the therapist assesses how the relationship has changed as a result. This information can be integrated into exploring the general relationship history. The following questions might be posed in terms of how the disorder has impacted the relationship: Has either person's overall satisfaction changed? How has the couple's interaction style shifted? Have roles and responsibilities changed? Has there been conflict between the partners or with other people as a result? If there has been conflict, what specifically has it been about? If the onset of the current disorder occurred prior to the relationship, clinicians should assess the degree to which the couple's interactions have evolved to accommodate the disorder, even if the couple (or the partner) is unaware of this association. Thus, these couples might not have a full awareness of the degree to which the disorder impacts their lives, because "that is the way things have always been." In such instances, the therapist might need to ask more specifically about the typical patterns and avoided activities that often emerge for a given disorder (see Chapters 10–13).

Structuring the task of conducting the relationship history

Although the length of time needed to carry out a relationship history will vary as a function of the duration of the relationship and the complexity of the circumstances the couple has faced, the relationship history can be structured around three overarching periods of time, adapted as applicable to a given couple: (a) the initial meeting, early interactions, and attraction; (b) the phase in which the relationship became "serious" but prior to an explicit commitment; and (c) the relationship and notable life events occurring subsequent to marriage, civil partnership, or committed cohabitation (Epstein & Baucom, 2002). A summary of the main themes to explore in each of these areas is provided in the interview outline in Appendix 4, and each of these three phases is described in more detail below.

THE INITIAL MEETING, EARLY INTERACTIONS, AND ATTRACTION

Understanding each individual's circumstances when the couple met, the couple's early interactions, and what attracted them to each other is important in establishing the context for their early relationship. Therefore, the therapist's first question about the history is usually some variant of, "Tell me about the first time you met. Where were you; what happened, and what initially attracted you to each other?" Because many couples experienced positive interactions early in their relationship, focusing on the positives and enjoying the couple's memories with them can allow the therapist to establish rapport, decrease initial anxieties about how painful couple therapy is going to be, and create a sense of hope. It also provides an opportunity for each person to say caring things about their partner. For example, when Sonia met Richard, she was drawn to his apparent stability, which in turn helped her feel more secure. Among other attractions, Sonia believed that Richard could offer her financial security—something she had never experienced in her childhood and an area with which she had struggled in her adult life. The therapist noted that Richard's perceived financial contribution to Sonia's well-being was driven primarily not by material concerns but rather by her experience of him as "a reliable person," which helped her feel safe and secure with him. Frequently, over time couples develop conflicts based on characteristics that initially attracted them to each other. For example, a "fun, spontaneous" person might later be seen as unreliable and childish. Understanding how the early relationship evolved can provide information about the early risk factors for current distress (such as personality differences), as well as a developmental lens through which the current distress can be viewed in a more balanced manner.

Following the discussion of initial interactions, the therapist asks the couple about their early times together and how the relationship evolved to the point when they knew it was serious. The therapist should inquire about their communication early in the relationship. Questions might include: How did the couple handle initial disagreements? Did arguments occur? Were the partners able to confide in each other? If so, did it take a long time to develop this kind of mutual trust? Or did it never evolve? Were there any early signs of the types of issues that the couple is now confronting? How did the couple learn to balance individual needs and differences, and what types of activities helped them foster a sense of intimacy? If either of the partners has experienced psychopathology, the therapist should inquire about its occurrence during the early relationship (i.e., were symptoms present, at what point did the other person become aware of them, and how easy or difficult was it to talk about these issues?). Contextual factors might be important as well, such as first interactions with friendship groups and in-laws, or other challenges, such as dating while one or both partners were still closeted.

HOW AND WHEN THE RELATIONSHIP BECAME "SERIOUS"

Assessing this phase of the relationship allows the therapist to understand the priorities of each partner and how the couple made decisions about their life and future. In this phase, the therapist seeks to identify how the couple moved from their initial attraction and/or early contact to making a commitment to one another. Couples vary greatly in the degree to which they explicitly reflected on and discussed important relationship transitions and moved toward commitment in an intentional way, as discussed in Chapter 8. Thus, the therapist can gain an understanding of the degree to which the couple tends to "slide" versus "decide" regarding major decisions. Some couples seem to "slide" forward because circumstances facilitated staying together, without clearly deciding that the relationship was what they wanted in life (Stanley et al., 2006). As Paula remarked, "James was graduating and moving to take a new job, and I wasn't about to be a 'trailing' girlfriend. Plus, we each needed a new place to live. So, I basically told him we either decide to get married and we move together, or it's over. I think he loved me and didn't want to lose me, so he said okay. Not particularly romantic, but that is the reality." Such couples might continue this approach, moving forward in life without ever stepping back and thinking about what each person wants. Such an approach often does not bode well for their long-term well-being.

The therapist also attends to a variety of other factors related to the formation of a "couple identity" and the development of the couple as a system, such as each partner's effort and investment over time, the negotiation of important boundaries, and the development of roles and routines (see Chapter 8). For example, for many but not all couples, this stage of the relationship introduces exclusivity in the form of monogamy. Although for some partners this development is a welcome experience, others experience it as a loss of personal freedom. If a couple decided upon consensual non-monogamy, such an agreement might have been handled well to varying degrees. Additionally, increased contact with family members can introduce complexities into the relationship as a function of how relatives respond to the new family member, and as expectations concerning the frequency and nature of contact with the wider family become clearer. The response of family and friends can be particularly important if the couple is outside of societal "ideals" with regard to differences between partners in terms of age, ethnicity, socioeconomic status, religion, gender identity, disability status, national origin, or other factors. How couples responded to stressors from the environment or from within their own relationship helps in understanding how they deal with difficulties and whether maladaptive patterns of responses have been present throughout their relationship or have shifted over time.

In addition, the therapist inquires about the couple's communication patterns and the overall emotional tone of the relationship during this phase. The couple's account of important events they have experienced, along with their major ups and downs along the way, helps the therapist understand how their relationship continued to evolve. Typically by this time, most couples will have experienced notable disagreements, challenging life events, or other obstacles, and the couple's description of how they responded to these circumstances provides important insights into their coping abilities, strengths as a couple, and potential weaknesses. Information provided by the couple about how each person made sense of various events, changes in the relationships, and their partner's behaviours gives important insights into each partner's cognitions as the relationship evolved.

THE RELATIONSHIP AND NOTABLE LIFE EVENTS OCCURRING SUBSEQUENT TO MARRIAGE, CIVIL PARTNERSHIP, COHABITATION, OR OTHER COMMITMENT

Many couples have been together for a number of years when they seek treatment. Therefore, the therapist does not want a detailed account of everything that has occurred during their committed relationship. Instead, the therapist wants to learn about events, both good and bad, that aid in understanding the couple's current functioning. The therapist might orient the couple as follows:

Therapist: That is very helpful. You've given me a good sense of how things progressed until the time you got married, and you've been together for 10 years since then. So, we don't want to try to cover 10 years in great detail. What would be helpful is if you could tell me about major events and smaller changes, both good and bad, that can help me understand how you have arrived at where you are now. What do you think I should know to understand you and your relationship better? And I realize that the two of you might see this differently, so I want to hear both of your perspectives.

At times an event or time period marks a turning point in a couple's relationship. That is, the couple handled earlier phases of the relationship well, but new challenges proved problematic for them, such as becoming parents, professional difficulties, new financial obligations, or health concerns. At other times, no particular challenge marks the beginning of relationship distress, but the therapist can note a maladaptive coping style that persists across time.

If psychopathology has been a notable concern, beginning to live together can be a time when partners either become more aware of, or more "involved" with, the disorder. For some individuals, increased contact with the partner can lead to symptom improvements (e.g., regular mealtimes together might decrease binge eating). On the other hand, symptom accommodation or other responses might become more pronounced, or the partner might begin to struggle more as they realize the day-to-day implications of the impairment. In such cases, the therapist will make further inquiries about each partner's experiences and responses during this time, attending both to changes in the relationship and to possible impacts on the disorder.

Having established an understanding of how the couple's relationship has developed over time and what historical factors might have contributed to the presenting concerns, the therapist extends this perspective of historical, individual, couple, and environmental factors to include a more detailed assessment of the couple's current relationship functioning.

Current relationship functioning

This conjoint interview with the couple seeks to develop a more in-depth understanding of the couple's presenting concerns along with other aspects of the couple as a unit, resources available to them, and any individual factors (including psychopathology), couple factors, or environmental factors that are negatively impacting the couple's ability to manage their current circumstances.

The therapist might choose to employ several strategies to obtain information about current functioning. In addition to the conjoint interview, couples are asked to complete brief self-report measures about their relationship (and individual psychopathology, if relevant) which provide an overall sense of relationship adjustment and identify specific areas of concern to the couple (e.g., finances, in-laws, chores, etc.). Table 14.1 includes a list of potentially helpful measures (also see Epstein & Baucom, 2002, for a detailed description of a variety of additional measures developed for both research and clinical practice), which will be discussed further below.

Table 14.1 Overview of self-report questionnaires to assess general relationship factors and factors central to psychopathology in a couples context

Relationship Satisfaction	Couples Satisfaction Index (CSI)	The CSI exists in 32, 16, 8, and 4-item versions and measures overall relationship satisfaction. The shorter versions can be used on a session-by-session basis to assess ongoing change.	Funk and Rogge (2007)
	Dyadic Adjustment Scale (DAS)	The DAS is a 32-item measure that often is considered the gold standard self-report of relationship adjustment. In addition to an overall score, the individual items (e.g., how often couple disagrees about finances, amount of time spent together, etc.) can be identified for further discussion with the couple.	Spanier (1976)
	Marital Satisfaction Inventory-Revised (MSI-R)	The MSI-R is a comprehensive, 150-item measure that assesses a wide range of domains of couple functioning, as well as an index of overall relationship distress.	Snyder (1997)
Specific Concerns	Areas-of-Change Questionnaire (A-C)	The A-C is a 34-item measure listing specific content areas of concern that can be identified for further discussion with the couple.	Weiss, Hops, and Patterson (1973)

(continued)

Table 14.1 (continued)

Interaction Patterns	Communication Patterns Questionnaire (CPQ)	The CPQ provides a brief perspective on how each partner perceives their interaction patterns, such as demand–withdraw and mutual avoidance.	Christensen and Heavey (1990, 1993); Crenshaw, Christensen, Baucom, Epstein, and Baucom (2017)
	Revised Conflict Tactics Scale (CTS2)	The CTS2 measures psychological and physical attacks of varying severity on partners, as well as the use of negotiation.	Straus, Hamby, Boney-McCoy, and Sugarman (1996)
Symptom Accommodation (partner report)	Family Accommodation Scale (FAS)	The FAS is a 13-item questionnaire to be completed by a family member of someone with OCD and has been adapted in wording for the use with partners specifically.	Abramowitz, Baucom, Boeding, et al. (2013); Calvocoressi et al. (1999)
	Significant Others' Responses to Trauma Scale (SORTS)	The SORTS is a 14-item measure of partner accommodation of PTSD symptoms. Items are summed to yield a total score, frequency subscale score, and intensity subscale score.	Fredman, Vorstenbosch, Wagner, Macdonald, and Monson (2014)
	Accommodation and Enabling Scale for Eating Disorders (AESED)	The AESED is a 33-item questionnaire that assesses caregivers' accommodation of eating disorder symptoms (applicable to all eating disorders). Several items capture the extent to which a partner might generally help the patient avoid distressing situations, whereas other items are focal to the eating disorder, such as accommodation of maladaptive meal routines.	Sepulveda, Kyriacou, and Treasure (2009)
Perceived Criticism		Perceived Criticism can be reliably assessed using one item ("How critical do you think this person is of you?"), answered on a scale of 1 (not at all critical) to 10 (very critical). This item tends to correlate highly with more extensive measures of Expressed Emotion.	Hooley and Teasdale (1989)

In addition to conducting a conjoint interview and obtaining self-report information from each partner, the therapist also directly observes the couple's communication. Using information obtained from all sources thus far, the therapist next seeks to obtain further information from the couple in order to understand their current concerns and relationship functioning more fully. When exploring the current relationship in detail, the therapist typically talks to one person at a time with both partners present, to obtain each person's perspective about current concerns, just as in the beginning of the assessment. Because most self-report measures and the couple's own focus tend to emphasize problematic areas, it is important to ask about areas of strength as well. Furthermore, the therapist will inquire about topics that many couples might not raise on their own, including patterns of substance use, physical intimacy, and aggression. Of course, therapists might skip aspects of the assessment if sufficient information was already gathered in the relationship history or they might inquire further about specific areas if more in-depth information is needed. Below are particular foci and strategies to employ in obtaining this fuller assessment of current functioning.

Further assessment of presenting concerns

If a relationship history has already been conducted, the therapist likely has gained a good understanding of the couple's main concerns and functioning. If needed, further details can be assessed when discussing the couple's current relationship. At this time, a more detailed conversation might occur regarding how the concerns are manifest on a day-to-day basis, as couples were previously asked to present only overview information. For example, the therapist might ask the couple to describe an instance in which a concern has arisen ("Walk me through what happens when this issue actually comes up. Who raises it, what happens next?"), or provide more clarification regarding the frequency and severity of the concern (e.g., "How often does this tend to happen in a given week?"). Also, the therapist might fill in some gaps regarding important associated cognitions (e.g., "How have you made sense so far of why this pattern occurs?"), behaviours (e.g., "What, if anything, have you tried so far that has helped?"), and emotions (e.g., "We've talked so far mostly about things that are not going well. Give me a sense of how this translates into what life feels like at home. What kind of emotional response do you tend to have when this happens?").

ASSOCIATIONS BETWEEN PSYCHOLOGICAL SYMPTOMS AND INTERPERSONAL PATTERNS

If psychopathology is a notable aspect of the presenting concerns, the therapist will gather more in-depth information regarding the functional associations between psychological symptoms, patient responses, partner responses, and relationship factors. It is important to understand how the relationship and the disorder have influenced each other not only on a broad level, but also the specific behavioural responses of each partner and their short- and long-term consequences. Such functional associations are central in maintaining maladaptive responses such as disorder-specific behaviours and symptom accommodation (e.g., drinking as a way to cope with stress; avoiding social situations to prevent anxiety; partners' attempts at caring for a depressed person by allowing them to stay in bed, leading to short-term decreases in distress for the patient and increases in positive feelings toward each other for both partners). As in individual therapy, couples might only have limited awareness of the functional connections between their behaviour, cognitions, and emotional responses.

If the patient and partner are unable to report on these patterns, the therapist might offer more structure in exploring the issues. For example, a clinician might inquire about the symptoms most commonly experienced by the patient, ask for recent examples, and then ask the partner if they noticed the patient's distress or behaviour, how they responded themselves, and how the interaction between the partners then unfolded and impacted each partner's experience. Particular attention should be given to symptom accommodation, expressed emotion, and other partner responses that can maintain symptoms; a variety of self-report measures can further support this assessment (see Table 14.1). Additionally, attention should be given to the impact on the partner. For example, some partners might experience notable caregiver distress or burnout, with emotional consequences as well as shifts in other areas of life (e.g., discontinuing individual activities, hobbies, and social connections).

Responses to the presence of a disorder vary, depending on each partner's prior knowledge and awareness of the disorder. Thus, therapists might ask a series of questions to assess potential misconceptions and levels of insight. What do the patient and partner each know about the disorder and the indicated treatment? Do they have any misconceptions or biases (e.g., someone who is depressed just needs to "snap out of it;" mental illness is a life sentence; bipolar disorder means the person is going to be violent)? Attributions regarding locus of control (i.e., how much control the patient has over their symptoms) are particularly important, given that attributions about controllability (e.g., the patient could decide to behave/feel differently) are associated with higher rates of criticism and hostility, which predict worse outcomes long term (Hooley & Miklowitz, 2018).

Additional substantive areas of couple functioning

In addition to the discussion of the presenting concerns as described above, the therapist needs to inquire about other areas that might be important to understand in terms of maintaining factors or potential resources and strengths. The therapist adapts this portion of the interview depending upon the content that has already been discussed, with the goal to "fill in gaps." Here, self-report questionnaires can be useful sources of information as well.

OVERALL RELATIONSHIP ATMOSPHERE/SATISFACTION

Self-report questionnaires (see Table 14.1) can be a source of information in assessing overall relationship satisfaction, but it is not essential that scores on these measures are discussed with the couple. If there are any obvious discrepancies, however, it might be important to explore them (e.g., "The two of you have let me know that overall things are going okay with you, except for a few 'sticking points' that you'd like assistance with. However, in looking at your questionnaires, I see that your responses were actually similar overall to others who report that they are very unhappy in their relationship. Can you help me understand this better? Is there something that we haven't discussed yet that was important in how each of you responded to the questionnaires?").

As previously discussed, psychopathology poses a risk for relationship distress, but on a more immediate basis, it can also affect the overall atmosphere at home. Therefore, the therapist should assess the extent to which the relationship atmosphere is due to relationship conflict or a direct result of the disorder (e.g., "Since you've been depressed, it feels like there's just no life at home anymore, and we've all given up on trying to cheer you up so now nobody is talking!" or "I can never tell when you are going to be happy and when you are going to be upset; anything can set you off. I know this is your PTSD, but now I'm tense all the time, walking on eggshells, trying not to say anything wrong").

CONTENT AREAS IMPORTANT TO EACH PARTNER

For some couples, major presenting concerns are stated at a process level, such as issues related to communication. Given that the treatment will also address substantive areas, it is helpful to get a better understanding of specific areas of dissatisfaction for each partner. Using the Areas-of-Change Questionnaire (see Table 14.1), the clinician can note items reflecting the concerns of each partner and use this information as the basis for the clinical interview (e.g., "Iona, you mentioned on one of the questionnaires that you and Samara often disagree about finances. Can you take a minute or two to clarify what aspects of finances you see as problematic and how that plays out between the two of you?").

CONTENT AREAS THAT COUPLES OFTEN OMIT FROM DISCUSSION

In addition to concerns raised directly, the therapist should inquire about areas which might be uncomfortable for the couple to discuss and therefore did not volunteer as an area of concern. These topics can include:

- The couple's physical relationship: The therapist inquires about preference for and satisfaction with the type, frequency, and quality of physical contact (comfort, physical affection, and sexual intimacy; see Chapter 11).
- Instances of aggression or violence: The therapist inquires with each partner in the individual interviews about forms of IPV that might be occurring (this topic is addressed individually for safety reasons). In addition, distressed couples might engage in milder forms of physical aggression that can be discussed with both partners present.
- Substance use: Due to the comorbidity between relationship conflict and substance misuse, therapists should inquire about substance use, including alcohol, illicit substances, and prescription drugs. In addition to gaining clear information regarding frequency of use, therapists should assess the context of usage and how it might impact the couple (e.g., intense conflict after a night of drinking together; neglect of adaptive couple activities in favour of drug use).
- Strengths: Couples typically focus on areas of dissatisfaction or difficulty at the expense of areas that are currently satisfying or have historically worked well. Similarly, the self-report measures described in Table 14.1 also focus on concerns without inquiring about strengths. Thus, it is important for the therapist to ask directly about strengths of the couple as a unit as well as the positive attributes and behaviours of each partner. If one or both partners are unable to note positives about each other or the relationship even when coaxed by the therapist, it can indicate how entrenched the couple is in their negative experience of the relationship.
- The environment: In addition to overlooking the good in each other, many couples tend to overlook sources of environmental support; therefore, it is useful for therapists to inquire about potential resources that could assist the couple, including extended family, friendship networks, professional agencies, social networks, and religious communities. It also is helpful to check with distressed couples regarding their knowledge of local statutory, regulatory, and voluntary services that might offer additional sources of

support. Additionally, couples might experience notable environmental stressors (e.g., financial strain, discrimination, safety concerns) with notable impact on relationship and individual functioning, which are important for the therapist to recognize.

Behavioural observation of communication

In order to understand more about the couple's patterns of communication, if time allows, it is preferable to obtain a sample of the couple's interactions as they discuss relevant topics. This goal is usually achieved by asking the couple to engage in a structured conversation while the therapist observes the interactions as they unfold. These short, structured discussions (typically 7–10 minutes each) provide information on the couple's strengths and limitations in relation to particular types of conversation as discussed in Chapter 4. Thus, these brief behavioural observations of couple interaction map onto three forms of communication:

- sharing thoughts and feelings about an issue in the relationship (including the disorder if appropriate);
- decision-making about an issue in the relationship (including the disorder if appropriate); and
- offering individual support to one partner regarding areas of non-relationship concern.

Appendix 5 illustrates how to introduce these tasks to the couple. If a psychological disorder is the primary reason for the couple to seek treatment, the first two topics might be adapted to focus on an issue related to the disorder that has been a problem in the relationship, in order to assess communication around the disorder specifically. Including all three types of conversations is typically not preferable because having all of these conversations will likely take too long and will exhaust the couple. Therefore the therapist might select one or two types of conversation, based on the therapist's emerging conceptualization of a couple's primary areas of need. Also, in selecting topics for discussion, the therapist asks the couple to select topics of moderate difficulty. The issues discussed need to be of sufficient concern to provide a useful sample of how the couple interacts when distressed, yet not be so difficult that the interaction is highly aversive to the couple or results in a heated argument. Following each conversation, the therapist asks the couple how representative the conversation was of how the couple interacts in everyday life. Often couples report that they were "a bit nicer" to each other while the therapist was watching, but their main ways of interacting came through in the conversation. These conversations often provide valuable information that helps the therapist know how to focus communication training if it is needed. Although most clinicians will not learn detailed, complex coding systems of couple communication for routine clinical use, some familiarity with some of the major coding systems can sensitize the clinician to nuanced ways that couples might communicate with each other; see, for example, Hahlweg, Reisner, et al. (1984) for a description of the Kategoriensystem fur partnerschaftliche Interaktion (KPI) and Heyman (2004) regarding the Rapid Marital Interaction Coding System (RMICS).

Special considerations for assessing risk of suicide

Beach and Gupta (2003) suggest that when a partner presents with a heightened risk of attempting suicide, formal couple therapy (focused on relationship distress) might be inappropriate and should be delayed until the risk has been reliably reduced. However, this perspective might be moderated when considering couple-based interventions explicitly focused on depression or other disorders. In such instances, the perspectives and observations of the partner can be taken into account, along with potential plans that involve the partner in an attempt to reduce or respond to heightened risk. The general principles of risk assessment and risk management apply in a couple context as well. Readers unfamiliar with best practices of suicide risk assessment should familiarize themselves or seek further training, as appropriate. In addition to assessing the typical individually based information as part of a risk assessment, therapists also include questions and domains relevant to a couple-based format, such as:

- Has suicidal ideation and/or intent been communicated to the partner? How has the partner responded in the past?
- Was the partner present or in some way involved when previous attempts occurred (such as finding the patient after a past attempt)? Does the partner experience some degree of trauma-related symptoms stemming from past attempts? To what extent is the partner hypervigilant for signs of possible new attempts in a dysfunctional manner (e.g., engaging in persistent checking)?
- To what extent is the relationship with the partner experienced as a protective or risk factor?
- Does the partner also experience depressive symptoms and/or suicidal ideation, and what level of resilience is displayed by the partner more generally?
- To what degree is a larger social support network available to both partners? Are there other members of the couple's family and social network who are aware of past and current suicidal ideation and/or attempts? How have these individuals responded in the past?

When an increased risk of suicide is present, safety planning procedures need to be constructed and agreed upon with each partner and also potentially communicated to other involved professionals. This issue is discussed further in Chapter 11 on depression, although it might also arise in couples without a depressed partner. In addition to the risk assessment with the partner present, the therapist should inquire again in the individual interview to avoid a situation in which the person with suicidal ideation minimizes risk while in the presence of the partner.

Up to this point in the assessment, the primary focus has been on the couple as a unit, although information about each individual and the couple's environment are obtained throughout the process. In addition, it is valuable to obtain more detailed information about each partner, with the goal of understanding how each individual's characteristics and unique history contribute to the current relationship functioning.

Individual interviews

Although pertinent information about each individual is obtained during the joint sessions, brief interviews without the other partner present allow the therapist to learn more about how each person influences the couple's relationship. Unless a partner has a particularly complicated history or a complex mental or physical health concern, each interview often can be completed in approximately 30 minutes. A summary of some of the main themes to explore in each of these interviews is provided in the interview outline in Appendix 6. The individual interview is not intended as an opportunity for one partner to complain about the other or explain to the therapist "what is really going on in the relationship." Instead, the focus is on obtaining a better understanding of the individual who is meeting with the therapist.

Typically, the therapist asks the individual to provide a brief historical overview of their life from childhood until the present time, seeking to identify past and present demands and resources that might impact current functioning. Topics to be explored in this overview generally include early childhood experiences and family of origin (particularly early relationship models), issues surrounding physical health, experiences of interpersonal trauma, personal characteristics impacting the current relationship, previous experiences in friendships and intimate relationships, educational and work history, and notable use of substances and psychopathology, including any current or historical suicidal thoughts or intent.

The therapist also addresses any concerns about risk to the individual's well-being and safety related to stated or suspected IPV. If substance use and/or psychopathology have already been assessed in the joint portions of the assessment, the individual interview also focuses on the past history of the disorder. For example, the therapist ascertains whether a current episode of depression is part of a long-standing history of mood disturbances since childhood, or whether depression emerged for the first time in the context of relationship distress. A range of self-report measures specific to relevant disorders and more general screening tools also can be beneficial. Clinicians can consult applicable specialty literature for additional tools for specific disorders.

A breadth of issues is likely to arise in a limited amount of time. Therefore, the therapist asks for brief information about each domain and then focuses the conversation on areas that have greater importance in understanding how the individual's history and personal characteristics impact current relationship functioning (e.g., having poor role models from parents regarding conflict, with parents' negative feelings typically having resulted in frightening arguments).

Complicating issues that can arise in the individual sessions

The individual interviews might include a discussion of sensitive information that the person is reluctant to share in detail with the partner, such as experiences with previous sexual partners or a history of early abuse. When these experiences are not implicated in the couple's current issues and are part of a personal history that the individual wishes to keep private, they do not need to be shared in the conjoint sessions. However, it will be important to consider the effects of these past experiences on current issues and to consider the potential benefits and costs of sharing this information with a partner. For example, Ken's tendency to walk away from Sheila when they had even a mild difference of opinion left Sheila feeling irritated and devalued. Having discussed the potential benefits and costs of self-disclosure in the individual interview, Ken chose to share with Sheila the extent of the random violence that he had witnessed his father mete out to his mother. This disclosure helped Sheila appreciate that for Ken, differences of opinion were interpreted as dangerous, with the potential to lead to violence. This history was taken into account as the couple learned to share negative thoughts and feelings, recognizing Ken's vulnerabilities and the reality that such discussions evoked long-term frightening feelings for him.

The individual interviews also create the potential for one person to reveal "confidential" information in such a way that it puts the therapist in the position of being asked to keep a secret from the other partner. In such instances, the therapist needs to be guided by their clinical judgment regarding how best to respond. If it appears that the past experiences are unrelated to current concerns, the individual's privacy is respected, and the issues are not shared with the partner. However, complications arise if the individual provides information that is contrary to what the person has shared with the partner. For example, if one partner states a commitment to the relationship during a conjoint interview but reveals an intention to leave the relationship during their individual interview, the therapist is in an untenable position. Given the potential complications resulting from such disclosures, it is important for the therapist to establish the boundaries of confidentiality with both partners present beforehand. In particular, partners are asked to avoid sharing information in their individual interviews that directly contradicts what has been said in joint sessions and are reminded that information revealed in individual interviews *might* be appropriate to share with the partner, if it is relevant to the couple's concerns. The therapist explains that confidential or contradictory disclosures work against developing a shared agenda for any treatment that might follow and potentially undermines the perceived trustworthiness of the therapist in the eyes of the partner who has been excluded from the confidence. Should one person disclose such information anyway, the therapist typically talks with the disclosing person about how this information might be shared openly in the session with the partner present. If it is not possible to share the information, the therapist and that individual explore together how the sessions can be brought to an end. In essence, the therapist must avoid colluding with one partner in keeping relevant secrets from the other. Because of the risk of such complications, some therapists avoid conducting individual interviews. However, we have found that including these interviews often provides valuable information relevant to couple functioning, and that most complications can be avoided with initial boundary setting prior to the interview or reminders during the interview if the conversation starts to veer off course.

The exception to the therapist "keeping secrets" involves concerns regarding IPV. In such instances, the therapist seeks information about the extent, severity, and impact of such behaviours in a way that does not expose the partner to further risk. If the therapist suspects that abusive behaviour has been denied or minimized during conjoint sessions, then it is appropriate to follow up with more specific questions in the individual interview, where it is safe for the endangered partner to reveal experiences that would be potentially unwise to share in front of an abusive partner. For example, some abusive individuals have warned partners that such issues are not to be discussed in couple therapy, with a warning that the partner will "pay the price" if they tell the therapist about the abuse. When there are significant concerns, it is important for the therapist to conduct a risk assessment, talk with the individual about options to ensure personal safety, and, if necessary, find a way to terminate further couple sessions until the therapist and both partners believe that such work can be resumed safely.

Summary

The assessment progresses through a series of distinct stages in which the therapist draws on a range of methods to create an emerging understanding of the couple's current functioning, including both areas of concern and areas of strength. The assessment has a clear structure, through which some of the fundamental principles and style of working in CBCT are introduced and maintained throughout treatment. The next sections present an overview of how a conceptualization is developed based on this information and then is shared with the couple as a means of providing feedback and guiding subsequent treatment planning, should intervention prove to be appropriate.

Case conceptualization

A case conceptualization involves integrating the information obtained during the assessment in order to highlight the factors most central to the couple's functioning, with particular focus on factors that contributed to the development and maintenance of individual and relationship distress. This conceptualization, along with initial treatment recommendations, is then shared and discussed with the couple in a feedback session with the goal of reaching a shared understanding of the couple's concerns and a mutually agreed-upon treatment plan. As described in this chapter, the initial assessment provides a vast amount of information. Consequently, attempting to integrate every detail could seem overwhelming to the therapist, and few couples could comprehend or make use of such a full explanation. Fortunately, that is not the task at hand; the topics discussed in this book are relevant for many couples but never are *all* factors central for a given couple. Instead, in most instances, three or four major themes or overarching issues are most relevant to the couple at the current point in time and to their treatment.

Within the CBCT framework, there is no fixed template for the conceptualization; instead, it is idiographic and tailored to each couple. This flexible approach flows from a recognition of the complexity of relationship functioning and psychopathology within an interpersonal context. It also is important to realize that the conceptualization is subjective, as it is based on information provided by the couple and observed by the clinician. That is, the themes that evolve from the assessment are influenced by the manner in which the clinician, guided by the couple, makes sense of a plethora of information, emphasizing certain themes while minimizing others. Thus, in line with the notion of "collaborative empiricism" in CBT, the conceptualization is a set of informed hypotheses that must be open to revision when shared with the couple as discussed below, along with ongoing modifications as the treatment proceeds and new information and insights emerge.

In developing a case conceptualization, the clinician takes several frameworks into account. These frameworks include the two perspectives discussed throughout this book: (a) the contextual model, i.e., the roles of the individual, the couple, and their environment; and (b) a CBT perspective, including both partners' cognitions, emotions, and behaviours (see Figure 2.1). These factors come together in different ways to understand each couple as a unique unit.

For example, a dominant theme in Mara and Anthony's current relationship distress was the difficulties they experienced in transitioning from being a couple to becoming a family with the birth of their first child, Anita (an environmental factor). This broader theme incorporated a number of their presenting complaints. The transition to parenthood involved changes in the roles for both partners (couple factor), less time and energy focused on them as a couple and each other (couple factor), and extreme fatigue, with both often awake for many hours each night with Anita (environmental factor). Within this context, Anthony's strong need for social engagement with groups of friends and colleagues had become minimized (individual factor) as both he and Mara wanted to stay home with Anita, rarely asking available family members to help out and babysit (environmental factor). Likewise, their typical way of staying close through long, open conversations was now a thing of the past (couple factor). At the same time, they experienced difficulty with boundaries in their social environment as Anthony's parents frequently dropped by unannounced, offering strong, unsolicited parenting advice (environmental factor).

On a different front, another couple included one partner who had a long history of depressive episodes that predated the couple's relationship, perhaps due to a biological vulnerability to depression along with an extensive family history of mood disorders. Within the context of that vulnerability, the current depression was precipitated by a shift in roles in the family in which the depressed partner experienced a loss of control over important aspects of life. (For example: "Although I value being the main breadwinner, it feels like that is all I am at this point. Everything seems to be so fixed in terms of what I do every day from the time I get up until I go to bed. I don't even think about what I might want; it is irrelevant because it won't happen anyway.")

In essence, within the context of the comprehensive CBCT model described throughout this book, the therapist selects the three or four major themes that appear to be most central to the maintenance of relationship distress, individual distress, or psychopathology, and then elaborates on some of the nuances within this theme to incorporate additional factors. Typically, this elaboration includes the specifics of how broader themes are manifest on a day-to-day basis in terms of behaviours, cognitions, and emotions. Then, in most cases the therapist explores how these major themes are interrelated as well. For example, a change in roles leads to a sense of loss of control and contributes to depression in one person, and then the partner accommodates to the depressed person's withdrawal by taking over more responsibilities. This dynamic in turn leaves less time for the couple to engage in relaxing times together, thus fuelling the depression due to a loss of intimacy for the depressed person. Poor communication, which has always been a problem for the couple, now becomes even more problematic because both partners are struggling and have no way to discuss how to make life better.

The above example might be the conceptualization for one couple's current distress and the partner's depression. It does not attempt to explain every facet of the couple's life; yet, it captures the essence of their current functioning and can lead to a well-articulated treatment plan with clear targets. The goal of the conceptualization is to be parsimonious, which allows both the therapist and the couple to grasp the fundamental themes without getting lost in detail and complexity. The case conceptualization can be built around the contextual model presented throughout this book; that is, the central individual, couple, and environmental factors interact in a reciprocal manner to create and maintain the couple's and each individual's current state. Within this model, these three elements can be of differential importance for any given couple.

Feedback to the couple

Once the therapist has developed the initial case conceptualization, the therapist conducts a feedback session with the couple to share initial perspectives and discuss what types of interventions might be indicated and if appropriate to proceed, what the treatment plan might involve. The therapist presents the conceptualization, noting that it is tentative, and asking for the couple's perspective, with the couple adding information or offering alternative perspectives in a collaborative manner. Also, the therapist is explicit that most of what the therapist says has been provided by the couple; what might be new is how the therapist has attempted to integrate the information and identify overarching themes that might have been difficult for the couple to see. Presenting the feedback typically takes at least half of a session or perhaps an entire couple session, depending on whether an extensive discussion develops. A typical feedback session includes the following elements, in the following order:

- a presentation of the therapist's understanding of why the couple has sought assistance;
- a discussion of the couple's strengths, assets, and resources, along with how they have used them adaptively at different points in their relationship;
- an elaboration of the major themes the therapist has noted that make up the substance of the conceptualization, taking them one at a time and addressing how the problematic areas have developed and what appears to maintain them at present; and
- a discussion of possible treatment modalities (couple intervention, individual intervention, medical intervention, etc.) and an initial treatment plan, either following a discussion of all the major themes or integrated with each theme as it is discussed.

While the initial feedback involves a fair amount of content provided by the therapist, it should not be presented as a lengthy monologue, but rather with frequent opportunities for the couple to react to what was said. A portion of how the therapist might provide feedback to Mara and Anthony is as follows:

Therapist: One of the most striking things is that you came here while you both still have such positive feelings for each other. You realized you needed to step back and figure out how to do things differently because many of the good things you've enjoyed in your relationship seem to have diminished. And it does sound like you have had a really sound, rewarding relationship for most of your time together until you became parents, is that right? Would you say that becoming parents was a major turning point, and you've been struggling somewhat since then?

Mara: In some ways, yes, but I don't want to blame Anita. She's a blessing to us, and we should be able to handle it. I mean, we're both bright, well educated, and have more resources than most people, and this is one child. We should be able to do this, but somehow we can't.

Anthony: I agree that we should be able to handle it better than we are, but this is hard. Everybody told us it would be hard, and we knew that, but living it is something else. So, yes, I agree that is when things definitely took a turn for the worse.

Therapist: Right, I certainly don't want to blame Anita; she sounds like a wonderful child, and the two of you are very loving parents. It's more that the two of you as a couple and individually have had difficulty figuring out how to adapt and balance the new demands that arise when a child comes along, is that right?
[Couple agrees.]

Therapist: And it looks like the main thing you've struggled with is how to stay close to each other during this time as new parents. You used to do almost everything together and really enjoyed it—grocery shopping and cooking together, all the routine daily tasks were also a time to connect. And you miss that, which in one way is nice to hear, in that you really still like and enjoy each other. But now you've divided up roles and responsibilities, which is very common and often necessary when a child comes along, so now one of you cooks while the other person runs errands. It's more efficient that way, but it means the routine day-to-day ways in which you used to connect aren't there any more, is that right? [Couple agrees and elaborates on how they still want that time together.]

Therapist: So that means that one of the things we'll focus on is how to give you at least some brief times together during the week; nothing big, just some way to be together, get something accomplished together, or have a brief time to chat. Of course, that won't be the only thing we'll do, but starting to find new, sustainable routines for you as a couple will be really important. What do you think? [Couple affirms they would like that but that it will be a challenge.]

Therapist: I agree it will be a challenge because you're both so tired much of the time. A couple of other things struck me about this transition, in addition to no longer doing day-to-day tasks together. You had developed such a lovely relationship where you spent good leisure time together, really enjoyed long walks, talking openly about important things, your hopes and dreams for the future. And now those close, connecting times seem rare, right? [Couple strongly agrees how they miss such times.]

Therapist: So that means we'll want to attend to that aspect of your relationship as well, whether we call it date nights, couple time, or whatever. Understandably, you've been focused on getting things done with a young child, and the more emotional, caring aspects of your relationship have taken a back seat. It won't be as easy or as frequent as in the past when you could often decide on the spot what you wanted to do. Now, it will take more planning, but I'd suggest we take time to problem-solve on how you might create those times. Before, that kind of time just seemed to be there automatically; now you might need to create it. [Couple briefly responds and strongly indicates they want that time with each other with some brief differences of opinion about which of them still makes the most effort.]

Therapist: Not everything is about your transition to parenthood, but there are lots of aspects to this. From what you've said, it sounds like you're struggling with how to deal with Anthony's parents coming over unannounced and offering parenting advice. And it is made more complicated because you both really love them, but the way it is playing out is making it hard to predict what will happen at home. So one issue you're facing is how to create "boundaries" or set limits between you and other people, even people you love. It sounds like whenever Mara brings it up, Anthony, you think that she must not really like your parents, is that right? Even though Mara says that's not it. Is that what happens? [Couple has lengthier input, affirming that it is a problem not only about Anthony's parents but also their differences in how to interpret each other's displeasure.]

Therapist: Let's not get into it now, but it does seem like this is an area that might require attention, both so you can openly discuss with each other how you feel and clear up misunderstandings, and then at some point decide how you want to handle things with Anthony's parents. Would that be helpful? [Couple affirms the need for addressing this as a difficult area that divides them more than other aspects of parenthood.]

Therapist: So there really are several aspects of this transition, aren't there, including how to find time together in small ways on a day-to-day basis, particularly with new responsibilities and fatigue; how to find longer, more special couple time; and how to interact with Anthony's parents, trying to get you both on the same page or at least clear regarding how you both feel, as well as how to set appropriate boundaries with people you love. Does that make sense?

This brief segment of discussing the conceptualization with the couple includes several noteworthy elements: an emphasis on what is good in their relationship and the couple's ongoing wish to spend time together; a developmental perspective and normalization of their current concerns which still are problematic for them, even if common; a specification of which aspects of the transition to parenthood are difficult for them, along with broad treatment approaches that might be employed to address the different domains; and an effort to seek input and discussion with the couple at each point to develop a shared perspective. Of course at times, the couple might see things differently from how the therapist has conceptualized them. In such a situation, the couple and the therapist discuss their perspectives further and either reach a consensus or agree that additional thought will be needed to understand the area better as treatment proceeds.

In the example above, the therapist also approached the couple's concerns in a given manner. Although the therapist had the contextual and CBT frameworks in mind when developing the conceptualization, the therapist did not provide feedback to the couple in these theoretical, conceptual terms. Instead, the therapist presented the feedback in terms of the couple's own experience regarding the concrete areas of concern which brought them to therapy. While doing so, the therapist began to infuse the feedback with brief mentions of the importance of expressing their feelings, clarifying misunderstandings (their cognitions), and noting their needs to stay close and connected. As therapy evolves, the therapist has ongoing opportunities to present a more systematic framework for the couple to consider as they address various concerns.

The above example focuses on relationship distress. If Anthony was also depressed, this factor would be woven into the conceptualization, perhaps noting that his depression has happened before in his adult life at times of high stress, but particularly when he feels more isolated from close social contacts such as since Anita's birth. Thus, helping the couple reconnect might help their relationship and Anthony's depression as well. In addition, other strategies for addressing Anthony's depression, such as behavioural activation, would also be taken into account.

At the end of the feedback and discussion of initial treatment recommendations, the therapist asks the couple for their overall reactions, including their perspectives on which aspects seem to "fit," what aspects might have been missed, or if there are different ways to think about their situation. Once the couple and therapist have solidified their conceptualization, they engage in an important discussion of whether all three of them think that working together would be beneficial, perhaps as follows:

Therapist: Good, it sounds like we're pretty much on the same page with some additional thought needed to understand your sexual relationship better and how it fits into all this. So let's think about where we want to go from here. I've given you my thoughts and how we might proceed if we work together, which I think could be beneficial. We could go a couple of ways with this. One strategy would be

> that you two go home, talk about it, and decide whether you want to pursue this work and whether it seems like the three of us would be a good fit. We can set up a session for next week, and you can let me know then, or if you both are pretty clear about what you want to do, we can decide now and take it from there. What would you like to do?

Providing the couple with an opportunity to make their decision explicit serves several purposes. They have just heard, for the first time, the therapist's perspectives on their relationship and how treatment might proceed, so they should have an opportunity to think about whether they want to pursue treatment and whether this therapist seems to be a good match for them as they consider engaging in this difficult and likely vulnerable task. Second, the therapist wants to endorse the notion of "deciding" and not "sliding" when the couple is making noteworthy decisions. Thus, the couple is asked to commit to the therapeutic process before treatment begins. Third, such an approach models the collaborative manner in which the therapist and couple will approach the couple's relationship throughout treatment.

If the couple and therapist decide to work together, developing a more detailed initial treatment plan is needed to guide the work. In the feedback session, the treatment plan is often provided in a somewhat general manner, without specifying which interventions might be used or the sequence that might be followed. Having a more detailed plan in mind can be valuable to the clinician to guide treatment. Given the diverse conceptualizations that evolve, the treatment plan must also be flexible. Below are general guidelines to consider in planning the sequence of interventions, taking into account both relationship distress and psychopathology.

Sequencing interventions

The treatment plan flows directly from the initial assessment. It is an initial plan in that it provides a road map to begin treatment; yet, it is likely to evolve and be revised as a fuller understanding develops over the course of treatment, new issues arise, and other issues are resolved. Sequencing depends on the specifics of each issue and how the issues are related. In addition, both relationship functioning and individual psychopathology must be taken into account, as appropriate. Below is a set of broad guidelines and factors to consider in developing the treatment plan. A typical flow of treatment is as follows:

- initial assessment;
- feedback session;
- psychoeducation about relationship distress and psychopathology, tailored to a couple's particular situation and needs (often begun during the feedback session as well);
- communication skills training applied to relationship and individual psychopathology, as needed;
- addressing major themes and central domains relevant to the couple's situation, including relationship distress and psychopathology, as appropriate; and
- relapse prevention.

Because the initial assessment and feedback session have been discussed above, the following section addresses the remaining major phases of the treatment planning.

Psychoeducation

Depending on the couple's reasons for seeking assistance, the therapist often provides brief psychoeducation about relationship distress and/or one individual's psychopathology and the interplay between them. This process is an extension of putting the couple's concerns in context which was begun during the assessment and feedback process. The primary goals are to make certain that the therapist and couple have a shared perspective on current concerns, how that perspective leads to the major strategies to be employed, and what will be asked of the couple during treatment (e.g., requests to extend the focus of sessions into the couple's everyday world on an ongoing basis). Particularly when psychopathology is the primary focus of treatment, such a discussion might require an entire session (see Chapters 10–13).

Communication training

Whether a couple has communication deficits and long-standing limitations or whether communication has deteriorated as relationship distress has increased, by the time the couple seeks assistance, their communication typically needs to improve. Even if the couple is satisfied with their relationship and is seeking assistance primarily for one partner's psychopathology, typically they can benefit from spending at least some time solidifying their communication, employing the interventions described in Chapter 4. Because the ability to share thoughts and feelings about an area of concern is a part of problem-solving, basic communication skills in sharing thoughts and feelings typically are taught first, followed by problem-solving. These skills are then applied to the major substantive issues to be addressed in treatment.

Addressing major themes and central domains of individual and relationship functioning

As noted throughout the book, each couple is unique, and the treatment plan and sequencing of interventions reflect this diversity. Yet, several broad factors are generally pertinent and need to be considered regarding when to address psychopathology relative to relationship distress. Likewise, various factors can guide sequencing within relationship distress as well. Moreover, there are sequencing issues specific to each type of psychopathology which go beyond the current discussion and can be constructed from a careful consideration of the issues noted in the earlier chapters on psychopathology.

Sequencing the focus on relationship distress versus psychopathology

When both relationship distress and psychopathology are present in a couple, rarely does a session focus solely on one of these issues. Either the therapist is addressing aspects of each factor separately within a given session, or a single intervention directly impacts both domains. Therefore, the main consideration involves the relative attention given to psychopathology versus relationship distress when both are present. Below are some broad guidelines that can assist the therapist in making these decisions, while always noting why couples have sought intervention and, when possible, attending to those concerns early in treatment. Give early, primary attention to psychopathology if:

- current symptoms involve danger to the patient or others;
- current symptoms would prevent effective intervention on relationship distress or are a major driving force for relationship distress (e.g., PTSD with very frequent flashbacks and angry outbursts);
- the patient and the partner are willing to address the psychopathology and work together as a team to address individual functioning in a relationship context;
- the couple needs early attention to relationship distress (see below) before focusing fully on the psychological disorder, but some symptoms are amenable to early improvement with limited intervention (e.g., psychoeducation and interoceptive exposure for panic disorder); or
- the couple is distressed but the form of distress involves a lack of positives without excessive hostile, critical interchanges.

The final point above is the guideline that might be the least obvious. Even if the couple is distressed, as long as they are not engaging in frequent destructive, negative interactions, often the couple can focus on one partner's psychopathology early in treatment. Having a common focus provides the couple with an issue and shared goal around which they can work together, which might in and of itself improve relationship functioning. This suggestion is consistent with findings from Ireland, Sanders, and Markie-Dadds (2003), indicating that distressed couples who had a child with behaviour problems significantly improved in relationship satisfaction as a result of behavioural parent training focused exclusively on assisting the child. Thus, providing the couple with an issue around which they can unite, when that issue does not pose a threat to their relationship, can at times prove valuable. Give early, primary attention to relationship distress if:

- the couple has a high level of hostility, criticism, or other forms of overt negativity that will impede their ability to address psychopathology without such efforts being dominated by relationship concerns;
- other factors, such as infidelity or other relational traumas, impede the couple's ability to focus on the psychopathology; or
- relationship distress is a primary precipitating and maintaining factor in the psychopathology.

In some cases, the therapist might decide that the relationship distress requires primary attention but the psychological disorder cannot be left untreated in the meantime; in such cases, collaborating with an individual therapist might be warranted. Or, the couple therapist might focus on interventions intended to alleviate relationship distress while simultaneously addressing psychopathology (e.g., helping the couple to build in more positive activities together to improve intimacy can also serve as behavioural activation for depression). Issues related to individual versus couple-based treatments (and possible combinations) as well as sequencing within treatments primarily focused on psychopathology are addressed in more detail in Chapter 10.

Sequencing within the treatment of relationship distress

Although a unique treatment plan for relationship distress is created for each couple, the following broad guidelines can be useful, again recognizing that a variety of interventions overlap during a given session or build on each other over time across sessions. For example, a couple who has been engaging in "caring days" might continue their caring activities as communication training is introduced in a subsequent session.

In general:

- First address issues requiring immediate attention due to detrimental practical or emotional impact.
- If the couple has a high level of hostility, criticism, or other forms of overt negativity, focus early attention on decreasing negatives (and later give more emphasis to increasing positives).
- If the couple is distant and disengaged with few negatives but also few positives, emphasize increasing positives early in treatment.
- Provide the couple with success experiences, working through a progression from less difficult to more difficult issues.
- Address issues early that maintain or exacerbate other areas of concern, thereby improving treatment efficiency.

Perhaps one of the broadest differentiations among distressed couples is whether the couple experiences an excess of negatives or a paucity of positives in their relationship, or both. When partners engage in highly aversive or frequent negative behaviour, decreasing or eliminating such behaviour is an immediate goal early in therapy. Such negative behaviours have a pervasive damaging effect on both individual and relationship well-being, so it is important to halt them as soon as possible. In addition, it often is difficult for partners to increase positive or caring behaviours if they are "at war" with each other. On the other hand, if such negative behaviours are not present but the couple presents with few positive behaviours and exchanges, the therapist can help the couple focus early in treatment on increasing positive behaviours, targeting these behaviours according to the case conceptualization and the couple's sense of how broad relationship principles apply to them specifically.

The therapist also tries to structure single sessions and the sequence of interventions over the course of therapy to provide success experiences for the couple whenever possible, particularly when a couple is discouraged about the likelihood of improving their relationship. In many instances, this approach involves working up a hierarchy from less difficult to more difficult issues or tasks across sessions. Thus, suggesting a long, relaxing dinner in a quiet restaurant for a couple who is disengaged and has difficulty talking to each other is probably not an appropriate starting point for rebuilding closeness.

In addition, areas of concern often are interrelated. With thoughtful planning, the therapist can either (a) employ interventions in one domain in order to help increase the likely success of addressing a second issue subsequently, or (b) address two issues simultaneously. As an example of the first circumstance, some couples feel distant from each other in general and also note the absence of a rewarding sex life. Although responses differ, many individuals do not want to engage in sex when they feel distant from their partner. If that is the case, a wide range of interventions might be introduced to increase an overall sense of closeness before addressing the couple's sexual relationship.

In these and all sequencing decisions, the therapist is simultaneously attending to individual, couple, and environmental factors, along with relevant cognitive, emotional, and behavioural aspects of both partners' functioning. In many instances, the explicit focus during one or more sessions revolves around a given "theme" (e.g., increasing intimacy or negotiating roles and responsibilities); yet, while addressing that given topic or theme, multiple behavioural, cognitive, and emotional interventions are utilized in an integrated manner.

Adapting the treatment plan

Just as the initial treatment planning and sequencing of interventions are flexible and responsive to numerous factors, so too the treatment plan continues to shift over the course of therapy. At times, new concerns arise as life for the couple continues to unfold. Also, issues that were initially scheduled to be addressed in treatment might resolve of their own accord or as a result of related matters being addressed. Moreover, as the couple's relationship or psychopathology improves, the couple might develop a different overall perspective, and circumstances that were initially upsetting are no longer distressing (e.g., "You falling asleep beside me as we watch television doesn't infuriate me any longer. It kind of reminds me of the decades we've been fortunate to be together on that same worn sofa; either awake or asleep, I think I'll keep you!").

Relapse prevention

As treatment moves toward an end, helping the couple prepare for terminating treatment and proceeding on their own is the next step in the therapeutic process. Relapse prevention often is included in individual CBT approaches and can be broadened for application to CBCT. Couples are attempting to avoid relapse in two domains: relationship discord and psychopathology. Even if only one domain has been the focus of treatment, relapse prevention is broadened in that two persons' behaviours are important in preventing relapse and monitoring ongoing functioning. However, the logic is the same as relapse prevention applied to individual therapy.

First, it is essential that couples are able to differentiate between (a) small lapses which are inevitable for most people and (b) relapses which signify more notable deterioration in functioning that might call for professional assistance. The therapist discusses this broad distinction and helps the couple clarify what to look for that would signify a lapse versus a relapse and what to do if either appears to be developing or is present, with regard to both the relationship distress and the psychopathology, as relevant.

Second, given that both partners are participating in treatment, there are two sets of eyes to attend to possible lapses and relapses. In many instances, this reality is a true asset, yet often it is helpful for the couple to discuss how input from both persons might be provided in an effective fashion. For example, an observation similar to the following is very likely to be ineffective: "You have become so irritable; you are impossible. I can't say anything without you jumping down my throat. You need to up your meds." Whether the topic is the relationship or either partner's well-being, the couple needs to discuss how they can share their thoughts and feelings appropriately and problem-solve accordingly. Furthermore, given that many couples and individuals use the structure of therapy and frequent check-ins with the therapist as a way to monitor their progress, many couples benefit from deciding upon regular times after therapy terminates when they will check in with each other, to discuss how things are going and what to increase, maintain, or alter to optimize functioning.

Main points

- The assessment has multiple aims, including establishing whether CBCT is appropriate for a couple and developing a case conceptualization and a tailored treatment plan.
- In order to carry out a comprehensive assessment, the therapist makes use of: (a) joint interviews with the couple; (b) self-report questionnaires; (c) observations of couple interactions; and (d) individual interviews with each partner.
- The assessment progresses through a series of distinct stages in which the therapist draws on a range of methods to create an understanding of the couple's current functioning and needs.
- When assessing a couple and conceptualizing their needs, it is important for therapists to remain attentive to strengths and potentially helpful resources, as well as areas of concern that are likely to dominate a couple's thinking.
- There is no "standardized" approach to conceptualization; instead, it is tailored to each individual couple while taking into account the fundamental principles of the CBCT model.
- The case conceptualization often emphasizes three or four major themes that capture the essence of the couple's current functioning and that serve as the basis for a clear and coherent treatment plan.
- The conceptualization, along with initial treatment recommendations, is shared and discussed with the couple in a feedback session, with the goal of developing a shared understanding of the couple's concerns and a mutually agreed-upon treatment plan.
- The sequencing of interventions is always important and deserves additional consideration when both relationship distress and psychopathology are present.
- As in all forms of psychological treatment, assessment is an ongoing activity. Therapists need to take numerous factors into account, and the treatment plan might need to be adapted as new information comes to light.

Chapter 15

Concluding comments

This book focuses on two domains which are central in the lives of most adults: (a) intimate, committed relationships and (b) individual mental health. Human beings are social creatures, and meaningful connections with others are essential for most people to live their lives to the fullest. Likewise, most adults experience some form of psychopathology at some point in their lifetime, either themselves or among their loved ones. Most importantly, relationship functioning and psychopathology are inexorably intertwined, and a significant goal of this book is to enhance our understanding of the intricate ways in which intimate relationships and individual functioning impact each other in an ongoing, reciprocal manner.

The findings noting the importance of each of these two domains and their association raise an important clinical question: What is the most effective way to treat relationship distress and psychopathology? Interventions for relationship distress must take into account the well-being and functioning of each of two partners. Likewise, because the course of individual psychopathology is greatly influenced by the couple's relationship, including the couple in the treatment of individual psychopathology mirrors how they live their lives. As a result, often both relationship difficulties and psychopathology can be addressed simultaneously by working with a couple together as a unit, taking into account the two individuals, the couple, and the broader environment in which they live. These intervention strategies include not only couple therapy to improve the relationship but also couple-based interventions for psychopathology which are targeted to address specific disorders, as appropriate.

Working with two partners to treat relationship distress can be a complex and challenging undertaking. The rewards include the potential to transform the lives of the two individuals, their relationship, and their family unit in profound, lasting ways. The interventions described in this book include the most recent developments in CBCT, a form of behaviourally based couple therapy which has received strong empirical support for decades. The current model demonstrates a continuing evolution of CBCT, reflecting the most recent theoretical, empirical, and clinical perspectives.

As described throughout this book, CBCT is a comprehensive model which makes it possible to address a wide range of concerns experienced by a variety of couples living in diverse contexts. This flexibility derives from the integration of (a) the contextual framework, which includes the individual, the couple, and their environment, along with (b) the CBT perspective, which addresses behavioural, emotional, and cognitive factors of relevance to a couple's relationship. For example, the contextual perspective allows for a rich understanding of the ways in which possible barriers and discrimination might impact couple functioning for various types of minority couples, a topic that is explored in this book.

Additionally, although the role of emotions in many CBT models has been acknowledged, *cognitive-behavioural* therapy has its title for a reason. To a large degree, cognitions and behaviours are the primary foci of intervention in many individual CBT treatments, with the rationale that emotions will change as a result. The focus on emotions as a distinct target of intervention in CBCT has continued to increase (Epstein & Baucom, 2002). The current CBCT model discussed in this book greatly expands on the centrality of emotions in intimate relationships, placing this domain on par with behaviours and cognitions. Thus, there is an in-depth discussion of the experience and expression of emotions by partners and the ways in which these emotions are manifest in the therapy room and in the couple's everyday lives. Many couple therapists experience that managing high levels of emotion during the therapy session is one of the most challenging aspects of treatment. Therefore, we have included a detailed discussion of working with emotions during therapy sessions. Finally, from a CBCT perspective, behaviours, emotions, and cognitions are integrally related both within and between individual partners; this integration and how to employ it in treatment is central to the current work.

Thus, the comprehensive CBCT model leads to a wide variety of interventions that can be tailored to the needs of a specific couple. Yet, these interventions alone are not enough for optimal treatment. As we tell couples, "It is not just what you do, but how you do it that matters." Couple therapy involves an important relationship between the therapist and the couple as well as the therapist and each partner. Therefore, how the therapist interacts with the couple is of great importance in providing effective treatment. As a result, Chapter 3 involves a concerted effort to articulate what CBCT actually looks like in the therapy room—how the therapist interacts and relates with the couple. In doing so, we rely on what we know regarding common factors in (a) therapy in general, (b) CBT in particular, and (c) couple therapy in general, leading to a discussion of the common factors that are integral to CBCT. Getting across what CBCT "feels like or looks like" in the therapy session is challenging. In many ways, the work of a skilled, experienced CBCT therapist appears intuitive in a way that cannot be described in words. However, as Kahnemann (2011) notes, intuition from an expert often involves some cue that triggers immediate access to a large set of experiences relevant to the current context which then become enacted. We have attempted to articulate what those "intuitive" factors are, as they relate to the common factors of CBCT. Employing empirically supported interventions within a comprehensive relationship model delivered by a skilled therapist who is sensitive to the therapist-couple relationship is the goal of CBCT.

While employing couple therapy to treat relationship distress has decades of support, working with the couple has not been a prominent form of intervention for treating psychological disorders in adults. Yet, working with the two partners together to address one person's psychopathology provides a number of potential benefits. First, effective therapy often requires patients to engage in difficult tasks as they confront aspects of their disorders that create distress. For many people, going through a difficult process is less upsetting or they can cope with the distress better if a caring, loving person is on the journey with them.

Second, helping both partners understand the disorder, how to approach it as a team, and what each partner's role will be in the process can create the context for increasing a patient's motivation to change and confront difficult issues. Motivation to change is important in the initiation of therapy, and it continues to be essential when the process of therapy takes a toll on patients. As a result, a notable number of patients drop out of treatment before it is complete. Our research and that of others indicates that in many instances, having a partner in treatment decreases patient dropout. One of the possible explanations for these findings is that when a patient's motivation begins to lag, the encouragement of a partner who is attending sessions with the patient helps keep the patient in treatment.

Third, much of the work of therapy occurs outside of the therapy session; patients need to make changes in their everyday lives. A partner is a central part of a patient's social environment, and incorporating a partner in treatment can create an ongoing environment in the couple's natural world that supports adaptive change. The partner can help to create that adaptive social environment but only if they know how to be of assistance. In our collective experience, partners frequently comment that they greatly appreciate being included in treatment because they want to be of help, but they do not know what to do, and they do not want to make things worse inadvertently. Additionally, partners can experience a significant burden and distress secondary to the patients' difficulties but often have little professional support themselves. As a result, many partners' ability to be patient with the suffering of their loved one and offer support declines over time as their own distress increases and important needs go unmet. As support decreases, negative interactions often increase. Although no one thrives in an environment filled with criticism and hostility, couples likely do not have the ability to find a way out of these types of communication once they have become ingrained. Such communications are among the most destructive forms of interpersonal interaction that impact the course of a patient's disorder. Furthermore, few loving partners realize the detrimental effects of accommodation that lowers the patient's distress at the moment, yet contributes to long-term maintenance of the disorder. Once the couple can understand these concepts, see how they occur in their lives, and receive appropriate support, they are in a position to make changes accordingly.

Fourth, some issues are inherently dyadic and are best addressed with the partner present. For example, couples' physical relationships are impacted by various disorders, whether it is an increased sexual drive as a part of mania or body image concerns related to an eating disorder that results in avoidance of intimate settings. Similarly, if a depressed person's withdrawal has resulted in decreased social time for the couple or a shift in roles and responsibilities, helping the couple navigate those dyadic processes together is optimal.

Finally, the partner without the disorder can be notably affected by the patient's disorder. Partners worry about the patient; that person is their partner for life. Moreover, partners take on added responsibilities, impacting their lives in a myriad of ways. In addition, the cost of quality care is high in many settings, often contributing to financial pressures and concerns. In couple-based treatments for psychopathology, the partner's concerns, needs, and preferences are addressed as well. Healthy relationships contribute to the growth and development of both partners, and while the couple's focus might shift somewhat when one person has a notable disorder, having both partners participate in treatment can help to ensure that some sense of balance is maintained in addressing the needs of both persons.

Thus, in many ways we are proposing a paradigm shift in the treatment of adult psychopathology. The modern treatment of adult psychopathology developed largely within the context of a medical model: If an individual has a disease, you treat the individual. Although various theoretical models such as CBT have moved away from the medical model, the predominant approach of treating only the individual has largely been retained. In treating children and youth, many interventions include parents or caregivers as a central and essential part of treatment. However, in the treatment of adults, the role of the family is de-emphasized, perhaps because many western cultures are individualistic in orientation and have a model that emphasizes *independence* in adulthood. Although interventions must take cultural factors into account, we would propose that, in general, healthy adults are *interdependent* as they proceed through life. Psychotherapeutic interventions should reflect this broader interpersonal perspective and consider including partners, or perhaps other loved ones, in treatment.

Such an approach means neither casting aside individual treatments, nor casting aside the vast knowledge we have gained from individual treatments as part of couple-based interventions. Drawing principles and specific interventions from empirically supported individual therapies and incorporating them into couple-based interventions is central in the treatment of every disorder described in this book. These interventions derived from individual therapy are then adapted to become interventions for the two partners together, working with a relational lens. For example, how do we engage in couple-based exposures for anxiety disorders? How is behavioural activation employed within a relationship when one partner is depressed? How does a partner contribute to healthy emotion regulation when the patient is struggling? How does a partner avoid accommodating to the patient's maladaptive use of alcohol and allow natural consequences to take place?

Well-articulated couple-based interventions have been developed for many disorders, as described in this book; however, much work is still needed to further develop and evaluate these treatments. As with all forms of psychotherapy, existing interventions can be fine-tuned and improved. Each time, after we have developed and initially applied a couple-based intervention for a specific disorder, we have found it necessary to revise the treatment, and this pattern will continue in the years ahead. Our hope is that while incorporating the empirical status of our field into our clinical work, we have spurred the reader to think in new ways about providing treatment that respects the complexity and interconnected nature of people's lives—lives that include the individual, their close relationships, and their social and physical environment. As Sarason (1971, p. 190) concluded many years ago, "If instead of putting one rat in the maze they had put two or more in the maze, the history of . . . psychology would have been quite different."

References

Abramowitz, J. S. (2006). *Understanding and treating obsessive-compulsive disorder: A cognitive-behavioral approach*. Mahwah, NJ: Lawrence Erlbaum Associates Publishers.

Abramowitz, J. S. (2018). Presidential address: Are the obsessive-compulsive related disorders related to obsessive-compulsive disorder? A critical look at DSM-5's new category. *Behavior Therapy*, *49*(1), 1–11. doi:10.1016/j.beth.2017.06.002

Abramowitz, J. S., Baucom, D. H., Boeding, S., Wheaton, M. G., Pukay-Martin, N. D., Fabricant, L. E., . . . Fischer, M. S. (2013). Treating obsessive-compulsive disorder in intimate relationships: A pilot study of couple-based cognitive-behavior therapy. *Behavior Therapy*, *44*(3), 395–407. doi:10.1016/j.beth.2013.02.005

Abramowitz, J. S., Baucom, D. H., Wheaton, M. G., Boeding, S., Fabricant, L. E., Paprocki, C., & Fischer, M. S. (2013). Enhancing exposure and response prevention for OCD: A couple-based approach. *Behavior Modification*, *37*(2), 189–210. doi:10.1177/0145445512444596

Acitelli, L. K., Rogers, S., & Knee, C. R. (1999). The role of identity in the link between relationship thinking and relationship satisfaction. *Journal of Social and Personal Relationships*, *16*, 591–618.

Ackerman, S. J., Benjamin, L. S., Beutler, L. E., Gelso, C. J., Goldfried, M. R., Hill, C., . . . Rainer, J. (2001). Empirically supported therapy relationships: Conclusions and recommendations of the Division 29 Task Force. *Psychotherapy: Theory, Research, Practice, Training*, *38*(4), 495–497. doi:10.1037/0033–3204.38.4.495

Algoe, S. B., & Zhaoyang, R. (2016). Positive psychology in context: Effects of expressing gratitude in ongoing relationships depend on perceptions of enactor responsiveness. *The Journal of Positive Psychology*, *11*(4), 399–415. doi:10.1080/17439760.2015.1117131

Allport, G. W. (1937). *Personality: A psychological interpretation*. New York, NY: Holt, Rinehart, & Winston.

Amato, P. R. (2001). Children of divorce in the 1990s: An update of the Amato and Keith (1991) metaanalysis. *Journal of Family Psychology*, *15*, 355–370.

American Psychiatric Association. (2013). *Diagnostic and statistical manual of mental disorders* (5th ed.) [DSM-5]. Washington, DC: American Psychiatric Publishing.

Antony, M. M., & Swinson, R. P. (2000). *Phobic disorders and panic in adults: A guide to assessment and treatment*. Washington, DC: American Psychological Association.

Balderrama-Durbin, C., Snyder, D. K., Cigrang, J., Talcott, G. W., Tatum, J., Baker, M., . . . Smith Slep, A. M. (2013). Combat disclosure in intimate relationships: Mediating the impact of partner support on posttraumatic stress. *Journal of Family Psychology*, *27*(4), 560–568. doi:10.1037/a0033412

Barbato, A., & D'Avanzo, B. (2008). Efficacy of couple therapy as a treatment for depression: A meta-analysis. *Psychiatric Quarterly*, *79*, 121–132. doi:10.1007/s11126-008-9068-0

Barrowclough, C., Gregg, L., & Tarrier, N. (2008). Expressed emotion and causal attributions in relatives of post-traumatic stress disorder patients. *Behaviour Research and Therapy*, *46*(2), 207–218. doi:10.1016/j.brat.2007.11.005

Barton, A. W., Futris, T. G., & Nielsen, R. B. (2015). Linking financial distress to marital quality: The intermediary roles of demand/withdraw and spousal gratitude expressions. *Personal Relationships*, *22*(3), 536–549. doi:10.1111/pere.12094

Baucom, B. R., Atkins, D. C., Eldridge, K., McFarland, P., Sevier, M., & Christensen, A. (2011). The language of demand/withdraw: Verbal and vocal expression in dyadic interactions. *Journal of Family Psychology*, *25*(4), 570–580. doi:10.1037/a0024064

Baucom, B. R., Weusthoff, S., Atkins, D. C., & Hahlweg, K. (2012). Greater emotional arousal predicts poorer long-term memory of communication skills in couples. *Behaviour Research and Therapy*, *50*(6), 442–447. doi:10.1016/j.brat.2012.03.010

Baucom, D. H. (1999, November). *Therapeutic implications of gender differences in cognitive processing in marital relationships*. Paper presented at the 33rd annual meeting of the Association for the Advancement of Behavior Therapy, Toronto, Canada.

Baucom, D. H., & Aiken, P. A. (1984). Sex role identity, marital satisfaction, and response to behavioral marital therapy. *Journal of Consulting and Clinical Psychology*, *52*(3), 438–444. doi:10.1037/0022-006X.52.3.438

Baucom, D. H., & Boeding, S. (2013). The role of theory and research in the practice of cognitive-behavioral couple therapy: If you build it, they will come. *Behavior Therapy*, *44*(4), 592–602. doi:10.1016/j.beth.2012.12.004

Baucom, D. H., & Epstein, N. B. (1990). *Cognitive-behavioral marital therapy*. New York, NY: Brunner/Mazel.

Baucom, D. H., Epstein, N., Daiuto, A. D., & Carels, R. A. (1996). Cognitions in marriage: The relationship between standards and attributions. *Journal of Family Psychology*, *10*(2), 209–222. doi:10.1037/0893-3200.10.2.209

Baucom, D. H., Epstein, N., Rankin, L. A., & Burnett, C. K. (1996). Assessing relationship standards: The Inventory of Specific Relationship Standards. *Journal of Family Psychology*, *10*(1), 72–88. doi:10.1037/0893-3200.10.1.72

Baucom, D. H., Epstein, N., Sayers, S., & Sher, T. G. (1989). The role of cognitions in marital relationships: definitional, methodological, and conceptual issues. *Journal of Consulting and Clinical Psychology*, *57*(1), 31–38.

Baucom, D. H., Fischer, M. S., Worrell, M., Corrie, S., Belus, J. M., Molyva, E., & Boeding, S. (2018). Couple-based intervention for depression: An effectiveness study in the National Health Service in England. *Family Process*, *57*(2), 275–292. doi:10.1111/famp.12332

Baucom, D. H., Hahlweg, K., Atkins, D. C., Engl, J., & Thurmaier, F. (2006). Long-term prediction of marital quality following a relationship education program: Being positive in a constructive way. *Journal of Family Psychology*, *20*(3), 448–455. doi:10.1037/0893-3200.20.3.448

Baucom, D. H., Hahlweg, K., & Kuschel, A. (2003). Are waiting-list control groups needed in future marital therapy outcome research? *Behavior Therapy*, *34*, 179–188. doi:10.1016/S0005-7894(03)80012-6

Baucom, D. H., Kirby, J. S., Fischer, M. S., Baucom, B. R., Hamer, R., & Bulik, C. M. (2017). Findings from a couple-based open trial for adult anorexia nervosa. *Journal of Family Psychology*, *31*(5), 584–591. doi:10.1037/fam0000273

Baucom, D. H., Porter, L. S., Kirby, J. S., & Hudepohl, J. (2012). Couple-based interventions for medical problems. *Behavior Therapy*, *43*(1), 61–76. doi:10.1016/j.beth.2011.01.008

Baucom, D. H., Sayers, S. L., & Sher, T. G. (1990). Supplementing behavioral marital therapy with cognitive restructuring and emotional expressiveness training: An outcome investigation. *Journal of Consulting and Clinical Psychology*, *58*(5), 636–645. doi:10.1037/0022-006X.58.5.636

Baucom, D. H., Shoham, V., Mueser, K. T., Daiuto, A. D., & Stickle, T. R. (1998). Empirically supported couple and family interventions for marital distress and adult mental health problems. *Journal of Consulting and Clinical Psychology*, *66*(1), 53–88.

Baucom, D. H., Snyder, D. K., & Gordon, K. C. (2009). *Helping couples get past the affair: A clinician's guide*. New York, NY: Guilford Press.

Baucom, D. H., Whisman, M. A., & Paprocki, C. (2012). Couple-based interventions for psychopathology. *Journal of Family Therapy*, *34*(3), 250–270. doi:10.1111/j.1467-6427.2012.00600.x

Beach, S. R. H., & Gupta, M. A. (2003). Helping clients with coexisting mental and relationship disorders. In D. K. Snyder & M. A. Whisman (Eds.), *Treating difficult couples* (pp. 88–113). New York, NY: Guilford Press.

Beach, S. R. H., Hurt, T. R., Fincham, F. D., Franklin, K. J., McNair, L. M., & Stanley, S. M. (2011). Enhancing marital enrichment through spirituality: Efficacy data for prayer focused relationship enhancement. *Psychology of Religion and Spirituality*, *3*(3), 201–216. doi:10.1037/a0022207

Beach, S. R. H., & Whisman, M. A. (2012). Affective disorders. *Journal of Marital and Family Therapy*, *38*(1), 201–219. doi:10.1111/j.1752-0606.2011.00243.x

Beck, A. T., Emery, G., & Greenberg, R. L. (1985). *Anxiety disorders and phobias: A cognitive perspective*. New York, NY: Basic Books.

Beck, A. T., Rush, A. J., Shaw, B. F., & Emery, G. (1979). *Cognitive therapy of depression*. New York, NY: Guilford Press.

Beck, J. S. (2011). *Cognitive behavior therapy: Basics and beyond* (2nd ed.). New York, NY: Guilford Press.

Beckes, L., & Coan, J. A. (2011). Social baseline theory: The role of social proximity in emotion and economy of action. *Social and Personality Psychology Compass*, *5*(12), 976–988. doi:10.1111/j.1751-9004.2011.00400.x

Belus, J. M., Baucom, D. H., & Abramowitz, J. S. (2014). The effect of a couple-based treatment for OCD on intimate partners. *Journal of Behavior Therapy and Experimental Psychiatry*, *45*(4), 484–488. doi:10.1016/j.jbtep.2014.07.001

Bodenmann, G. (2006). Dyadic coping and its significance for marital functioning. In T. A. Revenson, K. Kayser, & G. Bodenmann (Eds.), *Couples coping with stress: Emerging perspectives on dyadic coping* (pp. 33–50). Washington, DC: American Psychological Association.

Bodenmann, G., Atkins, D. C., Schär, M., & Poffet, V. (2010). The association between daily stress and sexual activity. *Journal of Family Psychology*, *24*(3), 271–279. doi:10.1037/a0019365

Bodenmann, G., & Cina, A. (2006). Stress and coping among stable-satisfied, stable-distressed and separated/divorced Swiss couples. *Journal of Divorce & Remarriage*, *44*(1–2), 71–89. doi:10.1300/J087v44n01_04

Bodenmann, G., Plancherel, B., Beach, S. R., Widmer, K., Gabriel, B., Meuwly, N., . . . Schramm, E. (2008). Effects of coping-oriented couples therapy on depression: A randomized clinical trial. *Journal of Consulting and Clinical Psychology*, *76*(6), 944–954. doi:10.1037/a0013467

Boeding, S. E., Baucom, D. H., Cohen, M. J., Meltzer-Brody, S., & Brandon, A. (2017). Roles and postpartum distress: The mediating role of relationship adjustment. *Current Psychology: A Journal for Diverse Perspectives on Diverse Psychological Issues*. doi:10.1007/s12144-017-9728-z

Boeding, S. E., Paprocki, C. M., Baucom, D. H., Abramowitz, J. S., Wheaton, M. G., Fabricant, L. E., & Fischer, M. S. (2013). Let me check that for you: Symptom accommodation in romantic partners of adults with obsessive–compulsive disorder. *Behaviour Research and Therapy*, *51*(6), 316–322. doi:10.1016/j.brat.2013.03.002

Boss, P. (1988). *Family stress management*. Thousand Oaks, CA: Sage Publications, Inc.

Bradbury, T. N., Beach, S. R. H., Fincham, F. D., & Nelson, G. M. (1996). Attributions and behavior in functional and dysfunctional marriages. *Journal of Consulting and Clinical Psychology*, *64*(3), 569–576.

Bradbury, T. N., & Fincham, F. D. (1990). Attributions in marriage: Review and critique. *Psychological Bulletin*, *107*(1), 3–33. doi:10.1037/0033-2909.107.1.3

Bronfenbrenner, U. (1989). *Ecological Systems Theory* (Vol. 6). Greenwich: JAI.

Brown, S. L., & Lin, I. F. (2012). The gray divorce revolution: Rising divorce among middle-aged and older adults, 1990–2010. *The Journals of Gerontology Series B: Psychological Sciences and Social Sciences*, *67*, 731–741. doi:10.1093/geronb/gbs089

Brownley, K. A., Berkman, N. D., Sedway, J. A., Lohr, K. N., & Bulik, C. M. (2007). Binge eating disorder treatment: a systematic review of randomized controlled trials. *International Journal of Eating Disorders*, *40*(4), 337–348. doi:10.1002/eat.20370

Bulik, C. M., Baucom, D. H., & Kirby, J. S. (2012a). Couples therapy for anorexia nervosa. In J. Alexander & J. Treasure (Eds.), *A collaborative approach to eating disorders* (pp. 189–200). New York, NY: Routledge/Taylor & Francis Group.

Bulik, C. M., Baucom, D. H., & Kirby, J. S. (2012b). Treating anorexia nervosa in the couple context. *Journal of Cognitive Psychotherapy*, *26*(1), 19–33. doi:10.1891/0889-8391.26.1.19

Butler, E. A. (2011). Temporal interpersonal emotion systems: The "TIES" that form relationships. *Personality and Social Psychology Review*, *15*(4), 367–393. doi:10.1177/1088868311411164

Butler, E. A., & Randall, A. K. (2013). Emotional coregulation in close relationships. *Emotion Review*, *5*(2), 202–210. doi:10.1177/1754073912451630

Byers, A. L., Yaffe, K., Covinsky, K. E., Friedman, M. B., & Bruce, M. L. (2010). High occurrence of mood and anxiety disorders among older adults. *Archives of General Psychiatry*, *67*, 489–496.

Byrne, M., Carr, A., & Clark, M. (2004). The efficacy of couples-based interventions for panic disorder with agoraphobia. *Journal of Family Therapy*, *26*, 105–125. doi:10.1111/j.1467-6427.2004.00273.x

Calvocoressi, L., Lewis, B., Harris, M., Trufan, S. J., Goodman, W. K., McDougle, C. J., & Price, L. H. (1995). Family accommodation in obsessive-compulsive disorder. *American Journal of Psychiatry*, *152*(3), 441–443. doi:10.1176/ajp.152.3.441

Calvocoressi, L., Mazure, C. M., Kasl, S. V., Skolnick, J., Fisk, D., Vegso, S. J., . . . Price, L. H. (1999). Family accommodation of obsessive-compulsive symptoms: Instrument development and assessment of family behavior. *Journal of Nervous and Mental Disease*, *187*(10), 636–642. doi:10.1097/00005053-199910000-00008

Campbell, S. B., Renshaw, K. D., Kashdan, T. B., Curby, T. W., & Carter, S. P. (2017). A daily diary study of posttraumatic stress symptoms and romantic partner accommodation. *Behavior Therapy*, *48*(2), 222–234. doi:10.1016/j.beth.2016.04.006

Cao, H., Mills-Koonce, W. R., Wood, C., & Fine, M. A. (2016). Identity transformation during the transition to parenthood among same-sex couples: An ecological, stress-strategy-adaptation perspective. *Journal of Family Theory & Review*, *8*(1), 30–59. doi:10.1111/jftr.12124

Carson, J. W., Carson, K. M., Gil, K. M., & Baucom, D. H. (2004). Mindfulness-based relationship enhancement. *Behavior Therapy*, *35*(3), 471–494. doi:10.1016/S0005-7894(04)80028-5

Carson, J. W., Carson, K. M., Gil, K. M., & Baucom, D. H. (2006). Mindfulness-based relationship enhancement (MBRE) in couples. In R. A. Baer & R. A. Baer (Eds.), *Mindfulness-based treatment approaches: Clinician's guide to evidence base and applications*. (pp. 309–331). San Diego, CA: Elsevier Academic Press.

Carter, B., & McGoldrick, M. (Eds.). (1999). *The expanded family life cycle: Individual, family, and social perspectives* (3rd ed.). Boston, MA: Allyn and Bacon.

Cassin, S. E., & von Ranson, K. M. (2005). Personality and eating disorders: A decade in review. *Clinical Psychology Review*, *25*(7), 895–916. doi:10.1016/j.cpr.2005.04.012

Castellini, G., Mannucci, E., Mazzei, C., Lo Sauro, C., Faravelli, C., Rotella, C. M., . . . Ricca, V. (2010). Sexual function in obese women with and without binge eating disorder. *Journal of Sexual Medicine*, *7*(12), 3969–3978. doi:10.1111/j.1743-6109.2010.01990.x

Caughlin, J. P., Huston, T. L., & Houts, R. M. (2000). How does personality matter in marriage? An examination of trait anxiety, interpersonal negativity, and marital satisfaction. *Journal of Personality and Social Psychology*, *78*(2), 326–336. doi:10.1037/0022-3514.78.2.326

Chambless, D. L., Allred, K. M., Chen, F. F., McCarthy, K. S., Milrod, B., & Barber, J. P. (2017). Perceived criticism predicts outcome of psychotherapy for panic disorder: Replication and extension. *Journal of Consulting and Clinical Psychology*, *85*(1), 37–44. doi:10.1037/ccp0000161

Chambless, D. L., Floyd, F. J., Rodebaugh, T. L., & Steketee, G. S. (2007). Expressed emotion and familial interaction: A study with agoraphobic and obsessive-compulsive patients and their relatives. *Journal of Abnormal Psychology*, *116*(4), 754–761. doi:10.1037/0021-843X.116.4.754

Christensen, A. (2010). A "unified protocol" for couple therapy. In K. Hahlweg, M. Grawe-Gerber, & D. H. Baucom (Eds.), *Couples in despair: Evidence-Based interventions for treatment and prevention* (pp. 33–46). Göttingen, Germany: Hogrefe.

Christensen, A., Atkins, D. C., Baucom, B. R., & Yi, J. (2010). Marital status and satisfaction five years following a randomized clinical trial comparing traditional versus integrative behavioral couple therapy. *Journal of Consulting and Clinical Psychology*, *78*(2), 225–235. doi:10.1037/a0018132

Christensen, A., Doss, B. D., & Jacobson, N. S. (2014). *Reconcilable differences* (2nd ed.). New York, NY: Guilford Press.

Christensen, A., Eldridge, K., Catta-Preta, A. B., Lim, V. R., & Santagata, R. (2006). Cross-cultural consistency of the demand/withdraw interaction pattern in couples. *Journal of Marriage and Family*, *68*(4), 1029–1044. doi:10.1111/j.1741-3737.2006.00311.x

Christensen, A., & Heavey, C. L. (1990). Gender and social structure in the demand/withdraw pattern of marital conflict. *Journal of Personality and Social Psychology*, *59*(1), 73–81.

Christensen, A., & Heavey, C. L. (1993). Gender differences in marital conflict: The demand/withdraw interaction pattern. In S. Oskamp & M. Costanzo (Eds.), *Gender issues in contemporary society. Claremont Symposium on Applied Social Psychology* (Vol. 6, pp. 113–141). Newbury Park, CA: Sage.

Christensen, A., Jacobson, N. S., & Babcock, J. C. (1995). Integrative behavioral couple therapy. In N. S. Jacobson & A. S. Gurman (Eds.), *Clinical handbook of couple therapy* (pp. 31–64). New York, NY: Guilford Press.

Christensen, A., & Shenk, J. L. (1991). Communication, conflict, and psychological distance in nondistressed, clinic, and divorcing couples. *Journal of Consulting and Clinical Psychology*, *59*(3), 458–463.

Coan, J. A., Schaefer, H. S., & Davidson, R. J. (2006). Lending a hand: Social regulation of the neural response to threat. *Psychological Science*, *17*(12), 1032–1039. doi:10.1111/j.1467-9280.2006.01832.x

Cohen, S., O'Leary, K. D., & Foran, H. (2010). A randomized clinical trial of a brief, problem-focused couple therapy for depression. *Behavior Therapy*, *41*(4), 433–446. doi:10.1016/j.beth.2009.11.004

Cordova, J. D., & Scott, R. L. (2001). Intimacy: A behavioral interpretation. *The Behavior Analyst*, *24*(1), 75–86. doi:10.1007/bf03392020

Coyne, J. C., & Downey, G. (1991). Social factors and psychopathology: Stress, social support, and coping processes. *Annual Review of Psychology*, *42*(1), 401–425. doi:10.1146/annurev.ps.42.020191.002153

Crenshaw, A. O., Christensen, A., Baucom, D. H., Epstein, N. B., & Baucom, B. R. W. (2017). Revised scoring and improved reliability for the Communication Patterns Questionnaire. *Psychological Assessment*, *29*(7), 913–925. doi:10.1037/pas0000385

Cutrona, C. E. (1996). *Social support in couples*. Thousand Oaks, CA: Sage Publications.

Cutrona, C. E., & Suhr, J. A. (1994). Social support communication in the context of marriage: An analysis of couples' supportive interactions. In B. Burleson, T. Albrecht, & I. Sarason (Eds.), *The communication of social support: Messages, interactions, relationships, and community* (pp. 113–125). Newbury, CA: Sage.

Cutrona, C. E., Suhr, J. A., & MacFarlane, R. (1990). Interpersonal transactions and the psychological sense of support. In S. Duck & R. C. Silver (Eds.), *Personal relationships and social support* (pp. 30–45). Newbury Park, CA: Sage.

Daiuto, A. D., Baucom, D. H., Epstein, N., & Dutton, S. S. (1998). The application of behavioral couples therapy to the assessment and treatment of agoraphobia: Implications of empirical research. *Clinical Psychology Review*, *18*(6), 663–687. doi:10.1016/S0272-7358(98)00024-5

Daspe, M.-È., Sabourin, S., Péloquin, K., Lussier, Y., & Wright, J. (2013). Curvilinear associations between neuroticism and dyadic adjustment in treatment-seeking couples. *Journal of Family Psychology*, *27*(2), 232–241. doi:10.1037/a0032107

Davila, J., Bradbury, T. N., Cohan, C. L., & Tochluk, S. (1997). Marital functioning and depressive symptoms: Evidence for a stress generation model. *Journal of Personality and Social Psychology*, *73*, 849–861. doi:10.1037//0022-3514.73.4.849

Davila, J., Starr, L. R., Stroud, C. B., & Li, Y. I. (2019). Mood and anxiety disorders. In B. H. Friese (Ed.), *APA handbook of contemporary family psychology: Applications and broad impact of family psychology* (Vol. 2, pp. 21–36). Washington, DC: American Psychological Association.

Davila, J., Stroud, C. B., & Starr, L. (2014). Depression in couples and families. In I. Gotlib & C. Hammen (Eds.), *Handbook of depression* (3rd ed., pp. 410–428). New York, NY: Guilford Press.

Davis, S. D., Lebow, J. L., & Sprenkle, D. H. (2012). Common factors of change in couple therapy. *Behavior Therapy, 43*(1), 36–48. doi:10.1016/j.beth.2011.01.009

de Jong, K., & DeRubeis, R. J. (2018). Effectiveness of psychotherapy. In J. N. Butcher & J. Hooley (Eds.), *APA handbook of psychopathology: Psychopathology: Understanding, assessing, and treating adult mental disorders* (Vol. 1, pp. 705–725). Washington, DC: American Psychological Association.

Diamond, L. M., & Aspinwall, L. G. (2003). Emotion regulation across the life-span: An integrative perspective emphasizing self-regulation, positive affect, and dyadic processes. *Motivation and Emotion, 27*, 125–156. doi:10.1023/A:1024521920068

Ditzen, B., Hahlweg, K., Fehm-Wolfsdorf, G., & Baucom, D. (2011). Assisting couples to develop healthy relationships: Effects of couples relationship education on cortisol. *Psychoneuroendocrinology, 36*(5), 597–607. doi:10.1016/j.psyneuen.2010.07.019

Ditzen, B., Hoppmann, C., & Klumb, P. (2008). Positive couple interactions and daily cortisol: On the stress-protecting role of intimacy. *Psychosomatic Medicine, 70*(8), 883–889. doi:10.1097/PSY.0b013e318185c4fc

Doss, B. D., Rhoades, G. K., Stanley, S. M., & Markman, H. J. (2009). The effect of the transition to parenthood on relationship quality: An 8–year prospective study. *Journal of Personality and Social Psychology, 96*(3), 601–619. doi:10.1037/a0013969

Doss, B. D., Rowe, L. S., Morrison, K. R., Libet, J., Birchler, G. R., Madsen, J. W., & McQuaid, J. R. (2012). Couple therapy for military veterans: Overall effectiveness and predictors of response. *Behavior Therapy, 43*(1), 216–227. doi:0.1016/j.beth.2011.06.006

Doss, B. D., Simpson, L. E., & Christensen, A. (2004). Why do couples seek marital therapy? *Professional Psychology: Research and Practice, 35*(6), 608–614. doi:10.1037/0735-7028.35.6.608

Driver, J. L., & Gottman, J. M. (2004). Daily marital interactions and positive affect during marital conflict among newlywed couples. *Family Process, 43*(3), 301–314.

Dush, C. M. K., Arocho, R., Mernitz, S. E., & Rhoades, G. K. (2019). Cohabitation and single mothering in the United States: A review and call for psychological research. In B. H. Friese (Ed.), *APA handbook of contemporary family psychology: Foundations, methods, and contemporary issues across the lifespan* (Vol. 1, pp. 667–685). Washington, DC: American Psychological Association.

Dyrenforth, P. S., Kashy, D. A., Donnellan, M. B., & Lucas, R. E. (2010). Predicting relationship and life satisfaction from personality in nationally representative samples from three countries: The relative importance of actor, partner, and similarity effects. *Journal of Personality and Social Psychology, 99*(4), 690–702. doi:10.1037/a0020385

Eaton, W. W., Shao, H., Nestadt, G., Lee, B., Bienvenu, O., & Zandi, P. (2008). Population based study of first onset and chronicity in major depressive disorder. *Archives of General Psychiatry, 65*, 513–529. doi:10.1001/archpsyc.65.5.513

Egan, R., & Smith, D. (2017, November). *Marital quality and psychopathology: A meta-analysis*. Paper presented at the Annual Convention of the Association for Behavioral and Cognitive Therapies San Diego, CA.

Einhorn, L., Williams, T., Stanley, S., Wunderlin, N., Markman, H., & Eason, J. (2008). PREP inside and out: Marriage education for inmates. *Family Process, 47*(3), 341–356. doi:10.1111/j.1545-5300.2008.00257.x

Ekman, P. (1992). An argument for basic emotions. *Cognition and Emotion, 6*(3–4), 169–200.

Eldridge, K., & Christensen, A. (2002). Demand-withdraw communication during couple conflict: A review and analysis. In P. Noller & J. A. Feeney (Eds.), *Understanding marriage: Developments in the study of couple interaction* (pp. 289–322). New York, NY: Cambridge University Press. doi:10.1080/02699939208411068

Epstein, N. B., & Baucom, D. H. (2002). *Enhanced cognitive-behavioral therapy for couples: A contextual approach*. Washington, DC: American Psychological Association.

Epstein, N. B., Berger, A. T., Fang, J. J., Messina, L. A., Smith, J. R., Lloyd, T. D., . . . Liu, Q. X. (2012). Applying western-developed family therapy models in China. *Journal of Family Psychotherapy, 23*(3), 217–237. doi:10.1080/08975353.2012.705661

Epstein, N. B., Curtis, D. S., Edwards, E., Young, J. L., & Zheng, L. (2014). Therapy with families in China: Cultural factors influencing the therapeutic alliance and therapy goals. *Contemporary Family Therapy: An International Journal, 36*(2), 201–212. doi:10.1007/s10591-014-9302-x

Epstein, N. B., Werlinich, C. A., & LaTaillade, J. J. (2015). Couple therapy for partner aggression. In A. S. Gurman, J. L. Lebow, & D. K. Snyder (Eds.), *Clinical handbook of couple therapy* (5th ed., pp. 389–411). New York, NY: Guilford Press.

Falconier, M. K., Nussbeck, F., Bodenmann, G., Schneider, H., & Bradbury, T. (2015). Stress from daily hassles in couples: Its effects on intradyadic stress, relationship satisfaction, and physical and psychological well-being. *Journal of Marital and Family Therapy, 41*(2), 221–235. doi:10.1111/jmft.12073

Fincham, F. D., Beach, S. R., & Baucom, D. H. (1987). Attribution processes in distressed and nondistressed couples: IV. Self–partner attribution differences. *Journal of Personality and Social Psychology, 52*(4), 739–748. doi:10.1037/0022-3514.52.4.739

Fischer, M. S., & Baucom, D. H. (2018). Couple-based interventions for relationship distress and psychopathology. In J. N. Butcher & J. M. Hooley (Eds.), *Psychopathology: Understanding, assessing and treating adult mental disorders* (Vol. 1, pp. 661–686). Washington, DC: American Psychological Association.

Fischer, M. S., Baucom, D. H., Abramowitz, J. S., & Baucom, B. R. (2018). *Expressed emotional arousal, coregulation, and symptom accommodation in couples with OCD*. Paper presented at the 51st Annual Convention of the Association for Behavioral and Cognitive Therapies, Washington, DC.

Fischer, M. S., Baucom, D. H., Baucom, B., Weusthoff, S., Hahlweg, K., Atkins, D. C., . . . Zimmermann, T. (2015). Emotional arousal predicts observed social support in German and American couples talking about breast cancer. *Journal of Family Psychology, 29*(5), 744–754. doi:10.1037/fam0000092

Fischer, M. S., Baucom, D. H., Baucom, B. R., Abramowitz, J. S., Kirby, J. S., & Bulik, C. M. (2017). Disorder-specific patterns of emotion coregulation in couples: Comparing obsessive compulsive disorder and anorexia nervosa. *Journal of Family Psychology, 31*(3), 304–315. doi:10.1037/fam0000251

Fischer, M. S., Baucom, D. H., & Cohen, M. J. (2016). Cognitive-behavioral couple therapies: Review of the evidence for the treatment of relationship distress, psychopathology, and chronic health conditions. *Family Process, 55*(3), 423–442. doi:10.1111/famp.12227

Fischer, M. S., Kirby, J. S., Raney, T. J., Baucom, D. H., & Bulik, C. M. (2015). Integrating couple-based interventions into the treatment of adult anorexia nervosa: A case example of UCAN. In H. Thompson-Brenner (Ed.), *Casebook of evidence-based therapy for eating disorders* (pp. 220–245). New York, NY: Guilford Press.

Foa, E. B., Hembree, E. A., & Rothbaum, B. O. (2007). *Prolonged exposure therapy for PTSD: Emotional processing of traumatic experiences: Therapist guide*. New York, NY: Oxford University Press.

Ford, D. E., & Kamerow, D. B. (1989). Epidemiologic study of sleep disturbances and psychiatric disorders: an opportunity for prevention? *Journal of the American Medical Association, 262*(11), 1479–1484.

Frank, E. (2007). Interpersonal and social rhythm therapy: A means of improving depression and preventing relapse in bipolar disorder. *Journal of Clinical Psychology, 63*(5), 463–473. doi:10.1002/jclp.20371

Fredman, S. J., Baucom, D. H., Boeding, S. E., & Miklowitz, D. J. (2015). Relatives' emotional involvement moderates the effects of family therapy for bipolar disorder. *Journal of Consulting and Clinical Psychology, 83*(1), 81–91. doi:10.1037/a0037713

Fredman, S. J., Baucom, D. H., Miklowitz, D. J., & Stanton, S. E. (2008). Observed emotional involvement and overinvolvement in families of patients with bipolar disorder. *Journal of Family Psychology*, *22*(1), 71–79. doi:10.1037/0893-3200.22.1.71

Fredman, S. J., Beck, J. G., Shnaider, P., Le, Y., Pukay-Martin, N. D., Pentel, K. Z., . . . Marques, L. (2017). Longitudinal associations between PTSD symptoms and dyadic conflict communication following a severe motor vehicle accident. *Behavior Therapy*, *48*(2), 235–246. doi:10.1016/j.beth.2016.05.001

Fredman, S. J., Macdonald, A., Monson, C. M., Rhoades, G. K., Dondanville, K. A., & the Consortium to Alleviate PTSD (2018, November). *An open trial of cognitive-behavioral conjoint therapy for PTSD delivered in an intensive weekend format for military and veteran couples*. Paper presented at the Annual meeting of the International Society for Traumatic Stress Studies, Washington, DC.

Fredman, S. J., Pukay-Martin, N. D., Macdonald, A., Wagner, A. C., Vorstenbosch, V., & Monson, C. M. (2015). Partner accommodation moderates treatment outcomes for couple therapy for posttraumatic stress disorder. *Journal of Consulting and Clinical Psychology*, *84*(1), 79–87. doi:10.1037/ccp0000061

Fredman, S. J., Vorstenbosch, V., Wagner, A. C., Macdonald, A., & Monson, C. M. (2014). Partner accommodation in posttraumatic stress disorder: Initial testing of the Significant Others' Responses to Trauma Scale (SORTS). *Journal of Anxiety Disorders*, *28*(4), 372–381. doi:10.1016/j.janxdis.2014.04.001

Fredrickson, B. L. (1998). What good are positive emotions? *Review of General Psychology*, *2*(3), 300–319. doi:10.1037/1089-2680.2.3.300

Friedman, H. S., Tucker, J. S., Schwartz, J. E., Tomlinson-Keasey, C., Martin, L. R., & Wingard, D. L. (1995). Psychosocial and behavioral predictors of longevity. The aging and death of the "Termites." *American Psychologist*, *50*, 69–78.

Friese, B. H. (2019). *APA handbook of contemporary family psychology: Foundations, methods, and contemporary issues across the lifespan* (B. H. Friese Ed. Vol. 1). Washington, DC: American Psychological Association.

Frost, D. M., & Meyer, I. H. (2009). Internalized homophobia and relationship quality among lesbians, gay men, and bisexuals. *Journal of Counseling Psychology*, *56*(1), 97–109. doi:10.1037/a0012844

Fruzzetti, A. E., & Payne, L. A. (2015). Couple therapy and borderline personality disorder. In A. S. Gurman, J. L. Lebow, & D. K. Snyder (Eds.), *Clinical handbook of couple therapy* (5th ed., pp. 606–634). New York, NY: Guilford Press.

Funk, J. L., & Rogge, R. D. (2007). Testing the ruler with item response theory: Increasing precision of measurement for relationship satisfaction with the Couples Satisfaction Index. *Journal of Family Psychology*, *21*(4), 572–583. doi:10.1037/0893-3200.21.4.572

Gable, S. L., & Reis, H. T. (2001). Appetitive and aversive social interaction. In J. H. Harvey & A. Wenzel (Eds.), *Close relationships: Maintenance and enhancement* (pp. 169–194). Mahwah, NJ: Lawrence Erlbauum.

Gavin, N. I., Gaynes, B. N., Lohr, K. N., Meltzer-Brody, S., Gartlehner, G., & Swinson, T. (2005). Perinatal depression: a systematic review of prevalence and incidence. *Obstetrics and Gynecology*, *106*(5, Part 1), 1071–1083. doi:10.1097/01.AOG.0000183597.31630.db

Geffken, G. R., Storch, E. A., Duke, D. C., Monaco, L., Lewin, A. B., & Goodman, W. K. (2006). Hope and coping in family members of patients with obsessive-compulsive disorder. *Journal of Anxiety Disorders*, *20*(5), 614–629. doi:10.1016/j.janxdis.2005.07.001

Geiss, S. K., & O'Leary, K. D. (1981). Therapist ratings of frequency and severity of marital problems: Implications for research. *Journal of Marital and Family Therapy*, *7*(4), 515–520.

Glade, A. C., Bean, R. A., & Vira, R. (2005). A prime time for marital/relational intervention: A review of the transition to parenthood literature with treatment recommendations. *American Journal of Family Therapy*, *33*(4), 319–336. doi:10.1080/01926180590962138

Gordon, C. L., & Baucom, D. H. (2004, November). *Don't settle for "satisfied": Individual factors contributing to optimal relationship functioning*. Paper presented at the 38th annual meeting of the Association for the Advancement of Behavior Therapy, New Orleans, LA.

Gordon, C. L., & Baucom, D. H. (2005, November). *Happy marriages consist of happy partners: The individual's contribution to satisfying relationships*. Paper presented at the 39th annual meeting of the Association for Behavioral and Cognitive Therapies, Washington, DC.

Gordon, C. L., & Baucom, D. H. (2009). Examining the individual within marriage: Personal strengths and relationship satisfaction. *Personal Relationships, 16*, 421–435. doi:10.1111/j.1475-6811.2009.01231.x

Gordon, K. C., Khaddouma, A., Baucom, D. H., & Snyder, D. K. (2015). Couple therapy and the treatment of affairs. In A. S. Gurman, J. L. Lebow, & D. K. Snyder (Eds.), *Clinical handbook of couple therapy* (5th ed., pp. 412–444). New York, NY: Guilford Press.

Gotta, G., Green, R. J., Rothblum, E., Solomon, S., Balsam, K., & Schwartz, P. (2011). Heterosexual, lesbian, and gay male relationships: A comparison of couples in 1975 and 2000. *Family Process, 50*(3), 353–376. doi:10.1111/j.1545-5300.2011.01365.x

Gottman, J. M. (1979). *Marital interaction: Experimental investigations*. New York, NY: Academic.

Gottman, J. M. (1994). *What predicts divorce?* Hillsdale, NJ: Erlbaum.

Gottman, J. M. (1999). *The marriage clinic: A scientifically based marital therapy*. New York, NY: Norton.

Gottman, J. M., Driver, J., & Tabares, A. (2015). Repair during marital conflict in newlyweds: How couples move from attack-defend to collaboration. *Journal of Family Psychotherapy, 26*, 85–108. doi:10.1080/08975353.2015.1038962

Gottman, J. M., & Notarius, C. I. (2000). Decade review: Observing marital interaction. *Journal of Marriage and the Family, 62*, 927–947. doi:10.1111/j.1741-3737.2000.00927.x

Graham, J. M., & Barnow, Z. B. (2013). Stress and social support in gay, lesbian, and heterosexual couples: Direct effects and buffering models. *Journal of Family Psychology, 27*(4), 569–578. doi:10.1037/a0033420

Green, R.-J., & Mitchell, V. (2015). Gay, Lesbian, and Bisexual issues in couple therapy. In A. S. Gurman, J. L. Lebow, & D. K. Snyder (Eds.), *Clinical handbook of couple therapy* (5th ed., pp. 489–511). New York, NY: Guilford Press.

Greenberg, L. S., & Johnson, S. M. (1988). *Emotionally focused therapy for couples*. New York, NY: Guilford Press.

Griskevicius, V., Tybur, J. M., Delton, A. W., & Robertson, T. E. (2011). The influence of mortality and socioeconomic status on risk and delayed rewards: A life history theory approach. *Journal of Personality and Social Psychology, 100*(6), 1015–1026. doi:10.1037/a0022403

Gross, J. J. (2013). *Handbook of emotion regulation*. New York, NY: Guilford Press.

Hahlweg, K., & Baucom, D. H. (2008). *Partnerschaft und psychische Störung*. Göttingen: Hogrefe.

Hahlweg, K., Reisner, L., Kohli, G., Vollmer, M., Schindler, L., & Revenstorf, D. (1984). Development and validity of a new system to analyze interpersonal communication (KPI: Kategoriensystem fur partnerschaftliche Interaktion). In K. Hahlweg & N. S. Jacobson (Eds.), *Marital interaction: Analysis and modification* (pp. 182–198). New York, NY: Guilford Press.

Hahlweg, K., Schindler, L., Revenstorf, D., & Brengelmann, J. C. (1984). The Munich marital therapy study. In K. Hahlweg & N. S. Jacobson (Eds.), *Marital interaction: Analysis and modification* (pp. 3–26). New York, NY: Guilford Press.

Halford, W. K., Pepping, C. A., Hilpert, P., Bodenmann, G., Wilson, K. L., Busby, D. M., . . . Holman, T. (2015). Immediate effect of couple relationship education on low-satisfaction couples: A randomized clinical trial plus an uncontrolled trial replication. *Behavior Therapy, 46*(3), 409–421. doi:10.1016/j.beth.2015.02.001

Halford, W. K., Sanders, M. R., & Behrens, B. C. (1993). A comparison of the generalization of behavioral marital therapy and enhanced behavioral marital therapy. *Journal of Consulting and Clinical Psychology, 61*, 51–60.

Halford, W. K., & Snyder, D. K. (2012). Universal processes and common factors in couple therapy and relationship education. *Behavior Therapy, 43*, 1–12. doi:10.1016/j.beth.2011.01.007.

Hays, P. A. (2016). *Addressing cultural complexities in practice: Assessment, diagnosis, and therapy*, 3rd ed. Washington, DC: American Psychological Association.

Helm, J. L., Sbarra, D., & Ferrer, E. (2012). Assessing cross-partner associations in physiological responses via coupled oscillator models. *Emotion, 12*(4), 748–762. doi:10.1037/a0025036

Hetherington, E. M., & Elmore, A. M. (2004). The intergenerational transmission of couple instability. In P. L. Chase-Lindsdale, K. Kiernan, & R. Friedman (Eds.), *Human development across lives and generations. The potential for change* (pp. 171–203). Cambridge: Cambridge University Press.

Heyman, R. E. (2001). Observation of couple conflicts: Clinical assessment applications, stubborn truths, and shaky foundations. *Psychological Assessment, 13*(1), 5–35. doi:10.1037//1040-3590.13.1.5

Heyman, R. E. (2004). Rapid marital interaction coding system. In P. K. Kerig & D. H. Baucom (Eds.), *Couple observational coding systems* (pp. 67–94). Mahwah, NJ: Lawrence Erlbaum Associates.

Hirschfield, R. M. A. (2001). The comorbidity of major depression and anxiety disorders- Recognition and management in primary care. *Primary Care Companion to the Journal of Clinical Psychiatry, 3*(6), 244–254. doi:10.4088/pcc.v03n0609

Holt-Lunstad, J., Birmingham, W., & Jones, B. Q. (2008). Is there something unique about marriage? The relative impact of marital status, relationship quality, and network social support on ambulatory blood pressure and mental health. *Annals of Behavioral Medicine, 35*(2), 239–244. doi:10.1007/s12160-008-9018-y

Holt-Lunstad, J., Smith, T. B., Baker, M., Harris, T., & Stephenson, D. (2015). Loneliness and social isolation as risk factors for mortality: A meta-analytic review. *Perspectives on Psychological Science, 10*(2), 227–237. doi:10.1177/1745691614568352

Holt-Lunstad, J., Smith, T. B., & Layton, J. B. (2010). Social relationships and mortality risk: A meta-analytic review. *PLoS Medicine, 7*(7). doi:10.1371/journal.pmed.1000316

Holtzworth-Munroe, A., & Jacobson, N. S. (1985). Causal attributions of married couples: When do they search for causes? What do they conclude when they do? *Journal of Personality and Social Psychology, 48*(6), 1398–1412.

Hooley, J. M. (2007). Expressed emotion and relapse of psychopathology. *Annual Review of Clinical Psychology, 3*, 329–352. doi:10.1146/annurev.clinpsy.2.022305.095236

Hooley, J. M., & Miklowitz, D. J. (2018). Families and mental disorders. In J. N. Butcher & J. M. Hooley (Eds.), *APA handbook of psychopathology: Psychopathology: Understanding, assessing, and treating adult mental disorders* (pp. 687–703). Washington, DC: American Psychological Association.

Hooley, J. M., & Teasdale, J. D. (1989). Predictors of relapse in unipolar depressives: Expressed emotion, marital distress, and perceived criticism. *Journal of Abnormal Psychology, 98*, 229–237.

Huke, K., & Slade, P. (2006). An exploratory investigation of the experiences of partners living with people who have bulimia nervosa. *European Eating Disorders Review, 14*(6), 436–447. doi:10.1002/erv.744

Ireland, J. L., Sanders, M. R., & Markie-Dadds, C. (2003). The impact of parent training on marital functioning: A comparison of two group version of the Triple P-Positive Parenting Program for parents of children with early-onset conduct problems. *Behavioural and Cognitive Psychotherapy, 31*, 127–142. doi:10.1017/S1352465803002017

Jacobson, N. S., & Moore, D. (1981). Spouses as observers of the events in their relationship. *Journal of Consulting and Clinical Psychology, 49*(2), 269–277.

Jenkins, M. M., Baucom, D. H., Drummond, S., & Nappi, C. M. (2016). Partner-assisted cognitive behavioral therapy for insomnia. Unpublished manuscript. Monash University. Melbourne, Australia.

Jenkins, M. M., Nappi, C. M., Cassidy, J., Khosa, V., & Drummond, S. (2015). *Testing partner-assisted cognitive behavioral therapy for insomnia.* Paper presented at the Annual Meeting of the Associated Professional Sleep Societies, LLC, Seattle, WA.

Johnson, S. M. (1996). *The practice of emotionally focused marital therapy.* New York, NY: Brunner/Mazel.

Johnson, S. M., & Greenberg, L. S. (1985). Differential effects of experiential and problem-solving interventions in resolving marital conflict. *Journal of Consulting and Clinical Psychology, 53*(2), 175–184.

Johnson, S. M., & Greenberg, L. S. (1995). The emotionally focused approach to problems in adult attachment. In N. S. Jacobson & A. S. Gurman (Eds.), *Clinical handbook of couple therapy* (pp. 121–141). New York, NY: Guilford Press.

Jouriles, E. N., & Farris, A. M. (1992). Effects of marital conflict on subsequent parent-son interactions. *Behavior Therapy, 23*(3), 355–374. doi:10.1016/S0005-7894(05)80163-7

Kahnemann, D. (2011). *Thinking fast and slow*. New York, NY: Farrar, Straus and Giroux.

Kaniasty, K., & Norris, F. H. (2008). Longitudinal linkages between perceived social support and posttraumatic stress symptoms: Sequential roles of social causation and social selection. *Journal of Traumatic Stress, 21*(3), 274–281. doi:10.1002/jts.20334

Karney, B. R., & Bradbury, T. N. (1995). The longitudinal course of marital quality and stability: A review of theory, methods, and research. *Psychological Bulletin, 118*, 3–34. doi:10.1037/0033-2909.118.1.3

Karney, B. R., & Bradbury, T. N. (2005). Contextual influences on marriage: Implications for policy and intervention. *Current Directions in Psychological Science, 14*(4), 171–174. doi:10.1111/j.0963-7214.2005.00358.x

Kazantzis, N., Dattilio, F. M., & Dobson, K. S. (2017). *The therapeutic relationship in cognitive-behavioral therapy: A clinician's guide*. New York, NY: Guilford Press.

Kelly, S., Bhagwat, R., Maynigo, P., & Moses, E. (2014). Couple and marital therapy: The complement and expansion provided by multicultural approaches. In F. T. L. Leong, L. Comas-Díaz, G. C. Nagayama Hall, V. C. McLoyd, & J. E. Trimble (Eds.), *APA handbook of multicultural psychology, Vol. 2: Applications and training* (pp. 479–497). Washington, DC: American Psychological Association.

Kelly, S., & Iwamasa, G. Y. (2005). Enhancing behavioral couple therapy: Addressing the therapeutic alliance, hope, and diversity. *Cognitive and Behavioral Practice, 12*(1), 102–112. doi:10.1016/S1077-7229(05)80045-8

Kessler, R. C., Amminger, G. P., Aguilar-Gaxiola, S., Alonso, J., Lee, S., & Ustun, T. B. (2007). Age of onset of mental disorders: A review of recent literature. *Current Opinion in Psychiatry, 20*, 359–364. doi:10.1097/YCO.0b013e32816ebc8c

Kiecolt-Glaser, J., & Wilson, S. (2017). Lovesick: How couples' relationships influence health. *Annual Review of Clinical Psychology, 13*(7), 1–23. doi:10.1146/annurev-clinpsy-032816-045111

King, D. B., & DeLongis, A. (2014). When couples disconnect: Rumination and withdrawal as maladaptive responses to everyday stress. *Journal of Family Psychology, 28*(4), 460–469. doi:10.1037/a0037160

Kirby, J. S., & Baucom, D. H. (2007a). Integrating dialectical behavior therapy and cognitive-behavioral couple therapy: A couples skills group for emotion dysregulation. *Cognitive and Behavioral Practice, 14*, 394–405. doi:10.1016/j.cbpra.2006.09.006

Kirby, J. S., & Baucom, D. H. (2007b). Treating emotion dysregulation in a couples context: A pilot study of a couples skills group intervention. *Journal of Marital and Family Therapy, 33*(3), 375–391. doi:10.1111/j.1752-0606.2007.00037.x

Kirby, J. S., Runfola, C. D., Fischer, M. S., Baucom, D. H., & Bulik, C. M. (2016). Couple-based interventions for adults with eating disorders. In S. Murray, L. Anderson, & L. Cohn (Eds.), *Innovations in family therapy for eating disorders: Novel treatment developments, patient insights, and the role of carers* (pp. 135–143). Abingdon: Routledge.

Kline, G. H., Stanley, S. M., Markman, H. J., Olmos-Gallo, P. A., St. Peters, M., Whitton, S. W., & Prado, L. M. (2004). Timing is everything: Pre-engagement cohabitation and increased risk for poor marital outcomes. *Journal of Family Psychology, 18*(2), 311–318. doi:10.1037/0893-3200.18.2.311

Knobloch-Fedders, L. M., Caska-Wallace, C., Smith, T. W., & Renshaw, K. (2017). Battling on the home front: Posttraumatic stress disorder and conflict behavior among military couples. *Behavior Therapy, 48*(2), 247–261. doi:10.1016/j.beth.2016.08.014

Kurdek, L. A. (2005). What do we know about gay and lesbian couples? *Current Directions in Psychological Science, 14*(5), 251–254. doi:10.1111/j.0963-7214.2005.00375.x

Kurdek, L. A. (2008). Change in relationship quality for partners from lesbian, gay male, and heterosexual couples. *Journal of Family Psychology*, *22*(5), 701–711. doi:10.1037/0893-3200.22.5.701

Lambert, J. E., Engh, R., Hasbun, A., & Holzer, J. (2012). Impact of posttraumatic stress disorder on the relationship quality and psychological distress of intimate partners: A meta-analytic review. *Journal of Family Psychology*, *26*(5), 729–737. doi:10.1037/a0029341

Lavner, J. A. (2017). Relationship satisfaction in lesbian couples: Review, methodological critique, and research agenda. *Journal of Lesbian Studies*, *21*(1), 7–29. doi:10.1080/10894160.2016.1142348

Lawrence, E., Rothman, A. D., Cobb, R. J., & Bradbury, T. N. (2010). Marital satisfaction across the transition to parenthood: Three eras of research. In R. D. Parke (Ed.), *Strengthening couple relationships for optimal child development: Lessons from research and intervention* (pp. 97–114). Washington, DC: American Psychological Association.

Layard, R. (2005). *Happiness: Lessons from a new science*. London: Penguin Books.

Layard, R. & CEP Mental Health Policy Group (2006). *The depression report: A new deal for depression and anxiety disorders*. CEP Special Papers 15, Centre for Economic Performance, LSE. Retrieved from https://ideas.repec.org/p/cep/cepsps/15.html

Layard, R., & Clark, D. M. (2014). *Thrive: How better mental health care transforms lives and saves money*. Princeton, NJ: Princeton University Press.

LeBlanc, M., Beaulieu-Bonneau, S., Mérette, C., Savard, J., Ivers, H., & C. M. (2007). Psychological and health-related quality of life factors associated with insomnia in a population-based sample. *Journal of Psychosomatic Research*, *63*(2), 157–166. doi:10.1016/j.jpsychores.2007.03.004

Lebow, J. L. (2019). *Treating the difficult divorce: A practical guide for psychotherapists*. Washington, DC: American Psychological Association.

Lerner, J. S., Li, Y., Valdesolo, P., & Kassam, K. S. (2015). Emotion and decision making. *Annual Review of Psychology*, *66*(1), 799–823. doi:10.1146/annurev-psych-010213-115043

Levenson, R. W., Carstensen, L. L., & Gottman, J. M. (1993). Long-term marriage: Age, gender, and satisfaction. *Psychology and Aging*, *8*(2), 301–313.

Levenson, R. W., Haase, C. M., Bloch, L., Holley, S. R., & Seider, B. H. (2014). Emotion regulation in couples. In J. J. Gross (Ed.), *The handbook of emotion regulation* (2nd ed., pp. 267–283). New York, NY: Guilford Press.

Lewis, J. M., & Kreider, R. M. (2015). Remarriage in the United States: American Community Survey reports. Retrieved from www.census.gov/content/dam/Census/library/publications/2015/acs/acs-30.pdf

Linehan, M. M. (1993). *Cognitive-behavioral treatment of borderline personality disorder*. New York, NY: Guilford Press.

Linehan, M. M. (2015). *DBT skills training manual* (2nd ed.). New York, NY: Guilford Press.

Linville, D., Brown, T., Sturm, K., & McDougal, T. (2012). Eating disorders and social support: perspectives of recovered individuals. *Eating Disorders*, *20*(3), 216–231. doi:10.1080/10640266.2012.668480

Liu, R. T., & Mustanski, B. (2012). Suicidal ideation and self-harm in lesbian, gay, bisexual, and transgender youth. *American Journal of Preventive Medicine*, *42*(3), 221–228. doi:10.1016/j.amepre.2011.10.023

Maisel, N. C., & Karney, B. R. (2012). Socioeconomic status moderates associations among stressful events, mental health, and relationship satisfaction. *Journal of Family Psychology*, *26*(4), 654–660. doi:10.1037/a0028901

Manber, R., Edinger, J. D., Gress, J. L., San Pedro-Salcedo, M. G., Kuo, T. F., & Kalista, T. (2008). Cognitive behavioral therapy for insomnia enhances depression outcome in patients with comorbid major depressive disorder and insomnia. *Sleep*, *31*(4), 489.

Manning, W. D., & Stykes, B. (2015). Twenty-five years of change in cohabitation in the U.S., 1987–2013 (FP-15-01). Retrieved from www.bgsu.edu/content/dam/BGSU/college-of-arts-and-sciences/NCFMR/documents/FP/FP-15-01-twenty-five-yrs-change-cohab.pdf

Markman, H. J., Halford, W. K., & Hawkins, A. J. (2019). Couple and relationship education. In B. H. Fiese (Ed.), *APA Handbook of Contemporary Family Psychology* (Vol. 3, pp. 307–324). Washington, DC: American Psychological Association.

Martell, C., Dimidijian, S., & Herman-Dunn, R. (2013). *Behavioural activation for depression: A clinician's guide*. New York, NY: Guilford Press.

Matt, G. E., Vázquez, C., & Campbell, W. K. (1992). Mood-congruent recall of affectively toned stimuli: A meta-analytic review. *Clinical Psychology Review*, *12*(2), 227–255. doi:10.1016/0272-7358(92)90116-P

McClelland, D. C. (1987). *Human motivation*. Cambridge: Cambridge University Press.

McCrady, B. S. (2014). Alcohol use disorders. In D. H. Barlow (Ed.), *Clinical handbook of psychological disorders: A step-by-step treatment manual* (5th ed., pp. 533–587). New York, NY: Guilford Press.

McCrady, B. S., & Epstein, E. E. (2009). *Overcoming alcohol problems: A couples-focused program*. New York, NY: Oxford University Press.

McCrae, R. R., & John, O. P. (1992). An introduction to the five-factor model and its applications. *Journal of Personality*, *60*(2), 175–215. doi:10.1111/j.1467-6494.1992.tb00970.x

McKee, L., Jones, D. J., Forehand, R., & Cuellar, J. (2013). Assessment of parenting style, parenting relationships, and other parent variables in child assessment. In D. H. Saklofske, C. R. Reynolds, and V. Schwean (Eds.), *Oxford handbook of psychological assessment of children and adolescents* (pp. 788–821). New York, NY: Oxford.

McNulty, J. K. (2008). Neuroticism and interpersonal negativity: The independent contributions of perceptions and behaviors. *Personality and Social Psychology Bulletin*, *34*(11), 1439–1450. doi:10.1177/0146167208322558

Meis, L. A., Erbes, C. R., Kramer, M. D., Arbisi, P. A., Kehle-Forbes, S. M., DeGarmo, D. S., . . . Polusny, M. A. (2017). Using reinforcement sensitivity to understand longitudinal links between PTSD and relationship adjustment. *Journal of Family Psychology*, *31*(1), 71–81. doi:10.1037/fam0000195

Mercado, E., & Hibel, L. C. (2017). I love you from the bottom of my hypothalamus: The role of stress physiology in romantic pair bond formation and maintenance. *Social and Personality Psychology Compass*, *11*(2), e12298. doi:10.1111/spc3.12298

Mermelstein, R., Lichtenstein, E., & McIntyre, K. (1983). Partner support and relapse in smoking cessation programs. *Journal of Consulting and Clinical Psychology*, *51*(3), 465–466.

Meyer, I. H. (2003). Prejudice, social stress, and mental health in lesbian, gay, and bisexual populations: Conceptual issues and research evidence. *Psychological Bulletin*, *129*(5), 674–697. doi:10.1037/0033-2909.129.5.674

Miklowitz, D. J., George, E. L., Richards, J. A., Simoneau, T. L., & Suddath, R. L. (2003). A randomized study of family-focused psychoeducation and pharmacotherapy in the outpatient management of bipolar disorder. *Archives of General Psychiatry*, *60*, 904–912. doi:10.1001/archpsyc.60.9.904

Miklowitz, D. J., & Goldstein, M. J. (1997). *Bipolar disorder: A family-focused treatment approach*. New York, NY: Guilford Press.

Mineo, L. (2017). Good genes are nice, but joy is better. *The Harvard Gazette*. Retrieved from https://news.harvard.edu/gazette/story/2017/04/over-nearly-80–years-harvard-study-has-been-showing-how-to-live-a-healthy-and-happy-life

Monson, C. M., & Fredman, S. J. (2012). *Cognitive-behavioral conjoint therapy for PTSD: Harnessing the healing power of relationships*. New York, NY: Guilford Press.

Monson, C. M., Fredman, S. J., Adair, K. C., Stevens, S. P., Resick, P. A., Schnurr, P. P., . . . Macdonald, A. (2011). Cognitive-behavioral conjoint therapy for PTSD: Pilot results from a community sample. *Journal of Traumatic Stress*, *24*(1), 97–101. doi:10.1002/jts.20604

Monson, C. M., Fredman, S. J., Macdonald, A., Pukay-Martin, N. D., Resick, P. A., & Schnurr, P. P. (2012). Effect of cognitive-behavioral couple therapy for PTSD: A randomized controlled trial. *Journal of the American Medical Association*, *308*(7), 700–709. doi:10.1001/jama.2012.9307

Monson, C. M., Schnurr, P. P., Stevens, S. P., & Guthrie, K. A. (2004). Cognitive-behavioral couple's treatment for posttraumatic stress disorder: Initial findings. *Journal of Traumatic Stress*, *17*, 341–344. doi:10.1023/B:JOTS.0000038483.69570.5b

Monson, C. M., & Snyder, D. K. (2012). Couple-based interventions for Military and Veteran families: Evidence and rationale. In D. K. Snyder & C. M. Monson (Eds.), *Couples-based interventions for military and veteran families: A practitioner's guide* (pp. 3–12). New York, NY: Guilford Press.

Monson, C. M., Taft, C. T., & Fredman, S. J. (2009). Military-related PTSD and intimate relationships: From description to theory-driven research and intervention development. *Clinical Psychology Review*, *29*(8), 707–714. doi:10.1016/j.cpr.2009.09.002

Morin, C. M., Bootzin, R. R., Buysse, D. J., Edinger, J. D., Espie, C. A., & Lichstein, K. L. (2006). Psychological and behavioral treatment of insomnia: update of the recent evidence (1998–2004). *Sleep*, *29*(11), 1398–1414. doi:10.1093/sleep/29.11.1398

Morin, C. M., Hauri, P. J., Espie, C. A., Spielman, A. J., Buysse, D. J., & Bootzin, R. R. (1999). Nonpharmacologic treatment of chronic insomnia. An American Academy of Sleep Medicine review. *Sleep*, *22*(8), 1134–1156. doi:10.1093/sleep/22.8.1134

Murstein, B. I., Cerreto, M., & MacDonald, M. G. (1977). A theory and investigation of the effect of exchange-orientation on marriage and friendship. *Journal of Marriage and the Family*, *39*, 543–548.

Myers, S. M. (2006). Religious homogamy and marital quality: Historical and generational patterns, 1980–1997. *Journal of Marriage and Family*, *68*(2), 292–304. doi:10.1111/j.1741-3737.2006.00253.x

National Sleep Foundation. (2014). Adult sleep habits and styles sleep in America poll. Retrieved from http://sleepfoundation.org/sleep-polls-data/sleep-in-america-poll/2005–adult-sleep-habits-and-styles

Neff, L. A., & Karney, B. R. (2007). Stress crossover in newlywed marriage: A longitudinal and dyadic perspective. *Journal of Marriage and Family*, *69*(3), 594–607. doi:10.1111/j.1741-3737.2007.00394.x

NICE. (2017). NICE guideline (NG69): Eating disorders: Recognition and treatment. Retrieved from www.nice.org.uk/guidance/ng69

Nichols, M. P., & Schwartz, R. C. (2001). *Family therapy: Concepts and methods*. Boston, MA: Allyn and Bacon.

Norcross, J. C., & Wampold, B. E. (2011). Evidence-based therapy relationships: Research conclusions and clinical practices. *Psychotherapy*, *48*(1), 98–102. doi:10.1037/a0022161

Notarius, C. I., Benson, P. R., Sloane, D., & Vanzetti, N. A. (1989). Exploring the interface between perception and behavior: An analysis of marital interaction in distressed and nondistressed couples. Special Issue: Coding marital interaction. *Behavioral Assessment*, *11*(1), 39–64.

Office for National Statistics. (2015). Marriages in England and Wales. Retrieved from www.ons.gov.uk/peoplepopulationandcommunity/birthsdeathsandmarriages/marriagecohabitationandcivilpartnerships

Office for National Statistics. (2016). Women shoulder the responsibility of "unpaid work." Retrieved from www.ons.gov.uk/employmentandlabourmarket/peopleinwork/earningsandworkinghours/articles/womenshouldertheresponsibilityofunpaidwork/2016-11-10

Osgarby, S. M. (1998). Memory and positive exchange in marital satisfaction. Doctoral dissertation, School of Applied Psychology, Griffith University, Australia.

Overbeek, G., Vollebergh, W., de Graaf, R., Scholte, R., de Kemp, R., & Engels, R. (2006). Longitudinal associations of marital quality and marital dissolution with the incidence of DSM-III-R disorders. *Journal of Family Psychology*, *20*(2), 284–291. doi:10.1037/0893-3200.20.2.284

Owen, J., Chapman, L. K., Quirk, K., Inch, L. J., France, T., & Bergen, C. (2012). Processes of change in relationship education for lower-income African American couples. *Journal of Couple & Relationship Therapy*, *11*(1), 51–68. doi:10.1080/15332691.2012.639704

Palmer, C. A., & Baucom, D. H. (1997, November). *Components of long-term, healthy marriages*. Paper presented at the 31st annual meeting of the Association for the Advancement of Behavior Therapy, Miami, FL.

Palmer, C. A., & Baucom, D. H. (1998, November). How our marriages lasted: Couples' reflections on staying together. Paper presented at the 32nd annual meeting of the Association for the Advancement of Behavior Therapy, Washington, DC.

Paprocki, C., & Baucom, D. H. (2017). Worried about us: Evaluating an intervention for relationship-based anxiety. *Family Process*, *56*(1), 45–58. doi:10.1111/famp.12175

Payne, B. K., Brown-Iannuzzi, J. L., & Hannay, J. W. (2017). *Economic inequality increases risk taking*. Paper presented at the Proceedings of the National Academy of Sciences of the United States of America.

Perlis, M. L., Jungquist, C., Smith, M. T., & Posner, D. (2005). *Cognitive behavioral treatment of insomnia: A session-by-session guide*. New York, NY: Springer-Verlag.

Perry-Jenkins, M., Goldberg, A. E., Pierce, C. P., & Sayer, A. G. (2007). Shift work, role overload, and the transition to parenthood. *Journal of Marriage and Family*, *69*(1), 123–138. doi:10.1111/j.1741-3737.2006.00349.x

Pinheiro, A. P., Raney, T. J., Thornton, L. M., Fichter, M. M., Berrettini, W. H., Goldman, D., . . . Bulik, C. M. (2010). Sexual functioning in women with eating disorders. *International Journal of Eating Disorders*, *43*(2), 123–129. doi:10.1002/eat.20671

Planalp, S., Fitness, J., & Fehr, B. A. (2018). The role of emotions in relationships. In A. L. Vangelisti & D. Perlman (Eds.), *The Cambridge handbook of personal relationships* (2nd ed., pp. 256–267). Cambridge: Cambridge University Press.

Ragland, L., Baucom, D. H., Burnett, C. K., & Schilling, E. A. (1996, November). *Communication and relationship standards: Predicting marital satisfaction*. Paper presented at the 30th annual meeting of the Association for the Advancement of Behavior Therapy, New York, NY.

Rankin-Esquer, L. A., Burnett, C. K., Baucom, D. H., & Epstein, N. (1997). Autonomy and relatedness in marital functioning. *Journal of Marital and Family Therapy*, *23*(2), 175–190. doi:10.1111/j.1752-0606.1997.tb00242.x

Rankin-Esquer, L., Clayton, D., Baucom, D. H., & Mullens, J. A. (1997, November). *Individual versus relationship schema use: Replication of a priming procedure in an adult, married population*. Paper presented at the 31st Annual Convention of the Association for the Advancement of Behavior Therapy, Miami, FL.

Reis, H. T., & Shaver, P. (1988). Intimacy as an interpersonal process. In S. Duck (Ed.), *Handbook of personal relationships* (pp. 367–389). New York, NY: Guilford Press.

Renshaw, K. D., Allen, E. S., Carter, S. P., Markman, H. J., & Stanley, S. M. (2014). Partners' attributions for service members' symptoms of combat-related posttraumatic stress disorder. *Behavior Therapy*, *45*(2), 187–198. doi:10.1016/j.beth.2013.10.005

Renshaw, K. D., Chambless, D. L., & Steketee, G. (2003). Perceived criticism predicts severity of anxiety symptoms after behavioral treatment in patients with obsessive-compulsive disorder and panic disorder with agoraphobia. *Journal of Clinical Psychology*, *59*(4), 411–421. doi:10.1002/jclp.10048

Renshaw, K. D., Chambless, D. L., & Thorgusen, S. (2017). Expressed emotion and attributions in relatives of patients with obsessive-compulsive disorder and panic disorder. *Journal of Nervous and Mental Disease*, *205*(4), 294–299. doi:10.1097/NMD.0000000000000636

Reuman, L., & Abramowitz, J. S. (2018). Predictors of accommodation among families affected by fear-based disorders. *Child Psychiatry and Human Development*, *49*(1), 53–62. doi:10.1007/s10578-017-0728-x

Revenson, T. A., Kayser, K. E., & Bodenmann, G. E. (2005). *Couples coping with stress: Emerging perspectives on dyadic coping*. Washington, DC: American Psychological Association.

Revenstorf, D., Hahlweg, K., Schindler, L., & Vogel, B. (1984). Interaction analysis of marital conflict. In K. Hahlweg & N. S. Jacobson (Eds.), *Marital interaction: Analysis and modification* (pp. 159–181). New York, NY: Guilford Press.

Rhoades, G. K., Stanley, S. M., & Markman, H. J. (2012). The impact of the transition to cohabitation on relationship functioning: Cross-sectional and longitudinal findings. *Journal of Family Psychology*, *26*(3), 348–358. doi:10.1037/a0028316

Riener, R., Schindler, K., & Ludvik, B. (2006). Psychosocial variables, eating behavior, depression, and binge eating in morbidly obese subjects. *Eating Behaviours*, *7*(4), 309–314. doi:10.1016/j.eatbeh.2005.11.004

Riggs, D. S., Hiss, H., & Foa, E. B. (1992). Marital distress and the treatment of obsessive compulsive disorder. *Behavior Therapy*, *23*(4), 585–597. doi:10.1016/S0005-7894(05)80223-0

Rogojanski, J., Carney, C. E., & Monson, C. M. (2013). Interpersonal factors in insomnia: a model for integrating bed partners into cognitive behavioral therapy for insomnia. *Sleep Medicine Reviews, 17*(1), 55–64. doi:10.1016/j.smrv.2012.02.003

Rood, B. A., Puckett, J. A., Pantalone, D. W., & Bradford, J. B. (2015). Predictors of suicidal ideation in a statewide sample of Transgender individuals. *LGBT Health, 2*(3), 270–275. doi:10.1089/lgbt.2013.0048

Rosenthal, L., & Starks, T. J. (2015). Relationship stigma and relationship outcomes in interracial and same-sex relationships: Examination of sources and buffers. *Journal of Family Psychology, 29*(6), 818–830. doi:10.1037/fam0000116

Ross, J. M., Karney, B. R., Nguyen, T. P., & Bradbury, T. N. (2019). Communication that is maladaptive for middle-class couples is adaptive for socioeconomically disadvantaged couples. *Journal of Personality and Social Psychology, 116*(4), 582–597. doi:10.1037/pspi0000158

Rostosky, S. S., & Riggle, E. D. B. (2017). Same-sex couple relationship strengths: A review and synthesis of the empirical literature (2000–2016). *Psychology of Sexual Orientation and Gender Diversity, 4*(1), 1–13. doi:10.1037/sgd0000216

Runfola, C. D., Kirby, J. S., Baucom, D. H., Fischer, M. S., Baucom, B. R. W., Matherne, C. E., . . . Bulik, C. M. (2018). A pilot open trial of UNITE-BED: A couple-based intervention for binge-eating disorder. *International Journal of Eating Disorders, 51*(9), 1107–1112. doi:10.1002/eat.22919

Salk, R. H., Hyde, J. S., & Abramson, L. Y. (2017). Gender differences in depression in representative national samples: Meta-analyses of diagnoses and symptoms. *Psychological Bulletin, 143*(8), 783–822. doi:10.1037/bul0000102.supp

Sánchez-Ortuño, M. M., & Edinger, J. D. (2012). Cognitive-behavioral therapy for the management of insomnia comorbid with mental disorders. *Current Psychiatry Reports, 14*(5), 519–528. doi:10.1007/s11920-012-0312-9

Sanford, K. (2007). Hard and soft emotion during conflict: Investigating married couples and other relationships. *Personal Relationships, 14*, 65–90. doi:10.1111/j.1475-6811.2006.00142.x

Sarason, S. B. (1971). *The culture of the school and the problem of change*. Boston, MA: Allyn & Bacon.

Sayers, S. L. (2011). Family reintegration difficulties and couples therapy for military veterans and their spouses. *Cognitive and Behavioral Practice, 18*(1), 108–119. doi:10.1016/j.cbpra.2010.03.002

Sbarra, D. A., Bourassa, K. J., & Manvelian, A. (2019). Marital separation and divorce: Correlates and consequences. In B. H. Friese (Ed.), *APA handbook of contemporary family psychology: Foundations, methods, and contemporary issues across the lifespan* (Vol. 1, pp. 687–705). Washington, DC: American Psychological Association.

Sbarra, D. A., & Hazan, C. (2008). Coregulation, dysregulation, self-regulation: An integrative analysis and empirical agenda for understanding adult attachment, separation, loss, and recovery. *Personality and Social Psychology Review, 12*(2), 141–167. doi:10.1177/1088868308315702

Scherer, K. R. (2009). The dynamic architecture of emotion: Evidence for the component process model. *Cognition and Emotion, 23*(7), 1307–1351. doi:10.1080/02699930902928969

Schilling, E. A., Baucom, D. H., Burnett, C. K., Allen, E. S., & Ragland, L. (2003). Altering the course of marriage: The effect of PREP communication skills acquisition on couples' risk of becoming maritally distressed. *Journal of Family Psychology, 17*(1), 41–53. doi:10.1037/0893-3200.17.1.41

Schmaling, K. B., & Sher, T. G. (2000). *The psychology of couples and illness: Theory, research and practice*. Washington, DC: American Psychological Association.

Schmidt, U., & Treasure, J. (2006). Anorexia nervosa: Valued and visible. A cognitive-interpersonal maintenance model and its implications for research and practice. *British Journal of Clinical Psychology, 45*(3), 343–366. doi:10.1348/014466505x53902

Schumm, J. A., Fredman, S. J., Monson, C. M., & Chard, K. M. (2013). Cognitive-behavioral conjoint therapy for PTSD: Initial findings for Operations Enduring and Iraqi Freedom male combat veterans and their partners. *American Journal of Family Therapy, 41*(4), 277–287. doi:10.1080/01926187.2012.701592

Schumm, J. A., O'Farrell, T. J., & Andreas, J. B. (2012). Behavioral couples therapy when both partners have a current alcohol use disorder. *Alcoholism Treatment Quarterly, 30*(4), 407–421. doi:10.1080/07347324.2012.718963

Schumm, J. A., O'Farrell, T. J., Kahler, C. W., Murphy, M. M., & Muchowski, P. (2014). A randomized clinical trial of behavioral couples therapy versus individually based treatment for women with alcohol dependence. *Journal of Consulting and Clinical Psychology, 82*(6), 993–1004. doi:10.1037/a0037497

Seligman, M. E. P. (1975). *Helplessness: On depression, development and death.* San Francisco, CA: W. H. Freeman.

Sepulveda, A. R., Kyriacou, O., & Treasure, J. (2009). Development and validation of the accommodation and enabling scale for eating disorders (AESED) for caregivers in eating disorders. *BMC Health Services Research, 9*, 171. doi:10.1186/1472-6963-9-171

Shadish, W. R., & Baldwin, S. A. (2003). Meta-analysis of MFT interventions. *Journal of Marital and Family Therapy, 29*(4), 547–570.

Shafran, R., Ralph, J., & Tallis, F. (1995). Obsessive-compulsive symptoms and the family. *Bulletin of the Menninger Clinic, 59*(4), 472–479.

Sher, T., Braun, L., Domas, A., Bellg, A., Baucom, D. H., & Houle, T. T. (2014). The Partners for Life program: A couples approach to cardiac risk reduction. *Family Process, 53*(1), 131–149. doi:10.1111/famp.12061

Shoham, V., Butler, E. A., Rohrbaugh, M. J., & Trost, S. (2007). Symptom-system fit in couples: Emotion regulation when one or both partners smoke. *Journal of Abnormal Psychology, 116*, 848–853. doi:10.1037/0021-843X.116.4.848

Sillars, A. L., & Vangelista, A. L. (2018). Communication: Basic properties and their relevance to relationship research. In A. L. Vangelista & D. Perlman (Eds.), *The Cambridge handbook of personal relationships* (pp. 243–255). Cambridge: Cambridge University Press.

Simon, G. E., & VonKorff, M. (1997). Prevalence, burden, and treatment of insomnia in primary care. *American Journal of Psychiatry, 154*(10), 1417–1423. doi:10.1176/ajp.154.10.1417

Skerrett, D. M., Kõlves, K., & De Leo, D. (2016). Factors related to suicide in LGBT populations. *Crisis, 37*(5), 361–369. doi:10.1027/0227-5910/a000423

Snyder, D. K. (1997). *Marital satisfaction inventory revised.* Los Angeles, CA: Western Psychological Services.

Snyder, D. K., Baucom, D. H., & Gordon, K. C. (2007). *Getting past the affair: A program to help you cope, heal, and move on—together or apart.* New York, NY: Guilford Press.

Snyder, D. K., Castellani, A. M., & Whisman, M. A. (2006). Current status and future directions in couple therapy. *Annual Review of Psychology, 57*, 317–344. doi:10.1146/annurev.psych.56.091103.070154

Snyder, D. K., & Whisman, M. A. (Eds.). (2003). *Treating difficult couples.* New York, NY: Guilford Press.

Snyder, D. K., & Wills, R. M. (1989). Behavioral versus insight-oriented marital therapy: Effects on individual and interspousal functioning. *Journal of Consulting and Clinical Psychology, 57*(1), 39–46.

Spangler, A., & Payne, K. K. (2012). *Marital duration at divorce.* Report no. FP-14–11. Bowling Green, OH: National Center for Family & Marriage Research:

Spanier, G. B. (1976). Measuring dyadic adjustment: New scales for assessing the quality of marriage and similar dyads. *Journal of Marriage and the Family, 38*(1), 15–28. doi:10.2307/350547

Sparrevohn, R. M., & Rapee, R. M. (2009). Self-disclosure, emotional expression and intimacy within romantic relationships of people with social phobia. *Behaviour Research and Therapy, 47*(12), 1074–1078. doi:10.1016/j.brat.2009.07.016

Sprecher, S., Schmeeckle, M., & Felmlee, D. (2006). The principle of least investment: Inequality of emotional involvement in romantic relationships. *Journal of Family Issues, 27*, 1255–1280. doi:10.1177/0192513X06289215

Sprenkle, D. H., Davis, S. D., & Lebow, J. L. (2009). *Common factors in couple and family therapy: The overlooked foundation for effective practice.* New York, NY: Guilford Press.

Stanley, S. M., Rhoades, G. K., Loew, B. A., Allen, E. S., Carter, S., Osborne, L. J., . . . Markman, H. J. (2014). A randomized controlled trial of relationship education in the U.S. Army: 2-year outcomes. *Family Relations: An Interdisciplinary Journal of Applied Family Studies*, *63*(4), 482–495. doi:10.1111/fare.12083

Stanley, S. M., Rhoades, G. K., & Markman, H. J. (2006). Sliding vs. deciding: Inertia and the premarital cohabitation effect. *Family Relations*, *55*, 499–509. doi:10.1111/j.1741-3729.2006.00418.x

Story, L. B., & Repetti, R. (2006). Daily occupational stressors and marital behavior. *Journal of Family Psychology*, *20*(4), 690–700. doi:10.1037/0893-3200.20.4.690

Straus, M. A., Hamby, S. L., Boney-McCoy, S., & Sugarman, D. B. (1996). The Revised Conflict Tactics Scales (CTS2): Development and preliminary psychometric data. *Journal of Family Issues*, *17*(3), 283–316. doi:10.1177/019251396017003001

Stuart, R. B. (1969). Operant interpersonal treatment for marital discord. *Journal of Consulting and Clinical Psychology*, *33*, 675–682.

Stuart, R. B. (1980). *Helping couples change: A social learning approach to marital therapy*. New York, NY: Guilford Press.

Sue, D. W., & Sue, D. (2012). *Counseling the culturally diverse: Theory and practice* (6th ed.). Hoboken, NJ: John Wiley & Sons.

Sullivan, L. J. (1999, November). *Observational measurement of relationship schemas*. Paper presented at the annual meeting of the Association for Advancement of Behavior Therapy, Toronto, Canada.

Sullivan, L. J., & Baucom, D. H. (2004). The Relationship-Schematic coding system: Behavioral manifestations of thinking in relationships terms. In P. K. Kerig & D. H. Baucom (Eds.), *Couple observational coding systems* (pp. 289–304). Mahwah, NJ: Lawrence Erlbaum.

Sullivan, L. J., & Baucom, D. H. (2005). Observational coding of Relationship-Schematic Processing. *Journal of Marital and Family Therapy*, *31*(1), 31–43. doi:10.1111/j.1752-0606.2005.tb01541.x

Szmukler, G. I., Eisler, I., Russell, G. F., & Dare, C. (1985). Anorexia nervosa, parental expressed emotion and dropping out of treatment. *British Journal of Psychiatry*, *147*, 265–271.

Taft, C. T., Watkins, L. E., Stafford, J., Street, A. E., & Monson, C. M. (2011). Posttraumatic stress disorder and intimate relationship problems: A meta-analysis. *Journal of Consulting and Clinical Psychology*, *79*(1), 22–33. doi:10.1037/a0022196

Tarrier, N., Sommerfield, C., & Pilgrim, H. (1999). Relatives' expressed emotion (EE) and PTSD treatment outcome. *Psychological Medicine*, *29*(4), 801–811. doi:10.1017/S0033291799008569

Taylor, S. E. (2011). Social support: A review. In H. S. Friedman (Ed.), *The Oxford handbook of health psychology* (pp. 189–214). New York, NY: Oxford University Press.

Timmons, A. C., Arbel, R., & Margolin, G. (2017). Daily patterns of stress and conflict in couples: Associations with marital aggression and family-of-origin aggression. *Journal of Family Psychology*, *31*(1), 93–104. doi:10.1037/fam0000227

Timmons, A. C., Margolin, G., & Saxbe, D. E. (2015). Physiological linkage in couples and its implications for individual and interpersonal functioning: A literature review. *Journal of Family Psychology*, *29*(5), 720–731. doi:10.1037/fam0000115

Tozzi, F., Sullivan, P. F., Fear, J. L., McKenzie, J., & Bulik, C. M. (2003). Causes and recovery in anorexia nervosa: The patient's perspective. *International Journal of Eating Disorders*, *33*(2), 143–154. doi:10.1002/eat.10120

U.S. Census Bureau. (2018a). Current population survey, annual social and economic supplement. Retrieved from www.census.gov/cps/data/cpstablecreator.html?#

U.S. Census Bureau. (2018b). Estimated median age at first marriage: 1890 to present. Retrieved from www.census.gov/data/tables/time-series/demo/families/marital.html

Van den Broucke, S., Vandereycken, W., & Vertommen, H. (1995). Marital communication in eating disorder patients a controlled observational study. *International Journal of Eating Disorders*, *17*(1), 1–21. doi:10.1002/1098-108X(199501)17:1<1::AID-EAT2260170102>3.0.CO;2-3

Vater, A., & Schröder-Abé, M. (2015). Explaining the link between personality and relationship satisfaction: Emotion regulation and interpersonal behaviour in conflict discussions. *European Journal of Personality*, *29*(2), 201–215. doi:10.1002/per.1993

Vikas, A., Avasthi, A., & Sharan, P. (2011). Psychosocial impact of obsessive-compulsive disorder on patients and their caregivers: A comparative study with depressive disorder. *International Journal of Social Psychiatry*, *57*(1), 45–56. doi:10.1177/0020764010347333

Vittengl, J. J., & Jarrett, R. B. (2014). Major depressive disorder. In S. G. Hoffmann (Ed.), *The Wiley handbook of cognitive behavioural therapy* (Vol. 3, pp. 1131–1159). Chichester: Wiley-Blackwell.

Waldinger, R. (2015). What makes a good life? Lessons from the longest study on happiness. Retrieved from www.ted.com/talks/robert_waldinger_what_makes_a_good_life_lessons_from_the_longest_study_on_happiness?language=en

Walitzer, K. S., & Dermen, K. H. (2004). Alcohol-focused spouse involvement and behavioral couples therapy: Evaluation of enhancements to drinking reduction treatment for male problem drinkers. *Journal of Consulting and Clinical Psychology*, *72*(6), 944–955. doi:10.1037/0022-006X.72.6.944

Watson, D., & Tellegen, A. (1985). Toward the structure of affect. *Psychological Bulletin*, *98*, 219–235.

Weber, D. M., Fischer, M. S., Baucom, D. H., Baucom, B. R. W., Kirby, J. S., Runfola, C. D., . . . Bulik, C. M. (2018). The association between symptom accommodation and emotional coregulation in couples with binge eating disorder. *Family Process*. doi:10.1111/famp.12391

Weidmann, R., Ledermann, T., & Grob, A. (2016). The interdependence of personality and satisfaction in couples: A review. *European Psychologist*, *21*(4), 284–295. doi:10.1027/1016-9040/a000261

Weiss, R. L. (1980). Strategic behavioral martial therapy: Toward a model for assessment and intervention. In J. P. Vincent (Ed.), *Advances in family intervention, assessment and theory* (Vol. 1, pp. 229–271). Greenwich, CT: JAI.

Weiss, R. L., & Heyman, R. E. (1997). A clinical-research overview of couples interactions. In W. K. Halford & H. J. Markman (Eds.), *Clinical handbook of marriage and couples interventions* (pp. 39–41). Chichester: Wiley.

Weiss, R. L., Hops, H., & Patterson, G. R. (1973). A framework for conceptualizing marital conflict, a technology for altering it, some data for evaluating it. In M. Hersen & A. S. Bellack (Eds.), *Behavior change: Methodology, concepts and practice* (pp. 309–342). Champaign, IL: Research Press.

Whisman, M. A. (2019). Psychopathology and couple and family functioning. In B. H. Friese (Ed.), *APA handbook of contemporary family psychology: Applications and broad impact of family psychology* (Vol. 2, pp. 3–20). Washington, DC: American Psychological Association.

Whisman, M. A., & Baucom, D. H. (2012). Intimate relationships and psychopathology. *Clinical Child and Family Psychology Review*, *15*(1), 4–13. doi:10.1007/s10567-011-0107-2

Whisman, M. A., & Beach, S. R. (2015). Couple therapy and depression. In A. S. Gurman, J. Lebow, & C. R. Snyder (Eds.), *Clinical handbook of couple therapy* (pp. 585–605). New York, NY: Guilford Press.

Whisman, M. A., & Bruce, M. L. (1999). Marital distress and incidence of major depressive episode in a community sample. *Journal of Abnormal Psychology*, *108*, 674–678.

Whisman, M. A., Dementyeva, A., Baucom, D. H., & Bulik, C. M. (2012). Marital functioning and binge eating disorder in married women. *International Journal of Eating Disorders*, *45*(3), 385–389. doi:10.1002/eat.20935

Whisman, M. A., & Uebelacker, L. A. (2009). Prospective associations between marital discord and depressive symptoms in middle-aged and older adults. *Psychology and Aging*, *24*, 184–189. doi:10.1037/a0014759

Whisman, M. A., Uebelacker, L. A., & Bruce, M. L. (2006). Longitudinal association between marital dissatisfaction and alcohol use disorders in a community sample. *Journal of Family Psychology*, *20*(1), 164. doi:10.1037/0893-3200.20.1.164

Whitton, S. W., Scott, S. B., Dyar, C., Weitbrecht, E. M., Hutsell, D. W., & Kuryluk, A. D. (2017). Piloting relationship education for female same-sex couples: Results of a small randomized waitlist-control trial. *Journal of Family Psychology*, *31*(7), 878. doi:10.1037/fam0000337.

Whitton, S. W., Weitbrecht, E. M., & Kuryluk, A. D. (2015). Monogamy agreements in male same-sex couples: Associations with relationship quality and individual well-being. *Journal of Couple & Relationship Therapy*, *14*(1), 39–63. doi:10.1080/15332691.2014.953649

Williams-Baucom, K. J., Atkins, D. C., Sevier, M. I. A., Eldridge, K. A., & Christensen, A. (2010). "You" and "I" need to talk about "us": Linguistic patterns in marital interactions. *Personal Relationships*, *17*(1), 41–56. doi:10.1111/j.1475-6811.2010.01251.x

Williamson, H. C., Karney, B. R., & Bradbury, T. N. (2013). Financial strain and stressful events predict newlyweds' negative communication independent of relationship satisfaction. *Journal of Family Psychology*, *27*(1), 65–75. doi:10.1037/a0031104

Wilson, B. J., & Gottman, J. M. (2002). Marital conflict, repair, and parenting. In M. H. Bornstein (Ed.), *Handbook of Parenting* (2nd ed., Vol. 4, pp. 227–258). Mahwah, NJ: Lawrence Erlbaum Associates.

Winterheld, H. A., & Simpson, J. A. (2018). Personality in close relationships. In A. L. Vangelista & D. Perlman (Eds.), *The Cambridge handbook of personal relationships* (2nd ed., pp. 163–174). Cambridge: Cambridge University Press.

Witkiewitz, K., Donovan, D. M., & Hartzler, B. (2012). Drink refusal training as part of a combined behavioral intervention: Effectiveness and mechanisms of change. *Journal of Consulting and Clinical Psychology*, *80*, 440–449. doi:10.1037/a0026996

Woodside, D. B., Lackstrom, J. B., & Shekter-Wolfson, L. (2000). Marriage in eating disorders comparisons between patients and spouses and changes over the course of treatment. *Journal of Psychosomatic Research*, *49*, 165–168. doi:10.1016/S0022-3999(00)00154-9

World Health Organization. (2017). *Depression and other common mental disorders: Global health estimates*. Geneva: World Health Organization.

Worrell, M. (2015). *Cognitive behavioural couple therapy: Distinctive features*. London: Routledge.

Young, J. E. (1999). *Cognitve therapy for personality disorders: A schema-focused approach* (3rd ed.). Sarasota, FL: Professional Resource Exchange.

Zabala, M. J., Macdonald, P., & Treasure, J. (2009). Appraisal of caregiving burden, expressed emotion and psychological distress in families of people with eating disorders: A systematic review. *European Eating Disorders Review*, *17*(5), 338–449. doi:10.1002/erv.925

Zaider, T. I., Heimberg, R. G., & Iida, M. (2010). Anxiety disorders and intimate relationships: A study of daily processes in couples. *Journal of Abnormal Psychology*, *119*(1), 163–173. doi:10.1037/a0018473

Zimet, D. M., & Jacob, T. (2001). Influences of marital conflict and child adjustment: Review of theory and research. *Clinical Child and Family Psychology Review*, *4*, 319–335. doi:10.1023/A:1013595304718

Zizza, C. A., Ellison, K. J., & Wernette, C. M. (2009). Total water intakes of community-living middle-old and oldest-old adults. *The Journals of Gerontology Series A: Biological Sciences and Medical Sciences*, *64A*(4), 481–486. doi:0.1093/gerona/gln045

Appendices

APPENDIX 1: GUIDELINES FOR SHARING THOUGHTS AND FEELINGS CONVERSATIONS

Skills for sharing thoughts and feelings (the speaker)

Express yourself in a way that makes it as easy as possible for your partner to listen and understand.

- Talk about your experiences *subjectively*, not as absolute truths.
- Include your *emotions or feelings.*
- Make your statement *specific*, both in terms of specific feelings and thoughts.
- Speak in "paragraphs." Give your partner a chance to respond to *one main idea* at a time.
- When you share negative emotions or concerns, try to include *positive feelings* you have as well.
- Discuss how you feel *about your partner* and not just an event.
- Express your feelings and thoughts with *tact* and *timing.*

Skills for listening to partner (the listener)

Your goal is to understand your partner's experience and help your partner feel understood.

When your partner is speaking . . .

- Try to put yourself *in your partner's place.* Think about the situation from your partner's perspective without adding your own point of view.
- Show that you understand and accept what your partner has to say, even if you do not agree. *Remember, acceptance is NOT agreement.*

When your partner finishes speaking . . .

- *Summarize* your partner's most important feelings, desires, conflicts, and thoughts in a way that shows you truly listened.

Do not . . .

- Express your own viewpoint or opinion.
- Judge what your partner has said.
- Interpret or change the meaning of your partner's statements.
- Attempt to solve a problem if one exists.

APPENDIX 2: GUIDELINES FOR DECISION-MAKING OR PROBLEM-SOLVING

1. State the issue

- Express the issue in terms of behaviours.
- Do not include solutions in the description of the problem.
- Break down larger problems into smaller issues and talk about one at a time.
- Make sure both people agree on the description of the problem and are ready to talk about it.

2. Talk about why the issue is important—what do you need?

- Share your understanding of the issue. Include why it is important to you.
- Explain which of your *needs, desires, or challenges* are important for a good solution.
- Do not give any solutions yet.

3. Discuss possible solutions

- Think of solutions that include both partners' needs and preferences.
- Focus on how to do things differently in the future.
- If you feel stuck, brainstorm anything that comes to mind, even if it seems silly.
- Focus on the solution. Do *not*:
    - Judge who is right and wrong.
    - Try to find the "truth" about what happened.

4. Decide on a solution that works for both of you

- Find a compromise if there is no perfect solution.
- Repeat your final decision in terms of specific behaviours each person will carry out.
- Do *not* make a decision that:
    - You will not actually do.
    - Will make you angry or resentful.

5. Decide on a trial period to try out the solution or decision

- Set a trial period that is long enough to give the new way of doing things a fair chance.
- Review how the solution is working at the end of the trial period.
- Revise the solution if needed and set a new trial period.

APPENDIX 3: EMOTIONS LIST

Positive emotions					
Happy/joyful		*Close/warm*		*Energy/vigour*	
Cheerful	Happy	Loving	Warm	Active	Lively
Excited	Pleased	Devoted	Safe	Adventurous	Vigorous
Amused	Hopeful	Secure	Tender	Energetic	Enthusiastic
Delighted	Thrilled	Sexy	Affectionate		
Glad	Joyful	Close	Friendly		
		Proud			
Relaxed/calm		*Other positive moods*			
Gentle	Peaceful	Agreeable	Cooperative		
Calm	Relaxed	Confident	Inspired		
Contented					
Negative emotions					
Depressed/Sad		*Anxious*		*Angry*	
Sad	Bored	Shaky	Tense	Angry	Frustrated
Blue	Gloomy	Restless	Nervous	Resentful	Enraged
Helpless	Grim	Anxious	Fearful	Furious	Irritated
Hopeless	Low	Panicky	Insecure	Disgusted	Outraged
Miserable	Dejected	Terrified	Frightened	Annoyed	
Discouraged	Hurt	Confused	Shy		
Unhappy		Bashful			
Contemptuous		Fatigue		Other negative moods	
Critical	Disdainful	Exhausted	Listless	Bewildered	Lonely
Contemptuous	Hostile	Fatigued	Sluggish	Jealous	Guilty
		Weary	Wilted	Ashamed	Stupid

APPENDIX 4: RELATIONSHIP HISTORY INTERVIEW OUTLINE

The initial meeting, early interactions, and attraction

1 How and where the couple met; other people involved in their meeting.
2 Each person's positive and negative life circumstances at the time.
3 Characteristics of the partner that attracted each person to the other.
4 Shared activities and how each person felt about them.

How and when the relationship became "serious" (i.e., serious relationship prior to marriage or comparable committed relationship)

1 Amount and quality of the couple's interaction (shared time and activities, affection, arguments, quality of communication and decision-making).
2 Positive and/or negative thoughts and emotions about forming a committed relationship.
3 Involvements with each other's families, friends, etc.
4 Significant events that had positive or negative effects on the relationship.

The relationship and notable life events occurring subsequent to marriage or comparable committed relationship

1 Circumstances surrounding the decision to get married or make a similar explicit commitment.
2 Any differences in the partners' levels of readiness to make the commitment; each person's feelings about life changes that they anticipated would result from the commitment.
3 Degrees to which the partners' initial positive qualities are still present.
4 Degree of support for the relationship from other important people in each partner's life (e.g., family, friends, co-workers).
5 Significant changes that occurred in the relationship (e.g., one person moving into the other's home, formation of stepfamily relationships, merging of partners' financial assets).
6 Major positive and negative events involving either individual, the couple, or the environment that have impacted the relationship and the couple's responses to those events.
7 Management of differences of opinion and conflict (positive and negative coping strategies).
8 Signs each person noticed indicating difficulties in the relationship, actions taken to deal with the problems, and changes in the issues over time.

APPENDIX 5: BEHAVIOURAL OBSERVATIONS OF COMMUNICATION

Instructions for the therapist

There are several different types of conversations that you might want the couple to have so you can observe their patterns of communication. Select the types of conversations that are most relevant for this couple; attempting to have all of these conversations will likely require too much time and will be exhausting for the couple. If you can video record these interactions and you have the couple's consent to do so, this can be very helpful, allowing you to review the interactions after the session. However, if this is not possible, explain to the couple that you will remain quiet in the role of observer and that they should have a conversation as though you were not present.

Read the instructions below or describe to the couple what you want them to do. Make certain that they are clear about the task and have selected their topic. Let them know that when the time is up or if they finish earlier, they can notify you of this.

Instructions to the couple

- Sharing thoughts and feelings
  - "Select some area of concern in your relationship and spend about 10 minutes sharing your thoughts and feelings with each other about this issue. Don't attempt to resolve it, just let each other know what you think and feel."
- Decision-making
  - "Select a moderate size problem in your relationship and attempt to resolve it or make a decision about it. Take about 10 minutes and get as far as you can. If you don't reach a final decision, that is okay."
- Focus on the individual (support)
  - "I would like for one of you to select something that is of concern to you as an individual that you would be willing to discuss with your partner, not something about your relationship. The other person's role is to respond like you normally would. We'll do that for about 5 minutes, and then we'll switch roles with the other person talking about an area of personal concern. Who would like to start?"

APPENDIX 6: INDIVIDUAL INTERVIEW OUTLINE

Demographic information

1 Age, ethnicity, religious affiliation, country of origin (and immigration history if relevant), education, current employment.

Family of origin

1 Members of family of origin, birth order, members currently alive, where they live.
2 Quality of relationships among members of family of origin during individual's childhood and currently.
3 Any notable stressful events affecting family of origin during childhood and subsequently (e.g., illnesses, disabilities, deaths, financial problems, unemployment, estranged relationships, substance abuse problems, criminal and legal problems).

Physical health

1 Past and current health problems and physical disabilities; impact on daily functioning (job, interpersonal relationships, etc.).
2 Treatments, medications (and any side effects).
3 Past and current use of tobacco, caffeine, alcohol, drugs; impact on daily functioning (job, interpersonal relationships, etc.).

Developmental history

1 Educational history (performance in each level of schooling, any learning disabilities, experiences of being bullied or other interpersonal difficulties).
2 Interests and leisure activities (individual and with other people); special talents.
3 History of psychopathology (e.g., anxiety, depression, behavioural problems); any formal diagnoses and treatments received; association of symptoms with particular life experiences (follow-up with more detailed assessment of psychopathology if warranted).
4 Personality characteristics and motives (screening for consistencies in cognitive, emotional, and behavioural response patterns to life events).
5 Perceived personal strengths (including values).
6 Job history (types of jobs, performance, job satisfaction, career goals).
7 Relationship history (friendships, prior romantic relationships); how relationships tended to begin and end; quality of current relationships.
8 Past and current demands involving own characteristics, relationships with significant others, and other aspects of the person's environment; past and current traumatic experiences (e.g., physical and sexual abuse, psychological abuse, abandonment).
9 Personal, relationship, and environmental resources previously used to adapt to life demands (their degree of effectiveness; the individual's attitudes about using resources).

Current relationship

1 Additional specific information about current relationship requiring elaboration.
2 Global perspective on relationship.

Index

Page numbers in *italics* refer to figures and tables.